J

N

THE CONCISE ENCYCLOPEDIA of SPORTS

THE CONCISE ENCYCLOPEDIA of SPORTS

SECOND REVISED EDITION

Edited By GERALD NEWMAN

Franklin Watts

New York | London | Toronto | 1979

Mr. Newman gratefully acknowledges the assistance of Shelley Hendlin, Ph.D., who helped with the compilation of this volume.

Printed in the United States of America
6 5 4 3 2 1

Library of Congress Cataloging in Publication Data

Main entry under title:

The Concise encyclopedia of sports.

Ed. of 1970 edited by K. W. Jennison
Includes bibliographical references and index.
SUMMARY: Discusses more than 85 sports, including their history, development, rules, statistics, and outstanding athletes.
1. Sports—Dictionaries, Juvenile. [1. Sports—Dictionaries] I. Newman, Gerald. II. Jennison, Keith Warren. The concise encyclopedia of sports.
GV567.J46 1979 796'.03 79-10260
ISBN 0-531-02391-5

Introduction

Did you know:

- In 1823, William Webb Ellis, a student at the Rugby School in England, failed to kick the ball in an interclass soccer game. He became so incensed that he picked up the ball and ran with it across the goal line. Thus, the game of rugby was born.
- There is archeological evidence that as early as 1500 B.C. boxing was a sport in Crete.
- In the 15th century, the Scottish parliament tried to ban the playing of golf because Scottish citizens were losing interest in archery. Fewer archers meant fewer men to defend the land against invaders.
- The first bowl game was part of the Tournament of Roses in 1902. But it was discontinued in favor of Roman Chariot Races until 1916.

These facts are just a sampling of the information to be found in this newly revised edition of *The Concise Encyclopedia of Sports.* This volume has been expanded to include the history, development, and rules of more than 85 internationally played sports, as well as information about sports equipment and its use, the dimensions of playing areas, and the official scoring of games and competitions.

Some topics are discussed briefly, offering concise information, while others—especially the more popular sports—are covered in greater detail. In addition, there is a great deal of statistical information, plus numerous charts, diagrams, and photographs. Many articles are cross-referenced and offer "See also" listings as well as texts to consult for further reading.

Because sports records change constantly, no attempt has been made to include every victory or every broken record. But each entry about a particular sport notes those who have made outstanding contributions in that area. This enlarged edition also includes more than 135 capsule biographies ot people who have helped make athletics the world's most popular leisure-time activity. It is to these men and women that *The Concise Encyclopedia of Sports* is gratefully dedicated.

A

AARON, HENRY LOUIS (HANK) (1934–), U.S. baseball player, who in Atlanta on April 8, 1974, hit his 715th home run to break Babe Ruth's record and become the leading home-run hitter in baseball history. Born in Mobile, Ala., Aaron entered the big leagues in 1954 as right fielder with the Milwaukee Braves, and he moved with the team as it became the Atlanta Braves in 1966. The low-keyed, modest Aaron won the National League's most valuable player award (1957) and its batting championships (1956 and 1959). In his best season for homers, he hit 47 in 1971.

In 1958, 1959, and 1960, Aaron received the Golden Glove award for fielding, and from 1955 to 1974 he was a member of the National League All-Star team.

ACROBATICS. *See* GYMNASTICS.

ALEXANDER, GROVER CLEVELAND (1887–1950), American baseball player who shares with "Christy" Mathewson the National League record for pitching victories (373) during a lifetime career. He was born in St. Paul, Nebr., and threw and batted right-handed. He played for three National League teams: Philadelphia (1911–17, 1930), Chicago (1918–26), and St. Louis (1926–29). He established the major-league record for shutouts in a single season (16), and the National League records for games pitched in a lifetime career (696), innings pitched (5,189), complete games (437), and shutouts (90). He was elected to the National Baseball Hall of Fame in 1938.

ALLEN, FORREST C. ("PHOG") (1885–1974), innovative American college basketball coach, born in Jamesport, Mo. He coached for 49 years, the last 39 at the University of Kansas. Earlier he coached at Haskell Institute, Baker University, and Central Missouri College. When he retired in 1956, his teams had won 31 conference championships. He founded the National College Basketball Coaches' Association in 1929, and was instrumental in having basketball added to the program of the Olympic Games in 1936. In 1960 he was elected to the Basketball Hall of Fame.

AMATEUR ATHLETIC UNION OF THE UNITED STATES (AAU), nationwide, nonprofit organization whose aim is the promotion and improvement of athletic sports and games among amateur participants. It was founded in 1888, and maintains headquarters in New York City. By the early 1960's, the volunteer membership had grown to about 10,000. At the same time the organization included 51 component groups, or associations, throughout the United States. These comprised about 3,500 member units (athletic clubs or educational institutions, permanent in nature and interested in amateur athletics). The AAU claims jurisdiction over, and sets amateur standards for, the following U.S. sports: track and field, basketball, boxing, gymnastics, handball, swimming, water polo, wrestling, weight lifting, volleyball, bobsledding, ice hockey, judo, horseshoe pitching, and baton twirling. It participates in international amateur sports competition as the sole U.S. member of the international amateur federations governing 9 of 21 sports on the program (present or past) of the Olympic Games. The AAU also serves as a clearinghouse for competition involving U.S. amateurs abroad and foreign amateurs in the United States. In the 1960's its authority in this area was challenged by the N.C.A.A.

AMERICA'S CUP, most famous prize in yachting. It was first placed in competition as the Hundred-Guinea Cup in 1851 by Great Britain's Royal Yacht Squadron. It was first

Australia's *Gretel* trailing *Weatherly* in 1962 America's Cup race.

Morris Rosenfeld

won by the schooner *America*, representing the New York Yacht Club, in a 58-mi. race with British craft around the Isle of Wight. Subsequently the trophy was renamed the America's Cup. Between 1870, when the competition was resumed, and 1937, yachtsmen from England, Scotland, and Canada made 16 unsuccessful attempts to regain the cup from the New York Yacht Club in races in U.S. waters. In 1958, after an interval of 21 years, the competition was resumed with yachts that were smaller than earlier entries and more economical to operate. U.S. boats continued to dominate the races. As the competing sloops became more and more alike in design, the races became true tests of the seamanship of captain and crew.

ANSON, ADRIAN CONSTANTINE ("CAP") (1852–1922), American baseball player and manager, one of the game's foremost pioneers. He was born in Marshalltown, Iowa. He played and managed for 27 years in the National Association and National League (1871–97). A first baseman, and a right-handed hitter and thrower, he led the National League in batting four times, and hit .407 in 1879 and .421 in 1887. His lifetime average was .331. He was the first player to get more than 3,000 hits during his career, achieving a total of 3,081. He managed the Chicago Cubs (1879–97), winning five National League pennants. He was elected to the National Baseball Hall of Fame in 1939.

ARCARO [*är-kăr'ō*], **GEORGE EDWARD ("EDDIE")** (1916–), American jockey born in Cincinnati, Ohio. He was the leading stakes-winning jockey in the history of thoroughbred racing. During a 31-year career (1931–61) he rode 4,779 winning mounts which earned $30,039,543. In 1941 he rode Whirlaway to the "Triple Crown" (victories in the Kentucky Derby, Preakness Stakes, and Belmont Stakes); riding Citation, he repeated the feat in 1948, making him the only jockey win the "Triple Crown" twice.

ARCHERY, a modern sport employing bows and arrows for either target shooting or hunting. (The bow and arrow was an important weapon of warfare for many centuries until the invention of firearms made it obsolete.) Archery became established as a sport in Europe in the 17th century. In the United States its popularity was furthered by the formation, in 1879, of the National Archery Association, which governs all organized target shooting in the country. The National Field Archery Association was organized in 1939, and controls all field and hunting activities associated with the sport. Field archery employs

Bowhunting Magazine, Riderwood, Md.

Line-up of archers competing in a National Field Archery Association championship tournament at Grayling, Mich.

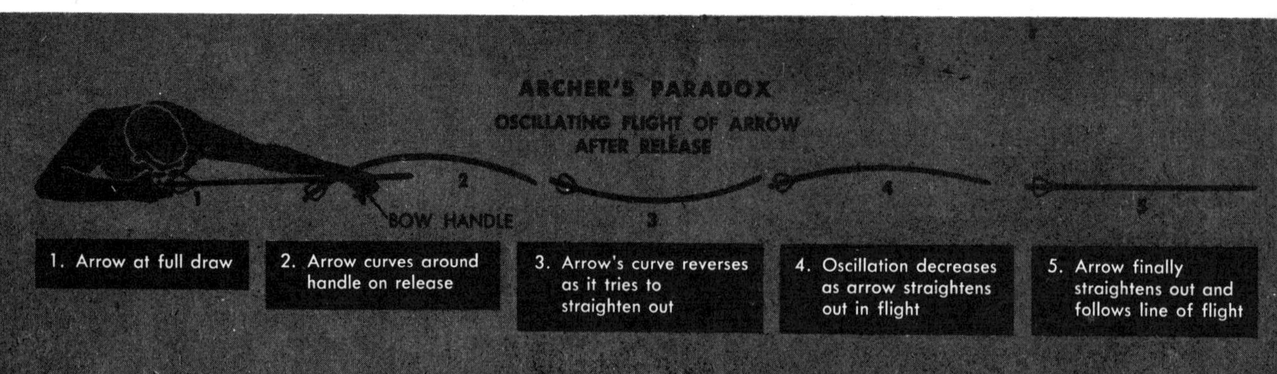

PARTS OF THE BOW

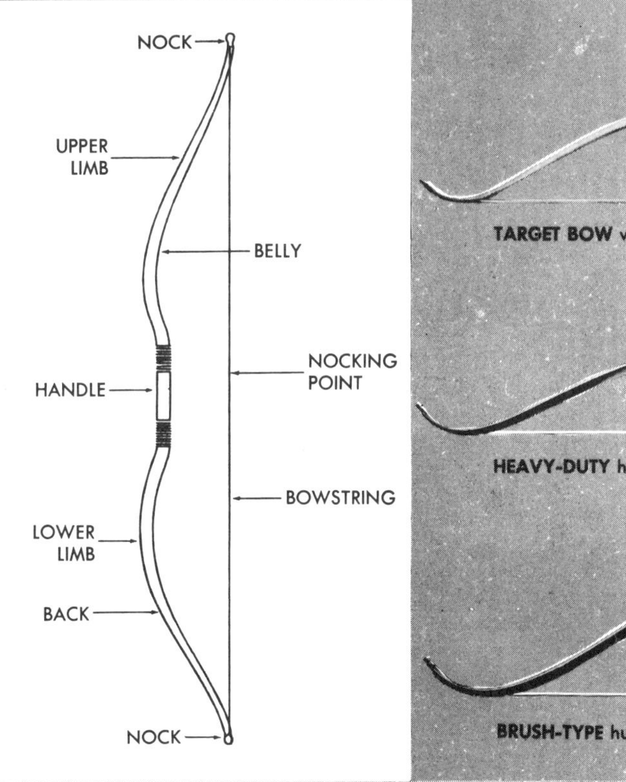

THREE KINDS OF BOWS

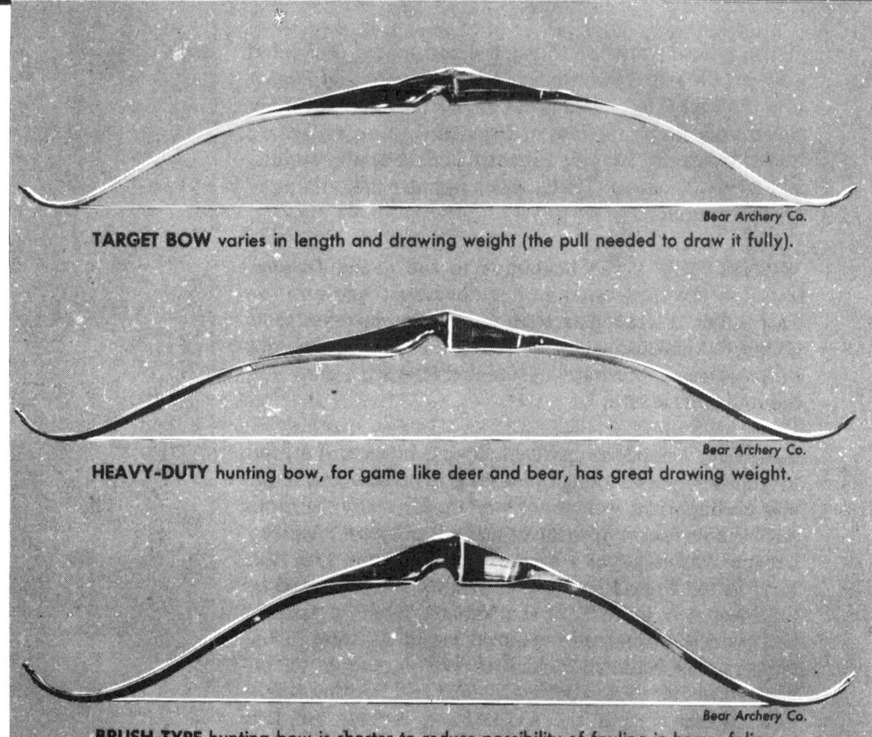

TARGET BOW varies in length and drawing weight (the pull needed to draw it fully).

HEAVY-DUTY hunting bow, for game like deer and bear, has great drawing weight.

BRUSH-TYPE hunting bow is shorter to reduce possibility of fouling in heavy foliage.

FOUR KINDS OF ARROWHEADS

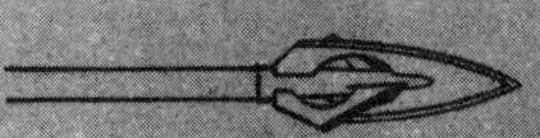

The razorhead arrow is designed for big-game hunting. The sharp head is made of steel.

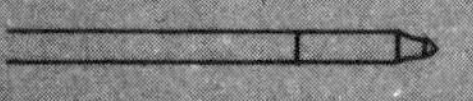

This head is easily recoverable because a ridge near the tip reduces penetration.

The blunt shape of this arrowhead ensures a powerful impact when small game is hit.

The insert target point, used in target practice, enables archer to achieve accuracy.

PARTS OF THE ARROW

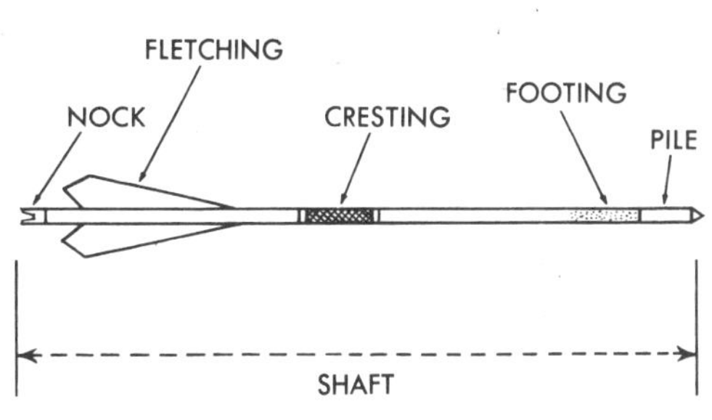

ARCHERY ACCESSORIES

Accessories for archers include leather tabs or gloves to protect the fingers pulling the bowstring; arm guards, also made of leather, to shield insides of forearms from the sting of released string; and quivers, worn either on hips or shoulders, to carry arrows.

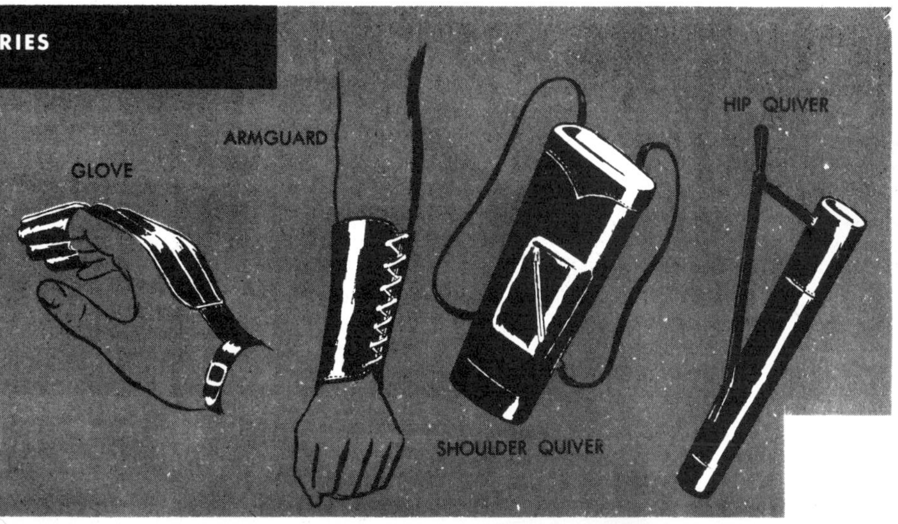

Jim Leder, champion at archery, now mainly a sport but once man's chief means of hunting and warfare. (BOWHUNTING MAGAZINE)

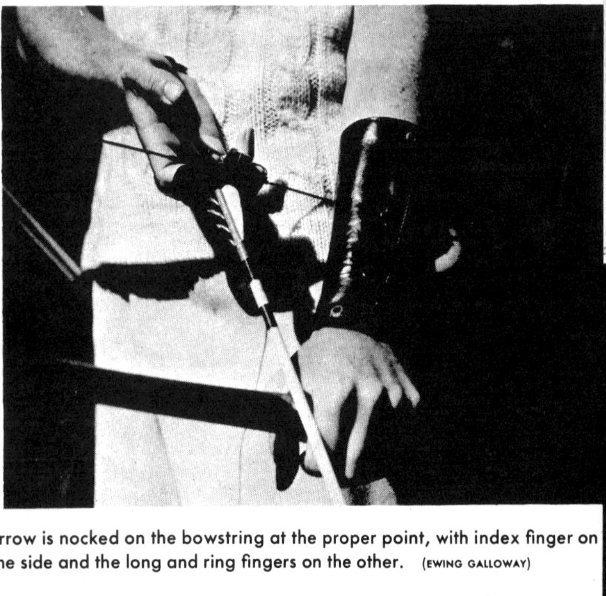

Arrow is nocked on the bowstring at the proper point, with index finger on one side and the long and ring fingers on the other. (EWING GALLOWAY)

Vicki Cook, an expert archer, displays perfect stance in a target-shooting demonstration. (BOWHUNTING MAGAZINE)

targets, living or otherwise, in natural surroundings. It is estimated that over 4,000,000 persons participate in present-day archery as a sport in the United States.

The basic equipment of archery includes a strung bow, a supply of suitable arrows, and a target. The most common woods in use in manufacturing bows are yew, lemonwood, Osage orange, sassafras, and hickory. Within recent years Fiberglas bows have been made, but the vast majority of bows are still made of the traditional woods. There are five basic types of arrows: target, field, hunting, flight, and fishing. The best woods for arrows are cedar, pine (Norway), Douglas fir, and spruce. Aluminum arrows are available but very expensive.

The standard archery target is 4 ft. in diameter, circular in shape, and made of canvas or other durable cloth, with backing of woven march grass or rye straw about 6 in. thick. On the face of the target are painted five concentric circles. The center one (the bull's-eye) is gold, and has a 9.6-in. diameter. From the gold outward, the other concentric circles are painted red, blue, black, and white, respectively, and are 4.8 in. wide. Arrows hitting within the gold circle score 9 points; those hitting the other circles score as follows: red, 7 points; blue, 5; black, 3; white, 1. Arrows that pass completely through the face of the target, or bounce off it, score 5 points no matter where they hit. The target is hung or supported so that the bull's-eye is exactly 4 ft. above the ground. It is usually supported on a firmly anchored tripod so that it will not slip or be upset by the wind. National championship matches in both men's and women's divisions are held annually in the United States.

From the gold bull's-eye (9 points) outward, circles are red, blue, black, and white, respectively denoting scores of 7, 5, 3, and 1. (BOWHUNTING MAGAZINE)

ARMOUR, THOMAS DICKSON ("TOMMY") (1894–1968), American golfer, born in Edinburgh, Scotland. He won the French amateur championship in 1920 and turned professional in 1924. In 1927 he won the United States Open and Canadian Open tournaments. Other notable victories came in the Professional Golfers Association (PGA) tournament (1930) and British Open (1931). One of the greatest iron players during his competitive career, Armour became equally renowned as an instructor beginning in the 1940's. He was elected to golf's Hall of Fame in 1942.

ARMSTRONG, HENRY, ring name of Henry Jackson (1912–), American boxer, noted for his extremely aggressive style. He was born in Columbus, Miss., and began boxing professionally in 1932. In 1938 he had the rare distinction of holding three championships simultaneously—the featherweight, which he had won in 1937, and the lightweight and welterweight titles, won in 1938. After retiring from boxing in 1945, Armstrong entered the clergy. He was elected to boxing's Hall of Fame in 1954.

ATHLETICS, a term used in the broad sense to cover all competitive individual and team games and sports depending upon feats of physical strength or skill. In England, however, athletics is generally construed as covering only track and field events.

Athletic sports were practiced in various forms by the ancient Egyptians and Asian races. They were brought to a high standard of development by the establishment of the Olympic Games in 776 B.C. in Greece. The Tailteann games were established in Iceland some 3,000 years ago, making them the most ancient known organized games.

AUTOMOBILE RACING, sport involving either speed competition among racing cars of various designs, or racing "against the clock" for individual performance records. The vehicles may be specially designed racing cars, sports cars, stock cars (standard passenger cars), midget cars, sprint cars, jalopies, or "karts" (small vehicles consisting of a chassis, a seat, and an engine mounted over the rear axle).

At one time automobile racing was allowed on public roads under proper supervision. That type of racing was banned about the time of World War I, however, and most organized auto racing in the United States and Canada is now confined to "closed-circuit" tracks, specially built for the sport.

Automobile racing has grown tremendously in the United States since the end of World War II. Up to that time it had been carried on on a small scale except for the Indianapolis 500-mi. race. There were several reasons for this increase in interest and participation. Some returning servicemen had become accustomed to operating fast airplanes, speedy PT boats, and maneuverable jeeps. Many of these men had admired and acquired small foreign sports cars, and were anxious to test the cars in competition. There were numerous unused airstrips that served in many cases as temporary race courses until per-

Contestants dash across the track toward their sports cars, entered in a 12-hour endurance test in Sebring, Fla. (GULF OIL CORPORATION)

manent ones could be built. Tires were safer for high-speed driving, brakes were more efficient and reliable, and higher-octane gasoline was more readily available. All these factors contributed to increased participation in the sport by men and women from every walk of life.

Early History. There were not many horseless carriages, or mechanized buggies, in the world before the men wealthy enough to own them, and daring enough to drive them, decided to test them in competition with other vehicles. The first organized automobile race in the world was held in France in 1894. The course was a 78-mi. stretch of road from Paris to Rouen. Over 100 vehicles with various types of motive power entered, but only 21 actually started. Some were propelled by gasoline engines, some by steam, and others by electricity, compressed air, huge sails, or even large coiled-steel springs. A De Dion steam-powered vehicle crossed the finish line first, but was disqualified because it was not a strictly self-propelled vehicle. The winner's prize was divided between a Peugeot and a Panhard-Levassor. The maximum speed was about 11 mph.

Although there was a "reliability run" in Chicago in 1895 over a 54-mi. course, the first real automobile race in the United States was held on Apr. 15, 1900, in Springfield, N.Y. It was won by A. L. Riker in an electric car, averaging about 25 mph for the 50-mi. run.

Automobile racing came of age when the first of the annual Vanderbilt Cup races was held on Oct. 8, 1904, sponsored by William K. Vanderbilt. It was held over a 28-mi. stretch of public roads on Long Island and attracted more than 25,000 spectators. The race, involving 18 cars, was won by A. L. Campbell in a Mercedes.

Another milestone was the great "around the world" race. It began in New York City on Feb. 12, 1908, when six cars—French, Italian, German, and American—headed for Paris via Alaska and Siberia. The German car, a Protos, and the American car, a Thomas Flyer, arrived in Paris in that order on July 30. The German entry was disqualified, however, because it had traveled part of the distance in a railroad car, and the American entry was declared the winner.

Indianapolis Race. Shortly after the Vanderbilt Cup road races were abandoned in 1908 because of the number of injuries incurred by spectators, and possibly because of the frequency with which Europeans were winning, a group of men headed by Carl G. Fisher opened the Indianapolis Speedway in Aug., 1909. It was built originally for stock-car racing, as a place to test the endurance of the products of the infant automotive industry. But the idea was not very popular with the manufacturers, who realized that the races served to reveal basic defects of their vehicles in addition to testing mechanical innovations. Gradually the track became a course for racing cars only. It has featured such famous drivers as Berner Eli ("Barney") Oldfield, Ralph DePalma, Tommy Milton, Ray Harroun, and, more recently, Wilbur Shaw, three-time winner of the "500."

The first of the annual 500-mi. Memorial Day races was run in 1911. The winner was Ray Harroun who drove a six-cylinder Marmon Wasp at an average speed of 74.59 mph. Since that time the race has become the world's best-attended sporting event, attracting crowds of about 200,000. The 2½-mi. track, once known as the "brickyard" because of its original paving, has since been resurfaced with asphalt. The cars travel counterclockwise around the rectangular, curved-corner track, which is banked at a 16-degree angle. The front and back stretches measure 3,300 ft.; the short straightaways at the north and south ends are each 660 ft.

The Indianapolis 500-mi. race was the first automobile racing event in the United States to receive international recognition. It is sanctioned by the United States Auto Club, under the supervision of the international governing body for the sport, the Fédération Internationale de l'Automobile. The starting field for the classic race is limited to the 33 fastest cars, determined by four-lap qualification runs conducted prior to the race.

Measured-Mile Racing. Since the early automobile

Line-up in Chicago for performance tests of electric cars during the early days of motoring. (SY SEIDMAN)

A tense moment during the 1908 Briercliffe Road Race held in Westchester County in New York. (SY SEIDMAN)

Start of a Ford marathon from New York to Seattle in 1909. Typical speed limits of the time were 15 to 25 mph. (CULVER PICTURES, INC.)

The finish of the 1912 Indianapolis 500-mi. classic. Joe Dawson, the winner, averaged 78.72 mph. (CULVER PICTURES, INC.)

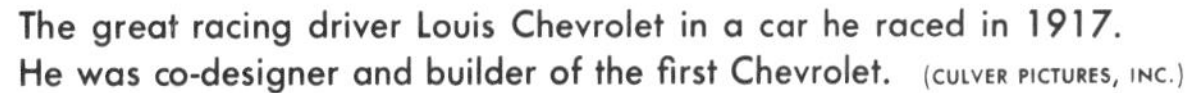

The great racing driver Louis Chevrolet in a car he raced in 1917. He was co-designer and builder of the first Chevrolet. (CULVER PICTURES, INC.)

Ray Harroun won the first Indianapolis "500" in 1911.
(FIRESTONE TIRE AND RUBBER COMPANY)

Wilbur Shaw, a three-time winner, in 1937, 1939, and 1940.
(FIRESTONE TIRE AND RUBBER COMPANY)

races were run over rough, unsurfaced roads, it was not always possible to find out the top speed of the vehicle because of the road hazards. Soon the idea of testing cars on a smooth-surfaced stretch of road became popular. Such testing was conducted by cars employing a "flying start," and was in reality racing against the clock. The first driver to reach the speed of a mile a minute was Camille Janatzy, a Frenchman. Driving an electric-powered car, he averaged 65.79 mph in 1899. Five years later, a Frenchman named Rigolly became the first driver to be officially credited with bettering the 100-mph mark. On July 21, 1904, Rigolly drove a four-cylinder Gobron-Brillie along a road at Ostend, Belgium, at an average speed of 103.56 mph for 1 km.

Fred Marriott, an American, was the first to go 2 mi. a minute, when he drove a Stanley Steamer at 127.66 mph in Daytona Beach, Fla., in Jan., 1906. The last of the "normal" racing cars to attain a world speed record was Maj. H. O. D. Segrave's V-12 Sunbeam, which reached 152.33 mph in Mar., 1926. Thereafter, specially built, aircraft-engined giants set the records for the measured mile, which became steadily more impressive. An Englishman, Sir Malcolm Campbell, reached 301.129 mph with his Bluebird vehicle in 1935 at the Bonneville Salt Flats in Utah. In 1947 a new official world record, 394.196 mph, was set by John Cobb of England in his Railton Special at the Salt Flats. This record continued to stand in the early 1960's. The mark was his two-way average. In order to establish an official record, the driver must traverse the course twice.

In 1963 the American Craig Breedlove achieved an average speed of 407.75 mph over the same course. He drove a vehicle radically unlike any previously used in racing—a jet-driven, three-wheel machine. Consequently his mark stood in a special category. In 1964 this record was bettered both by Breedlove himself and by other racers who drove jet-powered, four-wheel vehicles. By 1965 the record had been pushed to more than 600 mph by Breedlove driving his Spirit of America.

Racing Cars. Most of the racing cars used in international competition are in one of the following six categories set up by the Fédération Internationale de l'Automobile:

Formula I, cars of the type used in Grand Prix competition (*see* INTERNATIONAL RACING below). There is no restriction as to their design, but the engine must not exceed 1,500 cc. (91.5 cu. in.) without a supercharger. This type of car is a single-seater with no fenders, headlights, bumpers, starters, or reverse gear.

Formula Junior, very small racers that are limited to an engine size of 1,000 cc. (61 cu. in.). Also, engine parts are limited to those from touring cars of standard makes. These too are stripped single-seaters.

Formula IC (Intercontinental), a recently sanctioned racing category designed as a concession to devotees of cars larger and faster than the Formula I machines. This group is allowed power plants up to 3,000 cc. (183 cu. in.). There are few races for this type of machine.

Formula Libre, cars of almost any design and with engines of unlimited capacity. The term is also used to describe a race in which there are no restrictions as to the capacity of the cars entered.

Gran Turismo (Grand Touring), cars that are actual production vehicles. They must conform to models well defined in manufacturers' sales catalogues. To qualify for this category, a car must be one of at least 100 models (with identical mechanisms and coachwork) constructed within a period of 12 consecutive months.

Sport Cars, specially designed production road vehicles that are suitable for racing competition. This category covers a wide range of machines, and includes the types most commonly used in present-day competition.

In addition to the above, there are various types of very small (midget) cars. Sprint cars are modeled on large cars of the type used in the Indianapolis "500" but are more maneuverable than the latter. Jalopies are dilapidated but operable stock cars that are driven in a careless manner, and are often crashed deliberately for the delight of a particular type of racing fan. "Karts," the most recent type of racing cars to be organized in national competition, are tiny vehicles consisting of little more than an engine, four wheels, and a frame only a few inches above the ground. They attain very high speed (60–70 mph) for their size.

International Racing. The international racing program in any one year consists of scheduled speed competitions, sanctioned by the Fédération Internationale de l'Automobile, and regularity, or rally, competitions. (Rallies are tests of driving and navigational ability conducted at controlled speeds). There are usually about 10 speed events that count in determining the world drivers' championship, and these are designated as Grand Prix events. There is one such event yearly in each country represented in the Fédération Internationale de l'Automobile. Formula I autos are used in such competition.

There are also about the same number of speed races to determine the sports-car constructors' world championship. In the regularity, or rally, competition, there are about a dozen events that count in determining the European

WINNERS OF THE INDIANAPOLIS "500"			
DATE	DRIVER	CAR	AVERAGE MPH
1911	Ray Harroun	Marmon	74.59
1912	Joe Dawson	National	78.72
1913	Jules Goux	Peugeot	75.933
1914	Rene Thomas	Delage	82.47
1915	Ralph DePalma	Mercedes	89.84
1916	Dario Resta	Peugeot	84.00*
1919	Howard Wilcox	Peugeot	88.05
1920	Gaston Chevrolet	Monroe	88.62
1921	Tommy Milton	Frontenac	89.62
1922	Jimmy Murphy	Murphy Special	94.48
1923	Tommy Milton	H.C.S. Special	90.95
1924	L. L. Corum and Joe Boyer	Duesenberg Special	98.23
1925	Peter DePaolo	Duesenberg Special	101.13
1926	Frank Lockhart	Miller Special	95.904†
1927	George Souders	Duesenberg Special	97.545
1928	Louis Meyer	Miller Special	99.482
1929	Ray Keech	Simplex Piston Ring Special	97.585
1930	Billy Arnold	Harry Hartz Special	100.448
1931	Louis Schneider	Bowes Seal Fast Special	96.629
1932	Fred Frame	Miller-Hartz Special	104.144
1933	Louis Meyer	Tydol Special	104.162
1934	William Cummings	Boyle Products Special	104.863
1935	Kelly Petillo	Gilmore Speedway Special	106.240
1936	Louis Meyer	Ring Free Special	109.069
1937	Wilbur Shaw	Shaw-Gilmore Special	113.580
1938	Floyd Roberts	Burd Piston Ring Special	117.200
1939	Wilbur Shaw	Boyle Special	115.035
1940	Wilbur Shaw	Boyle Special	114.277
1941	Floyd Davis and Mauri Rose	Noc-Out Hose Clamp Special	115.117
1946	George Robson	Thorne Engineering Special	114.820
1947	Mauri Rose	Blue Crown Spark Plug Special	116.338
1948	Mauri Rose	Blue Crown Spark Plug Special	119.814
1949	Bill Holland	Blue Crown Spark Plug Special	121.327
1950	Johnny Parsons	Kurtiss-Kraft Wynns Special	124.002**
1951	Lee Wallard	Belanger Special	126.244
1952	Troy Ruttman	Agajanian Special	128.922
1953	William Vukovich	Fuel Injection Special	128.740
1954	William Vukovich	Fuel Injection Special	130.840
1955	Robert Sweikert	Zink Special	128.209
1956	Pat Flaherty	Zink Special	128.490
1957	Sam Hanks	Belond Exhaust Special	135.601
1958	Jimmy Bryan	Belond Special	133.791
1959	Rodger Ward	Leader Card Special	135.856
1960	Jim Rathmann	Ken Paul Special	138.767
1961	A. J. Foyt	Indianapolis Bowes Special	139.131
1962	Rodger Ward	Leader Special	140.292
1963	Parnelli Jones	Agajanian-Willard Battery Special	143.137
1964	A. J. Foyt	Offenhauser Special	147.350
1965	Jim Clark	Lotus-Ford	150.686
1966	Graham Hill	Lola-Ford	144.317
1967	A. J. Foyt	Coyote-Ford Special	151.207
1968	Bobby Unser	Offenhauser Eagle	152.882
1969	Mario Andretti	Hawk Ford	156.867
1970	Al Unser	P. J. Colt-Ford	155.749
1971	Al Unser	P. J. Colt-Ford	157.735
1972	Mark Donahue	Penske McLaren Offenhauser	163.465
1973	Gordon Johncock	Eagle-Offenhauser	159.014††

*300 mi. †400 mi. **345 mi. ††332.5 mi.

championship. In addition to the events enumerated, there are hundreds of other organized auto races throughout the world for vehicles in the Formula I and Sports-Cars categories, and for the Formula Junior, Gran Turismo, and Formula IC categories.

In the races that determine the drivers' world champion-

Straightaway in Daytona Beach, Fla., scene of automobile racing since 1903. (GOODYEAR TIRE AND RUBBER CO.)

Left, drivers of "midget" cars round a turn in a pacing demonstration. (CULVER PICTURES, INC.)

Sports cars in the 24-hour endurance contest at Le Mans, France. (MARVIN E. NEWMAN)

ship, points are awarded as follows: 1st place, 8 points; 2d place, 6 points; 3d place, 4 points; 4th place, 3 points; 5th place, 2 points. The driver (placed or not) who achieves the fastest lap is awarded 1 point.

In the regularity, or rally, competition, any type of automobile is generally acceptable. In a race, the purpose is to reach the finish line as quickly as possible. In a rally, the purpose is to arrive at the finish line at exactly the proper time according to the given instructions. The main portion of a rally is over public roads, and the maintaining of a time schedule forms a substantial part of the competition. There are straightforward rallies, and also trick rallies in which the instructions are purposely confusing or ambiguous. The outstanding international rallies are the Monte Carlo (Switzerland), Acropolis (Greece), Midnight Sun (Scandinavia), and Royal Automobile Club (England).

Racing Drivers. In many foreign countries champion drivers are treated as national heroes. Since 1906, when Grand Prix racing originated, international competition has been marked by the emergence of outstanding figures. Tazio Nuvolari (1892–1953) is often called the finest of the Grand Prix drivers. This temperamental Italian from Mantua was unorthodox in his driving habits, but his record of victories was impressive. Some authorities claim that the German perfectionist Rudolf Caracciola (1901–59) was the most brilliant of all. Juan Manuel Fangio (1911–)

of Argentina, five times world champion, compiled one of the greatest records of all time. Stirling Moss (1929–) of England was outstanding in the early 1960's until he was severely injured in a crash in 1962.

A list of other outstanding drivers would include Barney Oldfield, Wilbur Shaw, Walter Hansgen, Phil Hill, Alphonse de Portago, Briggs Cunningham, and Masten Gregory, all of the United States; Pierre Levegh, Jean Behra, and Maurice Trintignant, France; Richard Seaman, John Cobb, and Peter Collins, England; and Alberto Ascari and Piero Taruffi, Italy.

Racing in the United States. In recent years almost all organized automobile racing in the United States has been controlled or supervised by three governing bodies for particular types of racing competition: the Sports Car Club of America, the United States Auto Club, and the National Association for Stock Car Auto Racing. All these groups have come into existence since the sport was revived and expanded after World War II. What little auto racing there was in the United States up to that time had been under the supervision of the Contest Board of the American Automobile Association (AAA), but the AAA decided to disassociate itself from all forms of speed competition involving the automobile, effective Jan. 1, 1956. This stimulated the growth of the three present supervisory bodies which are represented on the Automobile Competition Committee for the United States, an affiliate of the Fédération Internationale de l'Automobile.

Sports Car Club of America (SCCA). This organization was established in 1945 by a small group of sports-car owners "to encourage the preservation, ownership, and operation of sports cars." The membership of the club has grown to about 13,000, including many regional organizations throughout the United States. The club is concerned with amateur racing only, but allows any member holding an SCCA competition license to accept remuneration, when racing abroad, without loss of amateur status. In the United States and certain nearby places, such as the Bahamas, Mexico, and Canada, drivers may compete in approved events against professionals, but may not accept prize money. The headquarters of the club are in Westport, Conn.

United States Auto Club (USAC). This body was formed in 1955 as a nonprofit organization to succeed the Contest Board of the American Automobile Association. Its purpose is to provide qualified leadership and competent officiating personnel at the major automotive competitions in the United States. The club co-operates with the Fédération Internationale de l'Automobile, and operates within its rules, in an effort to promote international competition. Included in the club's activities are five divisions of racing, plus certified automotive tests and runs aimed at bettering the world's straightaway speed record. The five divisions include competition under the following headings: National Championship, Sprint, Late Model Stock, Midget, and Sports Cars. Some of the most important events are the Indianapolis "500" and 16 other races for Indianapolis-type cars; the Pikes Peak Hill Climb; the Mobilgas Economy Run; the Bonneville Salt Flats speed trials for world records; and numerous automotive certification test runs. Headquarters are in Indianapolis, Ind.

National Association for Stock Car Auto Racing (NASCAR). This organization was established in 1947 by William H. G. France, and has its headquarters in Daytona Beach, Fla. A stock car is any standard passenger model that can be purchased from any dealer. Stock-car racing was stimulated enormously when the Automobile Manufacturers' Association decided in 1957 to de-emphasize the racing aspects and speed capacities of American cars. The effect was to increase the number of individual, or independent, competitors.

NASCAR is the world's largest professional organization devoted solely to automobile racing. In 1960 it sanctioned 1,156 races, and its membership reached 7,550. The total amount of prize money for its sanctioned events reached almost $2,000,000 for the same year. NASCAR functioned on 93 race tracks throughout the United States and Canada in 1960. The outstanding racing installation in this category is the Daytona Speedway near Daytona Beach, Fla. This $3,000,000 speedway, opened in 1959, includes three turns and three straightaways. It is a 2½-mi. track with an infield sports-car course (making the over-all circuit 3.81 mi.). The turns are well banked, and maximum speeds 20 mph in excess of those attainable at the Indianapolis Speedway are possible.

Outstanding U.S. Races. The first U.S. Grand Prix auto race was held in 1959 in Sebring, Fla. In 1960 and 1961 the event was transferred to a track at Riverside, Calif.

The 12-hour endurance race in Sebring, Fla., was inaugurated in 1951. It is the foremost sports-car race in the United States and the longest auto race of any type.

The Pikes Peak Hill Climb is held annually on July 4, near Colorado Springs, Colo. It is a 12½-mi. event for special cars and stock cars.

The Road America 500-mi. race for sports cars is held annually at Elkhart Lake, Wis. It comprises 125 laps over hilly, twisting roads, and is sponsored by the Sports Car Club of America.

The first U.S. postwar road race was run in Watkins Glen, N.Y., in 1948. It was initially held on public roads of the town, but has been conducted subsequently on a specially built closed-circuit course just outside the community. It features both Formula Libre and Grand Prix competition.

HOT RODDING

The classic definition of a hot rod is a standard automobile that has been improved and modified to provide better performance and handling characteristics. The average passenger car represents a large number of compromises in efficiency made for convenience, appearance, or comfort. The art and, to a great degree, science of hot rodding is to sacrifice or reduce these compromises in favor of functionalism. Its extreme is seen in the bare, for-performance-only competition hot rod. Its mildest degree is in the late-model street hot rod. There are a number of stages between the two extremes.

The hoary old British admonition to the racing car builder: "Simplificate and add lightness . . ." aptly if ungrammatically describes the basic process by which the hot rodder approaches his goal. Depending on the degree of performance desired, the original automobile is relieved of many of its built-in compromises and its engine and suspension system tuned to a much tauter state than would be saleable to the average buyer. Gentle control operation, smooth engine idling, and silence are sacrificed for precise suspension control, quick steering and shifting, and raw engine performance. Unnecessary (to the hot rodder) weight in the form of trim, standard bumpers, and side window glass is removed. The possible changes are many, varied, and often expensive. The accompanying bibliography gives an introduction to the vocabulary of the art. Rare is the high school freshman who does not have at least a nodding acquaintance with such items as headers (racing exhausts), superchargers, cams, alloy wheels, and the host of other devices in the modern hot rodder's arsenal.

History. Many of the classic racing cars that thundered over the roads and tracks of the United States and Europe in the first decades of the 20th century were actually stripped and "hot rodded" versions of the stock production cars of that era. Most of this work was carried out by the factories or privately by wealthy owners. Hot rodding, as we know it today, had its beginnings with the production automobiles of the 1920's and '30's.

Hot rodding for the street began with the Ford Model T. There was, in the 1920's, a kind of professional racing that required modified production-type engines. Some of the equipment developed for this filtered down to the nonprofessional enthusiast. It was expensive, however, so early hot rodders began building their own. Among these was a young La Canada, Calif., man named Ed Winfield, now considered the father of hot rodding. So successful was his home-built equipment that he found himself in business making similar material for his friends. He founded a business field that 40 years later burgeoned into a complex multimillion-dollar industry supported by enthusiastic customers all over the world.

Hot rodding as a sport began with an unknown enthusiast on a Mojave desert outing. He drove over a small rise to view a vast alkali flat marked on the map as Muroc Dry Lake (now Edwards Air Force Base). From helter-skelter groups running "on the floor and flat out" came a gradual organization that produced, on Mar. 25, 1931, the first formal lakes meet. At first these meets consisted of multicar dashes of similar cars lined abreast toward a finish line, winner take all. In the mid-1930's, electric timers were developed, and the cars run through a measured flying mile one at a time in a race against the clock. Hot rodding had assumed the form in which we see it today at lakes meets, the Bonneville National Speed Trials in Utah, and in somewhat modified form in the tremendously popular sport of drag racing.

World War II ended the early era of hot rodding. After the war, unorganized street racing returned, and the law cracked down. In response the hot rodders reorganized the Southern California Timing Association (SCTA) and sought out a new place to race. They found it at El Mirage dry lake.

Their publicity, both good and bad, brought hot rodding into national scope. Through the efforts of such organizers as Robert E. Petersen and Wally Parks, then executive secretary of SCTA, hot rodders were brought to the most famous straightaway in the world—Bonneville. During the last week of Aug., 1949, the first hot rod roared down the black line over the glistening field of salt that long had been the private province of professional world-record drivers. Hot rodders had made the big time, and the Bonneville Nationals continues to this day.

But what of the rest of the United States, unblessed with dry lakes and salt deserts? Hot rodding had gone national and, out of the reach of the SCTA, street racing became a hazard. The answer came out of the form that street racing had taken. The usual illegal race was between two cars beginning from a standing start and going from stop light to stop light. Since the distance from light

An altered roadster crossing the starting line on a speed run at a major hot rod competition. (PETERSEN PUBLISHING CO.)

to light was roughly a quarter of a mile, why couldn't an exact quarter-mile be laid out off the streets? The first track was on a strip of two-lane road at the Goleta Airport just north of Santa Barbara, Calif. Almost immediately afterward Chief Ralph Parker and Sergeant Bud Coons of the Pomona, Calif., Police Department obtained permission to use the abandoned Fontana airstrip. They successfully halted street racing in their city. The cry of "Drag it out!" had moved off the street to supervised strips of pavement out of harm's way, and a new sport was born. Drag racing has since, under the guidance of the National Hot Rod Association, become the most popular form of automotive competition of all time.

The Drag Race. Essentially simple, a drag race consists of cars accelerating one at a time from a standing start against the clock over a measured quarter-mile, or two at a time against each other over the same distance. From its small beginning in 1949, drag racing has grown into a nationwide activity attracting hundreds of thousands of enthusiasts every weekend. Part of this popularity lies in the simplicity of the physical layout and control of the drag strip raceway, and part in fact that virtually any licensed driver with almost any sort of motor vehicle that will pass a safety inspection can find satisfactory competition at the strip.

The few original classes of cars based on those used in dry lakes competition have grown to about 100. They range from showroom standard, or pure stock automobiles, through various forms of modified production cars (those with essentially standard bodies but with modified engines). The all-out dragster is essentially a light tubular frame, with a cockpit at the extreme rear, powered by a modified engine producing more than 1,000 hp. These are capable of covering the 1,320-ft. distance in seven seconds from a standing start, attaining terminal speeds of more than 200 mph. Not only is every piece of hardware in the hot rodder's arsenal used, but also exotic fuels based on methyl alcohol mixed with nitromethane.

While the less powerful classes of car are largely run by amateurs, the exotic dragsters and the newer exhibition cars are virtually the private preserve of the professional. A prerequisite to drive in this company is the possession of a National Hot Rod Association license and a Federal Aviation Authority medical fitness certificate.

Hot rodding has come a long way from mad dashes in fenderless roadsters across a desert alkali bed. Today it is an organized, creative activity.

B

BADMINTON [*băd'mĭn-tən*], game similar to tennis, in which two or four players bat a shuttlecock back and forth over a net, using very light racquets. The regulation playing area measures 44 by 17 ft. for singles play, and 44 by 20 ft. for doubles. The length is divided by a net suspended across the middle of the court between two posts placed on the side lines. At its center, the net is suspended so that its top is 5 ft. above the level of the court; at the posts, the height is 5 ft. 1 in. The game may be played indoors or outdoors. Badminton rackets weigh about 5 oz. The shuttlecock is a half sphere to which feathers have been attached on the flat side. It is made of cork, rubber, or plastic, and weighs ⅙ oz.

Rules of Play. The object of the game is to bat the shuttlecock over the net in such a way that it cannot be hit for a return by the opposing player. The sudden plummeting action of the shuttlecock in flight makes its trajectory difficult to judge in attempting the return hit. In singles, play begins with a serve by one of the players, who must stand in the serving area with both feet in contact with the court until the racket hits the shuttlecock. The first serve of every game is from the server's right-hand service court into the receiver's right-hand service court. If the shuttlecock falls outside the latter area, a fault results. A good serve must be returned by the opposing player, by hitting the shuttlecock back over the net. Points go to the server only—one for each time his opponent is unable to return the shuttlecock successfully. Unsuccessful returns include hitting the shuttlecock into the net in such a way that it does not go over the net, or hitting it out of bounds. The server continues in that capacity until he commits a fault, or fails to return the opponent's volley. The winner is the player who scores either 15 or 21 points, as arranged before the start of play. In women's competition, the corre-

Backhand smash. Other common strokes are the lob and drive.

Post Dispatch—Black Star

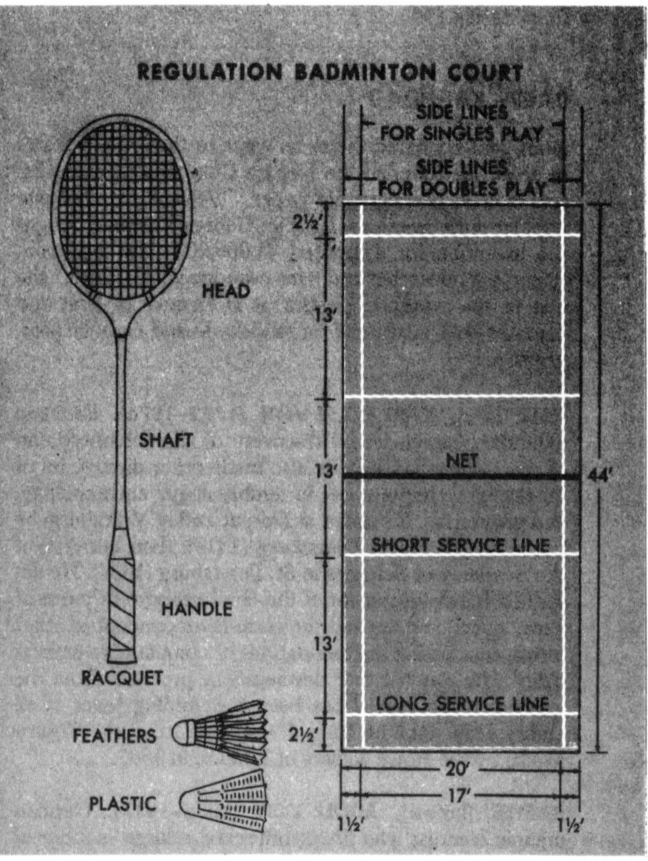

sponding figure is 11 points. In doubles, the service alternates between partners.

History. Badminton takes its name from the country estate of the Duke of Beaufort in Gloucestershire, England. It came about through a combination of two games, poona, and battledore and shuttlecock, about 1873. In poona, an Indian game, a parchment ball is batted over a net with rackets. It was learned by British army officers stationed in India, and subsequently brought back to England by them. Battledore and shuttlecock has been played in Europe and the Orient for at least 2,000 years. In it, contestants bat a shuttlecock back and forth, without permitting the shuttlecock to touch the ground, and without use of a net.

Shortly after its origin in England, badminton spread to the United States and Canada, where it has had its greatest popularity since 1930. The American Badminton Association is the governing body for the sport in the United States. International match competition for the Thomas Cup began in 1948.

BAKER, JOHN FRANKLIN ("HOME RUN") (1886–1963), American baseball player who was the foremost home-run hitter before the present era of the lively baseball. He was born in Trappe, Md. During a 13-year career in the American League as a third baseman with Philadelphia and New York, beginning in 1908, he hit 93 home runs. He led the league in home runs during three consecutive seasons beginning in 1911, and tied for the lead in 1914.

BANNISTER [*băn'ĭs-tər*], **ROGER GILBERT** (1929–), English middle-distance and mile runner, first man to run a mile in less than four minutes in accredited competition. He established the record, 3:59.4 (since surpassed), in Oxford, England, in 1954. He became a practicing physician in 1954, when he retired from athletic competition.

BASEBALL, an outdoor sport played in the United States, Canada, and other parts of the world. Millions of fans watch major-league baseball games in parks or on television during each season, which lasts from early April to late September. The World Series, played annually in October between the champions of the two major leagues, the American and National, is one of the most important sports events in the world.

There are also minor professional leagues that serve as a training ground for the "majors," many semiprofessional teams, and thousands of college, high school, and other amateur teams.

Baseball has been a leading American sport since shortly after the formation of the National League in 1876. It evolved in the last half of the 19th century from two slow-paced English games, cricket and rounders. Its emphasis on skill and on clean, hard play, strictly governed by officials of unquestioned honesty and authority, did much to raise the level of all professional athletics in the United States. It was beset by scandal on one noteworthy occasion—in 1919—but moved quickly to set its house in order.

A baseball team has nine players: pitcher, catcher, first baseman, second baseman, third baseman, shortstop, left fielder, center fielder, and right fielder. The game is played by two teams, and the object of the game is to score more runs than the opposition. A run is scored when a player makes a complete circuit of the bases. A game includes nine innings, in each of which both opposing teams have turns at bat. If both teams have the same score after nine innings, play continues until the tie is broken.

The field of play is divided into two areas: infield, the territory within and immediately surrounding the 90-ft (27.4 m) square formed by the four bases (home plate, and first, second, and third bases); and outfield, the area beyond the infield or specifically, between the infield and the outlying boundaries of the field, usually marked by fences. Foul lines are drawn with chalk from home plate through first and third bases and on to the outfield fences to divide fair territory from foul. In the major leagues, in parks built before June 1, 1958, outfield fences must be at least 250 ft (76.2 m) from home plate at all points in fair territory. All major league parks built after that date must have a minimum distance of 325 ft (99.1 m) on both the first-base and third-base foul lines to the outfield fence. The distance to the center field fence must be at least 400 ft (121.9 m)

Early History of the Game

In 1905 a commission was appointed at the suggestion of Albert Goodwill Spalding, a leading 19th-century player and manager (who was also a sporting goods manufac-

UPI

Babe Ruth, one of baseball's immortals, broke many batting records with his powerful swing and perfect timing.

turer), to delve into the history of baseball and to endeavor to discover its exact origin. Patriotic Americans interested in the game had rejected the suggestion of British-born Henry Chadwick, baseball's first historian, that it was derived from cricket and rounders. The commission reported its findings two years later and, largely on the evidence of one Abner Graves, declared that baseball had been invented by Abner Doubleday, an American Army officer, at Cooperstown, N.Y., in 1839. Graves and Doubleday had been schoolmates at the time.

For many years this was the generally accepted version of baseball's origin, though it was questioned by some, and it formed the basis for a centennial celebration in 1939, at which time the National Baseball Hall of Fame was dedicated with great ceremony at Cooperstown. The final blow to the Doubleday myth was delivered almost simultaneously with the publication of two bulletins by the New York Public Library. In these, and in his later scholarly study of the history of all ball games, *Ball, Bat and Bishop* (1947), Robert William Henderson proved (1) that Doubleday was not even at Cooperstown in 1839, but at West Point as a cadet ineligible for summer leave; and (2) that the word "baseball" had been used in the 18th century in both England and colonial America to describe the games from which modern baseball grew.

Henderson gave credit to the Knickerbocker Club of New York, and particularly to Alexander Cartwright, a civil engineer and member of the club, for developing the first set of codified baseball rules in 1845. It was Cartwright who set the dimensions of the baseball "diamond" (as the infield square is sometimes called in popular usage) at approximately 90 ft (27 m) on a side.

There were 15 sections in the Knickerbocker rules, and about half of them have become permanent parts of baseball law. One major innovation was the specific ban against throwing a ball at a runner to put him out. The

Knickerbocker rules required another fielder to catch the throw and tag or touch the runner with the ball before he reached the safety of a base. The rules also defined a foul ("a ball knocked outside the range of the first or third base"); limited a batter to three "strikes" and a team to three "outs"; reduced the number of players to nine and required them to bat in turn; and set a game's limit at 21 "aces" (runs).

The first interclub game played under these rules took place on June 19, 1846, when the New York Nine (so named because of the number of players) defeated the Knickerbockers, 23–1, in four innings. Before long, other clubs in the New York area switched from cricket to baseball under the Knickerbocker rules. In 1853 the first advance write-up of a game appeared in the New York *Sunday Mercury*, and by 1858 Chadwick was writing regular reports for the sporting press.

As the game spread to Philadelphia, Boston, and Chicago in the 1850's, arguments developed over the playing rules. Originally, a batter was out if his fly ball was caught even on one bounce. The Knickerbockers eliminated that provision in 1857, and the ensuing controversy led to the establishment of the first baseball league.

Spread of the Game. The National Association of (amateur) Baseball Players was organized on Mar. 18, 1858, by 24 clubs from New York and New Jersey. A formal set of rules had been adopted a year earlier, largely based on those of the Knickerbockers. One major change set the game's limit at nine innings rather than 21 runs. In the three years prior to the Civil war, three more "firsts" were recorded: (1) admission was charged on July 28, 1858, for an all-star game at Jamaica, N.Y.; (2) the Excelsiors of Brooklyn made a tour of upstate New York in 1860; (3) the game spread to the West Coast (San Francisco) and the South (New Orleans).

Although competition between teams languished during the Civil War, the game itself received a great boost as soldiers from baseball centers played the game in camps and taught it to men from other areas. After the war new teams sprang up in almost every major city. In 1867, 237 clubs from eight states sent delegates to the convention of the National Association. In the same year, the Washington Nationals made the first coast-to-coast tour.

Competition between cities inevitably led to the practice of importing players, and to the surreptitious payment of money to the better ones. The amateur status of the game became a farce that ended when Alfred James Reach, later a well-known manufacturer of sporting goods, openly signed a professional contract with the Philadelphia Athletics in 1865.

In 1869 the Cincinnati Red Stockings fielded the first all-professional baseball team, whose aggregate payroll was $9,500. Captain Harry Wright signed the best available players, including his brother George, the game's first great star. Cincinnati won 68 games and tied one in 1869, and won 23 more the next year before losing to the Brooklyn Atlantics, 8–7.

The financial success of the Cincinnati club led to the organization of the National Association of Professional Baseball Players in 1871. This pioneer professional league lasted only five seasons. The game it played was still primitive—the pitching distance was 45 ft, or 14 m (the distance from the pitcher's mound to home plate is now 60 ft 6 inches, or 18.4 m), and all throws had to be underhand; players had no gloves, and the umpire was hired by the home team. Gambling on the outcome and rowdiness were features of almost every game.

Still, the National Association left its mark upon baseball. It standardized the size of the ball in 1872. In 1874 Spalding took the Boston Red Stockings and Philadelphia Athletics on an overseas tour (England and Ireland), a practice followed often in later years. During the league's last season, 1875, players began to experiment with gloves, and a college athlete, Fred W. Thayer of Harvard, invented the catcher's mask.

In addition to gambling and rowdiness at the games, the big problem of the National Association was "revolving," the shifting of players from one team to another at the end of each season. When William A. Hulbert, president of the Chicago team, signed Boston's four star players, including Spalding, to contracts for 1876 during the season of 1875, the premature release of the story in the newspapers produced a furor and a threat to bar Chicago from the league.

Negro Leagues. The rejection of black players by organized baseball after 1884 led to the formation the next year of the first all-black independent team. In 1920, a Negro National League was formed in Kansas City; the next year a Negro Eastern League arose. The champions of both met in a World Series from 1924 to 1932, when the depression killed both leagues. A few years later, Negro American and National Leagues were organized. They flourished, often playing their games in organized baseball's parks, until the latter lifted its ban after World War II. Some of the great stars of the Negro Leagues were pitchers Joe (Cyclone) Williams and Dick Redding, shortstop John Henry Lloyd and sluggers Home Run Johnson and Josh Gibson. Pitcher Leroy (Satchel) Paige was the only one of the fabled Negro League stars to play in organized baseball, but all of the first group of blacks

Sy Seidman

Intercity baseball competition predates the formation of leagues. Brooklyn v. Philadelphia in 1865.

Sy Seidman

Cincinnati Red Stockings, the first all-professional baseball team. (SY SEIDMAN)

Culver Pictures, Inc.

Albert Spalding, famous pitcher of early baseball and one of the organizers of the National League. (CULVER PICTURES, INC.)

to enter the major league—Jackie Robinson, Roy Campanella, Sam Jethroe, Larry Doby, and Monte Irvin among them—got their start in those leagues.

Formation of Modern Major Leagues

Origin of the National League. Hulbert took the initiative in forming the new National League in 1876 as a means of forestalling the attack on his Chicago franchise. Morgan Gardner Bulkeley of Connecticut was elected league president, but resigned in Dec., 1876, and was succeeded by Hulbert. The latter launched an immediate attack against gamblers and, in 1877, expelled four Louisville players accused of "throwing" games (allowing opponents to win). This sharp, decisive action ended gambling's threat to baseball for the next 40 years.

The charter members of the National League were Chicago (which won the first pennant, symbolic of the league championship), St. Louis, Hartford, Boston, Louisville, New York, Philadelphia, and Cincinnati. There were many changes of franchises in the next 25 years and the league had 12 teams from 1892 to 1899.

During the last two decades of the 19th century three other leagues also claimed "major" status, but only one lasted more than a single season. This was the American Association, which was organized as a minor league in 1881 and advanced to major-league standing the follow-

Sy Seidman

Three studies of Cornelius McGillicuddy, better known as Connie Mack, "the grand old man of baseball." Mack managed the Philadelphia Athletics from 1901 to 1950 and was president of the same club from 1950 to 1954.

Judge Kenesaw Mountain Landis, first commissioner of baseball. He ruled the major leagues with forcefulness and impartiality from 1920 until his death in 1944.

UPI

ing year. It had two advantages over the older league: (1) it charged only 25 cents for tickets to its games, half the National League admission fee, and (2) it permitted Sunday baseball, forbidden to National League teams.

Player raids by members of the two leagues ended with an agreement establishing peace in 1884. The champions of each league met in a play-off that year and annually thereafter until 1890. According to terms of the agreement, each league was to respect the other's territorial and player rights. Such provisions have been part of all interleague agreements since that time. The National League had already moved to halt the practice of "revolving" by allowing each member team to "reserve" a certain number of players at the end of each season. The club then had the sole right to bargain for the services of those players for the next season. Teams were allowed to reserve only four players at first, but the number gradually was increased to include the entire membership.

This reserve clause and the power it gives clubs to set contract terms for its players has been argued in baseball councils, courts, and the United States Congress ever since it was adopted. It has been called an instrument of monopoly by those who attack it, and has been labeled the only practical solution to baseball's unique personnel problems by its defenders.

The first attack on the reserve clause came in 1884 when Henry V. Lucas of St. Louis organized the Union Association and placed most of its eight teams in National League or American Association cities. Though about 50 players joined the new league, it lasted only one season.

In 1885 a players' organization, the Brotherhood of Baseball Players, was formed by John Montgomery Ward, shortstop of the New York Giants. It won approval from the existing leagues and negotiated several concessions for the players. But when a salary-classification system was adopted after the 1888 season, establishing wage standards, a split developed between the leagues and the Brotherhood, which broke into open war in Dec., 1889. Members of the Brotherhood formed a rival league, the Players League, in 1890. It had the services of most of the National League stars, but still lost money and was disbanded after operating a single season.

Controversy developed between the National League and American Association over the rights to players returning from the Players League. This eventually led to the end of the American Association, which had been losing money in most cities due to its low admission fee and the two baseball "wars," at the close of the season of 1891.

One of baseball's great problems in this period was the lack of a strong executive. Hulbert had died in 1882 and his successor, A. G. Mills (later head of the commission inspired by Spalding to report on the game's origin), resigned in 1885 during the league's settlement with the defunct Union Association. Nicholas ("Nick") Young, league secretary from 1876 to 1884, was elected president and served from 1885 through 1902. But Young was no Hulbert, and baseball's next strong leader came from another direction.

Origin of the American League. In 1893 the Western League, a minor league, elected a former sports writer, Byron Bancroft ("Ban") Johnson, as president. He recog-

nized the cumbersomeness of the 12-team National League, whose increase in size had resulted from the disbanding of the American Association. During the next seven years, with the assistance of men such as Charles Comiskey and Cornelius McGillicuddy ("Connie Mack"), Johnson made the series of moves that led to the formation of the American League in 1900. These moves included the securing of new financial backing, switching the location of several franchises of the Western League, and renaming the revamped organization the American League. In 1901 the American League attained major-league status, though it was not until two years later that the status was given full recognition by the rival league. The membership of the American League in 1901 included Chicago, Boston, Detroit, Philadelphia, Washington, Cleveland, Milwaukee, and Baltimore. In 1900 the National League, reduced again to eight teams, had franchises in Brooklyn, New York, Philadelphia, Boston, Pittsburgh, Chicago, Cincinnati, and St. Louis.

A bitter battle over personnel broke out between the two leagues after the formation of the American. Of 182 American League players in 1901, 111 had come from the National League, and this list included such giants of the game as Denton T. ("Cy") Young, Napoleon Lajoie, and Clark Griffith. Another former National League leader, John McGraw, was manager and part owner of Baltimore of the American League in 1901, but returned to the National League and became manager of the New York Giants midway in the 1902 season. (Baltimore had been a member of the National League from 1892 through 1899.)

The year 1903 proved a historic one for major-league baseball. It brought a truce between the American and National leagues, negotiated by Johnson and the new president of the older league, Harry C. Pulliam. The first World Series was played in that year between Boston of the American League and Pittsburgh of the National. A three-man National Commission was formed to govern all organized professional baseball; its membership at the outset included Johnson, Pulliam, and Gary Herrmann, owner of the Cincinnati club. In 1902 the American League replaced Milwaukee with St. Louis; in 1903 it replaced Baltimore with New York, thus giving major-league baseball a geographical pattern that remained unchanged for the next 50 years.

Both leagues adopted 154-game schedules for the 1904 season, which established a standard used by eight-team major and minor leagues ever since. Attendance increased rapidly in both leagues, the combined totals rising from 3,500,000 to 7,000,000 between 1901 and 1908. In no small measure this was due to the new authority Johnson gave to his umpires. The game earned the public's trust, and increased attendance led to larger stadiums being erected between 1910 and 1920, including the Polo Grounds in New York, Ebbets Field in Brooklyn, Comiskey Park in Chicago, and League Park in Cleveland. The steel of these parks, replacing the old wooden grandstands, symbolized the game's new permanency.

Increased prosperity brought another challenge when, in 1914, a group of millionaires, headed by the oilman Harry Sinclair, backed the Federal League as a rival to the American and National. It lasted two seasons (1914–15), lured several famous players from the other leagues, and unsuccessfully challenged the reserve clause in the courts. But the threat of World War I helped to force the Federal League out of existence.

World War I had only a minor effect on baseball otherwise, cutting attendance and forcing an early closing of the season of 1918. But the arrival of peace also brought about great increases in attendance, and the ill-fated World Series of 1919 drew receipts of $722,414. Even greater prosperity resulted from the arrival of the era of the lively baseball, typified by the home runs of George Herman ("Babe") Ruth, in the 1920's. In 1920 the New York Yankees of the American League drew a total attendance of 1,289,422, which remained a major league record for more than 25 years.

Modern Governing Body. The selection of a new "czar" to rule the game after World War I was the result of these developments: the "Black Sox scandal" of 1919, which involved the conspiracy of members of the Chicago White Sox of the American League and gamblers to bring about the defeat of Chicago in the World Series of that year, and which did much to blacken the game's name; the weakness of the National Commission; and the challenge to the reserve clause in the courts. On Nov. 12, 1920, the American jurist Kenesaw Mountain Landis was named ruler of organized baseball by its leaders, who gave him the title of "commissioner." The National Commission was dissolved in 1921 and was succeeded by an Advisory Council headed by Landis.

After the U.S. Supreme Court upheld the reserve clause in 1922, baseball entered a new era of prosperity, symbolized by the opening of Yankee Stadium a year later.

Landis ruled baseball with an iron hand until his death in 1944. He was joined by the two league presidents in forming the Advisory Council, but there was never any doubt about where true authority resided. Landis' successors, Albert B. ("Happy") Chandler, Ford Frick, William

D. Eckert, and Bowie Kuhn did not enjoy such absolute rule, but the commissioner still holds the chief executive power in professional baseball.

Leading Club Executives. Three baseball executives left a strong imprint on the game in the period between the two World Wars. The first was Edward G. Barrow, who, as manager of the Boston Red Sox in 1918, transformed Babe Ruth from pitcher into an outfielder, thus paving the way for the fulfillment of the most striking individual career in the game's history. Barrow then went with Ruth to the New York Yankees. As head of that team, Barrow built the most successful empire baseball has ever known. A quiet, efficient workman, he produced fabulous results.

The second of the trio was Branch Rickey, who twice changed the course of the game's history. In the 1920's he built baseball's first "farm system" for the St. Louis Cardinals, organizing a structure of minor-league teams that developed players for the parent club with almost machinelike precision. In 1946 Rickey signed the first black player in the history of organized baseball, Jack Roosevelt ("Jackie") Robinson. In 1947 Robinson became the first member of his race to play in the "majors," and since that time blacks have been an increasingly important source of the game's talent. In late 1974, Frank Robinson became the first black manager in major league history.

Leland Stanford ("Larry") MacPhail, general manager of the Cincinnati Reds in the 1930's, and later an executive of the Brooklyn Dodgers and the New York Yankees, introduced night baseball to the major leagues in 1935. (It had already become common in the "minors.") The Reds started with seven night games in 1935; eventually, more than half of all games were played at night.

Baseball peace was broken in 1946 when a prominent Mexican sportsman, Jorge Pasquel, lured several leading players to his Mexican League. Commissioner Chandler levied a five-year suspension on all players who broke their contracts, and lawsuits resulting from this action renewed the interest of the courts and Congress in the reserve clause. Several of the lawsuits were settled out of court, but Congressional investigations so worried baseball owners that henceforth they showed more interest in the applications of new cities to join the major leagues.

All-Star Game. In 1933 Arch Ward, sports editor of the Chicago *Tribune*, suggested that a game involving the outstanding players of the American League against those of the National League be played in conjunction with his city's exposition, Chicago's Century of Progress. The idea was accepted; teams representing each league were chosen, and the game was played in that year at Comiskey Park, Chicago. The rival managers were Connie Mack (American League) and John J. McGraw (National). The game became an annual event in July thereafter, except in 1945. Between 1959 and 1962 two such games were played each year; in 1963 the leagues returned to a single annual contest.

Recent Shifts of Franchises. After 50 years of stability, the major league map began to change in the 1950's. In the National League, the Boston Braves moved to Milwaukee in 1953 and the New York Giants and Brooklyn Dodgers to San Francisco and Los Angeles, respectively, in 1958. In the American League, the St. Louis Browns became the Baltimore Orioles in 1954 and the Philadelphia Athletics moved to Kansas City in 1955.

In the 1960's, both leagues expanded, first to 10 teams and then to 12. In 1961, the American League moved the old Washington Senator franchise to Minnesota and placed new franchises in Washington and Anaheim, Calif. The next year, the New York Mets and Houston Astros joined the National League. The season was expanded from 154 to 162 games in both circuits.

Milwaukee, the first city to benefit from a franchise shift, was also the first to lose its team; the Braves moved to Atlanta in 1966 after a bitter legal fight that reached the U.S. Supreme Court. Kansas City was next; the Athletics moved to Oakland in 1968. The two leagues then expanded to 12 teams in 1969, the National League adding San Diego and Montreal and the American League adding Seattle and Kansas City. But the Seattle teams had a poor year and, after another court case, moved to Milwaukee in 1970. New stadiums were eventually erected for all of these teams, Houston's being a roofed, air-conditioned dome. In the following years, the composition of the league continued to change.

Outstanding Teams and Players

The history of major-league baseball is often divided into four eras: (1) 1876–99, the period of growth and development; (2) 1900–19, the "dead ball" era; (3) 1920–45, the "lively ball" era, when the ball in use was constructed so as to travel great distances when struck solidly by the batter; (4) 1946– , the "two-platoon" era, in which teams employ many players to capitalize on their particular skills in given situations.

Some of the individual playing records compiled in the first era are fantastic, when judged by modern standards. Charles ("Hoss") Radbourne won 60 games pitching for Providence of the National League in 1884. In recent years the number of pitchers who win as many as 20 games in a single season seldom exceeds two or three in each major league. James ("Tip") O'Neill of the St. Louis

Sy Seidman

UPI

Above, Ty Cobb, expert as a batter and a base runner, is shown stealing third base in a 1909 photograph.

Left, Christy Mathewson of the New York Giants was one of baseball's outstanding pitchers.

Right, Rogers Hornsby, a great hitter, had a lifetime batting average of .358.

Hollis—National Baseball Hall of Fame

Browns had a batting average of .492 in 1887; nowadays the major leagues produce only a small minority who achieve averages over the .300 level during the course of a full season. (Batting averages are figured by dividing a player's number of hits by the number of times he has batted.) However, playing conditions have changed greatly since this earliest period. Originally the distance between pitcher and batter was 40 ft (12 m). By 1871 it had grown to 45 ft (14 m). In 1881, as an aid to the batter, the distance was increased to 50 ft (15 m), and eventually it grew to 60 ft, 6 inches (18.4 m). After 1884, the overhand delivery of the ball by the pitcher was permitted; before that time all deliveries were made underhand. The year in which O'Neill compiled his great batting record was the only one in which bases on balls were counted as hits.

The dominant teams of the earliest period were the Chicago White Stockings, who won six National League pennants between 1876 and 1886; the Boston Red Stockings, who won eight National League pennants from 1877 to 1898; and the Baltimore Orioles, who won that league's championship in 1894, 1895, and 1896. The White Stockings were the first team to travel to southern areas of the United States for spring training, a practice that is followed by all modern major-league clubs.

Stars of the period from 1900 to 1919 included a number of players from the earlier era: "Cy" Young, Napoleon Lajoie, William Henry ("Wee Willie") Keeler, and Edward J. Delahanty. John J. McGraw and Wilbert Robinson, who had been Keeler's teammates on the Baltimore Orioles, gained fame during the first two decades of the century as managers of the National League teams in New York and Brooklyn, respectively. Among the newer stars of the National League were Christopher ("Christy") Mathewson of the New York Giants and Grover Cleveland Alexander of the Philadelphia Phillies, pitchers; and John Peter ("Honus") Wagner, shortstop of the Pittsburgh Pirates. In the American League the outstanding players included Walter Johnson, pitcher of the Washington Senators, Tyrus Raymond ("Ty") Cobb of the Detroit Tigers, and Tristram E. ("Tris") Speaker of the Cleveland Indians, outfielders.

"Scientific" vs. "Power" Baseball. During the period between 1900 and 1919, low-scoring games were the rule; for that reason the era was known as one of "scientific" baseball in which speed and resourcefulness were more important than the batting prowess that became the hallmark of the era of the lively baseball. The ball was not lively during the 1900–19 period, and it was used during the course of a game until it was battered out of shape. (This is in decided contrast with present-day practice, which dictates the prompt replacement of the ball when it becomes scarred or stained from contact with bat, glove, or fences.) Moreover, pitchers were permitted to use "trick deliveries" during the earlier period. By applying saliva to the ball, or rubbing the ball with substances such as emery, they were able to make it travel in unpredictable paths, thus making it increasingly difficult for the batter to hit. Few home runs (hits enabling the batter to make the complete circuit of the bases) were made. During the period from 1901 through 1918, only two players —Frank Schulte of the Chicago Cubs and Clifford C. Cravath of the Philadelphia Phillies—hit more than 20 home runs during the course of individual seasons.

The leading teams of that era were New York and Chicago in the National League, and Philadelphia and Boston in the American. Chicago won four pennants between 1906 and 1910, and Philadelphia achieved the same record between 1910 and 1914.

The era of the lively baseball was ushered in during the

season of 1920, when "trick deliveries" were banned (although pitchers who had been using the spitball up to that time were permitted to continue the practice for the duration of their careers). In 1920 the legendary Babe Ruth hit 54 home runs, and the home run became the dominant offensive feature of the game.

During the early 1920's New York teams dominated both leagues. In the National, the Giants, led by John J. McGraw, won four consecutive championships beginning in 1921. In the American the Yankees, under the management of Miller J. Huggins, won championships in 1921, 1922, 1923, 1926, 1927, and 1928. The New York Yankees of the latter part of the 1920's were among the game's greatest teams. In 1927 Ruth hit 60 home runs during a 154-game season, a record that stood for four decades until Roger Maris of the Yankees hit 61 in 1961 on the final day of the first 162-game season in American League history—the year in which the league expanded to include 10 teams. Ruth was joined in his batting feats by Henry Louis ("Lou") Gehrig, the Yankees' first baseman throughout most of Ruth's era.

Other outstanding batters of the era were George Sisler of the St. Louis Browns, Rogers Hornsby of the St. Louis Cardinals, Paul Waner of the Pittsburgh Pirates, and James Emory ("Jimmy") Foxx of the Philadelphia Athletics. Among the top pitchers were Robert Moses ("Lefty") Grove of the Philadelphia Athletics and Carl Hubbell of the New York Giants.

In the American League, Philadelphia teams led by Foxx, Grove, and Al Simmons, and managed by Connie Mack, put a halt to the Yankees' domination by winning three championships of their own, beginning in 1929. (These were the last of nine pennants won by Mack's teams.) In the National League, Branch Rickey's "farm system" in St. Louis began to pay dividends, and the Cardinals won five pennants between 1926 and 1934.

An even greater period of domination by the Yankees began in 1936. In the next 25 years the New York team of the American League won 18 pennants and 14 World Series. Joseph Vincent ("Joe") McCarthy managed the Yankees during their triumphs in the 1930's. Although Ruth went into a decline midway in the decade, Joe DiMaggio arrived on the scene at about the same time.

The caliber of major league play declined sharply during World War II as 75% of the outstanding players entered military service. Stan Musial, who won seven batting titles in a 22-year career, led the St. Louis Cardinals to four pennants and three World Series titles between 1942 and 1946. Branch Rickey had moved to the Brooklyn Dodgers by the latter year and signed organized baseball's first black player, Jackie Robinson. With the help of black stars like Robinson, Roy Campanella, and Don Newcombe, the Dodgers won six pennants between 1947 and 1956. The New York Giants also tapped this new source and obtained Willie Mays, who paced them to pennants with his hitting and fielding in 1951 and 1954.

Another black star, Hank Aaron, led the Milwaukee Braves to pennants in 1957 and 1958. By 1974, while he was with the Atlanta Braves, Aaron surpassed Babe Ruth's career record of 714 home runs.

The Yankees resumed domination of the American League in 1949, winning 14 pennants and nine World

Atlanta Braves

Hank Aaron hitting Home Run No. 715, breaking Babe Ruth's career record. The historic homer was made on April 8, 1974, in Atlanta, on a fast ball thrown by Al Downing of the Los Angeles Dodgers.

Lou Brock of the St. Louis Cardinals stealing his 105th base of 1974, setting a record (raised to 118 by season's end). Philadelphia's Larry Bowa is covering second base.

UPI

Series in 16 years. Casey Stengel managed the first 10 of these teams, making extensive use of the two-platoon system to get the most out of his 25-player squad. The three stars were pitcher Ed (Whitey) Ford, catcher Lawrence (Yogi) Berra, and outfielder Mickey Mantle, who replaced DiMaggio in 1951. Stengel's 10 pennants matched McGraw's record.

Los Angeles gave the West Coast its first pennant and Series title in 1959, repeating in 1963 and 1965 behind the strong pitching of Sandy Koufax. Mays led San Francisco to its first pennant in 1962. With both leagues split into six-team divisions in 1969, the New York Mets became the first expansion team to win a World Series, taking four of five games from highly favored Baltimore.

In 1971, in a case brought by Curt Flood of the St. Louis Cardinals, the Supreme Court upheld the reserve clause. But later rulings and events substantially weakened the effectiveness of this clause.

Digest of Equipment and Rules

There is only one set of rules in baseball, compiled and administered by the major leagues. The rules are extremely detailed and cover every situation that arises on the field of play. They are reviewed regularly by officials of the leagues, and their complexity occasionally demands summary conferences by umpires during the progress of a game to determine the proper ruling in a given situation. The following is a brief summary of high points.

Equipment. The baseball has a core of cork and rubber, which is bound with yarn and an outer covering of leather. The ball must weigh between 5 and 5½ oz (142 and 148.8 grams) and must be between 9 and 9¼ inches (23 and 23.5 cm) in circumference.

The bat must be round and made entirely of wood. It must be not more than 2¾ inches (7 cm) in diameter at its thickest part nor longer than 42 inches (107 cm).

When a team is not taking its turn at bat during an inning, its members are stationed at assigned positions in the field, where they function defensively, attempting to keep the team at bat from scoring runs. Players of the team in the field wear leather gloves to assist them in catching the ball. Gloves other than those worn by catchers are carefully limited in size. The larger and thicker ones worn by catchers and first basemen are called mitts. The catcher

KEEPING YOUR SCORE CARD

Keeping a score card during a ball game enables the spectator to review every play that has taken place. This record reveals almost any statistic, such as strike-outs and consecutive putouts. The columns at the right show totals for the day: AB—times at bat; R—runs scored; H—base hits; PO—putouts; A-assists; and E—errors.

BRUINS	1	2	3	4	5	6	7	8	9	10	AB	R	H	PO	A	E
JONES, 2B	O 6	X	O 7	X	1-3	X	X	=	6-3		5	0	1	2	3	0
WILSON, CF	1-3	X	X	≡ ⊖ —	X	K	X	O 3	X		4	1	1	4	0	0
WOOD, RF	—	X	X	— =	X	O 8	X	O 7	X		4	0	2	2	0	0
SMITH, LF	5-3	X	X	—	X	O 7	X	K	X		4	0	1	4	0	0
BROWN, 1B	X	1-3	X	K	X	X	(≣)	X	⊖ BB		3	2	1	8	1	0
CHARLES, 3B	X	O 8	X	K	X	X	S —	X	— —		4	0	2	1	4	0
FOX, C	X	O 9	X	K	X	X	4-3	X	K		4	0	0	2	5	0
OWENS, SS	X	X	6-3	X	6-3	X	1-3	X	K		4	0	0	4	3	0
FLYNN, P	X	X	5-3	X	K	X	0-8	X	—		4	0	1	0	2	0
HITS / RUNS	1 / 0	0 / 0	0 / 0	3 / 1	0 / 0	0 / 0	2 / 1	1 / 0	2 / 1	/	36	3	9	27	18	0

NUMBER PLAYERS AS FOLLOWS:

PITCHER 1	SECOND BASEMAN 4	LEFT FIELDER 7
CATCHER 2	THIRD BASEMAN 5	CENTER FIELDER 8
FIRST BASEMAN 3	SHORTSTOP 6	RIGHT FIELDER 9

SYMBOLS FOR PLAYS

Single —	Reached Base on Error ....E	Stolen Base ....S	Struck Out ....K
Double =	Fielder's Choice ....FC	Sacrifice Hit ....SH	Base on Balls ....BB
Triple ≡	Hit by Pitcher ....HP	Passed Ball ....PB	Forced Out ....FO
Home Run ≣	Wild Pitch ....WP	Balk ....BK	

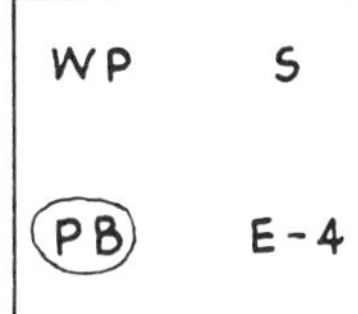

SCORING BLOCK, left, is from score card above. Code numbers and symbols are used to record a runner's progress on bases. Home plate is represented by the lower left corner of the block. Counterclockwise, the lower right corner is first base; upper right is second; and upper left, third. In this example batter reached first because of an error (signified by letter E) on the part of the opposing second baseman (player's code number 4). Runner then stole second base (S), went to third on a wild pitch (WP), and got home on a passed ball (PB). Circling symbols at home plate pinpoints all scoring plays.

also wears a mask, chest protector, and shin guards for protection against injury. Batters wear plastic batting helmets for protection against possible head injuries caused by contact with the pitched ball.

Baseball uniforms even now resemble the ones first worn by the New York Knickerbockers in the game's pioneer days, in most respects. The shirt carries a large numeral to identify the player to the spectator, whose score card carries a list of all players' numerals. The players' shoes have sharp metal spikes to gain secure footing.

Rules. Once a game starts, it is entirely in the control of the umpires. In major-league games, four umpires are used—one at each base, and the fourth behind home plate, the focal point of play. The umpire behind home plate is the chief umpire, and his duties include "calling balls and strikes" (determining whether the pitcher's deliveries are within suitable range of the batters, as explained in the following section).

The visiting team has the first turn at bat. As the game starts, the home team takes up defensive positions in the field, and its pitcher prepares to face the first batter of the visiting team. The batter steps into one of two areas, each 4 by 6 ft (1.2 by 1.8 m) on either side of home plate, depending on whether he bats right- or left-handed. Home plate is a flat piece of rubber 17 inches (43 cm) wide over which the pitcher is required to throw the ball. The pitcher stands on an elevated slab, measuring 6 by 24 inches (15 by 64 cm), while throwing the ball.

If the batter fails to swing his bat at the ball after it is thrown by the pitcher, the umpire calls the pitch a "strike" or a "ball," depending upon whether the ball has passed through the "strike zone." (The strike zone is that space over home plate which is between the batter's armpits and the top of his knees when he assumes his natural stance. The umpire determines the strike zone according to the batter's usual stance when he swings at a pitch). If, in the judgment of the umpire, the pitch is within that area, it is a strike; otherwise it is a ball. Strikes also are recorded on missed swings by the batter, or on foul balls (balls hit into the area beyond the foul lines) when less than two strikes have been recorded. If the batter receives four pitches judged balls, he can advance to first base. He is "out" (retired from his turn at bat) if he accumulates three strikes. The batter also is retired if he hits the ball into the air in foul territory and the ball is caught by an opposing player before it strikes the ground.

There are three basic possibilities if the batter hits the ball into "fair territory" (area within foul lines):

(1) The ball may be hit in the air. If it is caught by an opposing player before it touches the ground, or before it strikes one of the barriers in the outfield, the batter is declared "out."

OFFICIAL MEASUREMENTS OF THE DIAMOND

BATTER'S BOX (2) 60 ft (18.3 m) from home plate to backstop
8 ft (2.4 m) from umpire to home plate
6 ft (1.8 m) long by 4 ft (1.2 m) wide
29 in (74 cm) between left and right boxes

COACH'S BOX (2) 20 ft (6.1 m) long

CATCHER'S AREA 8 ft (2.4 m) long by 43 in (109 cm) wide

1ST, 2D, AND 3D BASES 15 in (38 cm) square

HOME PLATE 17 in (43 cm) wide

PITCHER'S PLATE 24 in (61 cm) by 6 in (15 cm)

1ST BASE TO 3D BASE 127 ft 3⅜ in (38.79 m)

HOME PLATE TO 2d BASE 127 ft 3⅜ in (38.79 m)

HOME PLATE TO PITCHER'S PLATE 60 ft 6 in (18.4 m)

PITCHER'S PLATE TO 2D BASE 66 ft 3⅜ in (20.29 m)

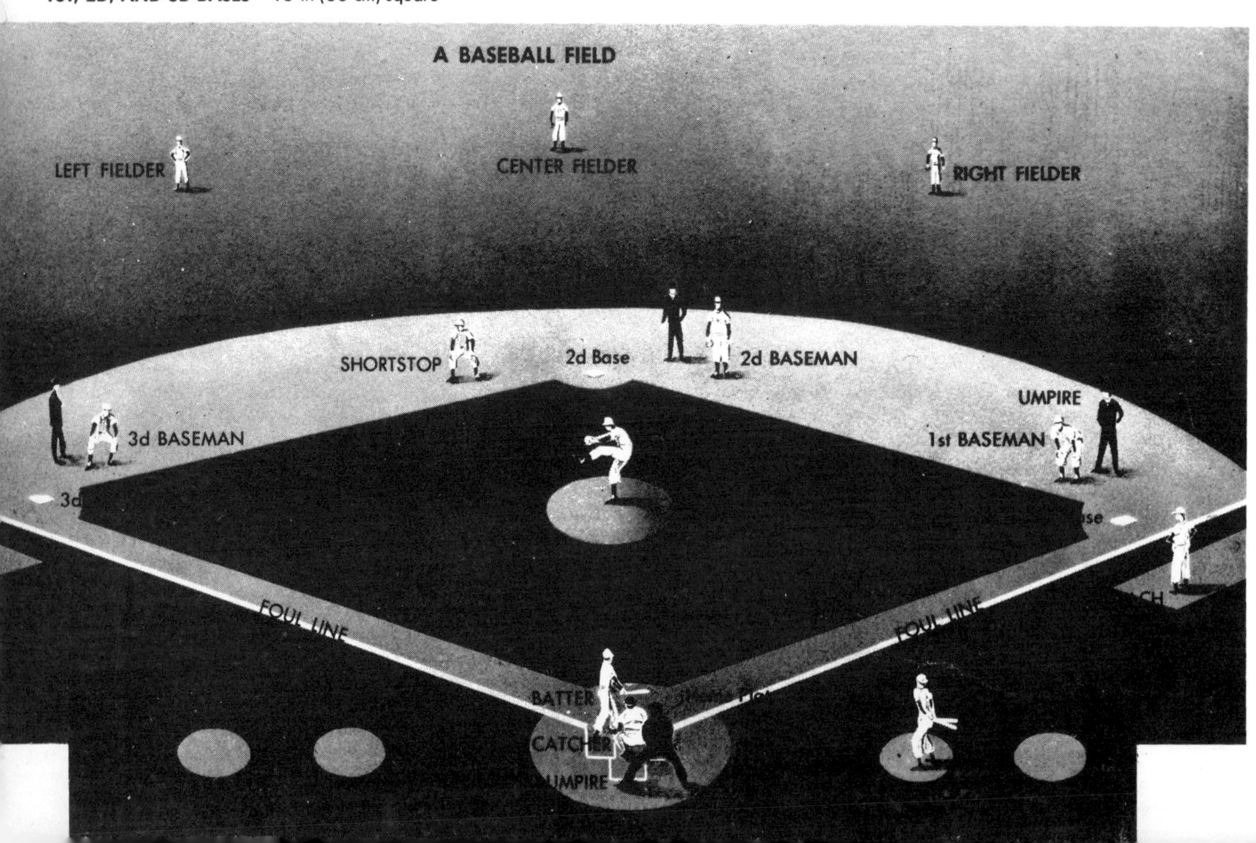

BASEBALL GLOSSARY

Bullpen, area where pitchers warm up before entering game.
Bunt, an attempt to hit the ball with shortened grip on the bat so that it will not reach an infielder in time for him to make a play on a runner already on base or the batter himself.
Cleanup man, the fourth batter in the lineup; usually the best hitter on the team.
Designated Hitter, a batter who hits for the pitcher throughout the game, but does not take a fielding position. Also known as designated pinch hitter.
Fielder's choice, a play in which a batter reaches first base only because the fielder elects to retire another runner.
Full count, three balls and two strikes.
Grand slam, a homerun with the bases loaded.
Hit and run, play in which the runner (usually on first base) breaks for the next base with the pitch, and the batter tries to hit the ball behind him to right field.
Infield fly, a fair fly ball, hit with men on first and second base or the bases loaded and less than two out, which can be easily caught by an infielder; the batter is automatically out.
Interference, any unfair obstruction by a player. Offensive interference puts the batter or runner out; defensive interference allows the batter or runner to advance one base.
Leadoff man, the first batter in the lineup.
Passed ball, failure by the catcher to hold a pitch, allowing a runner to advance one or more bases.
Perfect game, a game where a pitcher goes at least nine innings without letting a single runner reach base.
Pinch-hitter, a player who bats in a teammate's place.
Rookie, a first-year player in the major leagues.
Sacrifice, a bunt or long fly ball that advances a runner one or more bases.
Southpaw, a lefthanded thrower or batter.
Squeeze play, an attempt to bunt a man home from third base; on a *suicide squeeze* the runner takes off with the pitch and the batter must try to bunt the ball.
Switch hitter, a batter who can hit from either side of the plate.
Texas leaguer, a short fly ball that falls safely between the infield and the outfield.
Triple play, same as double play, except three men are put out; a very rare occurrence.
Twin bill, another name for a doubleheader.
Wild pitch, a pitch that is too low, high or wide for the catcher to hold, allowing a runner to advance.

(2) The ball may be hit on the ground. If one of the players comprising the defensive team's infield (the first baseman, second baseman, shortstop, and third baseman), or the pitcher or catcher can secure the ball and throw it to one of his teammates standing on first base so that the ball arrives at that base before the batter, the batter is out. If, in the judgment of the umpire stationed at that base, the batter arrives first, he is entitled to possession of the base.

(3) The ball may be hit, on the ground or in the air, in such a way that it cannot be caught before it touches the ground, and cannot be thrown to first base before the batter arrives at that station. In such an event, the batter has made a "hit," and is entitled to try to progress around the base paths as far as he can. If the defensive team can gain control of the ball so that it arrives at second base or third base before the batter reaches that base, the batter is out if he is tagged with the ball by a defensive player at that base. If the batter drives the ball over one of the fences, he has made a "home run" and is entitled to make a complete circuit of the bases. In that case he scores a run, and any of his teammates occupying the bases when he hits the home run also are entitled to cross home plate and score runs.

The batter also can reach first base safely if he is hit by a delivery of the pitcher or if the catcher (stationed behind the batter) interferes in any manner with the batter's swing.

Each team continues its turn at bat until three outs have been made—that is, until three of its men have been put out by the opposition. A hit enabling the batter to reach first base is called a "single"; one enabling the batter to reach second base is a "double"; one enabling him to reach third base, a "triple." An offensive player who reaches any one of the bases safely is termed a "base runner," and his objective is to reach home plate safely. He advances around the bases (from first base to home plate) principally by virtue of hits by members of his team or through errors by members of the defensive team. He may advance while a teammate is being put out after hitting the ball on the ground; he may also seek to advance by running to the next base after a member of the defensive team (usually an outfielder) has caught a ball, hit by one of his teammates, before the ball strikes the ground. The base runner also may advance by "stealing" (running to the next base while the pitcher is in the process of delivering the ball to a batter). If he arrives at the next base before the defensive team succeeds in getting the ball to that base, he is entitled to occupancy of the base that is his objective; if the ball arrives at the base ahead of him, and one of the defensive players tags him with the ball, the base runner is out.

Basic Skills of the Game

Throwing. A strong, accurate arm is one of the first requirements of a youth seeking to make baseball his career. Infielders must be able to throw quickly and accurately as part of their defensive play. Of great importance is the infielder's ability to field a ball hit on the ground and to throw it to a teammate with a minimum of delay. An outfielder must be able to throw the ball great distances with accuracy, and he must also be able to make his throws with a minimum of delay after catching the ball.

In the case of pitchers, special skills are required. The pitcher's aim is to prevent the batter from hitting the ball; yet he also must keep his pitches within the strike zone with a high degree of consistency. The basic skills for pitchers include control (the ability to throw the ball within the strike zone), speed (the ability to throw it so that it travels toward the batter at great velocity and thus is difficult to hit), and deception (the ability to make the ball travel in other than straight paths on its trip toward the batter, and to vary the speeds of successive deliveries so that the batter is thrown off stride). The basic pitches include the "fast ball," "curve," and "change of pace" (or "slow ball"). Many pitchers without outstanding "fast

PITCHING

A team's first line of defense is a good pitching staff. Sandy Koufax of the Los Angeles Dodgers demonstrates the delivery.

UPI

POSITION OF A RIGHT-HANDED PITCHER ON THE MOUND

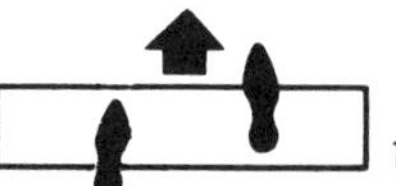

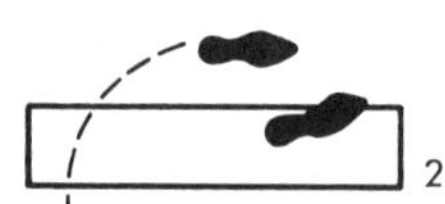

The delivery begins with both feet on the rubber, the left foot slightly behind the right (Fig. 1). During the windup the pitcher steps forward with the left foot (Fig. 2). After the ball is released, the momentum of the follow-through carries the pitcher another step forward (Fig 3).

PITCHING FORM

One purpose of the windup is to produce a smooth and natural delivery of the pitch. A smooth delivery helps to ensure control, the most important element in the art of pitching. Following through after delivery, the pitcher should be facing the plate squarely, so that he will be able to field any ball hit at or near him.

BASIC PITCHING GRIPS

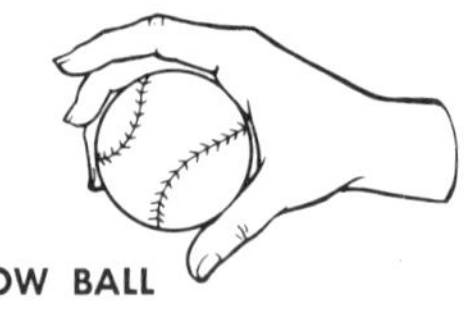

SLOW BALL

For a slow ball, grip tightly with fingers and palm. On release, lift first two fingers a bit to reduce spin and cause ball to "float."

FAST BALL

Grip the ball with the thumb and fingers. Snap wrist forward and down to backspin it off the fingers, so as to impart the needed "hop."

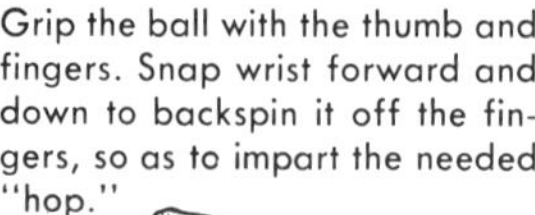

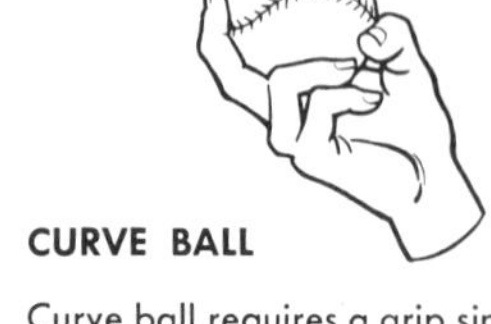

CURVE BALL

Curve ball requires a grip similar to the fast ball. Snap wrist and spin ball between first finger and thumb to roll it off sides of fingers.

BATTING

A batter has a fraction of a second to decide on a pitch. The Giants' Willie Mays, one of baseball's best hitters, in action.

UPI

THREE POSITIONS OF BATTER AT PLATE

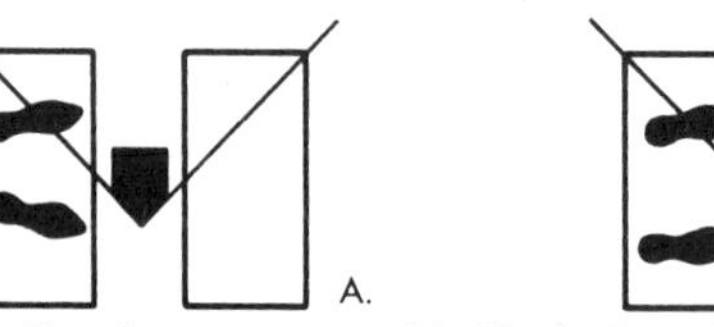

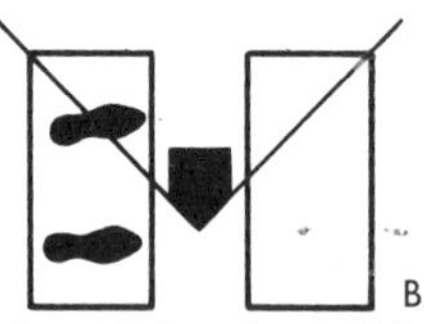

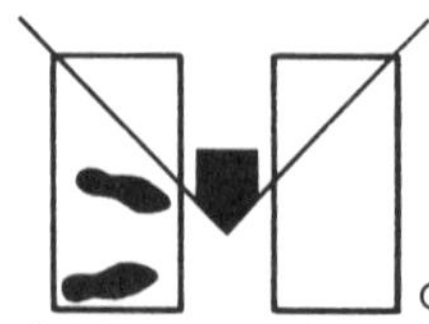

First, batter must stand inside the batter's box; beyond that, ease and effectiveness are the deciding factors in the choice of stance. Many batters stand at box center, feet slightly apart (A). Others spread them wider, but never at loss of ease (B). Some batters draw feet together at rear of box (C).

BATTING FORM

To have good batting form, the entire body must be poised for utmost ease and effect. Bent slightly from the waist, with elbows crooked outward, batter holds bat high. Uncoiling hips and arms, he steps "into the pitch," snapping wrists and following through.

BUNTING

In the drop bunt (Fig. 1) the batter allows the ball to meet a bat which he holds stationary at the time of impact. In the drag bunt (Fig. 2) the batter guides, or "drags," the ball to the right side of the infield as he runs toward first base.

NATIONAL LEAGUE PENNANT WINNERS (1876–1900)

1876—Chicago
1877—Boston
1878—Boston
1879—Providence
1880—Chicago
1881—Chicago
1882—Chicago
1883—Boston
1884—Providence
1885—Chicago
1886—Chicago
1887—Detroit
1888—New York
1889—New York
1890—Brooklyn
1891—Boston
1892—Boston
1893—Boston
1894—Baltimore
1895—Baltimore
1896—Baltimore
1897—Boston
1898—Boston
1899—Brooklyn
1900—Brooklyn

PENNANT AND WORLD SERIES WINNERS SINCE 1901

(Note: Capitalized names indicate World Series winners; number following each team signifies games won.)

NATIONAL LEAGUE	AMERICAN LEAGUE
1901—Pittsburgh (no series played)	Chicago
1902—Pittsburgh (no series played)	Philadelphia
*1903—Pittsburgh (3)	BOSTON (5)
1904—New York (no series played)	Boston
1905—NEW YORK (4)	Philadelphia (1)
1906—Chicago (2)	CHICAGO (4)
1907—CHICAGO (4) (one tie)	Detroit (0)
1908—CHICAGO (4)	Detroit (1)
1909—PITTSBURGH (4)	Detroit (3)
1910—Chicago (1)	PHILADELPHIA (4)
1911—New York (2)	PHILADELPHIA (4)
1912—New York (3) (one tie)	BOSTON (4)
1913—New York (1)	PHILADELPHIA (4)
1914—BOSTON (4)	Philadelphia (0)
1915—Philadelphia (1)	BOSTON (4)
1916—Brooklyn (1)	BOSTON (4)
1917—New York (2)	CHICAGO (4)
1918—Chicago (2)	BOSTON (4)
*1919—CINCINNATI (5)	Chicago (3)
*1920—Brooklyn (2)	CLEVELAND (5)
*1921—NEW YORK (5)	New York (3)
1922—NEW YORK (4) (one tie)	New York (0)
1923—New York (2)	NEW YORK (4)
1924—New York (3)	WASHINGTON (4)
1925—PITTSBURGH (4)	Washington (3)
1926—ST. LOUIS (4)	New York (3)
1927—Pittsburgh (0)	NEW YORK (4)
1928—St. Louis (0)	NEW YORK (4)
1929—Chicago (1)	PHILADELPHIA (4)
1930—St. Louis (2)	PHILADELPHIA (4)
1931—ST. LOUIS (4)	Philadelphia (3)
1932—Chicago (0)	NEW YORK (4)
1933—NEW YORK (4)	Washington (1)
1934—ST. LOUIS (4)	Detroit (3)
1935—Chicago (2)	DETROIT (4)
1936—New York (2)	NEW YORK (4)
1937—New York (1)	NEW YORK (4)
1938—Chicago (0)	NEW YORK (4)
1939—Cincinnati (0)	NEW YORK (4)
1940—CINCINNATI (4)	Detroit (3)
1941—Brooklyn (1)	NEW YORK (4)
1942—ST. LOUIS (4)	New York (1)
1943—St. Louis (1)	NEW YORK (4)
1944—ST. LOUIS (4)	St. Louis (2)

NATIONAL LEAGUE	AMERICAN LEAGUE
1945—Chicago (3)	DETROIT (4)
1946—ST. LOUIS (4)	Boston (3)
1947—Brooklyn (3)	NEW YORK (4)
1948—Boston (2)	CLEVELAND (4)
1949—Brooklyn (1)	NEW YORK (4)
1950—Philadelphia (0)	NEW YORK (4)
1951—New York (2)	NEW YORK (4)
1952—Brooklyn (3)	NEW YORK (4)
1953—Brooklyn (2)	NEW YORK (4)
1954—NEW YORK (4)	Cleveland (0)
1955—BROOKLYN (4)	New York (3)
1956—Brooklyn (3)	NEW YORK (4)
1957—MILWAUKEE (4)	New York (3)
1958—Milwaukee (3)	NEW YORK (4)
1959—LOS ANGELES (4)	Chicago (2)
1960—PITTSBURGH (4)	New York (3)
1961—Cincinnati (1)	NEW YORK (4)
1962—San Francisco (3)	NEW YORK (4)
1963—LOS ANGELES (4)	New York (0)
1964—ST. LOUIS (4)	New York (3)
1965—LOS ANGELES (4)	Minnesota (3)
1966—Los Angeles (0)	BALTIMORE (4)
1967—ST. LOUIS (4)	Boston (3)
1968—St. Louis (3)	DETROIT (4)
1969—NEW YORK (4)	Baltimore (1)
1970—Cincinnati (1)	BALTIMORE (4)
1971—PITTSBURGH (4)	Baltimore (3)
1972—Cincinnati (3)	OAKLAND (4)
1973—New York (3)	OAKLAND (4)
1974—Los Angeles (1)	OAKLAND (4)
1975—CINCINNATI (4)	Boston (3)
1976—CINCINNATI (4)	New York (0)
1977—Los Angeles (2)	NEW YORK (4)

In 1903, 1919–21, World Series victor won five of nine games; in other years, four of seven.

ALL-STAR BASEBALL GAMES

Year	Location	Winner	Score
1933	Chicago	American	4–2
1934	New York	American	9–7
1935	Cleveland	American	4–1
1936	Boston	National	4–3
1937	Washington, D.C.	American	8–3
1938	Cincinnati	National	4–1
1939	New York	American	3–1
1940	St. Louis	National	4–0
1941	Detroit	American	7–5
1942	New York	American	3–1
1943	Philadelphia	American	5–3
1944	Pittsburgh	National	7–1
1945	Not played		
1946	Boston	American	12–0
1947	Chicago	American	2–1
1948	St. Louis	American	5–2
1949	Brooklyn	American	11–7
1950	Chicago	National (14 innings)	4–3
1951	Detroit	National	8–3
1952	Philadelphia	National (5 innings; rain)	3–2
1953	Cincinnati	National	5–1
1954	Cleveland	American	11–9
1955	Milwaukee	National (12 innings)	6–5
1956	Washington, D.C.	National	7–3
1957	St. Louis	American	6–5
1958	Baltimore	American	4–3
1959	Pittsburgh	National	5–4
	Los Angeles	American	5–3
1960	Kansas City	National	5–3
	New York	National	6–0
1961	San Francisco	National (10 innings)	5–4
	Boston	Tie (9 innings; rain)	1–1
1962	Washington, D.C.	National	3–1
	Chicago	American	9–4
1963	Cleveland	National	5–3
1964	New York	National	7–4
1965	Bloomington, Minn.	National	6–5
1966	St. Louis	National	2–1
1967	Anaheim, Calif.	National (15 innings)	2–1
1968	Houston, Tex.	National	1–0
1969	Washington, D.C.	National	9–3
1970	Cincinnati	National (12 innings)	5–4
1971	Detroit	American	6–4
1972	Atlanta	National (10 innings)	4–3
1973	Kansas City	National	7–1
1974	Pittsburgh	National	7–2
1975	Milwaukee	National	6–3
1976	Philadelphia	National	7–1
1977	New York	National	7–5

balls" or "curve balls" have achieved success, or prolonged their careers, by mastering specialized pitches: "knuckle balls," "sliders," and the like, all of which are thrown by gripping the ball in unorthodox fashion.

Fielding. In fielding a ball hit on the ground, the successful player manages to get his body fully behind the ball so that if it eludes his hands, he will be able to stop the ball by blocking it, and retrieve it quickly. Outfielders must develop the knack of judging the flight of a ball shortly after it leaves the opponent's bat, since a false start may deprive them of the opportunity to be in the proper area when the ball descends. If the ball is hit in such a way that it falls in front of him, the outfielder must be able to judge quickly whether he can run in fast enough to make the catch, or whether he must be content to field the ball on the bounce. Like the infielder, he must strive to be in position to block balls hit on the ground in the event he is unable to pick them up cleanly.

Batting. The keys to successful hitting are a relaxed position at home plate, the ability to keep the eyes on the ball as it travels from the pitcher's hand, and a fast, level swing of the bat. Strong wrists are another major asset to successful batting, and they can be developed by special exercise. It is important to choose a bat of proper weight, and to learn to utilize skills other than sheer power in swinging the bat. Many players who lack great physical strength have become skilled batters by becoming expert judges of the strike zone and by learning to adapt their swings to the deliveries of particular pitchers and the position of the ball as it approaches the plate.

Running. There is no substitute for natural speed of foot, but through practice it is possible to improve one's ability as a base runner, which involves special techniques along with speed. Of great importance is the ability to know when to run, and to be ever alert to capitalize on a lapse in the play of the defensive team.

BASEBALL HALL OF FAME, shrine of U.S. baseball in Cooperstown, N.Y. The building houses a museum, and its Hall of Fame wing features plaques dedicated to the greats of baseball. Candidates to the Hall of Fame are elected by three bodies. A committee on veterans selects players who have not played in at least 25 years, and managers, coaches, umpires, and executives who have been retired at least five years. Members of the Baseball Writers' Association of America select players who have been active within the last 20 years, but have ceased playing at least five years.

Because black players had not played in major league baseball until 1947, many failed to qualify for the Hall of Fame. A special committee now selects players who have had at least 10 years' experience in the Negro leagues.

BASEBALL HALL OF FAME MEMBERS

1936

Ty Cobb
Walter Johnson
Christy Mathewson
Babe Ruth
Honus Wagner

1937

Morgan G. Bulkeley
Ban Johnson
Nap Lajoie
John J. McGraw
Connie Mack
Tris Speaker
George Wright
Cy Young

1938
- Grover C. Alexander
- Alexander Cartwright
- Henry Chadwick

1939
- Adrian C. (Cap) Anson
- Eddie Collins
- Charles A. Comiskey
- Candy Cummings
- Buck Ewing
- Lou Gehrig
- Willie Keeler
- Old Hoss Radbourne
- George Sisler
- A. G. Spalding

1942
- Rogers Hornsby

1944
- Kenesaw Mountain Landis

1945
- Roger Bresnahan
- Dan Brouthers
- Fred Clarke
- Jimmy Collins
- Ed Delahanty
- Hugh Duffy
- Hugh Jennings
- Mike Kelly
- Jim O'Rourke
- Wilbert Robinson

1946
- Jesse Burkett
- Frank Chance
- Jack Chesbro
- Johnny Evers
- Clark Griffith
- Tom McCarthy
- Joe McGinnity
- Eddie Plank
- Joe Tinker
- Rube Waddell
- Ed Walsh

1947
- Mickey Cochrane
- Frank Frisch
- Lefty Grove
- Carl Hubbell

1948
- Herb Pennock
- Pie Traynor

1949
- Three-Finger Brown
- Charley Gehringer
- Kid Nichols

1951
- Jimmy Foxx
- Mel Ott

1952
- Harry Heilmann
- Paul Waner

1953
- Edward G. Barrow
- Charles A. Bender
- Thomas H. Connolly
- Dizzy Dean
- William J. Klem
- Al Simmons
- Roderick J. Wallace
- William H. Wright

1954
- Bill Dickey
- Rabbit Maranville
- Bill Terry

1955
- J. F. (Home Run) Baker
- Joe DiMaggio
- Gabby Hartnett
- Ted Lyons
- Raymond W. Schalk
- Dazzy Vance

1956
- Joe Cronin
- Hank Greenberg

1957
- Sam Crawford
- Joe McCarthy

1959
- Zach Wheat

1961
- Max Carey
- Billy Hamilton

1962
- Bob Feller
- Bill McKechnie
- Jackie Robinson
- Edd Roush

1963
- John Clarkson
- Elmer Flick
- Sam Rice
- Eppa Rixey

1964
- Luke Appling
- Urban Faber
- Burleigh Grimes
- Miller Huggins
- Tim Keefe
- Heinie Manush
- John Montgomery Ward

1965
- Jim Galvin

1966
- Ted Williams
- Casey Stengel

1967
- Branch Rickey
- Red Ruffing
- Lloyd Waner

1968
- Kiki Cuyler
- Goose Goslin
- Joe Medwick

1969
- Roy Campanella
- Stan Coveleski
- Waite Hoyt
- Stan Musial

1970
- Lou Boudreau
- Earle Combs
- Ford Frick
- Jesse Haines

1971
- Dave Bancroft
- Jake Beckley
- Chick Hafey
- Harry Hooper
- Joe Kelley
- Rube Marquard
- Satchel Paige
- George Weiss

1972
- Yogi Berra
- Josh Gibson
- Lefty Gomez
- Will Harridge
- Sandy Koufax
- Buck Leonard
- Early Wynn
- Ross Youngs

1973
- Roberto Clemente
- Billy Evans
- Monte Irvin
- George Kelly
- Warren Spahn
- Mickey Welch

1974
- James (Cool Papa) Bell
- Jim Bottomley
- Jocko Conlan
- Whitey Ford
- Mickey Mantle
- Sam Thompson

1975
- Earl Averill
- Bucky Harris
- Billy Herman
- William (Judy) Johnson
- Ralph Kiner

1976
- Oscar Charleston
- Roger Connor
- Cal Hubbard
- Bob Lemon
- Fred Lindstrom
- Robin Roberts

1977
- Ernie Banks
- Martin Dihigo
- John Henry Lloyd
- Al Lopez
- Amos Rusie
- Joe Sewell

BASKETBALL, game played by two teams composed of five members each. The object is to score points by tossing a ball into the opposing team's basket, while preventing the opposing team from scoring. Each successful toss (field goal) counts two points; a successful attempt to throw the ball into the basket from the free-throw line, after an illegal play, counts one point. The game is played in 20-minute halves, separated by an intermission. The team with the higher total at the conclusion of the regulation period of play is the winner. In the event of a tie at the 40-minute mark, a 5-minute overtime period is played—or as many as are necessary to determine the winner. Professional teams play 12-minute quarters.

The regulation playing area is a rectangular indoor court with a hardwood surface whose maximum dimensions are 94 by 50 ft (28.6 by 15.2 m). Smaller courts are usually employed when the contestants are girls or women or young boys. The boundaries of the court are marked by two pairs of parallel lines called side lines and end lines. The court is divided in half by a center line parallel to the end lines. At the start of play each team occupies one half of the court, defending the goal, or basket, at its end of the court and trying to toss the ball into the basket at the other end of the court.

The two baskets are suspended from 4 by 6 ft (about 1.2

Diagram of a Regulation Basketball Court

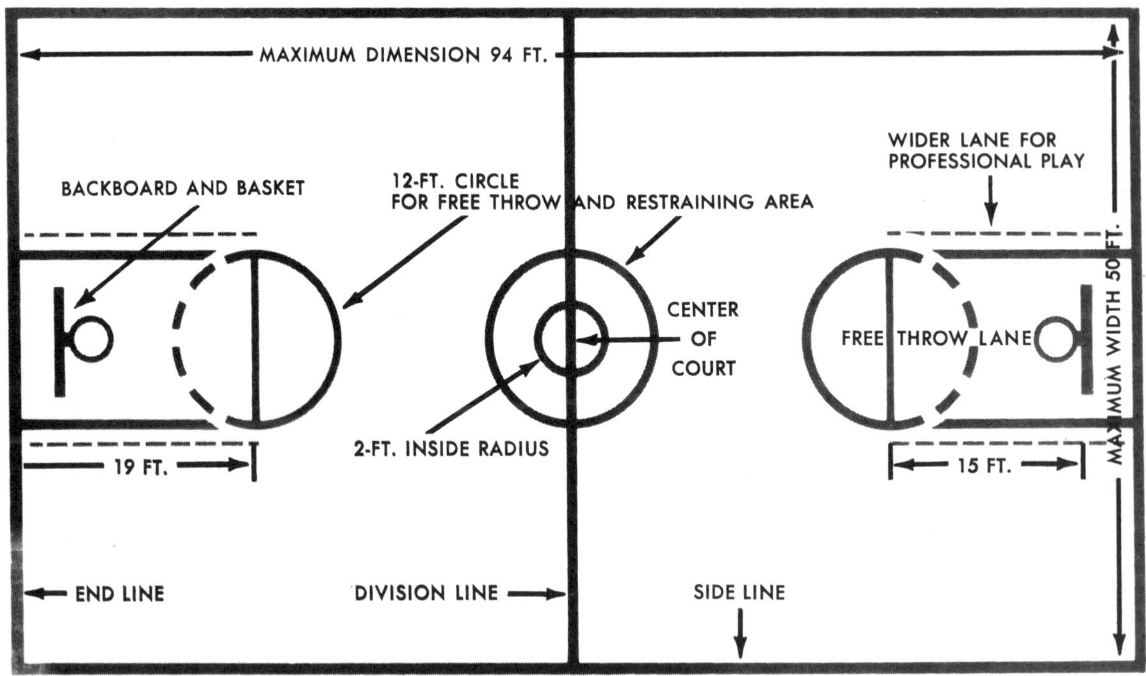

by 1.8 m) backboards, set parallel to the end lines and 4 ft (1.2 m) inside them. The backboards are midway between the sidelines. The baskets are metal rings, 18 inches (45.7 cm) in diameter with bottomless netting. The rings are parallel to the court surface and are attached to the backboards 1 ft (.3 m) from the bottom, midway between the sides, and 10 ft (3 m) above the court surface.

In the center of the court is a circle with a radius of 2 ft (.6 m) surrounded by another (restraining line) with a radius of 6 ft (1.8 m). Play begins in each period at this center when the referee throws the ball into the air between two rival players. The rival players, usually the tallest on each team, jump into the air and try to bat the ball with their hands to one of their teammates, to inaugurate some offensive maneuver.

The two free-throw lines are 12 ft (3.7 m) long, parallel to the end lines, and 15 ft (4.6 m) in front of each backboard. Each free-throw line is actually the diameter of one or another of two other circles marked on the court surface. After an illegal play, the player against whom a foul has been committed stands alone in this circle, at the free-throwline, and, depending on the nature of the offense, takes one or two unobstructed shots at the basket.

The ball is an inflated sphere made of rubber casing and covered with leather. It has a 30-inch (76-cm) circumference and weighs from 20 to 22 ounces (567 to 624 grams).

After one team has gained possession of the ball following the jump ball in the center of the court, it may advance in the direction of the opponent's goal by passing the ball among its members or by dribbling—bouncing the ball on the court surface. Once a player has completed his dribble, however, he must either pass the ball to a teammate or attempt a field goal. He may not advance by holding the ball and running. Players may not impede the progress of opponents by holding, pushing, blocking, or tripping. Such offenses are called personal fouls, and result in the violated player being given one or two free throws. When a player commits his fifth personal foul (sixth, in professional play), he is disqualified from further competition in the game being played, and a substitute takes his place.

After a field goal has been scored, the team scored upon puts the ball in play from the out-of-bounds area behind the end line where the last score was made. The ball is also put in play, from out-of-bounds, by one team when the opponents have committed infractions of the rules known as violations—punching, kicking, or running with the ball. Other infractions of the rules, called technical fouls, do not involve personal contact with an opponent. These result in the fouled team getting a free throw.

In the girls' or women's game, there are five or six players on each side. In boys' high-school games, play is divided into eight-minute quarters; overtime periods are three minutes.

Origin. Basketball was conceived by James Naismith, a Canadian by birth, and was first played in 1891 in Springfield, Mass.

Naismith studied for the Presbyterian ministery. In 1890 he enrolled at the Springfield, Mass., Young Men's Christian Association Training School (now Springfield College) because he felt that "there might be more effective ways of doing good besides preaching." The students of the school were studying to become YMCA athletic directors or secretaries. Since they took a strong dislike to

WILT CHAMBERLAIN

Chamberlain about to score for Philadelphia against the Boston Celtics. He was one of the greatest offensive players in the history of professional basketball.

United Press International

BILL RUSSELL

Boston's famous "No. 6" stealing a rebound from the St. Louis Hawks. The camera has caught the incomparable timing which has literally given him the jump on the game's other defensive stars.

United Press International

DRIBBLING PASSING FAKING PIVOTING

OFFENSIVE MANEUVERS

The two methods of advancing the ball are dribbling (bouncing it on the court with one hand in uninterrupted motion) and passing (throwing it to a teammate). Faking is the technique of giving an opponent the impression of moving in one direction, then moving in another. The final movement in such cases is usually a whirling one called a pivot.

SHOOTING

The four methods of shooting the ball. In the one-hand push the ball rests in the palm of one hand and is then pushed off with the other hand. In the jump, the ball is released at the height of the jump. The hook is made with either hand over the shooter's own shoulder. The two-hand set is made from a stationary position.

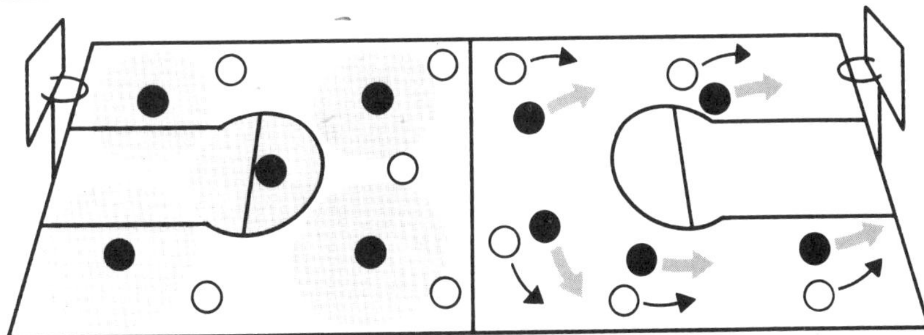

ZONE DEFENSE **MAN-TO-MAN DEFENSE**

In zone defense each player is assigned to guard a specific area of the court. In man-to-man defense, each player has an individual opponent and is responsible for covering him anywhere on the court.

REFEREE'S SIGNALS

Rules differ in high-school, college, and professional play, but the signals denoting rule violations are the same. If a spectator knows these signals, the game is more enjoyable.

the Swedish and German forms of calisthenics in their gymnastic classes, Luther Gulick, head of the department of physical education, asked his students to devise a game that would fill the void between the football and baseball seasons.

Naismith's original conception of basketball was embodied in 13 rules, five principles of which still govern the game today. These include the following: (1) the ball must be large, light, and easily handled; (2) the ball may not be advanced by running; (3) there must be no restriction on any player's getting the ball at any time; (4) bodily contact is not permissible; and (5) the goals must be horizontal and elevated.

Since the gymnastic class consisted of 18 students, the group was divided into teams of 9. In lieu of present-day baskets, the first game employed peach baskets that had been uncovered in the cellar by the school janitor. They were nailed to the boards of the running track in the gym, 10 ft (3 m) above the floor. Despite the ineptness of play, the game was an instant success, and Naismith received many requests for copies of the rules. When the participants in the original game accepted YMCA assignments in various parts of the country and overseas, the sport was on its way to wide popularity.

Within three years, however, basketball had fallen into disrepute for two reasons. One was that the games had become excessively rough and prompted ill feeling; the other had to do with its tendency to limit the use of gymnasiums. Whereas gyms were formerly used by as many as 60 persons at a given time, the new game restricted their use to 18 (and, a little later, to 14, when the teams were reduced to 7 players each) for prolonged periods. An adverse ruling by the YMCA led basketball-minded youths to drop their memberships so that they might pursue the new sport in dance halls and other places affording sufficient space. It also hastened the advent of professional basketball, because teams charged admission to pay the rentals of the halls, and split the profits among themselves.

By the beginning of the 20th century, the game was being played by more than 50 U.S. colleges. Because many areas modified the rules to their own liking, there was much confusion, and occasionally each half of a contest was played under a separate set of rules. The early history of basketball in the colleges followed a more or less basic pattern. Few schools had coaches. Usually the coach was the captain, the best player, a member of the faculty, a former athlete who served as an adviser, or even a basketball referee. The teams were not recognized by college athletic associations. Players were required to provide their own uniforms and defray all expenses incurred by travel. Uniforms consisted of jerseys and baseball or football pants or wrestlers' tights. As the game developed, short, padded pants became a standard part of the player's garb.

In the earliest games a soccer ball was used. By 1894 a slightly larger, laced ball was introduced. In 1937 the laceless ball was adopted, and, in 1941, the present-day molded ball.

The baskets, too, have changed through the years. In 1893, after the original peach baskets had been discarded, hammock-type baskets were used. When a player was successful in tossing the ball into the netting, someone had to climb a ladder to retrieve the ball. Later it became customary to use a pole to regain the ball, and then a device involving a chain that, when pulled, ejected the ball. The professional players were the first to cut an opening in the net to permit the ball to fall through.

Naismith Memorial Basketball Hall of Fame

The world's first basketball team posing in 1891 in Springfield, Mass. James Naismith is in street clothing.

During basketball's pioneer years, balcony spectators delighted in sitting directly behind the baskets and steering the ball into, or away from, the baskets, according to their loyalties. In 1895 a wire screen was introduced as a standard backboard, but since the home teams quickly learned how to take advantage of peculiarities in these wire backboards—how best to retrieve balls off the dented wire, for example—standard wooden backboards came into being. In 1909 the professionals introduced glass backboards. In 1940 fan-shaped backboards were legalized. Present-day backboards are either rectangular or fan-shaped, and made of plate glass, steel, or wood.

Early courts were small and irregular in shape, and play frequently was obstructed by pillars. In 1903, when the process of standardization of courts began, it was ruled that boundary lines had to be straight. Prior to 1915, when the National Joint Rules Committee was formed by representatives of colleges, the Amateur Athletic Union of the United States (AAU), and the YMCA, to set up a single code governing the game, as many as five different sets of rules were used.

Progress from the 1930's. The skill of players in passing, rebounding, and scoring has increased strikingly, largely as the result of expert coaching. Coaches have been aided in their work by the establishment of clinics which make possible the exchange of theories and practices. In addition, there has been much study of the techniques of leading players by boys entering the game.

Four factors were important in popularizing basketball on a national scale in the 1930's: the construction of large field houses, especially in the Midwest, many of which were capable of seating more than 15,000 spectators; the introduction of big-time collegiate basketball at Madison Square Garden in New York, which permitted the strongest regional teams to compete in a major sports area, and which also brought about standardization in officiating and rules interpretation; the introduction of the high-scoring game by coach Frank W. Keaney of the University of Rhode Island, which made basketball more exciting than it had been; and the wide acceptance and accuracy of the one-hand shot.

The game has been popularized still further by annual tournaments. The first of these were largely local in nature, even though they were called "national." The AAU held its first such tourney in 1897, and the YMCA in 1923. In 1937, Emil Liston founded the National Association of Intercollegiate Basketball (now the National Association of Intercollegiate Athletics, or NAIA) in Kansas City, Mo., from among the nation's smaller colleges. Its first tournament was held in that city in 1937. The Metropolitan Basketball Writers Association, a New York City group, was instrumental in founding the National Intercollegiate Tournament (more often called the National Invitation Tournament, or NIT) in 1938. The annual tournaments of the National Collegiate Athletic Association (NCAA) were begun in 1939; their success led to the formation of a competitive division for smaller schools in 1957. These and other tournaments provide goals for the outstanding U.S. college teams.

Professional Basketball. The contributions to the game made by professionals have never received full recognition. The reason has been largely that the early professional leagues suffered from lack of stability. They were short-lived, and players frequently showed little respect for contractual obligations, jumping from one team to another. The first semblance of order came in 1946 when Walter A. Brown, president of the Boston Garden, organized the Basketball Association of America. Players thereafter signed contracts identical to those used in professional baseball, thus assuring each team the exclusive services of its players until they were released or traded to rival clubs.

In 1949 that league and the older National Basketball League consolidated. The merger produced the National Basketball Association. In 1967, the American Basketball Association was formed. These two associations were known as the big leagues of basketball. However, in 1976 the ABA disbanded and four of its teams became members of the NBA.

Rick Barry, Golden State star, dribbles past a defender. *UPI*

Richard Lee—Queens College

A tense moment typical of the play in women's intercollegiate basketball. A Queens College player, closely defended, tries to pass to a teammate.

Outstanding professional teams of the past include the New York Wanderers, so called because they did not have a home court; the Buffalo Germans, who were organized in 1895 at the Buffalo, N.Y., YMCA and competed for 44 years, winning 792 of 878 games, including 111 consecutive games in 1912; and the New York-based Celtics—called the "Original" Celtics—who dominated the game in the 1920's, playing all comers under any set of rules proposed by the opposition, and sometimes winning as many as 200 games in a single season.

During the 1930's professional basketball lagged, but a revival took place following World War II. In the early postwar period the Minneapolis Lakers, led by George Mikan, Vern Mikkelsen, and Jim Pollard—three players of the giant variety now common to the professional game—was the dominant team. One of the greatest players in the history of basketball was Bill Russell, who retired after the 1969 season. In 13 years with the Boston Celtics he led the club to 11 world titles.

High School Basketball. The importance of high school basketball is evident from the fact that each year thousands of high schools have teams that compete in interscholastic competition. The popularity of basketball, especially in small schools, is increased by the relatively small number of players needed and the low cost of equipment.

Holyoke, Mass., High School and Central High (Philadelphia) are believed to have been the first to have basketball teams. In 1905 Wisconsin became the first state to conduct a tournament for high-school teams, a practice that is now general in the United States. Indiana is one of the most active.

Teams from two schools have become legendary. During the period from 1919 to 1925, the Passaic, N.J., High School teams won 159 consecutive games. During the 1927–28 season, the Carr Creek, Ky., High School team won national recognition for its feats, which included competition in the national high-school basketball tournament in Chicago, despite the fact that the players represented an extremely small rural community.

Women's Basketball. This phase of the game is almost as old as basketball itself. The first women to play were teachers from the Buckingham School in Springfield, Mass., one of whom was Maude Sherman, later the bride of James Naismith, basketball's inventor.

Smith College pioneered in basketball, among women's schools, introducing the game in 1892. Clara Baer of Newcomb College, New Orleans, La., formulated the first code of rules for women's competition in 1895.

However, almost from the very start of women's basketball, rules for the game have undergone many revisions. The major modern changes from six-player to five-player rules took place in 1971. The five-player adaptation abandoned the system of certain players being limited to playing offense and others only to defense. In addition to full court movement by all players, a 30-second clock and 20-minute quarters are now the standard. There are a few areas where the six-player rules are still being used.

Evidence of the growth of women's basketball is seen in the sold-out national tournaments of the Association of the Intercollegiate Athletics for Women, teams playing in the Madison Square Garden in New York City, and the addition of the sport to the Olympic games in 1976.

BAUGH [*bô*], **SAMUEL ADRIAN ("SLINGIN' SAMMY")** (1914–), American football player and coach, generally considered the greatest forward passer in the game's history. He was born in Temple, Tex., and attended Texas Christian University; in 1936 he was named quarterback of the All-American team chosen by Grantland Rice. In 1937 he began an outstanding career as a professional player with the Washington Redskins of the National Football League. When he retired after the 1952 season he had set NFL records for number of seasons played (16), passes attempted (3,016), passes completed (1,709), yards gained by passing (22,085), and touchdown passes thrown (187). He was head football coach of Hardin-Simmons University from 1953 through 1959.

BAYLOR [*bā'lər*], **ELGIN** (1935–), American basketball player born in Washington, D.C. He was one of the leading U.S. collegiate players from 1956 to 1958, at Seattle University. He was named to the all-star team of the National Basketball Association in his first season as a professional, 1958–59, as a member of the Minneapolis Lakers, and won the same honor during the next five seasons. During the 1960–61 season (the first in which the Lakers represented Los Angeles) he scored 71 points in a single game.

BERRA [*bĕr'ə*], **LAWRENCE PETER ("YOGI")** (1925–), American baseball player whose skill, sense of humor, and engaging personality made him one of the best-loved men in the game. He was born in St. Louis, Mo., and joined the New York Yankees in 1946. Primarily a catcher, he also performed as an outfielder and as an infielder. He retired as a player in 1963 to become manager of the New York Yankees.

BICYCLING. The bicycle is the principal means of individual mechanical transport in much of the world. In North America, unlike most other parts of the world, cycling has been primarily a form of recreation, and until the mid-1970's, when the first federal highway funds were earmarked for bikeway construction, even recreational cycling in the United States was impeded by the overwhelming impact of the automobile.

The following discussion deals with the purely recreational aspects of cycling.

Racing

The man who built the first self-propelled bicycle was also the first cyclist to race. In 1842, Kirkpatrick Macmillan (see BICYCLE) raced the Glasgow-Carlisle mail coach a distance of 70 mi (112 km) and won. But his invention failed to stir sustained interest.

Track Events. The first recorded bicycle race was held on May 31, 1868, when Napoleon III of France offered a gold medal to the winner of a 2-km race at the Parc de St. Cloud in Paris. James Moore, an Englishman living in Paris, took the prize. The very next day, June 1, Whit Monday, England held its first bicycle race, at Hindon,

All pictures courtesy of Arnold, Schwinn & Co.

Foot-driven "Dandy-horse," a hit with the dandies of 1816, was the first practical steering bicycle. Baron von Drais modernized the original two-wheeler, which was invented in Paris.

Middlesex, and every Whit Monday since has seen an annual event in that country.

The earliest racing cycles were "boneshakers," horizontal machines with wheels of roughly equal diameter. But after 1870 the boneshaker gradually yielded to the "ordinary," a high front-wheel, tiny rear-wheeled type, which became popular for more than two decades. Boneshakers and ordinarys competed together in the 1880's and 1890's. At the same time, however, separate championship races for ordinarys were established. In 1878 the National Cyclists' Union in England (formerly the Bicycle Union) was founded on the ordinary, and the universities of Cambridge and Oxford recognized the sport. Thereafter Albert A. Pope, a Boston merchant, commissioned an American ordinary, whereupon the Harvard Athletic Association quickly followed the British lead. On May 24, 1878, Beacon Park track in Boston saw C. Parker win the first track race in the United States. His time for the 3-mi (4.8-km) event was 12 min., 27 sec.

A combination of the "safety bicycle" (with chain drive and wheels of equal diameter), pneumatic tires, and American mechanical refinements gave cycling one of its proudest institutions, six-day bicycle racing. Champion William ("Plugger Bill") Martin inaugurated the event, which was to become a sensation, in Madison Square Garden in 1891 when he pedaled 1,466 mi (2 345 km) on a specially constructed velodrome. Fifteen years later more than 100 such tracks, both indoor and outdoor, had been built throughout North America.

Speed Records. H. L. Cortis, a star in the 1880's, was the first cyclist to exceed 20 mi (32 km) per hour. His feat launched a continuing competition in racing against time. On June 30, 1899, Charles M. ("Mile-a-Minute") Murphy rode on a wooden track laid between the rails of the Long Island Railroad. Using a train as a windbreak, he covered a measured mile (1.6 km) in $57\frac{4}{5}$ sec. Murphy's record stood for 42 years, until May 17, 1941, when former six-day bicycle racer Alfred ("Alf") Letourner used a Bakersfield, Calif., expressway and a midget racing car windbreak to cover the measured mile in a time of 33:05, or 108.92 mi (174.27 km) per hour. Thereafter Dr. Alan Abbott bettered the record to 138.67 mi (221.87 km) per hour, on the Bonneville Salt Flats, Utah, behind a specially designed pace car, on Aug. 25, 1973.

Both amateur and professional racing have known periods of great interest and subsequent decline. As the automobile developed, public interest switched from cycling to auto racing, and the numerous velodromes crumbled into decay. During the world wars both fields of competition were neglected, although amateur and professional bicycle racing were austerely maintained by cyclists in

The high wheel, or "ordinary," was the craze for parkside riding from 1872 to 1892 as cycling came of age. This high-wheeled model pioneered ball bearings, wire wheels, and ribbon tires.

By 1869 the "Dandy-horse" had sprouted cranks and pedals, thanks to the inventiveness of a Scottish blacksmith, Kirkpatrick Macmillan. Now it became the "boneshaker," a wayward Victorian toy.

love with the sport. Europe, lagging behind the United States economically, clearly became the center of organized cycling activity after World War II.

In the 1970's interest in energy conservation increased, and more people than ever turned to bicycle riding, which in turn stimulated a surge of racing activity throughout the world. Increased international competition via the Pan American Games, the world championships (conducted annually by the Union Cycliste Internationale, Paris), and the Olympic Games again prompted many nations to build velodromes for track racing.

Road Racing. The most famous international event in cycling is the Tour de France, originated in 1903 by the journalist Henri Desgrange. Roughly equivalent in public interest to baseball's World Series in the United States, this grueling three-week test attracts the world's foremost bicyclists, who compete over a course of more than 2,000 mi (3 200 km). The winner is acclaimed a hero throughout Europe. Other events of international significance include the Giro d'Italia (Tour of Italy), another three-week marathon; the 372.6-mi (596.2-km) Bordeaux-to-Paris race in France, which originated in 1891; and the 180.09-mi (288.14-km) Milan-to-San Remo race in Italy. Challenging Europe's long-established events in prominence are the new Tour of Egypt and Tour of Tunisia.

Major road-racing events in the Western Hemisphere are the 794-mi (1 270.4-km) Tour du St. Laurent; the 170-mi (272-km) Quebec-to-Montreal test sponsored by *La Presse*, a French-language newspaper in Montreal; the Tour of Mexico; and the Tour of Sommerville, N.J.

Competition Requirements. Women were admitted to American National competition in their separate division in 1937, and to world championship competition in 1958. However, they are denied recognition for Pan American and Olympic Games competition.

While there are local differences in the age groupings for racing, requirements for international events are standard throughout the world. All bicycle racing is controlled by each nation's parent racing organization, as recognized by the world governing body of cycling, the Union Cycliste Internationale (UCI) in Paris. In the United States the recognized body is the United States Cycling Federation (USCF), with headquarters in New York. The Canadian equivalent is the Canadian Cycling Federation (CCF), Toronto, Ont.

Racing programs for junior and senior high schools and colleges are rapidly becoming a part of physical fitness

The first "safety bicycle," equipped with a chain-drive throwback to Macmillan's rear-drive principle, was built by J. K. Starley. It sparked a bike-builders' boom in the late 1890's.

education, with ordinary stock bicycles accepted for use. This program also is supervised in the United States by the USCF. In licensed racing the USCF recognizes the following categories; veterans, 40 years of age or older; senior men and women, 18 years of age or older; junior men and women, 15 years to 18th birthday; intermediate boys and girls, 12 years to 15th birthday; and midget boys and girls, 8 years to 12th birthday. Canadians recognize only senior men and women and junior men categories.

Touring and Recreation

Touring by bicycle grew naturally as the developing velocipedes improved in design.

Organizations. The National Association of Velocipedists, founded in England in 1869, is recognized as the first bicycle touring organization. Nearly 10 years later the Bicycle Touring Club of England was organized (1878) with women admitted to membership a year later.

U.S. and other amateur cyclists organized within a few years thereafter. The League of American Wheelmen (LAW) was founded at Newport, R.I., in 1880. The French founded their first touring club in 1890, and in 1897 the International Touring Congress first offered information to cyclists of all countries who wished to tour abroad. By the beginning of the 20th century more than 200,000 Americans, and nearly 10 times that number of Europeans, were cycling for recreation and pleasure.

Trends. Thereafter cycling underwent an uneven growth—retarded by World War I, spurred by the economic depressions of the late 1920's and 1930's (when bicycles replaced automobiles as utility vehicles), retarded again by World War II and the automotive boom that followed it, and spurred once more by recession in the 1970's.

In the United States cycling proved particularly vulnerable to economic trends. At the bottom of the Depression in 1933 recreational cyclists and others organized the American Youth Hostels (AYH), patterned after European clubs that offered approved, inexpensive lodging to both cyclists and hikers who backpacked their bedding and equipment. Throughout the 1950's and 1960's, AYH was nearly defunct. But new, more sophisticated bicycles (at first almost wholly imported from Europe), rising consciousness of cycling's importance for health and fitness, improved bikeways, energy shortages, auto congestion, and recession all finally conspired to produce a startling rebirth of American cycling. U.S. bicycle purchases skyrocketed from an annual 7,000,000 at the beginning of the 1970's to 15,000,000 annually in the years 1972–74. Thus, by the middle of the decade nearly 80,000,000 bicycles were in use by an estimated 100,000,000 cyclists in the country.

Bikeways. At the same time a major breakthrough in bikeways development occurred when Congress, in the federal highway aid act of 1973, for the first time appropriated money—$120,000,000—for bikeway construction. The act provided, throughout its three-year life, up to $2,000,000 annually to each state on a 30%–70% matching fund basis for bikeways.

BILLIARDS, indoor game played with ivory or composition balls and a long slender stick, or cue, on a felt-covered rectangular table. The balls are struck against each other by means of the cue. In some forms of the game the aim is to propel the cue ball so that it hits, in succession, two other balls (object balls), thereby scoring a carom; in other forms the aim is to drive the object balls into pockets in the table or to combine these two objectives.

The history of the game is obscure. Many authorities believe it developed from efforts to play a variant of lawn bowls indoors. The name probably derived from the French word *bille* ("stick"). Billiards, in variations bearing some similarity to the modern game, was played in England and France in the 15th century. These variations, however, also had some resemblance to croquet. Within the past century the game has developed into its present form. Championship competition in the United States was first held in 1859. The present-day game includes three varieties:

Carom Billiards, played on a table twice as long as it is wide (usually 10 by 5 ft, or 3 by 1.5 m). There are no pockets on a carom table, and games are played with two white balls (one of which is marked with colored spots on two sides) and a red ball. Each carom counts as a single point, and the players take alternate turns with the cue, each retiring when he fails to make a carom. The most popular carom game is three-cushion billiards, in which

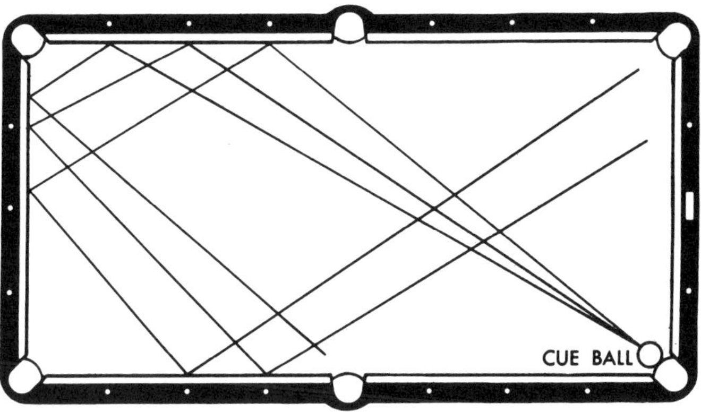

The spacing of the markers, usually diamond-shaped, in the rails of the billiard table is exact. Familiarity with the "connecting" diamonds assists a player in predetermining the path to be followed by a moving ball. Several such paths are illustrated. Though not infallible, the diamond system is used by many of the more skillful players.

the cue ball must touch a cushion (the felt-covered ridge inside the rails on carom tables) three times before it strikes the second object ball (and thus completes the carom). In championship play the winner is the first player to score 50 points. In straight-rail billiards, points are awarded for propelling the cue ball so that it strikes the two object balls, regardless of its contact with cushions. In balkline billiards, a game for experts, the table is divided into rectangular areas, and there are restrictions on the number of points a player may score in given areas.

Pocket Billiards (Pool), played on a table similar to that used in carom billiards except that there are pockets in each corner and at the center of each side rail. There are many variations, but all employ 15 object balls (numbered 1 to 15) and a cue ball. The aim is to pocket the object balls, that is to drive them into the pockets, using the cue to propel the cue ball into contact with the object balls. In advance of each shot, the player must announce the object ball and pocket he has in mind. Individuals or teams may compete; the first to pocket 8 of the 15 balls is the winner.

Snooker, played with 21 object balls and a white cue ball on a table similar to that used in pocket billiards. In American snooker, 15 of the object balls are red and have a scoring value of 1. The other six balls have the following colors and values: yellow, 2; green, 3; brown, 4; blue, 5; pink, 6; black, 7. Individuals or teams may compete. The higher score (based on the aggregate of the pocketed balls) determines the winner, the game ending when all the balls are off the table.

BLANCHARD [*blăn′chərd*], **FELIX ANTHONY, JR. ("DOC") (1925–),** American football player who won All-American rating as a fullback for the United States Military Academy (Army) in 1944, 1945, and 1946. Together with Glenn Davis, he led Army teams of those years to 28 consecutive victories, distinguishing himself through speed and power. In 1945 he won the John W. Heisman Memorial Trophy and the Robert Maxwell Memorial Trophy, awarded annually to leading players. He later became an outstanding fighter pilot in the U.S. Air Force.

BOATING. *See* CANOEING; MOTORBOATING; ROWING AND SCULLING; SAILING; WINTER SPORTS.

BOBSLEDDING, winter sport that involves downhill racing on a large four-runner sled over a specially constructed course covered with ice or snow. The sleds carry two to four persons. The sport evolved late in the 19th century; its name derived from a maneuver of the crew called "bobbing"—a concerted effort of the men to increase the speed of the sled by slowly leaning back to an almost horizontal position and then, on signal from the captain (the man in front), suddenly returning to an upright position. This technique has recently assumed less importance because improved design of the sleds increased their speed.

The sport was originated in Saint-Moritz, Switzerland, by tobogganers who sought to increase the speed and thrills of tobogganing by adding runners to their sleds and altering the course, or "run." The first national-championship competition was held in Austria in 1908 and the first European championships were decided in 1914. There was a cessation of bobsledding activity because of World War I, but interest revived after the war. The sport became a popular event at the first Olympic Winter Games in 1924 in Chamonix, France, and since that time has been part of the Winter Games in each Olympiad with the exception of those of 1960.

Participation in this dangerous sport is necessarily restricted because of the expensive equipment and, in the United States, by the scarcity of good runs. The only approved run in the United States is located at Mount Van Hoevenberg, near Lake Placid, N.Y. There are about 25 runs in Europe.

In approved competition the bobsled consists of a plain riding surface (once wood but now metal) that rests on two sets of runners, the front one being pivoted and used for steering. Sleds now average 500 lb. in weight. Recently a type of cowling has been added to the front to reduce wind resistance and increase speed. The finest sleds are made in Italy and cost more than $1,000. Speeds up to 90 mph are possible. Steering is accomplished by ropes attached to the front runners or by a steering wheel connected by cables to the front runners.

In four-man competition, the team captain, or skipper, steers. The rear man (brakeman) is responsible for checking skids and stopping the sled. The two middle men supply ballast and help "bob." A smaller sled is used in two-man competition, and the two riders perform the duties of the front and rear members of the four-man teams.

The international governing body for the sport is the Fédération Internationale de Bobsleigh et Tobogganing (F.I.B.T.). It was organized in 1923, and held the first world championships in 1927. Since that time it has sponsored annual two-man and four-man world-title competitions. In such races only one sled is permitted on the course at a given time. Each sled makes four trips down the course, and the fastest aggregate time determines the winner.

Publitoto—Pix

Two-man American team streaks around a turn on the bobsled run at Cortina, Italy.

Peter Anderson—Black Star

Argentine gauchos sharpening their skill with the bola.

BOCCIE [*bōt'chē-ā, Angl. bŏch'ē*], Italian game similar to bowls. Two players, or two teams of two to four each, compete on a level, grassy area; when defined, the court is approximately 10 by 60 ft. The game employs eight 4½-in. wooden or composition balls and a 2¾-in. *pallino*, or "jack" ball. In singles play the first player throws the *pallino* from one end of the court toward the opposite end; he then bowls a large ball from the same point, seeking to get it as close as possible to the *pallino*. The opposing player attempts to bowl a ball still closer and, if possible, to knock the opponent's ball farther away. The closer ball determines the next bowler and is worth one point. When all balls have been bowled, the player with a ball closest to the *pallino* has the option of throwing the *pallino* again. The first to score 12 points is the winner. The winner of two of three games wins the match. When more than two players are involved, partners alternate in performing.

BOLA [*bō'lə*] **or BOLAS,** weapon used for hunting, consisting of weights joined by cords or thongs. There may be two weights, usually stone or metal balls, at the end of one cord; or three weights and three cords may be used, the cords being joined at a common center. The bola is whirled around the head and thrown so as to entangle the legs of an animal. The Eskimos use it for hunting waterfowl, while the Indians of the South American pampas ensnare the flightless rhea and the guanaco with it. The gauchos of Argentina adopted this weapon from the Indians.

BOMAR [*bō'mər*], **HERBERT B. ("BUDDY")** (1916–), American bowler, voted "bowler of the year" in 1945 and 1947 by the Bowling Writers Association of America. He was born in Ardmore, Okla., but gained his fame while competing in Chicago, where he captained four teams that won national championships. In 1944 he won the National All-Star Individual Tournament sponsored by the Bowling Proprietors' Association of America.

BOWLING, indoor game in which contestants roll balls made of solid composition down wooden alleys toward groups of ten wooden pins, trying to knock down all of the pins in one or, if necessary, two attempts. In varying forms, bowling has existed throughout the world since ancient times. In the United States it has grown in popularity so markedly that it ranks among the top participant sports. In that country alone, nearly 20,000,000 persons were participating in the game during the early 1960's. The

Brunswick-Balke-Collender Co.

Bowling is a nationwide activity in the United States. Above, alleys typical of those in which the sport developed.

Brunswick-Balke-Collender Co.

The growth of the game has encouraged the development of large bowling establishments that feature automatic equipment.

American Bowling Congress, governing body of U.S. and Canadian competition in the game's most popular form—the one involving large pins—had a membership of more than 3,000,000 active participants. The Women's Interna-

Brunswick-Balke-Collender Co.

Bowling is a sport which appeals to millions of people in all age groups.

tional Bowling Congress, which performs a similar function in U.S. competition involving women, had nearly 1,000,000 members. Since World War II annual tournaments have attracted wide interest and large followings. In addition, coverage of major bowling events on television, and specially produced bowling shows on television, have widened the following of the game and provided a lucrative source of income for leading participants, several of whom have won national fame through such programs. Although bowling's greatest present-day popularity has been gained in the United States, it is also practiced in Canada, Central and South America, Great Britain, and a number of northern European countries.

Equipment and Rules of Play. The regulation alley is a smooth surface of wood; the player stands at one end, behind the foul line, and the pins rest in an upright position at the other. Behind the foul line there is a runway, or approach, with a minimum length of 15 ft. It is in this area that the player may take several steps before releasing the ball, but he must release the ball behind the foul line. The distance between the foul line and the center of the first, or head, pin is 60 ft. The width of the alley is between 41 and 42 in., and along each side is an indentation known as a gutter for retrieving misdirected balls. Balls are returned to the player via a separate chute.

The pins are 15 in. high and are arranged in a triangular pattern in four rows, the first consisting of the head pin, and the last row consisting of four pins approximately 3 ft. behind the head pin. The shape of the pins resembles that of a champagne bottle. The name "tenpins," sometimes used in place of bowling, derives from the use of ten pins in the game.

The regulation ball has a maximum diameter of 8.59 in., a maximum circumference of 27 in., and a maximum weight of 16 lb. There are usually either two or three holes for the participant's fingers.

The sport may be played by individuals or teams, the latter generally comprising five members.

A game in bowling constitutes ten "frames," in each of which the contestants bowl a maximum of two balls apiece. A single point is awarded for each pin toppled, and the highest total score for the ten frames determines the winner. When a contestant topples all the pins on his first try, he is credited with a "strike," and for that frame he receives ten points plus the number of pins he topples with the next two balls rolled. If he rolls a second strike in his next turn, he scores ten more points, which can be added to what he scores in his first roll in the third frame. If he scores a third consecutive strike, his total for the first frame is 30. Should he continue to roll strikes throughout the game (12 in consecutive attempts), he would finish with a total of 300 points (the maximum possible number) and thus achieve a perfect game.

If the contestant topples all the pins of a ten pin setup in two consecutive attempts, he scores a "spare," and is credited in that frame with ten points plus whatever he scores with the first ball in the next frame.

If the contestant fails to topple all pins in his two attempts within a given frame, he has committed a "miss" or "break." A "split" is a setup of pins, resulting from the first roll of the ball in a frame, in which two or more pins are left standing in positions spaced so widely that it is difficult to topple them in the second roll.

A contestant commits a foul if he permits any part of his body to come in contact with the foul line, or the area beyond it, during his delivery of the ball. He is penalized to the extent of receiving no credit for pins knocked down by the ball thus bowled, and he is permitted only one roll in that frame.

Early History. Research has established that bowling dates from ancient times, and that it has derived from games that were practiced in such widely spaced areas as Egypt and Polynesia. While examining the grave of a child whose burial was placed authentically at 5200 B.C., the English Egyptologist Sir Flinders Petrie discovered implements for playing a game similar to bowling. The game practiced by the Polynesians involved a type of alley in which the distance between the contestant and the object he was seeking to topple was 60 ft., identical with the corresponding distance in the present-day game.

The early history of bowling is often thought to parallel that of bowls, or lawn bowls, and its Italian variant, *boccie*, though bowling actually bears only limited resemblance to those games. The earliest comprehensive accounts of bowling center around Germany, where, by the 15th century, the game of ninepins had evolved. Before that time, according to the 19th-century German author William Pehle, medieval Germans practiced a form of bowling in which the target was a club (*Kegel*) that resembles the present-day bottle-shaped pin used in the sport. The keglers (a term still applied to bowlers in colloquial usage) commonly were participants in rites practiced in the cloisters of churches. Parishioners would place a *Kegel* at one end of the cloister and try to hit it with an object (usually a stone) thrown from the other end. Success was taken as an indication that the contestant was living a pure life. From the cloisters the game spread to the populace and soon gained popularity as a sport employing from 3 to 17 pins, the customary number varying with the section of Germany and the Low Countries in which the game was played. Another source of information, Joseph Strutt's *The Sports and Pastimes of the People of England* (1801), refers to 12th-century bowling tournaments in England. In most early forms of the game, boulders as nearly spherical as it was possible to obtain were bowled at wooden pins on outdoor alleys consisting of clay or cinders, or both. One of the early records of an indoor alley dates from 1455. Before that time bowling was primarily an outdoor game. By the early 19th century it was almost exclusively an indoor game.

The present-day game involving ten pins undoubtedly is a descendant of ninepins, as played by the Germans, Dutch, and Swiss. The Dutch introduced ninepins to colonial America in the 17th century. The game attracted a wide following in the United States, especially along the eastern seaboard, during the first half of the 19th century. Gambling for large stakes and rigged matches brought it into disrepute, however. About 1850, the Connecticut legislature outlawed ninepins. Shortly after the middle of the 19th century, the game made a comeback in a form employing ten pins, which has continued to be the number used in U.S. competition.

Modern Developments in the United States. By 1875 the need for uniformity in playing areas and rules was felt by the game's leaders. In that year the short-lived National Bowling Association was formed in New York. This was the first of several attempts to form a governing organization. Finally, in 1895, a successful effort along this line resulted in the formation of the American Bowling Congress (ABC). This organization formulated a code of rules and also standardized equipment, in addition to conducting a campaign to improve the surroundings in which the game was played. The organization prospered and grew. In 1901 it began its annual national tournament, awarding $1,592 in prizes. Fifty years later the ABC tournament's prize list totaled $576,730. The tournament ranks among the country's leading sports events and provides competition in singles (for individual bowlers), doubles (two-man teams), and five-man-team events. In the 1960's, more than 40,000 bowlers annually took part in this tournament.

Local associations affiliated with the ABC are located in Canada, Mexico, the Canal Zone, and Saudi Arabia. Services performed by the organization for its membership of more than 3,000,000 include bonding of officers of individual leagues, making awards for outstanding performances, providing aids to league secretaries, and distributing information concerning active leagues and tournaments.

Formation of the Women's International Bowling Congress (WIBC) in 1916 marked the growth of feminine participation in the game. This organization, too, has made steady progress. From about 200 members in 1917, it has grown to nearly 1,000,000 in the 1960's. Members compete in individual leagues throughout the United States and Canada, and also take part in annual WIBC national-championship competition.

Three other organizations have played major roles in the remarkable growth of bowling during more recent years of the 20th century.

The Bowling Proprietors' Association of America (BPAA) was organized in 1932 to provide organized promotion for the sport, to protect the investments of its members, and to encourage improvements in playing conditions. Within 20 years it had grown to the point that its membership included 80% of all commercial bowling establishments. Since 1941 the BPAA has conducted annual competitions to determine what are called All-Star Individual Championships; winners of these are recognized as the game's outstanding performers. Similar competitions for women were begun in 1949. Since that date the BPAA also has conducted regular tournaments for men and women in doubles and team competition, plus handicap competition.

The National Bowling Council (NBC), founded in 1943, includes representatives for all areas of the game: manufacturers and suppliers of equipment, proprietors of alleys, and actual participants. Its goals include promoting relations between these groups and protecting the welfare of the game as it is affected by legislation dealing with such matters as taxation. In 1946 the NBC took over direction and operation of the American Junior Bowling Congress, an organization of teen-age bowlers, whose membership has increased at an even greater rate than that of the ABC or WIBC during the postwar years.

The Professional Bowlers' Association was organized in 1959 by outstanding competitors in the sport. Additional members are admitted upon approval of the group's mem-

Don Carter, holder of many bowling records and honors. He bowled a four-game total of 1,084 during the 1962 ABC Masters Tournament and established a new world's record. He has also bowled more than a dozen perfect games.

Brunswick-Balke-Collender Co.

STRAIGHT BALL

Aimed directly from the right corner, this is considered the best delivery for a beginner.

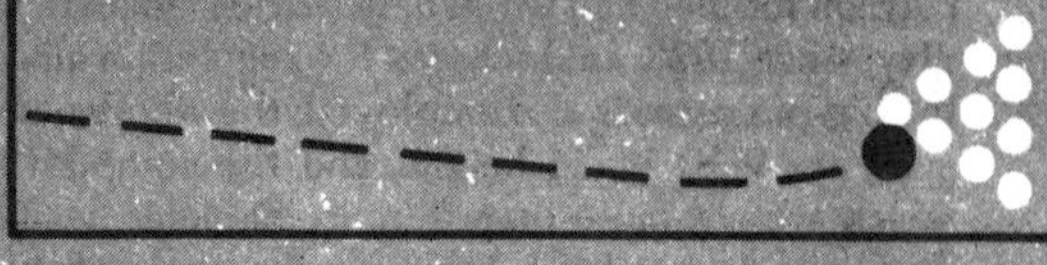

HOOK BALL

The hook is delivered from about the center, not from the corner.

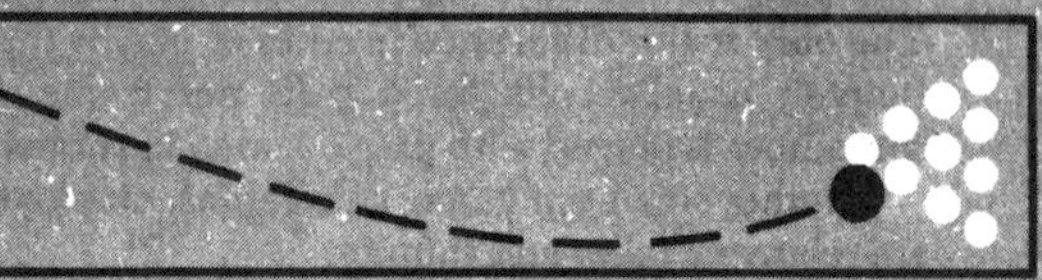

CURVE BALL

Hardest ball to control, this travels to the pins through a wide arc, like an exaggerated hook.

THREE-STEP DELIVERY

This approach relies almost entirely on strength. Bowler starts on the left foot, brings ball down and back fast, and then quickly pulls the ball through and forward.

FOUR-STEP DELIVERY

In four-step footwork the bowler starts on the right foot. A full, shoulder-level backswing and follow-through make this delivery the easiest and most popular approach.

FIVE-STEP DELIVERY

Five-step approach begins on the left foot and continues through backswing in next three steps to prepare for the last, long sliding step into straight-arm delivery.

LaVerne Carter, wife of Don Carter, demonstrates that bowling can be a family game professionally as well as recreationally. She finished 2d in the 1960 World's International Tournament.

Brunswick-Balke-Collender Co.

PICKING UP THE SPARES

LEFT-SIDE SPARE

To pick up left-side spares (4-7 below), bowler approaches from the right but angles across at pins.

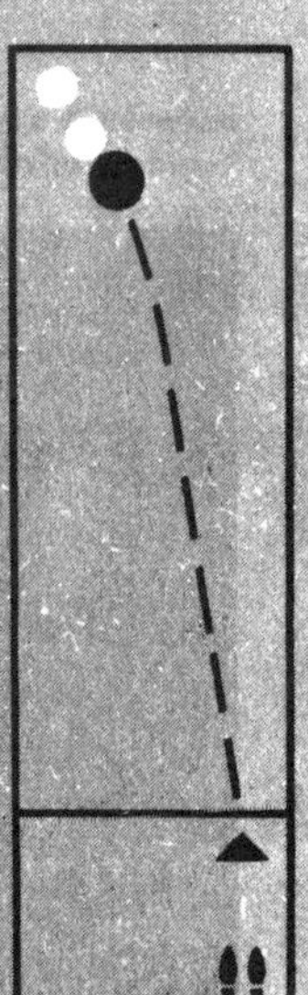

RIGHT-SIDE SPARE

When trying for right-side spares (3-6-10 combination shown), bowler angles ball across lane from left.

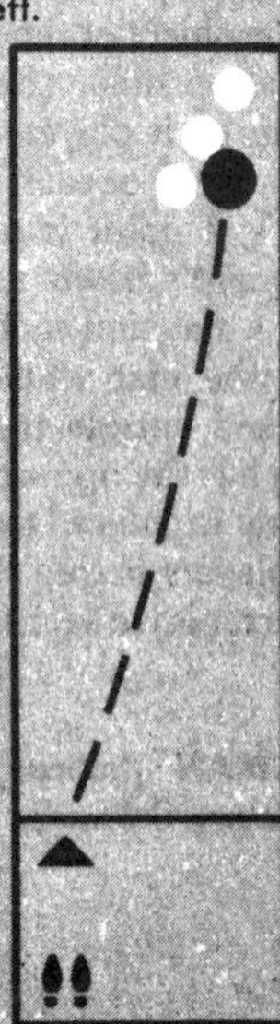

MIDDLE SPARE

In picking up middle spares (1-3-8 above), bowler stands a bit to the left of center to deliver.

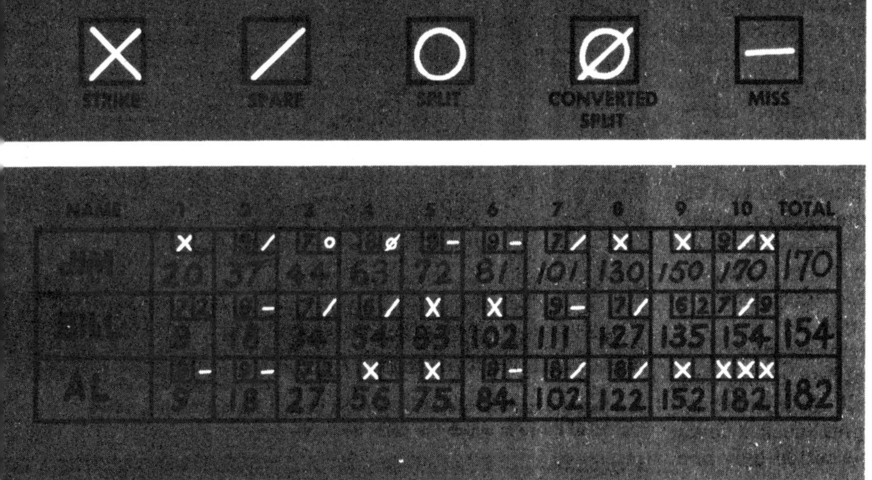

SCORING A TYPICAL GAME

A game consists of ten frames which are numbered on the scoresheet's first row. One point is scored for each downed pin. If all pins are knocked down with the first ball, the bowler has a "strike." If all pins are knocked down with two balls, the bowler has a "spare." Scores of 180 or more denote superior games; 300 is the highest possible score. Bill's score shows spares in the 3rd, 4th, 8th, and 10th frames, strikes in the 5th and 6th, and misses with his 2d turn in the 2d and 7th frames. In Jim's 4th frame, he was able to knock off a split (two or more pins, at least one which is not adjacent to another) to convert it to a spare. Thus, the "converted split" symbol is inserted.

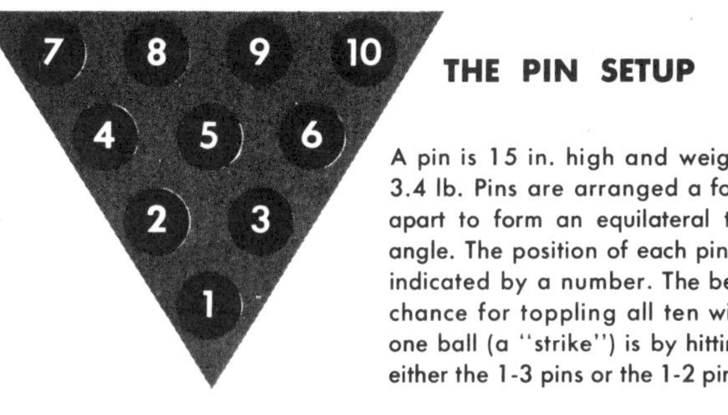

THE PIN SETUP

A pin is 15 in. high and weighs 3.4 lb. Pins are arranged a foot apart to form an equilateral triangle. The position of each pin is indicated by a number. The best chance for toppling all ten with one ball (a "strike") is by hitting either the 1-3 pins or the 1-2 pins.

bership committee. The association's primary aim is assisting its members financially by arranging endorsements of equipment and participation in exhibition matches and special tournaments.

Other manifestations of the growth of interest in bowling include the steady increase in the number of alleys, including those equipped with luxury items, and the popularity of television programs in which leading bowlers participate. In Aug., 1952, the first automatic pin setter was installed in a bowling establishment (in Brooklyn, N.Y.). Such devices have become standard features of the many ultramodern bowling establishments that have arisen since that time. The television shows command large audiences throughout the country, and in 1960 two participants earned a combined total of $145,000—a further indication of the sport's major proportions.

Small-Pin Bowling. In addition to the standard game employing large pins, there are variations using small pins. The most popular of these, duckpins, dates from the early 1900's. The game originated in the United States, and its governing body is the National Duck Pin Bowling Congress, which has conducted national-championship competition for men and women, in singles, doubles, and team play, since 1928. In duckpins the regulation alley used in the big-pin game is also employed; the wooden pins, however, are 9 13/32 in. in height, and the composition balls, which are not more than 5 in. in diameter, weigh 3¾ lb. The balls do not have holes for the contestants' fingers. The only major difference in rules of play is that the participant usually rolls three balls per frame. Duckpins sometimes is played with pins encased in rubber.

Another small-pin game, candlepins, employs pins that are relatively taller and thinner.

BOWLS, game for two, three, or four players, in which composition or wooden balls (bowls) are rolled toward a smaller ball (jack). The bowls are rolled on a greensward divided into six rinks 18 to 20 ft. in width, and 120 ft. in length. Bowls are 16½ in. in circumference and 3½ lb. in weight. The bowls are not perfectly round; consequently it is possible to make them curve. The jack is 8 in. in circumference and 10 oz. in weight.

The object of the game is to roll the bowl as close to the jack as possible. After the jack has been thrown down the green, each player rolls two bowls, alternating with his opponent. For each bowl closer to the jack than the opponent's, 1 point is scored. It is permissible to knock an opponent's bowls away from the jack. Bowls are rolled from a mat, and each player must have one foot in contact with the mat when bowling. In the event the jack is knocked outside the rink limits, the opposing player or team has the opportunity to throw the jack. Play may be for any stipulated time or number of rolls agreed upon by the players before the start of the game. In singles play, the first player scoring 21 points is the winner.

BOXING, the art of fighting with the fists, in which the fists and arms comprise the sole means of attack and defense. In modern practice the sport, also called pugilism and prize fighting, denotes fighting with padded gloves according to specified rules.

The popular definition, "the manly art of self-defense," offers a clue to the ancient origin of the sport, which can be traced to the Greeks and Romans but which undoubtedly goes back to the earliest period of man. The primitive laws of self-preservation very likely comprised the code of the forerunner of modern boxing.

Early Recorded History. The first recorded evidence of boxing is found in the civilization of Crete and dates from

United Press International

about 1500 B.C. It consists of unearthed stone slabs containing figures of men in the squared-off stance characteristic of boxers.

It was not until 900 B.C. that boxing was recorded on a regular basis. In ancient Greece, no sport was more popular or better known, since it was used to train youths to become warriors. Boxing was an instrument for building strength and endurance, which, along with courage, were stressed more than skill and agility. At first the hands of the young warriors were encased in leather thongs for protection; later a covering of hard leather, which extended halfway up the forearm, was used. Such was the origin of the cestus, which was first employed as a defensive device but which in time became a highly effective weapon.

When the Romans conquered Greece, they brought a number of the vanquished warriors to Rome as slaves. In the era when gladiators were the counterparts of modern boxers, wealthy Romans used their warrior-slaves to provide diversion for large audiences. Roman arenas were filled on holidays when gladiators engaged in matches that usually ended in the death of one of the contestants. And the cestus underwent a number of deadly embellishments. It was filled with iron or brass, or studded with metallic spikes or knobs. Few gladiators survived the vicious sport.

Eventually the cestus went out of use, and in the 1st century B.C. all boxing was banned. With the decline of the Roman Empire, the sport, too, went into eclipse. Its dark age continued until early in the 18th century.

Beginnings of Modern Boxing. The sport's renaissance came about in England, and was due to one man, James Figg, who was also highly proficient with the sword and cudgel. Figg, the first acknowledged boxing champion, who held that distinction from 1719 to 1730, has often been called "the father of modern boxing." He was the first to incorporate the tactics of swordplay and cudgel fighting into bare-knuckle fist fighting. When Figg first gained prominence, such tactics as gouging, hair-pulling, kicking, and hitting a downed opponent when he was in the act of regaining his feet were all considered fair means to an end. Figg capitalized on his huge fists, and on his ability to put them to devastating use, to popularize punching as the basic weapon of the sport. He met all comers for a purse and as many side bets as he could arrange, but his fistic ability soon discouraged challengers.

In 1719 the champion made a further contribution to the sport by opening a school for boxers in London. Figg taught his pupils the proper way to make a fist, the method of delivering a punch forcefully, and the location of an opponent's most vulnerable areas; the solar plexus and point of the chin. Within 10 years his graduates had spread throughout London and were conducting schools of their own. Figg continued to teach and fight until 1730, when he retired as an undefeated champion. He died in 1734.

Another Englishman of major importance, Jack Broughton, appeared on the scene while Figg was at the height of his power. Broughton became the champion after Figg, sometime between 1734 and 1740. A fine fighter, he is important in the annals of the sport to an even greater degree because he was a keen student of boxing, and because he was the first to attempt to refine its rules. Broughton discarded the brawling, free-for-all tactics that were prevalent when he entered competition. He established a code of rules that was in effect from 1743 until 1838, when the London Prize Ring rules came into existence. Under Broughton's rules a round (one of the periods of actual fighting, as distinguished from intervals of rest, into which a match is divided) lasted until one man was knocked down; there was a 30-second rest period following a knockdown, after which the fighters squared off a yard apart before resuming action; it was illegal to hit a downed foe; and wrestling or grappling an opponent below the waist was illegal. A referee was provided to "keep decorum."

Broughton also opened a boxing school, the Haymarket Academy, where he taught gentlemen and young nobles. It is believed that he first put gloves on the hands of his students as a means of protecting them. Thus he has been credited with inventing boxing gloves, though championship matches were still fought with bare fists, and boxing in general continued to be a much more rugged sport than it is in the 20th century.

The London Prize Ring rules, which underwent revision in 1853, were an outgrowth of Broughton's code. Under LPR rules, matches were fought in a ring, 24 ft. square, bounded by ropes; a knockdown terminated a round; a knockdown was followed by a 30-second rest period; and kicking, biting, gouging, butting, and hitting an opponent after he was downed were considered fouls. A key provision stipulated that following the 30-second rest period after a knockdown, the fighter had an additional 8 seconds in which to reach a spot marked in the center of the ring. If he failed to reach the mark within the time limit, he was declared "not up to scratch" and thus lost the match.

These rules governed the sport until the close of the era of bare-knuckle fighting. In the last such match on record, the American John L. Sullivan defended his championship by defeating Jake Kilrain in 1889.

Marquess of Queensberry Rules. About a quarter-century earlier, there occurred another major development in the sport's history. In 1865, Sir John Sholto Douglas, 8th Marquess of Queensberry and a patron of boxing, and Arthur Chambers, an English lightweight fighter, drew up the 12 rules, bearing the former's name, that have been the basic principles of all regulatory bodies of boxing since that time. The most important provided for the following: the wearing of "fair-sized" gloves; establishment of 3-minute rounds and 1-minute rest periods between rounds; the appointment of a referee to conduct each bout fairly; establishment of a 10-second period immediately following a knockdown during which a contestant must rise or be counted out by the referee and thus lose the match; a ban on wrestling, hugging, and hitting a fallen opponent; and a prohibition on the entry into the ring during the 3-minute rounds of seconds or any other persons connected with the contestants.

These rules were first followed in their entirety in a tournament in London in 1872. The tournament was also important historically because it classified contestants, a practice that was continued in much greater detail in later years. For the first time fighters were assigned to rivals of

A 19th-century English print of a boxing match in the Fives Court, a converted handball court in London.

New York Public Library—Picture Collection

GREAT HEAVYWEIGHT CHAMPIONS

John L. Sullivan (1882–92)

Rocky Marciano (1952–56)

The Ring

Jack Johnson (1908–15)

Jack Dempsey (1919–26)

Joe Louis (1937–49)

nearly equal weight. Lightweights were defined as fighters weighing 140 lb. or less; middleweights were 158 lb. or less, and all contestants over 158 lb. were classed as heavyweights.

Growth in the United States. The fact that the sport was in public disfavor during the Victorian era caused many English fighters to come to the United States during the 1850's and 1860's. But even in America boxing was not supported to a great extent; not until the rise to prominence of John L. Sullivan, "the Boston Strong Boy," did the sport begin to excite the American public.

After winning the bare-knuckle championship in 1882 by defeating another American, "Paddy" Ryan, Sullivan took the unprecedented step of offering to meet any opponent in a four-round bout conducted according to the Queensberry code, and to pay him $100 if he (Sullivan) failed to knock out the challenger. Later Sullivan increased his standing offer to $500 as he toured the nation's theaters, popularizing the sport and introducing it to spectators who as a group were socially many cuts above those who patronized earlier matches. The success of Sullivan and James J. Corbett of San Francisco, who knocked out Sullivan in New Orleans in 1892 and thus became the first heavyweight champion under the Marquess of Queensberry rules, marked the beginning of boxing's rise in America.

New York became the first state to legalize boxing (1896); Nevada did likewise a year later, and soon other states followed their lead. Most of them patterned boxing legislation on the Walker Law of 1920, which legalized the sport in New York through a newly created agency, the New York State Athletic Commission. Eventually most of the states banded together to regulate boxing through the World Boxing Association (WBA), formerly the National Boxing Association, created in 1920. In the early 1960's, New York, California, and Massachusetts were not members of that regulatory body, although the three generally follow the same rules observed by the WBA, and usually recognize its champions.

The British Boxing Board of Control regulates the sport in Great Britain and the Commonwealth. The European Boxing Union, comprising 16 countries, regulates it on the Continent.

Generally these groups and their American counterparts follow the same regulations with regard to purse distribution, suspensions of fighters, and recognition of champions. The prevailing rules follow those laid down by the Marquess of Queensberry.

Weight Divisions and Conduct of Matches. Professional boxers are classified in eight divisions having the following maximum weights: flyweight (112 lb.), bantamweight (118), featherweight (126), lightweight (135), welterweight (147), middleweight (160), light-heavyweight (175), and heavyweight (over 175).

In present-day competition bouts comprise a stipulated number of 3-minute rounds. Boxing programs usually include a series of preliminary matches of relatively short duration, leading up to the principal one, or "main event," usually 10 rounds in length, though championship matches are generally 15 rounds in duration. The winner is determined by a knockout, as stipulated under the Queensberry code; by a technical knockout (TKO), so declared by the referee when, in his opinion, one of the contestants is beaten so badly that he can continue no longer, even though he is not actually knocked out under terms of the code; or, when there is not a knockout or TKO, by the decision of the referee and two judges who score the match, awarding points for effective punching and deducting them for fouls defined by the code. A contestant who wins such a decision is said to "win on points." The referee and judges may also rule the match a draw.

The basic modern punches fall into three categories. Straight-arm punches include the left jab and straight right (the most powerful weapon of many fighters); hooks, which are bent-arm blows that travel in arcs and are usually delivered to the head; and uppercuts, bent-arm blows directed upward from waist level, and usually aimed at the opponent's body.

Modern Developments. The popularity of boxing has always depended on two elements: a plentiful supply of talented fighters, and promoters with the willingness to take large risks in "selling" fights to the public. In the early 1960's there was a scarcity of both. The great breeding ground of fighters, the small clubs that abounded in the United States during the 1920's and 1930's, was almost extinct. The short supply of boxers also inhibited the gambling instincts of promoters. The best-known Americans in that field had been George Lewis ("Tex") Rickard, Michael S. ("Mike") Jacobs, and James D. Norris.

Rickard began his successful promotions when the Walker Law came into existence in New York State. Most of his fights were staged in Madison Square Garden, in New York City, but among his successes was the second Gene Tunney–Jack Dempsey heavyweight title match in Chicago in 1927, which drew record gate receipts of $2,658,660—still the all-time high in the early 1960's.

Jacobs succeeded Rickard as the country's outstanding promoter in the 1930's. He was successful primarily because he had a contract giving him the exclusive services of Joe Louis, then the heavyweight champion. Jacobs also had similar arrangements with champions in other divisions.

Norris purchased Jacobs' Twentieth Century Sporting Club in 1949 and operated under the name of the International Boxing Club (IBC). He controlled a number of arenas throughout the country, and he was able to acquire the exclusive services of the prominent fighters in the years after World War II. During the most active years of his promotion, television rights to major bouts became a leading source of revenue in boxing. Ultimately the IBC's

GREAT MIDDLEWEIGHT CHAMPIONS

Stanley Ketchel (1908–10)

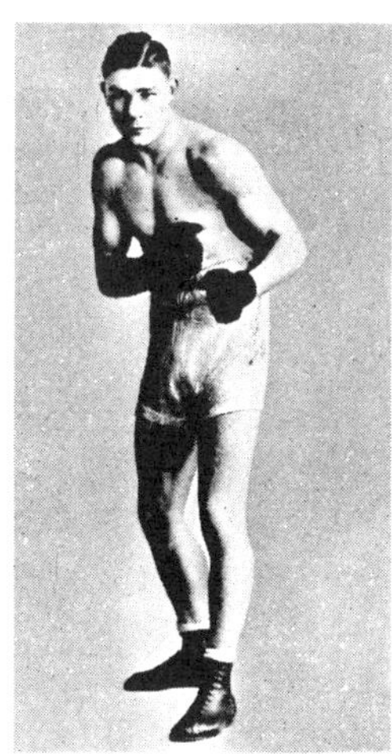

Harry Greb (1923–26)

Mickey Walker (1926–31)

Tony Zale (1940–47, 1948)

Sugar Ray Robinson (1951–52, 1955–59)

The Ring

BOXING

OFFENSE

Archie Moore became light-heavyweight champion in 1952. He was a durable fighter, able to withstand as well as to deliver hard punches.

The Ring

LEFT HOOK TO THE BODY:
Both knees should be slightly bent. The left shoulder is then brought forward as the arm is thrust to the opponent's midsection.

LEFT UPPERCUT:
A form of the hook delivered upward instead of sideways. Both are short arm punches used at close range, especially effective with crouching opponents.

LEFT JAB:
Used to slow the opponent and throw him off balance. The right hand is kept close to the body as the left arm is thrust forward with the wrist straight.

RIGHT HOOK TO THE JAW:
With left foot forward, the right arm lunges out but is still partially bent at the time the punch hits its mark.

DEFENSE

Willie Pep, featherweight champion (1942–48, 1949–50) earned a reputation as an expert boxer and a master of defense.

The Ring

PARRYING:
A means of deflecting the straight blow of an opponent by sharply striking his hand or forearm with the open-gloved hand.

BLOCKING:
Used to make the opponent's punch ineffective by stopping it close to the body with the arms, elbows, shoulders, or hands.

SLIPPING:
The body is moved to either side to avoid a lead or counter, causing the opponent's punch to brush by harmlessly.

DUCKING:
Lowering the head to avoid an opponent's lead, thus causing an intended blow to pass ineffectively over the head.

close control of the sport led to its downfall, for in 1957 the organization was declared a monopoly in violation of the Sherman antitrust law, and was ordered dissolved.

The promotion of boxing entered a new phase in the 1950's. By means of closed-circuit television, many thousands of fans were able to watch leading matches in theaters or other public places, each paying from $3 to $7 for the privilege and thus providing a new source of revenue beyond that furnished by broadcasters. The TelePrompTer Corporation of New York was foremost in the closed-circuit field. It reported that some 350,000 people paid about $1,400,000 to see the firm's telecast of the second Ray Robinson—Carmen Basilio match for the middleweight championship in 1958. The second Floyd Patterson—Ingemar Johansson match for the heavyweight title in 1960 was seen by more than 500,000 closed-circuit viewers, who paid $2,274,662.

An analysis of the receipts of that match indicates the extent to which revenue from sources other than spectators in the arena has become a key factor in boxing promotion. Various interests who covered the match by radio, motion pictures, and television for overseas viewers paid $450,000. Receipts at the box office were $824,814.

An important modern development is the steady progress of amateur boxing in the United States. Thousands of youths participate in this area of the sport; mainly through the Amateur Athletic Union of the United States (AAU) and the annual Golden Gloves competition.

Leading Heavyweights. Fighters in this division have always commanded the greatest share of public interest—and the highest purses. Since the time of John L. Sullivan, who spanned both the old (bare-knuckle) and modern eras, U.S. heavyweights have dominated competition in their class. Among the leaders were John A. ("Jack") Johnson, who in 1908 became the first Negro to win the title; Jess Willard, Johnson's successor; William Harrison ("Jack") Dempsey, who succeeded Willard in 1919 and did much to increase interest in the sport through his popularity; James Joseph ("Gene") Tunney, Dempsey's successor; and Joe Louis, who dominated the division throughout much of the 1930's and 1940's, defending his title successfully 25 times.

In the early 1930's, shortly before Louis' rise, Max Schmeling of Germany and Primo Carnera of Italy held the title briefly. From the time Max Baer of the United States knocked out Carnera in 1934 until Ingemar Johansson of Sweden dethroned the American Floyd Patterson in 1959 the championship remained in American hands. Patterson regained it in 1960. Charles ("Sonny") Liston succeeded Patterson in 1962, and was succeeded by Cassius Clay (Muhammad Ali) in 1964. Clay was stripped of his title by leading boxing associations in 1967 after refusing induction into the armed forces, and

Joe Gans
(1902–8)

Benny Leonard
(1917–24)

Tony Canzoneri
(1930–33, 1935–36)

Barney Ross
(1933–35)

Henry Armstrong
(1938–39)

The Ring

the title was contested until 1971 when he regained his license and lost to Joe Frazier.

BRAGG, DONALD (1935–), American pole vaulter. In 1959 he established a world indoor record, 15 ft., 9¾ in.; in 1960 he set a world outdoor record, 15 ft., 9¼ in., and an Olympic Games record, 15 ft., 5⅛ in. He was the National AAU indoor champion in 1959, 1960, and 1961, and National AAU outdoor and Pan American Games champion in 1959. Since that time, all of his records have been bettered.

BUDGE, JOHN DONALD ("DON") (1916–), American tennis player. In 1937 and 1938 he won the U.S. amateur men's outdoor singles title and Wimbledon men's singles championship. In 1938 he was the French and Australian men's singles champion. He also excelled in men's doubles and mixed-doubles competition in U.S. amateur outdoor and Wimbledon championship play. As a professional he won the U.S. men's singles title in 1940 and 1942, and was a member of the championship men's doubles teams in 1940, 1941, 1942, 1947, and 1949.

BULLFIGHTING, the spectacle that pits men against bulls, in an arena, for the diversion of an audience. It is known that ancient peoples, such as the Cretans, practiced games with bulls, leaping over their backs and doing acrobatic tricks, but the actual fighting of bulls had its origin in Spain because of the nature of the bull indigenous only to the Iberian Peninsula. The savage *toro bravo* (fighting bull) and the placid *toro manso* (domestic bull) are as different as a cobra and a gopher snake. The *toro bravo* has been specially bred for centuries with only one purpose—to kill men and horses.

History. Though it is said that Julius Caesar tried his hand at games involving bulls in ancient Seville, it was the Arabs, not the Romans, who gave real impetus to bullfighting, following their victory over the Goths in Spain in 711. It began as a sporting chase after herds of the vicious *toros bravos*, the horsemen lancing the animals as the bulls charged at them. Rodrigo Díaz de Vivar ("El Cid Campeador") is credited with being the first person to participate in organized bull festivals in enclosures, around 1090.

Bullfighting quickly became very popular; for centuries rich Moors and Christians, nobles and even kings, practiced it, no feast day being complete without the spectacle. Fatalities became so numerous that in 1567, Pope St. Pius V threatened excommunication to all Christians participating in the spectacle. (The proclamation was eventually canceled.) Isabella I, and several Spanish rulers after her, tried to discourage the nobles from risking their lives in this pursuit, but only the Frenchman Philip V, who founded the Bourbon Dynasty in Spain in 1700, was able to discourage the grandees.

About the same time, Spanish commoners, fighting the animals on foot with capes, began to overshadow the nobles' feats. Professional bullfighters began to emerge as a class, and the spectacle assumed the form it has retained, for the most part, to the present. About 1700 a carpenter, Francisco Romero, invented the muleta, a flaglike cloth attached to a staff, whose handling (in maneuvering the bull) is the most important phase of modern bullfighting He also was the first man to kill a bull in the modern manner—face to face, using a sword rather than a lance that had been employed by mounted toreadors during the preceding 600 years.

Bullfighting enjoyed a great revival in Spain in the 18th century, and has continued as the national pastime of that country to the present time, despite a setback during the period of civil war (1936–39). Elsewhere in Europe it has been confined to Portugal and southern France, where its popularity and influence are less. It is still popular in certain Spanish-speaking countries of the Western Hemisphere, however, notably Mexico and Peru. By the middle of the 20th century, there were more than 400 stadiums for bullfighting (*plazas de toros*) in Spain, ranging in capacity from 1,500 to 23,000 seats. The arena in Mexico city, which opened during the 1945–46 season, seats 47,-000 persons. The bullfighting season traditionally extends from March to October in Spain, and from February to November in Mexico; and programs are usually held on Sundays and festival holidays.

Along with the development of the art went the development of the bulls. Breeding became a highly specialized and profitable industry.

Bullfighting Procedure. The customary program includes appearances by three matadors (the principal members of the bullfighting team—the men appointed to kill the bulls), each opposing two of the animals in separate encounters. Usually they are between 19 and 30 years old if they are full-fledged matadors, or younger if they are *novilleros* (apprentices). They are the only performers who may handle the sword or go bareheaded in the arena. A successful matador can earn the equivalent of $10,000 during a single afternoon. The four most famous matadors of the 20th century became millionaires: Juan Belmonte, José Gómez Ortega ("Joselito"), Carlos Arruza, and Manuel Rodríguez ("Manolette").

Every matador has a team, or *cuadrilla*, including three *banderilleros*, who are in and around the ring for one purpose—to protect the matador and to help his performance. They place *banderillas* (darts thrust into the shoulders of the bull) if the matador doesn't place them himself, and they maneuver the bull into position for the matador by means of capes. *Banderilleros* are usually older men, often onetime matadors who early in the game realized that they did not have the nerve and skill necessary for success in that difficult calling.

Each matador also has two picadors—horsemen equipped with 8-ft. lances called *varas*, used to weaken the bull's neck muscles and prepare it for the last third of the fight.

The matador usually tries to rest as much as possible the day of the fight. There is a somber ritual of dressing a bullfighter in his intricate *traje de luces* ("suit of lights"), which takes about an hour and a half. When the matador is dressed, he prays, asking for protection and luck. Then he proceeds to the *plaza de toros*. Although bull rings vary slightly in area, most follow a basic plan. The arena invariably is enclosed by a wooden *barrera*, or barrier, about 4 ft. high.

The bullfighters arrive 10 or 15 minutes before the fight begins. At exactly the appointed hour the band strikes up a *pasodoble* (a two-step). The matadors stride out into the arena, followed by their *banderilleros* and the mounted picadors. Leading the parade are the *alguacils*, or constables, dressed in 16th-century costume. Their duty is to go through the ceremony of asking the *presidente*, or presiding official, for the key to the gate behind which the bulls are confined, and to carry out any other orders the *presidente* may give. The *presidente*, usually a town official, sits in a special box with one or more ex-bullfighters or experts, who serve as advisers.

After all the bullfighters have bowed to the *presidente*, the picadors and the drag mules leave the ring, and the matadors and *banderilleros* sling their ornate dress capes to friends in the first row, who display the capes. The *mozos de estoques* (sword boys) hand the *toreros* their big work capes, and then go back to setting up the muletas and preparing the other tools in the passageway.

The area is cleared, the kettledrum rumbles, a trumpet blares, the crowd hushes, and the gate of the *toril*, the pen where bulls are kept before the fight, is opened. Into the arena explodes the first bull, which is to be fought by the senior matador. At the nod of the matador, one of the *banderilleros* proceeds to do the initial maneuvering of the bull with the cape. This *doblando* process gives the matador a chance to see how the bull behaves. Next the matador maneuvers the bull with the cape, slowing the animal and giving the matador a chance to demonstrate his artistry with the cape. The standard movement of the cape (*lance* or *pase*) at this point is called *la verónica*.

By the time the last third of the bullfight arrives, less than 5 minutes of the total time of approximately 20 minutes has elapsed. Usually the matador is finishing his series of *verónicas* when the two picadors enter the ring. They jog counterclockwise around the arena on their horses, usually led by one of the ring servants called *monosabios* —"wise monkeys." When the first picador is within range of the bull, his horse is turned around so that its heavily mattressed side and blindfolded eye are facing the bull. The matador, or one of his *banderilleros*, lures the bull, by a series of passes with the cape, into position in front of the horse. This is known as *poniéndolo en suerte*.

When the bull spots the horse, he breaks into a hard charge. The picador thrusts his lance into the bull's withers as the horns hit the mattress-protected flank of his mount, putting his full weight on the bull.

After each of the three charges the bull is required to make at the picador, the animal is lured away by the three matadors in turn. Each tries to outdo the other in the gracefulness and risk-taking of his passes. This is often the most competitive and exciting part of the fight; it is in the *quites*, the sequence in which the bull is lured from the horse, that a matador can show the variety of his capework. The matador appointed to kill the bull performs the first *quite*, and the two others follow according to seniority. Regulations decree that a bull must take four *varas*, or thrusts from the picadors' poles, but custom—because of the decreasing size of the modern bull and the horses' protective mattresses—often reduces the number to three. The Mexicans give more importance to variety in the *quites* than do the Spaniards, and they have several passes that are rarely seen in Hispanic repertoires.

Approximately halfway through the 20-minute duration of the fight, the trumpet signals the picadors to retire from the ring. It is time for the *banderillas* to be placed. If the principal matador is not one of those who place their own *banderillas*, he withdraws to the *barrera* and studies the bull. The Mexicans give more importance to the *banderillas* than do the Spaniards, and hence have always been better at it. Most Mexican matadors know how to place their own darts; most Spanish matadors do not.

When the last pair of *banderillas* is placed, a trumpet announces the final phase of the fight—*la faena de muleta*, literally "the muleta task." The modern matador stands or falls on his performance in maneuvering the bull with the muleta; though not as obviously flashy as the manipulation of the cape, the *faena* is more dangerous because it presents a much smaller target to the bull, and most of the passes leave the matador's body exposed. The sword boy passes the folded muleta over the fence to his matador, who takes it in his left hand and then clamps the sword to it with his thumb. With the *montera* (hat) in his right hand, the matador asks the formal permission of the *presidente* to kill the bull; sometimes he rededicates the bull to someone in the audience. He then wheels and tosses his *montera* over his shoulder to the honored person in the stands.

The bull has now been maneuvered into the section of the arena where the matador wants to fight him. The two opponents are alone in the ring. There is no set way to commence a *faena*, since it depends upon the type of bull and the style of the matador. However, a very sound way of beginning is with the rough, wrenching *pases de castigo*—the punishing passes designed to gain control over the animal and let him know that he is confronted by his final enemy. Most wounds inflicted by the bull's horns occur during this last part of the fight, because, by now, the bull has learned a great deal about his opponent, and because the matador is exposed to danger to a greater degree while manipulating the muleta. Throughout the *faena*, the matador often embellishes his work with stunts known as *adornos* (such as resting his elbow on the bull's forehead), which are designed to demonstrate his courage and complete control over the bull.

There is no set time for a matador to kill. When he has drawn a very bad bull (one that has not made a good showing), his aim is to kill as soon as possible after the *banderillas* are placed. When the bull is good, the matador attempts to prolong the performance as long as possible. The first thing the matador must do is *cuadrar* ("square") the animal, so that its front feet are together (and its shoulder blades apart). Once the bull is "squared" the man furls the cloth of the muleta over its stick with his left hand, being careful to flick the cloth to the right so that the bull does not veer fenceward and into the man. The time of the sword thrust with the right arm—the *estocada*—is known as the "moment of truth" (so called because any faking or cowardice is immediately apparent to the crowd). The matador must run head on at the bull while plunging the sword into a small space between the shoulder blades. If he controls the animal sufficiently, and keeps its head down in the folds of the *muleta*, he will be able to pass over the right horn safely. If not, the animal will lift its head and gore him.

After the *coup de grâce* is administered by the *punti-*

A bullfight in Málaga, Spain.

Jane Latta

llero (another member of the bullfighting team) with a short dagger stroke at the base of the brain, mules are driven into the ring and chained to the bull's horns. If the animal has put up a fine fight, it will be given *una vuelta* —an honorary lap around the ring; otherwise it is dragged out of the ring immediately to be butchered.

Now it is the matador's turn to be applauded or booed. Depending on the poorness or excellence of his performance, indicated by the crowd, his award may be jeers or an ear of the bull. If the performance has been unusually good, the tail is also awarded—and very, very rarely, a hoof. If the applause is prolonged, the bullfighter will take a lap around the ring, but he cannot remain for long. Soon a trumpet blows, indicating that there are more bulls still to be fought in the afternoon.

C

CAMP, WALTER CHAUNCEY (1859–1925), American football coach and sports writer, born in New Britain, Conn. After a brilliant all-round athletic career at Yale University, he was football coach at that school (1888–92) and Stanford University (1894–95), where he did much to emphasize team strategy as a key factor of the game, rather than sheer force. He pioneered in naming annual All-American collegiate football teams comprising foremost players of each position. His first such selection was made in 1889 with Casper Whitney; from 1897 until his death, Camp's All-American teams were generally regarded as the official ones.

CAMPANELLA [*kăm-pə-nĕl'ə*], ROY (1921–), American baseball player, born in Homestead, Pa. In 10 seasons with the Brooklyn Dodgers (1948–57), he became one of the game's outstanding catchers, hitting 242 home runs, batting in 856 runs, playing in five World Series, and being named the National League's most valuable player three times. After his career was ended by a severe automobile accident in 1958, he became a sports commentator on television.

CAMPBELL, SIR MALCOLM (1885–1949), English automobile and speedboat racer. He set an automobile-racing record (174.22 mph) in 1927, and improved it steadily. In 1935 he became the first person to travel on land at more than 300 mph, when he drove at 301.1292 mph. In 1939 he set a world speedboat record, 141.74 mph. His achievements also contributed much to science and engineering.

CANOEING. The canoe, from the Stone Age on, was a common and useful means of transportation. As other modes of travel developed, its use became confined almost entirely to pioneers and explorers, and to guides and fishermen seeking virgin lakes or streams. Only late in the 19th century did canoeing become a competitive sport.

Although the New York Canoe Club was organized in 1871 and the American Canoe Association (ACA) came into being in 1880, it was not until 1936 that canoeing reached the status of an Olympic sport. The International Canoe Association, which today supervises most international competition, was organized in 1946 from the dormant remnants of a previous world group that dissolved during World War II.

Most canoeists rest on their knees as they propel their

EVOLUTION OF THE CANOE

Old Town

The earliest "canoes" were floating logs. In time man learned to shape and hollow the logs to make dugout canoes. Many modern sport models are constructed of canvas, aluminum, and light synthetic materials.

SOME CANOEING HINTS

ENTERING CANOE FROM BEACH

Sternman holds sides and crawls up to position.

Bowman remains astern of his position until under way.

ENTERING CANOE FROM DOCK

Sternman steadies canoe as bowman enters, balancing canoe with hand and foot on dock.

SINGLE-BLADE STROKE

Single-blade paddling is done more or less continually from one side. Form of the stroke is varied for the desired direction. Above, beginning of a "J" stroke.

As the upper arm finishes its initial drive and the lower follows through, the blade of the paddle is angled so as to sweep backward under the side of the canoe.

The stroke ends with lower arm behind hip and upper arm pressing the blade down to the left just above water level, and paddler prepares for sweep forward to repeat stroke cycle.

craft with either a single or double-blade paddle. The double-blade is perhaps best known as the type used by the Eskimo as he moves his kayak. Canoeists never use an oar, which is affixed to the craft by an oarlock. A sailing canoe is equipped with a sail, and the paddle is used primarily for steering.

The ACA supervises competitive canoeing in the United States, conducting national championships annually. The contests are set up for singles as well as for two- and four-man teams. Distances are 1,000 meters (about 3,325 ft.), 5,000 meters (about 3.2 mi.,), and 10,000 meters (about 6.3 mi.). The national winners of the United States and Canada also compete annually, alternately in each of the countries. Events in the Olympic games include both men's and women's races. Singles and doubles compete, and relay races are also featured. Both kayaks and Canadian, or open, canoes are used.

Ernest Riedel of Teaneck, N. J., is regarded by many as the greatest of all canoeists. In the competition between the United States and Canada he was one-man, double-blade champion from 1923 to 1941 except for 1936, 1937, and 1939, and he triumphed again in 1946 and 1947. The races were discontinued during World War II.

CHAMBERLAIN, WILTON NORMAN ("WILT") (1936–), American basketball player, born in Philadelphia. He won All-American rating playing for the University of Kansas in the 1956–57 and '57–'58 seasons. In professional play he went to the Philadelphia Warriors in 1959, San Francisco Warriors in 1963, and Philadelphia '76ers in Jan., 1965, at midseason. Chamberlain, 7 ft. 1 in. tall, led the National Basketball Association in scoring each season from 1959–60 through 1965–66, and is its leading all-time scorer (23,442 points at the end of the 1966–67 season).

CHANCE, FRANK LEROY (1877–1924), American baseball player and manager, born in Fresno, Calif. A right-handed thrower and batter, he played first base for the Chicago Cubs (1898–1912) and the New York Yankees (1913–14). He managed the Cubs (1905–12), the Yankees (1913–14), and the Boston Red Sox (1923). He was dubbed the "Peerless Leader" for managing the Cubs to four pennants in five years, 1906–8 and 1910. He was part of the famous "Tinker to Evers to Chance" double-play combination that included Joe Tinker and Johnny Evers. Chance was elected to the Baseball Hall of Fame in 1946.

CIRCUS, ROMAN, name applied to both the building and the chariot races and other contests held in it. The circus was brought to Rome by the Etruscans and quickly became one of the most popular activities of Roman life. The original, largest (seating some 250,000), and most important circus, the Maximus, was founded traditionally by Tarquinius Priscus, the first Etruscan King of Rome, in the 6th century B.C. in the valley between the Palatine and Aventine hills. The long narrow flat race course (1969 × 492 ft.) ran along the valley with seats for spectators along the slopes of the hills on both sides and in a semicircle around one end. At the open end was the starting line. An embankment (*spina*) down the center of the track divided it in half. Gradually there were built and rebuilt through Republican and especially Imperial times the spectators' seats, the Emperor's box, and 12 openings of the starting line with the judges' boxes above. On the *spina* were goal posts (*metae*) at each end, seven eggs and seven bronze dolphins (reversed to mark each of the seven laps of the race), two obelisks brought from Egypt by Augustus and Constantine, as well as many statues and shrines, including the very ancient altar of Consus around which the earliest races had been held. For the games were always religious, held at the numerous festivals of the gods. During the Empire their luxurious magnificence (at the Emperor's expense) was a means of keeping the populace happy and gave rise to the saying "the Roman longs for two things, bread and circuses." The Romans reveled in these races and in their partisanship of the rival parties (*factiones*) of charioteers (the Whites and Greens versus the Blues and Reds). The victorious charioteers were public heroes and amassed large fortunes as well as honor. Other circuses included the Circus Flaminius in the Campus Martius, built in 221 B.C., and the Circus Gai et Neronis, built by the Emperor Caligula on the Vatican hill; the obelisk from its *spina* now stands in front of St. Peter's.

CITATION, American race horse, first to win more than $1,000,000. Foaled in 1945 and owned by Calumet Farm, he won 32 of 45 races and finished out of the money only once. Citation's total earnings were $1,085,760. In 1948 he captured racing's "Triple Crown" by winning the Kentucky Derby, Preakness, and Belmont stakes.

COBB, TYRUS RAYMOND ("TY") (1886–1961), American baseball player also known as "The Georgia Peach." He was born in Narrows, Ga. A left-handed batter and right-handed thrower, he was an outfielder for the Detroit Tigers (1905–26) and the Philadelphia Athletics (1927–28), and managed the Tigers (1921–26). Cobb was one of the greatest and most colorful players in the history of the game; his daring base running and fiery competitive spirit led to constant feuds with rival players and even with his own teammates and fans. His lifetime batting average, .367, stood as a major-league record in the early 1960's, as did his career totals of 4,191 hits, 892 stolen bases, and 12 batting championships. He is included in the National Baseball Hall of Fame.

COCHRAN [kŏk'rən], JACQUELINE (1912?–), American aviatrix and business woman. She started her own successful cosmetics business in 1935. In 1932 she had begun flying and five years later achieved her first record in the air, an altitude flight to 33,000 ft. In 1938 she won the Bendix Transcontinental Air Race. During World War II she was commissioned a lieutenant colonel and commanded the WASPS. In 1953 she became the first woman to fly faster than sound. Her autobiography *The Stars at Noon* was published in 1954.

COCHRANE, GORDON STANLEY (MICKEY) (1903–62), American baseball player and manager. He was catcher for Philadelphia of the American League (1925–33), and catcher and manager of Detroit of the American League (1934–38), leading the team to two league championships (1934–35) and a World Series victory (1935). A brilliant defensive player, he also compiled a lifetime batting mark of .320. He is in the National Baseball Hall of Fame.

COCKFIGHTING, sport (popular in Asia and in Spanish-speaking areas of the world, but illegal in the United States and many other countries) in which two gamecocks, especially bred for pugnacity and usually equipped with sharp steel spurs, fight until one is the acknowledged victor. The contests, often brief because of the injuries inflicted, are held in a ring, or cockpit, and much money may be bet on the outcome. The sport is believed to have originated in Asia more than 3,000 years ago. Introduced by colonists into America, it was gradually outlawed in the United States but is still practiced secretly in some sections.

CODEBALL, game played either on an open field (codeball-on-the-green) or in an enclosed court (codeball-in-the-court). The object of the former is to kick a soft, rubber ball into a series of 7 to 14 bowls placed about an open field and ranging from 25 to 400 yd. apart. The ball is 6 in. in diameter and weighs 12 oz. The bowls, in the shape of inverted cones, have a base 41 in. in diameter, a 7-in. depth, and an 18-in. opening at the top. The game is played by two, three, or four players; it is scored the same as golf. The player requiring the least number of kicks is the winner.

Codeball-in-the-court, a variation of handball (q.v.), uses a ball with the dimensions given in the preceding paragraph. The ball is kicked. Hands or arms may not be used. Otherwise the basic rules follow those of handball. If the receiver is unable to return the kick, a point is scored for the server. The game is played on a handball court by two or four players. Codeball was originated in 1927 by Dr. William Code.

COLOSSEUM *[kŏl-ə-sē'əm],* Flavian amphitheater built in Rome by the Emperor Vespasian, 72 A.D., and completed by his sons Titus and Domitian. Erected on the site of the lake on the grounds of Nero's Golden House, it represented a powerful political move to replace the hated Emperor's private luxury with a building for the entertainment of the Roman people. Fifty thousand spectators (5,000 standing) could view the gladiatorial and wild beast combats provided by the Emperors. An architectural masterpiece, the Colosseum (so named for its huge size or because it stood beside the colossal statue of the Sun god, originally Nero) was the supreme expression of Roman engineering skill in supporting an auditorium on a framework of vaulted corridors. The oval plan measured 620 by 513 ft.; total height of the outer wall was 157 ft. Around the oval arena, 287 by 180 ft., radiating walls of concrete and three stories of concentric arcades of travertine stone supported vaults which carried the rows of seats and stairways. From the concentric corridors surrounding the building access was gained to the seats. The two lower zones of seats, of marble, were supported by the radiating vaults; the upper zones over the concentric corridors were of wood. The exterior wall of three superimposed arcades was decorated on the ground floor with Tuscan columns, on the second with Ionic, on the third with Corinthian; above the third floor of arcades rose a solid wall with Corinthian pilasters and with corbels for the masts of the awning habitually stretched over the spectators during the games. Under the arena were vaulted corridors and cells for wild animals used in

The Colosseum, Rome's most celebrated monument of antiquity.

Louis Renault—Photo Researchers

gladiatorial combats, with a mechanism to lift them up to the arena. Although the seats and parts of the supporting walls were dismantled during the Renaissance and their component materials taken for other buildings, most of this monument still remains and constitutes one of the most imposing and celebrated of all Roman landmarks.

COMISKEY [*kə-mĭs'kē*], **CHARLES ALBERT ("THE OLD ROMAN") (1858–1931),** American baseball player, manager, and executive, born in Chicago. He had an important part in the formation of the American League in 1900, and was owner and president of the Chicago White Sox of that league (1900–31). Earlier he played for, and managed, St. Louis of the American Association and Cincinnati of the National League.

COMPLEAT ANGLER, THE, dialogue on the pleasures of fishing, by Izaak Walton, published in 1653. The *Angler* is in the medieval tradition of treatises on outdoor sport. It celebrates the beauties of nature and the delights of recreation in the open country in so charming a manner that it has been reprinted more than 270 times.

CONACHER [*kŏn'ə-kŭr*], **CHARLES WILLIAM ("CHARLIE") (1909–67),** Canadian hockey player, born in Toronto. He had one of the hardest shots in the history of the sport. A right wing, he played with the Toronto Maple Leafs (1929–38), Detroit Red Wings (1938–39), and the New York Americans (1939–41) of the National Hockey League. He led the NHL in scoring twice and finished his career with a total of 225 goals. Conacher is a member of the National Hockey Hall of Fame.

COOK, WILLIAM OSSER ("BILL") (1896–   ), Canadian hockey player, born in Brantford, Ont. He played throughout Canada until he joined the New York Rangers in their first season (1926) in the National Hockey League. He played in the NHL 10 more years as a right wing, scoring 228 goals. He led the league in point scoring twice. Cook also coached the Rangers, 1951–53. He is a member of the National Hockey Hall of Fame.

COOPERSTOWN, resort village of central New York, and seat of Otsego County, on the Susquehanna River at its outlet from Otsego Lake. Cooperstown is famous as the home of baseball. Gen. Abner Doubleday is said to have invented the game here in 1839, and the National Baseball Museum and Hall of Fame here houses collections pertaining to the history of baseball and memorials honoring the outstanding players of the game.

CORBETT, JAMES J(OHN), known as "Gentleman Jim" Corbett **(1866–1933),** American boxer, born in San Francisco. A pioneer in scientific pugilism, Corbett won the world's heavyweight title in 1892 by knocking out John L. Sullivan; he lost it to Robert Fitzsimmons in 1897, and twice failed to regain it in matches with James J. Jeffries (1900; 1903). He made appearances in stage plays and films. In 1954 he was elected to boxing's Hall of Fame.

COURSING, a sport that originated as a form of hunting and from which the modern sport of greyhound racing developed. There are carvings on Egyptian tombs dating back about 4,000 years that show dogs being released for a coursing contest. Modern coursing involves the pursuit of live game (usually rabbits) by pairs of greyhounds that follow by sight rather than scent. It is confined mostly to England, Ireland, Australia, and the United States. Participation in the sport in the United States dates from colonial times but it was not well organized until late in the 19th century. At that time a smaller and slower breed, the whippet, was used instead of the greyhound.

The modern coursing field is a grass-covered enclosed area measuring 450 by 150 yd. At one end is a chute through which rabbits are released onto the field. At the opposite end are apertures through which the game can escape if they have not been caught by the dogs. A "slipper" holds the pair of dogs on a leash until the released hares are from 60 to 80 yd. down the field. Initial speed and the ability to alter the course of the hares are more important than the killing of the game to the judges who grade the performance of the dogs.

See also Dog Racing; Dog Shows; Field Trials.

COUSY [*ko͞o'zĭ*], **ROBERT JOSEPH ("BOB") (1928–   ),** American basketball player, born in New York. He graduated from Holy Cross in 1950 after achieving All-American rating in the sport during his senior year. In professional play with the Boston Celtics, he was named to the National Basketball Association all-star teams 10 consecutive seasons, beginning in 1951–52. He was noted for his ball-handling and play-making skill. In 1963 he became basketball coach of Boston College.

COY, EDWARD H. ("TED") (1888–1935), American football player, born in Andover, Mass. He attained All-American selection in 1908 and 1909 at Yale and coached the team in 1910. He was subsequently chosen as the fullback on the all-time All-American teams selected by Walter Camp and Parke H. Davis. Coy was famed for his high knee motion while carrying the ball.

CRICKET [*krĭk'ĭt*], outdoor bat-and-ball game that is played as extensively in the British Commonwealth as baseball is in the United States. Cricket is known to have been played in England since at least the 16th century. Formal rules first appeared about the middle of the 18th century. The name "cricket" is derived from an Anglo-Saxon word meaning "crooked stick," the instrument used as a bat in the early years of the game.

Rules and Equipment. Cricket is played on a large grassy field whose ideal dimensions are 525 by 550 ft. The center of activity is known as the pitch, an area measuring 10 ft. in width and 66 ft. in length. At either end of this pitch is a wicket, composed of three vertical sticks 28 in. high; the total width of the wicket is 9 in. Across the top of the wicket are placed two loose wooden pieces called bails, which are 4⅜ in. long and project about ½ in. above the top of the wicket.

The game is played by two teams of 11 players each, 10 of whom bat in turn until retired or put out during the course of an "innings." A match consists of two full innings. The team scoring the greatest number of "runs" is the

CRICKET

Diagram shows start of play during a cricket game. At position around the field are the 11 members of one team, with two batsmen of the opposing team at the wickets. A game in progress at Swan Green, Lyndhurst, England (*below*).

(J. ALLAN CASH—RAPHO-GUILLUMETTE)

winner. One batsman stands at one wicket and another batsman of the same team at the other wicket as play begins. After the bowler (pitcher) of the opposing team has bowled a ball toward one of the batsmen from the opposite wicket, that batsman tries to prevent the ball from knocking the bails off the top of the wicket just behind him by hitting the ball with his bat. There are no foul lines, and the batsman may attempt to score a run by hitting the ball in any direction. Runs are scored when the batter hits the ball far enough to enable him and the batsman at the other wicket to exchange places. If he feels he cannot safely exchange wickets with his batting partner, the batsman does not have to run. A batsman is out if the bails on his wicket are displaced by the bowled ball or if he hits a ball that is caught on the fly, as in baseball, by a member of the opposing (defensive) team. He is also out if he hits the ball, and it is recovered by the defensive team's players in time to knock down the bails of the opposite wicket before the batsman reaches the wicket. When the bowler has bowled a certain number of balls (six or eight, according to prior agreement) an "over" is declared, and another bowler then bowls from the opposite wicket to the opposite batsman.

The bat is a flat, wooden, paddlelike instrument with a round handle about 1 ft. long. The maximum length is 38 in., and the maximum width 4½ in. The ball, which has a hard leather cover, weighs between 5½ and 5¾ oz. and has a maximum circumference of 9 in.

International and U.S. Play. Most international competition is between various countries in the British Commonwealth, the most important being the biennial matches between Australia and England. Interest in these events is considerable. England's national game has never achieved wide popularity in the United States, however. In the early 1960's there were about 100 U.S. clubs located in California, Illinois, Massachusetts, Michigan, New Jersey, New York, and Pennsylvania.

CROQUET [*krō-kā'*], game played by two or more, in which a ball made of wood or hard rubber is propelled around a course, through a series of arches, in a specified sequence by means of a mallet. The standard court measures 60 by 30 ft (18 m by 9 m), but the game is often played in smaller areas—either lawns or hard surfaces. A croquet set usually contains four balls, four mallets, two wooden stakes, and nine wire arches (wickets). Each mallet is striped for identification, as are the corresponding balls. Wickets are 10 inches (25 cm) in height and about 5 inches (12.5 cm) wide.

At each end of the court is a stake; one of these provides the starting point of play. Taking alternate turns, players, competing individually or as teams, propel the

CROQUET

COMMON CROQUET TERMS

BOOBY — A ball that has failed in an attempt to pass through the first arch.
ROQUET — A ball that hits another player's ball.
CROQUET — A ball, having roqueted another, is placed in contact with the latter. The player sets his foot upon his own ball, and with a blow of the mallet, drives the other ball in any desired direction.
ROVER — A ball that has been through all arches and, at the choosing of the player, has not hit the home stake, but ranges over the field at his will, helping his partner and driving back his opponents.

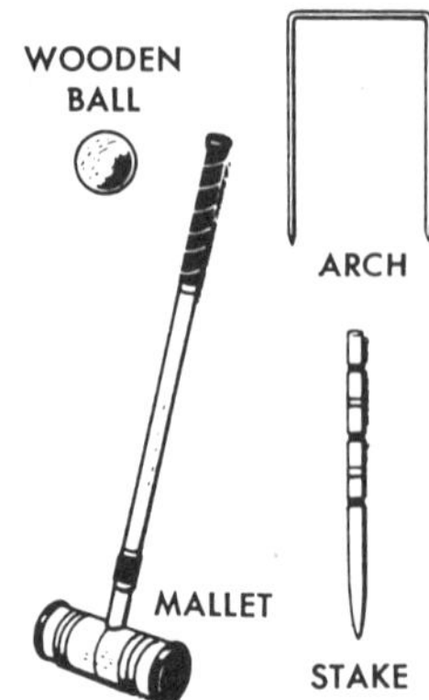

The Bettmann Archive

Croquet tournament in 19th-century England

DIAGRAM OF A STANDARD CROQUET COURT

Through the arch in a modern game

Strickler—Monkmeyer

ball through each arch in proper sequence, then hit the stake at the far end of the court, and continue the circuit of wickets until they hit the "home" stake.

Each player's turn comprises one chance to hit a stake, pass through a wicket, or hit his opponent's ball with his own ball. If he is successful, his turn continues. Two additional strokes with the mallet are given the player who hits an opponent's ball. If he wishes he may use one stroke to deprive the opponent of a good position. The first player (or team) to make the complete circuit is the winner.

CURLING, sport similar to bowls, in which teams, composed of four players each, slide heavy, polished stones over ice toward marked areas at each end of a rink. The marked area, known as the "house," is composed of four concentric circles having diameters of 2, 4, 8, and 12 ft. respectively. Their common center is called the "tee"; a distance of 38 yd. separates the tees.

Each player slides, or "curls," two stones, alternating with an opponent. The player begins his delivery at a "hack," or foothold, 12 ft. behind his team's tee. He must release the stone before crossing a "hog line" perpendicular to the sides of the rink and 21 ft. from his team's tee.

Each stone is 36 in. in circumference, 4½ in. in height, and has a maximum weight of 44 lb. The stone is usually rough on one side and smooth on the other and has a removable handle, so that either surface may be used. The stones are propelled with a motion similar to that used in bowling.

Curlers sweep the ice in the path of an approaching stone. (UPI)

Once the stone has been released and is past the team's hog line, the player who delivered it, or a teammate, may sweep the ice in front of the moving stone with a broom, permitting the stone to carry further down the rink than it would otherwise. Once the stone has passed the line running through the tee to each side of the rink, the players of the opposing team may begin sweeping in an effort to cause the stone to pass beyond the house and out of play. In neither case may the stone be touched by brooms. It is permissible to knock an opponent's stones out of the house.

Delivery of all 16 stones constitutes an "end," and a game usually comprises 10 to 14 ends. The final score is determined by the points scored in each end. In scoring, only those stones resting within the house are counted. One point is awarded for each stone closer to the tee than any one of the opponent's stones.

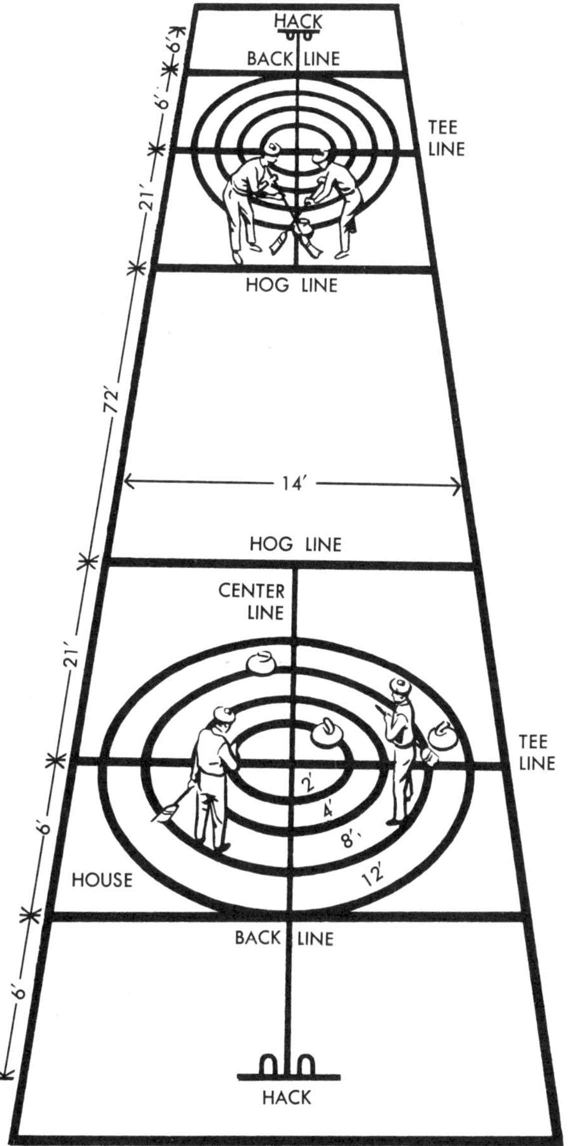

Diagram of a curling rink. Curling originated in Scotland. It was introduced into North America by Scottish settlers in Canada.

D

DAVIS, GLENN (1934–), American hurdler, born in Wellsburg, Va. He was twice Olympic games champion in the 400-meter hurdles; in 1956 he won in the record time of 50.1 seconds, and in 1960 he lowered his record to 49.3. In 1958 he set a world record in this event—49.2 seconds.

DAVIS, GLENN W. (1925–), American football player. After an outstanding high-school athletic career in La Verne, Calif., he won all-American rating as a halfback (1944–46) for the U.S. Military Academy. He and Felix ("Doc") Blanchard were principally responsible for making Army teams of that period among the greatest in the sport's collegiate history. He played professionally (1950–53) with the Los Angeles Rams of the National Football League.

DEAN, JAY HANNA ("DIZZY") (1911–74), American baseball player and sports broadcaster, born in Lucas, Ark. A colorful, flamboyant, right-handed pitcher, he played for St. Louis (1930, 1932–37) and Chicago (1938–41) in the National League. Employing a blazing fast ball, he won 30 games for St. Louis in 1934, when he was named the league's most valuable player. In the World Series that year, he and his brother Paul, also a right-handed pitcher, won two games each as St. Louis defeated Detroit. In 1941 "Dizzy" began a successful career as a broadcaster of baseball games. He was elected to the National Baseball Hall of Fame in 1953.

DEMPSEY, WILLIAM HARRISON ("JACK") (1895–), American boxer, born in Manassa, Colo. He won the world's heavyweight title in 1919 from Jess Willard and lost it in 1926 to Gene Tunney, who gained a 10-round decision over Dempsey. In 1927 Dempsey failed to regain the championship when he lost a controversial 10-round decision to Tunney. A savage puncher, Dempsey played the foremost role in popularizing U.S. boxing during its golden age in the 1920's.

DIMAGGIO [*dĭ-măj'ē-ō*], **JOSEPH PAUL** (1914–), American baseball player, born in Martinez, Calif. He spent his entire major-league career (1936–51) with New York of the American League, but missed three seasons (1943–45) because of Army service. A fine defensive center fielder and a powerful right-handed hitter, he won the league batting championship in 1939, with .381, and in 1940 with .352. He was voted the league's most valuable player in 1939, 1941, and 1947. His feat of hitting safely in 56 consecutive games, in 1941, still stands as a major-league record. He was elected to the National Baseball Hall of Fame in 1955.

DIVING. *See* SWIMMING AND DIVING.

DOG RACING. Dog racing is a sport in which greyhounds compete in pursuit of a mechanical rabbit. It is an outgrowth of one of the world's oldest sports, coursing. Dogs have been used for hunting and coursing since ancient times, but dog racing as it is known in the 20th century is comparatively new, dating from 1919.

Evolution and Present Extent. In coursing, dogs pursue live game, and in early U.S. dog racing, whippets chased live rabbits. Whippets gave way to speedier greyhounds, and opposition by humane organizations to the use of live rabbits led to the evolution of the sport in its present form. An American, Oliver P. Smith, devised and first employed the mechanical rabbit, which runs along the inner or outer rail of the track and serves as an artificial lure. It was introduced at a track built by Smith in Emeryville, Calif., in 1919. Soon other tracks were built in Florida, Oklahoma, Illinois, and Kentucky. Of these pioneers, only the St. Petersburg, Fla., Kennel Club's Derby Lane was still in operation in the 1960's. At the same time, there were 32 other tracks in operation in the United States, each with legalized pari-mutuel wagering. Florida led with 17, and others were located in Massachusetts, Arkansas, South Dakota, Arizona, Montana, and Oregon.

About 6,000,000 persons attended U.S. dog races annually in the early 1960's, and wagered $250,000,000. Tax revenue in the states in which they are located amounted to approximately $20,000,000. Although privately operated, the sport is supervised by state racing commissions.

Greyhound racing also flourishes in England and Australia, and exists on a smaller scale in Ireland, Italy, Germany, France, China, Mexico, Cuba, and South Africa.

Breeding and Conduct of Sport. The average greyhound used in racing weighs 65 lb. and measures about 28 in. at the shoulders. Most are brindled or red. The dogs are bred throughout the United States, but mostly in the Midwest, where coursing is a major sport. Dogs employed in U.S. racing and coursing are registered with the National Coursing Association, which has headquarters in Abilene, Kan. In the 1960's there were about 20,000 dogs in competition, representing about 900 owners or kennels. Greyhounds usually begin to race at the age of 14–16 months; their competitive careers seldom span more than three years.

In the United States the sport is largely conducted at night. A program consists of 10 or 11 races, each involving 8 or 9 dogs. The dogs are assembled in a starting box (or "trap," as it is known in some countries), from which they are released as the mechanical rabbit passes it. Races range in length from 330 yd. to more than a mile; many are conducted over courses measuring 5/16 or 3/8 mi.

The dogs compete for purses, as in horse racing. Purses range up to $50,000 in U.S. competition. The average annual gross earnings of kennel owners is $15,000, though some owners have grossed as much as $65,000.

See also COURSING.

DOG SHOWS. Many thousands of dog owners find competition, recreation, and social outlets through dog shows, and some find profit through sales and breeding. The shows set superior dogs ahead of inferior ones in a form of competition judged not on competitive performance alone, as in field trials, but on conformation, soundness, and gait. Several hundred are held each year in most parts of the United States, usually on weekends.

There are three major kinds. The most widely attended are the all-breed shows, which range in size from 200 or 300 dogs to 3,000. The specialty show is a one-breed event held either separately or in conjunction with an all-breed show. The match show may be either all-breed or one-breed, but has no formal status and carries no championship points. It is usually a medium for introducing new dogs or new exhibitors to the ring. All the shows are conducted by clubs, usually with the help of professional superintendents.

The most important single organization in dog shows is the American Kennel Club (AKC), New York City. It conducts no shows but adopts and enforces uniform rules for them and serves as a guardian against fraud. AKC's other functions include registering dogs and maintaining a stud book. Admission of a breed to the stud book is tan-

Ewing Galloway

Greyhounds leave the starting box at the beginning of a race at a Florida track.

tamount to "recognition" in the United States, although the AKC dislikes the use of the word. In 1961 there were 115 such "recognized" breeds.

The leading American show in terms of age and prestige is that of the Westminster Kennel Club, conducted in Madison Square Garden, New York City. It was held for the first time in 1877. Limited benching space restricts entries to 2,500 dogs. The country's largest show is the International in Chicago, which in the early 1960's had entries totaling over 2,900 dogs.

Procedure in Judging. Whether an all-breed dog show is large or small, it is one of the most orderly of sports enterprises, despite an appearance of utter confusion to the first-time visitor. Every dog has an assigned role in his own class, and there is an inexorable progression from competition involving the smallest puppies to the award of the title "best in show." There are usually five regular classes in each sex—"puppy," "novice," "American-bred," "Bred-by-exhibitor," and "open"—and a class known as "specials" for which only champions are eligible.

When all the classes have been judged, one dog emerges as "best of breed." That dog becomes eligible to compete against all the other breed winners in his variety. There are six "variety groups": "sporting dogs," "hounds," "working dogs," "terriers," "toys," and "nonsporting dogs." When the judging of the variety groups is complete, each of the six winners is judged once more for the title "best in show."

More highly desired by many exhibitors than any single honor is the designation "champion." It is indicated by the prefix "Ch." before the dog's name, and means a dog has won out over a specified number of others of his kind in competition. To attain a championship, a dog must win 15 points under different judges and under specific conditions prescribed by the AKC. The number of dogs that must be defeated differs from breed to breed and is different in various parts of the country where shows are held. The highest number of points that can be gained in any one show is five. Some exceptional dogs win championship rating in only three major shows, but usually competition in many times that number is required.

DOUBLEDAY, ABNER (1819–93), American army officer, born in Ballston Spa, N.Y. He served in both the Mexican and Civil wars. He has been credited with inventing baseball at Cooperstown, N.Y., in 1839, though most modern historians reject the contention.

DUROCHER [*də-rō'shər*], **LEO ERNEST ("LIPPY LEO") (1905–),** American baseball player and manager, born in West Springfield, Mass. He was a brilliant defensive shortstop for New York of the American League, and Cincinnati, St. Louis, and Brooklyn of the National League during his career as a major-league player, which began in 1925. As manager, he led Brooklyn to a pennant in 1941,

Evelyn M. Shafer

Judging entries in the working dog category during a show sponsored by the Westminster Kennel Club at Madison Square Garden in New York City.

and New York of the National League to championships in 1951 and 1954. He was a fiery, savagely articulate competitor. In 1961 he became a coach for the Los Angeles Dodgers; from 1966 to 1972 he managed the Chicago Cubs.

E

EDERLE [ĕd'ər-lē], **GERTRUDE CAROLINE** (1906–), American swimmer, born in New York. She was the first woman to swim the English Channel, crossing from France to England on Aug. 6, 1926, in 14 hours, 31 minutes.

F

FALCONRY, sport of training and employing falcons to capture game. Sometimes other birds, including short-winged hawks and eagles, are used. The sport is of ancient origin and was a popular method of hunting small game until the introduction of firearms. In modern times it is practiced mainly in Germany, England, Canada, and the United States.

The birds must be captured from the nest or trapped in migratory flight, since they do not breed in captivity. Only the females are used in falconry. The training of the bird is a long and complicated process. Well-trained falcons hover high over the prey and then swoop down to snatch it from the ground or while it is in flight. Hawks are flown from the fist, and their prey include grouse, ducks, pheasants, woodcocks, hares, rabbits, and squirrels.

FENCING, in its present form, a close-combat sport involving armed personal offense and defense between two persons using swords or foils.

Origin and Growth. Fencing originated long before the Christian era, as a form of life-and-death combat. As a sport, it got its start at the time when insults were avenged by means of duels fought with sabers or dueling swords. Although such duels are illegal throughout the present-day civilized world, the sport has become increasingly popular. Modern fencing dates from the 14th century and had its greatest early impetus in France, Italy, and Spain. Until 1952, France, Hungary, and Italy dominated the sport; since then the Soviet Union has successfully challenged France and Italy, and the United States and Poland have become strong contenders. The Soviet Union entered competitive fencing for the first time in the Olympic Games of 1952. In those of 1960 the Russians emerged as the most successful in over-all competition in the sport.

The growth of fencing throughout the world is best exemplified by the fact that in the early 1960's, 65 nations belonged to the Fédération Internationale d'Escrime (International Fencing Federation), governing body in international competition, and competed in the Olympic Games. In the United States, during the same period, the sport was taught and practiced extensively. Forty-two colleges competed in a tournament conducted by the National Collegiate Athletic Association, and 33 high schools took part in the annual tournament held at New York University. As a further indication of the growing strength of U.S. fencing, Miguel de Carpriles, former American Olympic fencer and champion, was elected president of the Fédération Internationale d'Escrime in 1960, thus becoming the first non-European to hold this highest post in the sport.

Equipment and Rules of Competition. Fencing is mostly an indoor sport and requires skill, stamina, grace, balance, speed, and a high degree of intelligence. Each participant wears a mask, glove, and uniform made of special cloth that affords maximum protection against injury. The blades of the weapons are flexible and the tips are blunt. Three weapons are used: foil, dueling sword (*épée*), and saber. Men use all three but women fence only with the foil. A bout takes place on a "strip" 40 ft. long and between 5 ft. 10⅞ in. and 6 ft. 6¾ in. wide, and is decided on the basis of five out of nine touches for men and four out of seven for women. There is a standard time limit of six minutes for each bout for men and five minutes for women.

The foil and *épée* are thrusting weapons, and touches can be scored only with the point of the blade. The saber is both a thrusting and cutting weapon so that valid touches are scored either with the point or with the cutting edge of the blade. Touches in all weapons count only if they are scored on the target area, which is different for each weapon. All matches are conducted under the supervision of a director. In foil and dueling-sword competition, the validity of a touch is determined with the aid of an electric machine connected to the specially wired weapons. Foil fencers wear over their uniforms a special vest made of metallic cloth and covering only the valid target area consisting of the trunk of the body and the groin. In dueling-sword competition the metallic jacket is unnecessary because the entire body is a valid target. The target in saber fencing is every part of the body above the imaginary horizontal line passing through the highest points of the folds in the thighs and trunk when the fencer is in the "on-guard" position.

The fencing strip is made of copper mesh and is grounded so as not to register touches that hit the floor. In saber fencing there is as yet no electric machine. The director is assisted by four judges, two of whom determine the validity of a touch. In the case of a disagreement each judge has one vote and the director has one and a half.

Actual fencing is preceded by the opponents saluting each other, the officials, and the spectators. Although the bout always starts from the basic position of on-guard, it

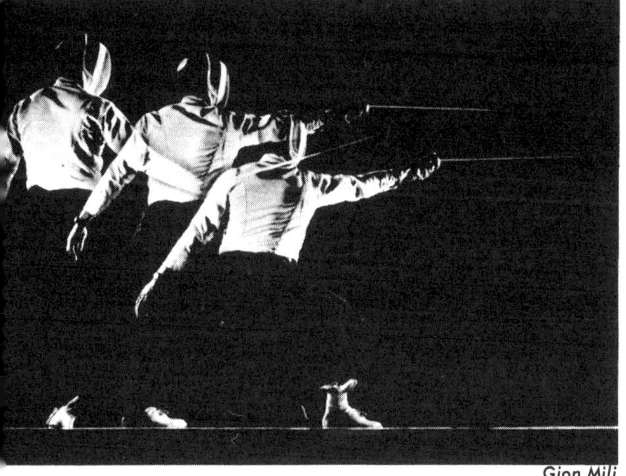

Gjon Mili

Action photograph shows a lunge performed by Michael Alaux, fencing master at New York Fencers' Club.

The art of fencing was revitalized when the Olympic Games were resumed in 1896. The international meet now includes individual and four-man-team contests in foil, épée, and saber for men and foil for women. In the United States this sophisticated sport is governed by the Amateur Fencers' League of America, and is popular in many educational institutions.

FENCING

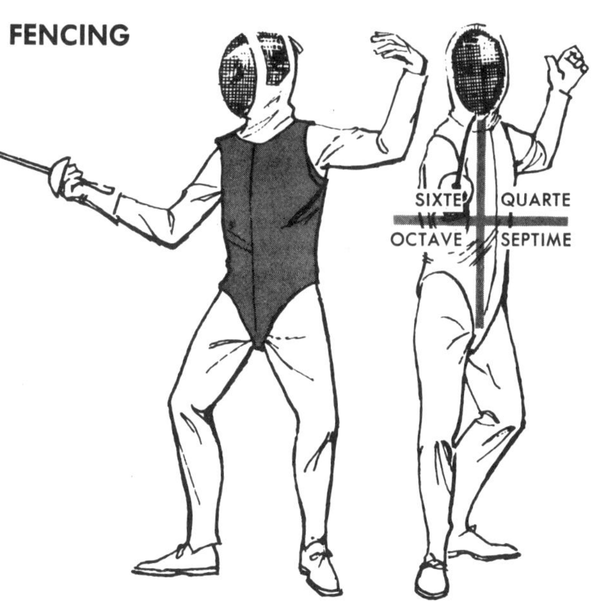

THE ON-GUARD POSITION

SIDE VIEW, SHOWING TARGET AREA IN GRAY

FRONT VIEW, SHOWING QUARTERS OF DEFENSE

LUNGE: from on-guard, fencer extends right arm and steps forward with right foot, left foot remaining in place.

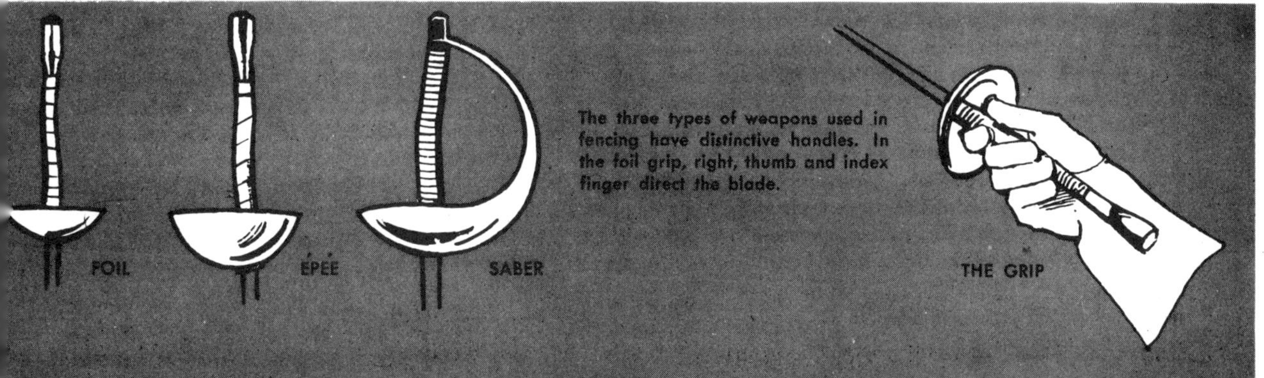

The three types of weapons used in fencing have distinctive handles. In the foil grip, right, thumb and index finger direct the blade.

immediately becomes a highly mobile sport within the confines of the strip. The basic aim is to hit one's opponent in the area of the prescribed target and to avoid being hit. This is achieved through a series of advances, lunges, and retreats. A sense of distance and timing is thus of the utmost importance.

Training. The development of a fencer is the responsibility of the coach or fencing master. The best masters have traditionally been developed in special academies in Europe, and they have carried the sport to the world. A fencer must spend a long period in perfecting his technique by working with a master before entering competition. A competitive peak is not usually reached until the early 30's, and it is not unusual to have fencers at the top level of competitive efficiency in their middle or late 40's. Loss of speed can be compensated for by experience.

FIELD HOCKEY, game played by two teams of 11 persons each. The modern game originated in England about the middle of the 19th century. Though field hockey, an Olympic sport, is popular with both men and women in many parts of the world, in the United States it is played almost exclusively by women.

Each player uses a curved stick to advance a ball toward—and into—the opponents' goal. The object of each team is to score more goals than the other in the 60-minute playing time (divided into halves). A goal counts one point.

The playing area is a rectangular turf field with side lines 100 yd. long and goal (end) lines 60 yd. wide. Two lines 25 yd. from the goal lines and a center line divide the field into quarters. The goal cage in the center of each end line has a mouth 4 yd. wide. A semicircle with a radius of 15 or 16 yd. (15 for women) marks off a striking area in front of each goal cage. Goals count only when the ball is hit from within this striking circle.

The end (head) of the curved wooden stick is rounded on its right side and flat on its left. Only the flat surface may be used to hit or stop the ball. In advancing the ball, a player may not raise any part of the stick higher than his shoulders. The ball, weighing about 5½ oz., has a cork center and leather or plastic cover.

Five members of each team comprise a forward line, three a halfback line, and two a fullback combination; the 11th player is the goalkeeper. All players may hit and pass the ball in any direction and stop the ball with stick, foot, or hand. The goalkeeper alone may kick the ball.

The game starts and restarts after each goal by putting the ball in play in the center of the field. If an attacker hits the ball over the goal line without a goal being scored, the ball is put in play on the nearer 25-yd. line. If a defender accidentally hits the ball over the goal line, the umpire awards the attackers a corner hit. For this infraction the defenders must stand behind the goal line until an attacker drives the ball in play from the corner of the field while his teammates are outside the striking circle. If a defender hits the ball over the goal line intentionally or commits a foul within the striking circle, the umpire awards a penalty corner hit. An attacker takes this hit from the goal line, 10 yd. from the nearer goal post. For other fouls, the team fouled receives a free hit at the spot where the infraction occurred. If the ball goes over the side line (out

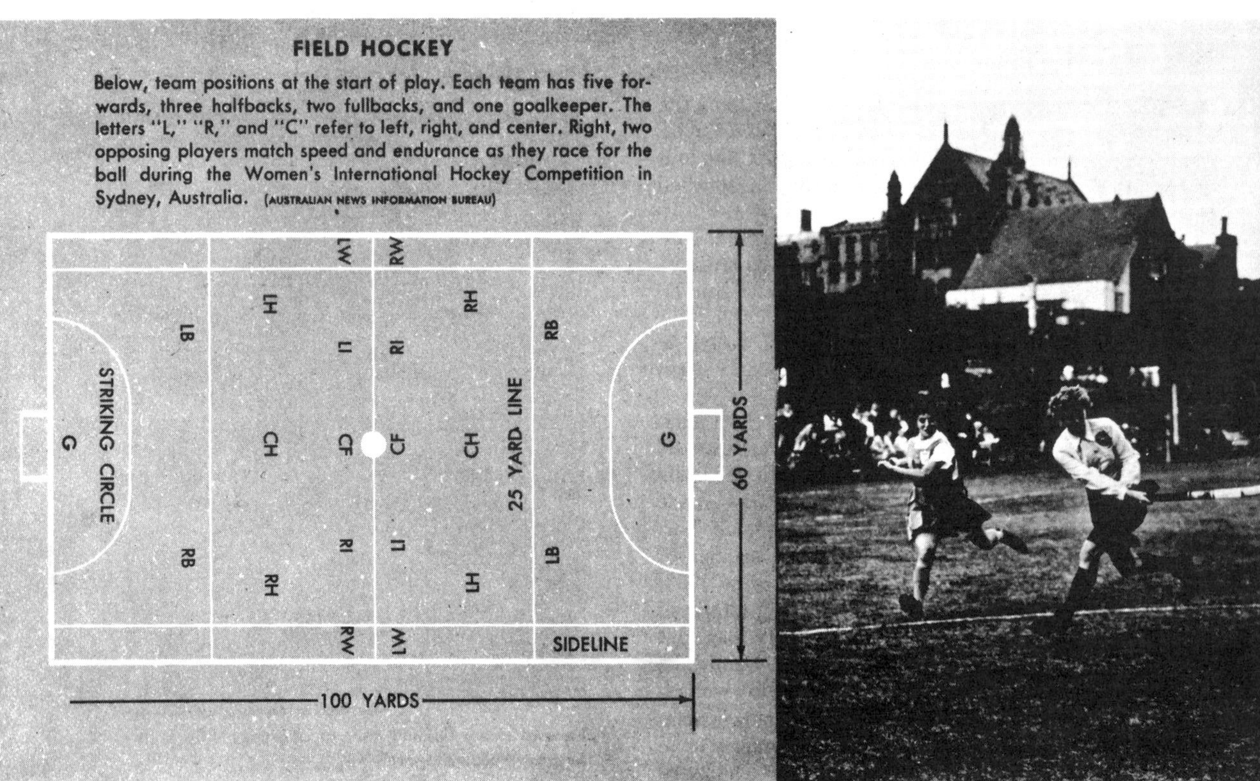

FIELD HOCKEY

Below, team positions at the start of play. Each team has five forwards, three halfbacks, two fullbacks, and one goalkeeper. The letters "L," "R," and "C" refer to left, right, and center. Right, two opposing players match speed and endurance as they race for the ball during the Women's International Hockey Competition in Sydney, Australia. (AUSTRALIAN NEWS INFORMATION BUREAU)

of bounds) a player opposed to the one who last touched it rolls it back into play by hand.

An umpire is stationed in each half of the field. Umpires may refrain from calling fouls if, through enforcement of the penalty, the offending team would gain an advantage.

FIELD TRIALS, competitions for sporting dogs in actual performance. Field trials are a formalized development of natural hunting with dogs. There are almost as many kinds of trials as there are kinds of hunting dogs, and each is adapted to a particular breed. There are competitive events for the pointing breeds, whose developed talent is pointing out where game birds hide; for spaniels and retrievers, whose functions are similar in some respects; and for various breeds of hounds, which pursue rabbits and hare according to their own particular code. The dogs are alike only in their common desire to bring game to the hunter. In no breed does it matter how the dog looks, as in bench-show competition; only results count in field trials. The dogs are entered in stakes according to age and experience. These are usually designated as puppy, derby, or all-age events, in that progression.

Bird-dog trials originated in 1874 with a competition held in Memphis by the Tennessee State Sportsmen's Association. Spaniel trials began in England in 1899 and spread to the United States in 1924. The most popular breed in U.S. field trials is the beagle, for which the first competition was held in Salem, N.H., by the National Beagle Club in 1890.

Conduct of Trials. As in bench-show competition, beagles run in two divisions according to size—those 13 in. and under and those measuring up to 15 in. at the shoulder. They run either in pairs, when pursuing rabbits, or in packs, when hare is the game. They are required to find game and then drive it "in an energetic and decisive manner and show an animated desire to overtake it," according to the American Kennel Club rules, which govern most contests for beagles. Speed and flashy driving are less important than accuracy in trailing, endurance, starting ability, style, and obedience to the handler's commands.

Trials for pointing breeds require the dogs to cover a great deal of ground in "races." Handlers and judges follow on horseback. A time limit (usually about 30 minutes) is imposed on each brace of dogs. At the end of the course is a special area of five acres or more, called the bird field or bird lot, where birds are planted. Pointers and setters are the chief breeds in this form of competition. The most important event is the national bird-dog championship in Grand Junction, Tenn., where three-hour heats and the country's most severe competition bring out the utmost in the dogs' capacities.

The function of the retriever is to seek and retrieve fallen game when ordered to do so. The dog should sit quietly in line or in the blind, walk at heel, or assume any station designated by his handler until sent to retrieve. When ordered, the dog should retrieve quickly and deliver with great care. (Birds must be delivered to hand.) Retrievers that bark or whine while awaiting orders are penalized. Dogs are judged on the basis of intelligence, attention, control, perseverance, and style. The usual trial consists of a specified number of land and water events.

Spaniel trials are similar to those for retrievers, but the dogs find and flush game, in addition to retrieving, and work close to the hunter. Emphasis is on land competition, although a test on water is frequently required. Handlers and judges follow on foot instead of on horseback. There is no bird field. Spaniels find their game anywhere along a course having considerable length and breadth.

See also HUNTING.

A field trial between a pointer and a setter begins as the two sporting dogs receive commands from their masters.

Percy T. Jones—F. Lewis

FISHING, as a sport or recreational activity, dates from prehistoric times. Early man in search of food found that he could devise means of catching fish, first by seizing them with his hands, then successively by spearing them, securing them in nets woven from grass, and hooking them with pieces of baited bone attached to strips of leather or lines woven from hair. One day he discovered that such activity yielded fun and excitement along with food, and sport fishing was born. There are accounts of sport fishing that date from Egypt in 2000 B.C. Angling, the sport of fishing with hook and line, is referred to in passages of the Bible, in the Greek of Plutarch, and in the works of numerous writers of Latin literature. A famous treatise on the subject was published in English in 1496 constituting a part of the second edition of the *Boke of St. Albans.*

Evolution of Modern Equipment

The first tackle employing hook and line was discovered in prehistoric caves. Early man coiled the primitive line at his feet, swung a length of it in a circle, and flung the baited hook out into the water. When the wheel was invented, the early angler placed the line, or cord, on the wheel; thus the reel was born. The evolution of the modern fishing rod from the early pole cut from a sapling and the growth of accessories has been a matter of constant brainwork, precision workmanship, much experience, and unending tests.

Basic Tackle and Refinements. The basic elements of modern tackle include the rod, by which the bait, or lure, is cast; the reel, on which the line is wound; the line and leader (used to join line and hook), employed in bringing the fish to the angler's station; and baits and lures, whose function is to attract the fish.

Among the earliest refinements was the addition of guides to the rod, which employed the basic winch-type reel. For convenience, rods were made in takedown design employing ferrule joints. Later the single-action-winch reel made possible faster retrieving of the line. Devices such as drags, attached to the reel to prevent too free spinning of the drum, gave the angler better control of his equipment.

Further refinement came as anglers found they needed heavy rods for throwing bait and lures (which simulate the animals on which fish feed, though they do not necessarily bear physical resemblance to such animals) made of metal and wood. Limber, thin, and light rods were needed for casting artificial flies (hooks fitted with feathers and yarn to simulate actual flies) and very light baits. In salt-water fishing, catching tuna and marlin called for very heavy rods and lines and for reels with great capacity. The early years of the 20th century witnessed the greatest advancement in the machining of reels and metal parts for rods and in precision cutting and matching of split bamboo for rods. Such developments were followed by the introduction of numerous accessories—such as gaffs (barbed spears or hooks used in securing heavy fish), elaborate boxes for tackle, and wading equipment.

Fishing Literature and Its Influence. Coincident with the development of specialized equipment was the emergence of fishing experts whose writings comprise both an exciting history of the sport and an invaluable body of practical information, ranging from the philosophical (Izaak Walton's *The Compleat Angler*, 1653) to the latest in "how-to-do-it" books. These works, moreover, had direct influence on actual practice of the sport. In England, for example, the 19th-century writer Frederic M. Halford was among the first to detail the art of fishing with dry flies, which simulate insects on the water's surface (in contrast with wet flies, which serve the same purpose when submerged). His works dealt with fishing for trout in English and European waters, but they spread to many corners of the earth where trout are found. North American fly-fishing (fresh-water or salt-water surface fishing with flies, natural or artificial) became the epitome of sport. Such present-day authors as Theodore Gordon, Ray Bergman, Charles M. Wetzel, Art Flick, and Albert J. McClane have furthered the cause championed by Halford.

In trout-fishing circles, the snobbishness of the period put the dry-fly man in a special class. Anyone who fished with a sunken fly or bait was considered a social outcast. It was only after the British expert G. E. M. Skues brought out several treatises on nymph fishing, employing artificial flies in imitation of insect larvae, that the sunken fly was considered fair tackle among expert fishermen. Fly-fishing for Atlantic salmon went through the same evolution as fishing for trout.

Further Developments. An important step in the development of modern tackle was the introduction of lures known as plugs (wooden or plastic objects equipped with hooks and painted to represent wounded bait fish or frogs). They were introduced in the Midwestern United States by James Heddon for use with relatively short bait-casting rods having multiplying reels (with spools that turn four times for every revolution of the reel handle), in fishing for large- and small-mouth bass. Another innovation was the use of artificial bugs in imitation of small bait fish or insects. These were heavier than large dry flies and lighter than the smallest plugs, and were cast with long fly rods.

Two other lures have become standard—spoons, revolving objects of polished metal that give the appearance of fish in motion as they are drawn through the water; and spinners, which are generally similar in design and function, and which, like spoons, can either be cast or trolled behind a boat or canoe.

Types of Fishing

Fishing is generally divided into two broad categories: fresh-water and salt-water. The fresh-water variety is subdivided into surface (fly) fishing; mid-water fishing, employing moving bait that is either natural (small fish) or artificial; and bottom fishing, employing bait (such as worms or paste) placed at or near the bottom of the water. Although they are not as sharply defined in salt-water fishing, these subdivisions also apply to that major category.

Fly-Fishing. This most highly developed variety is practiced in both fresh and salt water, in the former in fishing for trout, salmon, bass, and pan fish, and in the latter in catching bonefish, tarpon, snook, striped bass, bluefish, and pompano. The standard gear includes a fly rod of two or three sections, constructed of split bamboo or glass fiber; single-action reel; hard-finish, braided line of nylon or silk; and tapered leader of translucent monofilament

ROD-AND-REEL FISHING

(PHOTO RESEARCHERS, INC.)

FLY-CASTING

Left hand holds loop of line in readiness, but pulls line taut on rod to tense rod action.

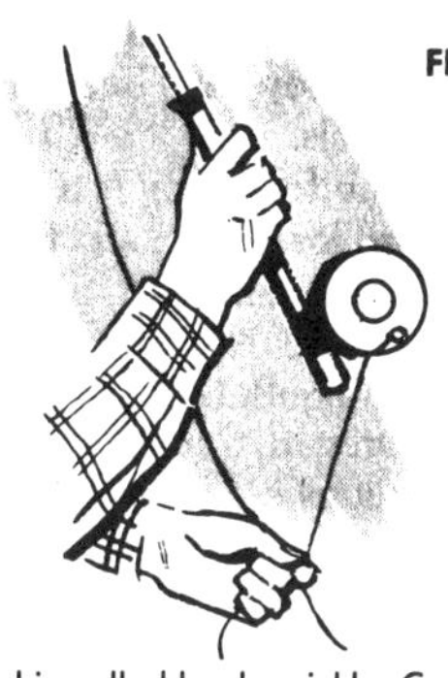

Rod is pulled back quickly. Caster pauses while back-cast line straightens.

With wrist locked, caster brings rod forward so line is driven parallel to water surface.

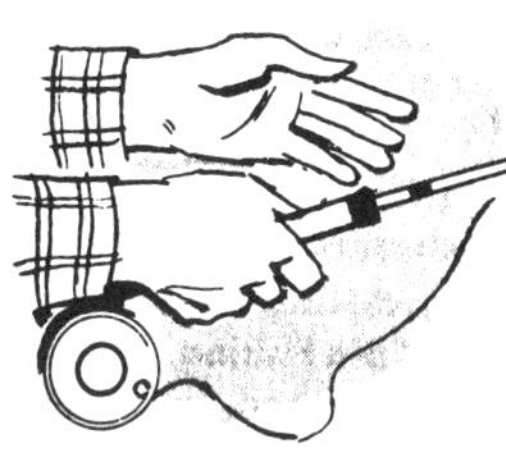

When forward movement of rod is halted, left hand releases reserve line, which shoots out.

SPINNING

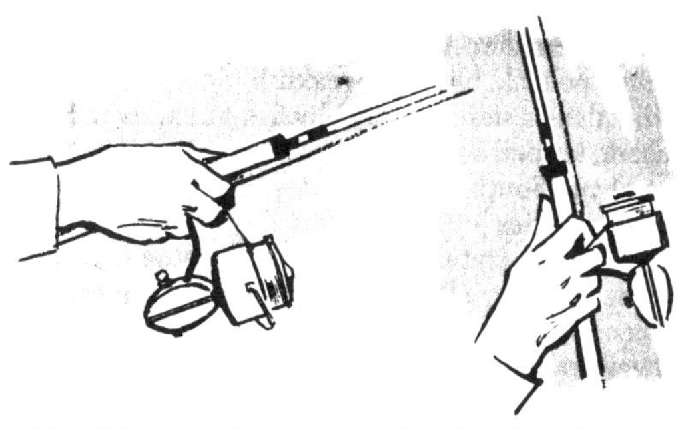

Rod is pointed toward and above target. Line is held by tip of forefinger, not by joint.

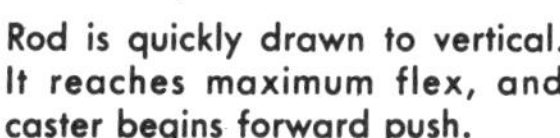

Rod is quickly drawn to vertical. It reaches maximum flex, and caster begins forward push.

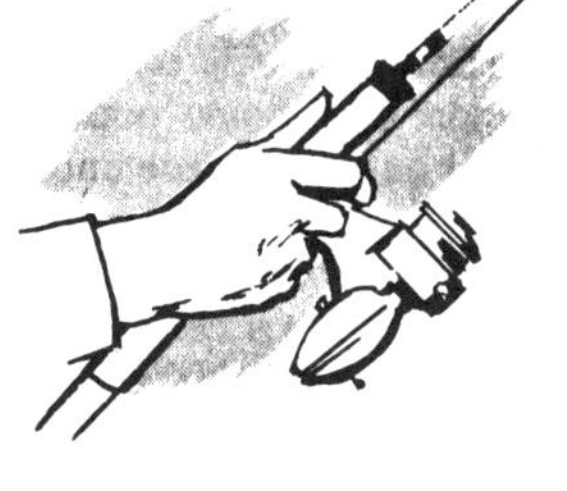

Caster stops rod in forward position. Line feeds out as lure shoots toward target.

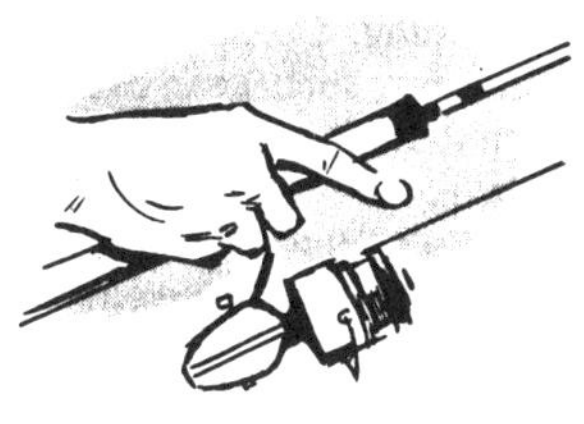

In follow-through rod is dropped toward target. Caster halts line with forefinger against spool.

BAIT-CASTING

Cast begins with rod pointed toward target, with wrist turned so reel handles are topside.

Rod is raised to vertical, momentarily halted, then allowed to drift back for forward push.

Rod is brought forward. Reel is released. Caster extends arm to lessen line friction on guides.

Reel is stopped by thumb. Rod is moved to left hand, where reel is palmed for retrieve.

nylon. Both wet and dry flies, and a variety of more specialized lures such as nymphs (in imitation of insect larvae) and streamers and bucktails (which resemble minnows), are employed. Fishing is done by wading in streams and lakes, casting from shore or boat, or trolling from boat or canoe.

Bait casting, by which live bait or artificial lures are cast and retrieved, requires a light line, relatively heavy lure, short rod, and reel that rotates with a maximum of ease; fly casting, in contrast, demands a very light lure.

Spin Fishing. One of the most important developments in the modern U.S. sport has been the introduction of "spin fishing," which actually was practiced in Europe as early as the 17th century. Spinning tackle came to America from Switzerland, France, and Italy in the 1930's and proved the most revolutionary development in the history of sport fishing in more than 100 years. Designed for use in both fresh and salt water, it employs a reel with a spool that remains fixed in casting. Unlike reels used in fly and bait casting, the spinning reel is constructed so that the line literally spins off the end of the reel, rather than unwinding. By making fishing technique much easier to master, such gear caused the sport to become popular with millions who otherwise might not have come under its spell.

Salt-Water Fishing. Aside from the gradual improvement of hand lines, nothing of great consequence happened in this form of fishing until the early 1900's when anglers such as Zane Grey popularized the sport of taking mighty game fish—swordfish, marlin, and tuna—with heavy gear from yachts. Soon thereafter, the International Game Fish Association was formed by sport fishermen and scientists eager to learn more about the habits and growth of salt-water species. Michael Lerner, S. Kip Farrington, Jr., Van Campen Heilner, Louis Mowbray, and many other present-day experts made big-game salt-water fishing a sport of international proportions, while other anglers helped to popularize the catching of bonefish and other smaller game fish. As a result, salt-water sport fishing is also a major business; entire communities make their livelihoods through fishing tournaments and contests.

Other Varieties. Still fishing, the most simple of all varieties, involves merely the lowering of baited hook into water; in contrast, casting requires both the specialized equipment described above and a highly developed technique involved in throwing out bait and lure and then retrieving them. A somewhat more advanced form of still fishing makes use of trotlines stretched across a stream and equipped with baited hooks. Trolling involves use of hook and lure drawn along or through the water by the fisherman in a boat or canoe.

Extent and Locales of North American Sport Fishing

In the 1960's more than 30,000,000 Americans participated in sport fishing, and the figure does not take into account the countless numbers (including salt-water anglers) who are not required to get licenses or permits, or who do not observe the requirement. With the industrialization of many parts of the country, fishing began to decline near centers of great population; consequent preemptying and polluting of streams presented a major problem to anglers. They have responded by forming conservation organizations designed to protect and promote the sport through research and law enforcement. In this effort they have been joined by government agencies on all levels.

The following is a guide to U.S. and Canadian areas noted for fishing, and to some of the types of fish for which they are famous:

Pacific Northwest: Pacific salmon, steelhead trout, smallmouth bass

Oregon, California: striped bass, trout, many salt-water varieties

Mountain states and adjoining Canadian areas: trout

North Central states and adjoining Canadian areas: musky, pike, largemouth and smallmouth bass

New York State, New England, Ontario, Quebec: musky, pike (including wolf-eyed pike), pickerel, trout, salmon (including landlocked salmon), largemouth and smallmouth bass

New England, New Brunswick, Nova Scotia, Newfoundland, Labrador: Atlantic salmon, squaretail or brook trout, tuna, pollack, bluefish, weakfish

North Atlantic states: fluke, bluefish, tuna, marlin, dolphin, shark, striped bass

Central and South Atlantic states: channel bass, many salt-water varieties

South Atlantic states: sailfish, wahoo, blue and white marlin, amberjack, albacore, barracuda, bonefish, sea trout, snook, tarpon, pompano, shark, dolphin

Midwestern states: bass, trout, channel catfish, pan fish

Tennessee, Georgia, Alabama, Florida: largemouth bass, crappie

Gulf Coast states: all but the deep Atlantic Ocean varieties.

FITZSIMMONS, ROBERT PROMETHEUS ("BOB") (1862–1917), boxer, born in Cornwall, England. He went to the United States in 1890 and won the world's middleweight championship in 1891 by knocking out Jack Dempsey, "the Nonpareil." In 1897 he won the heavyweight title by knocking out James J. Corbett and lost it in 1899 via a knockout by James J. Jeffries. Fitzsimmons won the light-heavyweight title from George Gardner in 1903 and lost it in 1905 to "Philadelphia Jack" O'Brien.

FOOTBALL, outdoor game played by two teams, each team attempting to carry or kick a ball over the other team's goal line. In most nations the word signifies soccer, rugby, or a variation of one or the other. In the United States football refers to a popular sport developed from soccer and rugby but with its own rules, traditions, and color. The same game, with some variations described later in this article, is played in Canada.

Football in the United States is played by hundreds of colleges and universities and by countless professional, semiprofessional, high school, grade school, and sand lot teams.

Large crowds are common at college and professional games. More than 100,000 spectators have seen contests in the Rose Bowl, Pasadena, Calif.; the Los Angeles Memorial Coliseum; the University of Michigan stadium in Ann Arbor; and the John F. Kennedy Memorial Stadium in Philadelphia, site of the annual Army-Navy game. Annual

Football attracts vast crowds in the United States and Canada. Throngs come to see star running backs like Tony Dorsett perform. Dorsett (No. 33) makes excellent use of a University of Pittsburgh teammate's block against a Penn State defender.

Wide World

attendance exceeds 32,000,000 for college games and 10,000,000 for professional games. Millions more watch the college and professional contests on television.

The games are often only parts of colorful spectacles. Marching bands, cheerleaders, cheering sections, and card stunts (performed by students who sit together and flash colored cards at a signal to form a pattern) add to the festive air.

History of Collegiate Football

American football stems from soccer, which probably was first played in England in the 11th century. Until the 19th century the game consisted solely of kicking a ball.

In 1823 soccer was revolutionized during an interclass game at Rugby School in England. William Webb Ellis, frustrated because he had missed a kick, picked up the ball and ran down the field with it. His team captain was so angry and embarrassed that he apologized profusely to the opposing team for this utter disregard of the rules.

Ellis' breach of soccer etiquette, however, was not forgotten. Some Rugby students liked it and in 1839 invented the game of rugby, named for their school. Thus football became two sports—soccer and rugby.

Beginning of Intercollegiate Play. The first intercollegiate game of American football was played on Nov. 6, 1869, in New Brunswick, N.J. Rutgers defeated Princeton, 6 goals to 4. The game was actually soccer, and only kicking was allowed. There were 25 men to a team.

The sport caught on quickly. Columbia played in 1870, Harvard staged class games in 1871, Yale played in 1872, and Cornell formed a team in 1873. In 1873 Princeton, Rutgers, Columbia, and Yale drafted rules primarily drawn from soccer.

In 1874 Harvard and McGill University met, employing "Boston game" rules. Their contests combined soccer and rugby; the players not only kicked the ball but advanced it by running with it and by passing it to teammates. Harvard and Yale met in 1875 for the first time, thus beginning a famous series. Harvard won, 4 goals to 0, under rules drawn mostly from rugby. The American Intercollegiate Football Association was founded the next year, and Yale claimed the association's championship. Rugby rules prevailed.

The sport received impetus in 1880 from Walter Camp, a 21-year-old Yale senior who later became one of the great figures in football. He reduced the number of players from 15 to 11 per team. He also replaced the rugby scrum, a semichaotic method of putting the ball in play, with something resembling the modern scrimmage, or the action between opposing lines of players.

In 1882 signals, as a method of directing a team's play, were originated and positions were standardized. At the same time it was decreed that to retain possession of the ball a team must gain 5 yd (4.6 m) in three downs (plays) or not lose 10 yd (9.1 m) in that time.

During its early years football was almost a private possession of the Eastern colleges that later formed the Ivy League. Of the 132 places on the All-America teams from 1889, when the first All-America was chosen, through 1900, 107 were filled by players from Yale, Harvard, and Princeton and 21 others by University of Pennsylvania athletes.

Early Criticism and Reform. Serious obstacles to continued growth of the game arose in the 1890's. In 1894 Harvard and Pennsylvania withdrew from the American Intercollegiate Football Association. The organization disbanded in 1895, leaving the game without a governing body. Playing rules were again revised, but football almost disappeared from the American scene.

The low point was reached in 1905 and 1906. Mass plays, notably use of the flying wedge, stressed sheer force rather than skill and resulted in many deaths and crippling injuries. Some schools were ready to abandon the game. President Theodore Roosevelt was foremost among those who declared that football must be made safer.

New rules banned most mass formations and permitted throwing the ball in a forward direction. The forward pass was tried in 1906 by Wesleyan University against Yale. In

UPI

Renowned coaches include Knute Rockne, left, a forward-pass pioneer, and Pop Warner, below, who devised the single-wing formation.

UPI

Wide World

Legendary players from football's early days include, clockwise from top right, Jim Thorpe, Harold (Red) Grange, and Bronko Nagurski.

Wide World

Wide World

a move to discourage power plays, which produced short gains, a team was required to gain at least 10 yd rather than 5, in three downs.

Football was saved, and it made rapid strides. In 1910 Glenn Scobey (Pop) Warner, then coach at the Carlisle (Pa.) Indian School, devised the single-wing formation, which became the basic offensive pattern for 30 years. In 1912 a team was given four downs to gain 10 yd, and a touchdown, or act of crossing the opponents' goal line while in possession of the ball, was valued at six points. These rules are still in effect. (Warner later coached at Pittsburgh, Stanford, and Temple.)

In 1913 the forward pass emerged as a potent weapon when Notre Dame upset Army, 35–7. Notre Dame scored one touchdown and set the stage for four others by employing passes. Its passing combination was Charles E. (Gus) Dorais to Knute Rockne. Rockne later became head coach at Notre Dame and was probably the most renowned coach the sport has seen.

Michigan, Washington, and Carlisle were among the leading teams early in the 20th century. Michigan's point-a-minute teams under coach Fielding H. (Hurry Up) Yost ran off plays with unbelievable speed. From 1901 to 1905 they played 56 games without a defeat. From 1908 to 1916 Washington went unbeaten in 61 straight games. Carlisle, a tiny school whose teams were led by the legendary Jim Thorpe, won against all comers.

The 1920's were the golden age of sports, including football. Notre Dame was the big team. Rockne was its coach, and its stars included the Four Horsemen. Although these four backfield men—Harry Stuhldreher, Jim Crowley, Elmer Layden, and Don Miller—averaged only 160 lb (73 kg), their running ability captivated the imagination of the public. This also was the era of Harold (Red)

Grange of Illinois and Bronko Nagurski of Minnesota, runners without peer.

Major Developments. In 1940 came a major development, the return of the T formation. The T is an offensive formation, previously used and abandoned, in which the quarterback stands directly behind the center, who hands the ball to him. It offered deception in contrast with the single-wing formation's power. Clark Shaughnessy, in his first year as Stanford's coach, brought back the T and added a man in motion—a halfback running laterally before the ball is passed back from the center. The T soon became the basic offensive weapon of football.

In 1941 Don Faurot, then coaching at the University of Missouri, devised the split-T formation. It varies the T by allowing the quarterback to run laterally with the ball behind the line of scrimmage. The quarterback then has these options: he can continue to run, he can throw a forward pass, or he can hand off or pass the ball laterally to a teammate, depending on how the defense has committed itself. The split T achieved popularity after World War II through two of Faurot's coaching disciples, Charles (Bud) Wilkinson at Oklahoma and Jim Tatum at Maryland.

Another landmark of the postwar era was two-platoon football. Unlimited substitution of players became legal in 1941, but despite this apparent aid, about 350 colleges gave up the sport during the war. In 1947 Michigan was the first to take full advantage of free substitution. It used separate units for offense and defense. Army adopted this system, and many others followed.

Extra coaches, extra players, and extra equipment were needed under the platoon system. Some 50 colleges abandoned football because platooning made it too expensive. The free-substitution rule, which had grown more and more controversial, was dropped in 1953. Professional football retained it, however, with notable success, and the college substitution rule was progressively liberalized until platoon football and free substitution returned in 1965.

The outstanding teams in the 1940's and 1950's included Army, Notre Dame, Michigan, Alabama, and Oklahoma. Army dominated the game from 1944 through 1946, the years of its fabled "Touchdown Twins," Glenn Davis and Felix (Doc) Blanchard. Wilkinson's teams at Oklahoma won or shared the Big Eight (previously, the Big Seven) Conference championship from 1947 through 1959, his first 13 years there.

In 1958 the first change in scoring values since 1912 was authorized. To increase interest, the conversion after touchdown, which had been worth one point, was altered. A team now has the option to try for one point, by place kick or drop kick, or two points, by a run or pass. The conversion attempt, previously made from the 2-yd (1.8-m) line, was moved back to the 3-yd (2.7-m) line. (See section on rules.)

In 1959 the colleges widened the goal posts from 18 ft 6 inches to 23 ft 4 inches, or 5.6 m to 7 m (inside measurements), to stimulate field-goal kicking, and the aim was quickly achieved.

Offensive formations changed slightly in the 1960's and 1970's. At least 90 percent of the college teams used some sort of triple-option offense—the veer, wishbone, split T, or wing T. The old single wing and double wing were no longer used.

The outstanding teams included Alabama, Nebraska, Ohio State, Notre Dame, Southern California, and Oklahoma. The most celebrated players were O. J. Simpson of Southern California, Archie Griffin of Ohio State, and Tony Dorsett of Pittsburgh, all running backs.

The cost of fielding college football teams rose dramatically. Most major colleges gave their players grants-in-aid (also known as athletic scholarships) that paid for tuition, books, room, and board. In 1974 the member colleges of the National Collegiate Athletic Association, the major governing body in college sports, voted economy restrictions. They limited the total number of football scholarships at each major college to 95 at one time and the number of new scholarships to 30 each year.

Rules and Progress of Game

The team that scores the most points is the winner. There are four types of scoring plays: touchdowns (worth six points each), conversions after touchdowns (one or two points), field goals (three points), and safeties (two points).

A touchdown is scored when a team advances the ball—by running, passing, or recovering an oppoenent's

UPI

UPI

Glenn Davis, far left, and Felix (Doc) Blanchard, called "The Touchdown Twins," made Army almost invincible from 1944 through 1946.

fumble—over the goal line defended by its opponent. Each touchdown is followed by an additional opportunity to score by the team that has made the touchdown—a conversion attempt from the 3-yd (2.7-m) line. The team attempting the conversion can try for one or two points.

A field goal is made from any place within the playing area by a place kick or drop kick that sends the ball between the goal-post uprights and over the crossbar.

A safety is scored by the defensive team when it tackles the ball carrier in his end zone, the area behind the goal line defended by his team. However, if the impetus that put the ball in the end zone came from the defensive team (via a kick, fumble, or intercepted pass, for example), it is a touchback, not a safety, and no points are scored.

The field, a rectangle of dirt covered by natural or artificial grass, measures 160 by 300 ft (48.8 by 91.4 m). In addition, there is an end zone 30 ft (9.1 m) deep at each end of the rectangle. The goal posts are stationed centrally on the back lines of the end zones. Each goal consists of two uprights, 20 or more ft (6 m) high, and a crossbar, 10 ft (3 m) above the ground.

The actual playing area is 100 yd (91.4 m) in length, from goal line to goal line; chalk marks, running from side line to side line and parallel to the goal lines, divide the playing area into 10-yd (9.1 m) segments, the distance necessary for a first down.

The ball is a pointed oval, technically a prolate spheroid. It has a leather or composition surface. It measures 11 to 11¼ inches (28 to 28.5 cm) in length, 6.73 to 6.85 inches (17.09 to 17.40 cm) in width, and 28 to 28½ inches (71.1 to 72.4 cm) in circumference. It weighs 14 to 15 oz (400 to 425 grams) when inflated to a pressure of 12½ to 13½ pounds (5.5 to 6 kg).

Make-up of Teams. Each team has 11 players on the field, seven in the line and four in the backfield. The linemen are the left and right ends (or tight end and wide receiver), left and right tackles, left and right guards, and center. The backs are the quarterback, left halfback, right halfback, and fullback (or quarterback, flanker, and two running backs).

Both offense and defense operate from a variety of formations. On offense the backs run with, pass, or kick the ball. Passing may be either forward or lateral. The center snaps, or passes, the ball between his legs to a back and then attempts to block the forward progress of opposing players. The guards and tackles block, and the ends block or run downfield to be in a position to catch forward passes.

On defense, every player attempts to prevent the other team from advancing with the ball. The defense does this by tackling the ball carrier and by breaking up attempts by the opponents to pass the ball or by intercepting the pass. A defensive player who intercepts such a pass while it is still in the air is entitled to run with the ball and to attempt to score a touchdown.

A game consists of four periods of 15 minutes each, with intermissions of one minute between quarters and 15 minutes at half time. The teams change goals each quarter.

A complex code of rules governs play. To enforce these rules the officials can call more than 60 types of penalties. The most common penalties result in losses of 5 to 15 yd (4.5 m to 13.7 m) by the offending team. Some result only in the loss of a down. Severe infractions can result in the loss of the ball or disqualification of a player.

The team captains and game officials meet immediately

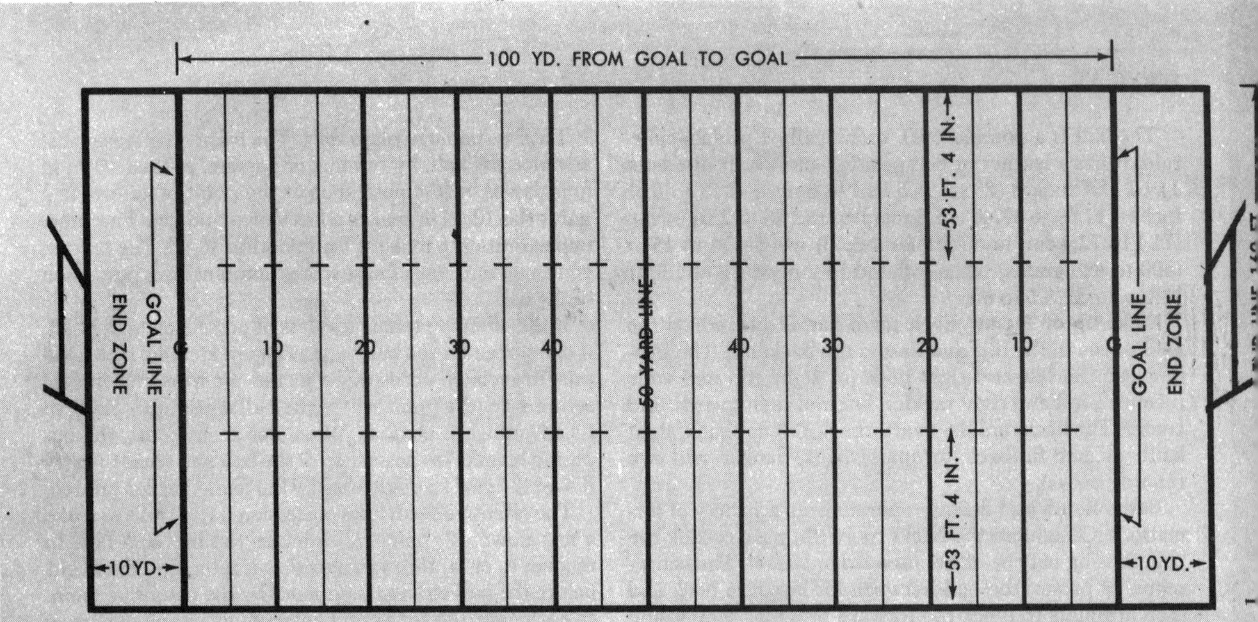

Diagram of a standard collegiate football field.

More than 100,000 persons crowd into the Rose Bowl at Pasadena, Calif., site of the oldest and most prestigious of the annual bowl games. The games often are accompanied by marching bands, organized cheering, and other festive activities.

UPI

OFFSIDE

ILLEGAL POSITION OR PROCEDURE

UNSPORTSMANLIKE CONDUCT

ILLEGAL MOTION OR SHIFT

CLIPPING

HOLDING

FORWARD PASS INTERFERENCE

INCOMPLETE PASS, PENALTY DECLINED

FIRST DOWN

TOUCHDOWN, FIELD GOAL

before a game. The captain who wins the toss of a coin has a choice of (1) kicking off or receiving the kickoff or (2) defending either goal.

Conduct of Play. The game starts with a kickoff—an unobstructed place kick—from the kicking team's 40-yd (36.5-m) line (40 yd from the goal line it defends) to the opponent's territory. (In professional football, the kickoff is made from the 35-yard line.) The receiving team runs back the kickoff as far as possible, thus becoming the offensive team.

Then scrimmage plays start. The team on offense must advance the ball, by running or passing, at least 10 yd in four downs or lose possession at the point of failure. If it gains the 10 yd, it makes a first down and gets four more opportunities to make at least another 10 yd. The process continues until the offense scores points or loses possession of the ball.

If the offensive team faces loss of possession of the ball, it can surrender the ball by punting, or kicking, it. A good punt travels 40 yd or more in the air from the line of scrimmage (the point where the ball was put in play), so its advantage is obvious. When one team punts, the opposing team takes possession of the ball and seeks to carry it over the goal line defended by the team that has punted.

The offensive team loses possession if it (1) fails to make a first down, (2) punts, (3) fumbles the ball and fails to recover it, or (4) throws a pass that is intercepted (caught before the ball strikes the ground) by the defensive team. In each case, the teams exchange offensive and defensive roles.

In collegiate football a running play stops when any part of the ball carrier's body except his feet and hands touches the ground. In professional football such a play continues if the ball carrier slips or falls without being touched by a defensive player.

Offensive plays and defensive formations are rarely improvised. They are selected (the offensive play usually by the quarterback) in a huddle immediately before the play is run. Plays are chosen from an intricate set memorized by each player.

American Professional Football

Professional football's first 30 years were marked by failure upon failure. But in the late 1920's, with the aid of exhibition tours of the Chicago Bears' Red Grange and imaginative leadership, the game achieved great popularity and financial success. In the 1970's the National Football League lifted its average attendance per game to more than 55,000.

The professionals, who emphasize passing, are more skilled than the collegians. Leading players earn up to $450,000 a year. The rules generally follow college rules with two major exceptions. The pros allow free substitution, permitting the use of offensive and defensive platoons, and all successful conversion attempts count one point.

The pioneers of professional football would have been amazed at the game's eventual acceptance by the public. The professional game started quite inauspiciously. On Aug. 31, 1895, the Latrobe, Pa., team needed a quarterback for its game with nearby Jeanette. It persuaded John Brallier, a former college player, to fill the position and paid him $10. Thus he became the first man known to have accepted money for playing football.

In 1902 and 1903 professional teams were formed in Massillon, Canton, and other communities in northern Ohio. Their rosters eventually included many college graduates, among them Knute Rockne and Jim Thorpe.

Colleges looked down on professional football, however, and discouraged their players from entering it. In 1920 the American Professional Football Association was founded with Thorpe as president. Franchises were sold for $100 each. The American Professional Football Association failed after one season.

National Football League. In 1921, from the association's remnants, Joseph F. Carr of Columbus, Ohio, formed a new league which in 1922 became the National Football League. Franchises cost as little as $50 apiece. The attendance at one game was only 30. Twenty-three teams played in 1921, some dropping out during the season and others replacing them. The first league championship was won by the Staley Athletic Club of Decatur, Ill., owned and coached by George Halas. The team's quarterback was Charles Dressen, later a major-league baseball player and manager. The next year the Staleys changed their name to the Chicago Bears and became one of the greatest teams in the annals of the sport.

In 1925 the professionals achieved success. For three years Red Grange's running exploits for the University of Illinois had captivated the sports world. Halas signed Grange immediately after Grange's last college game, and a tour filled stadiums and made considerable money for Grange and the Bears. It also made the public conscious of professional football.

In 1933 the National Football League held its first championship play-off game involving sectional leaders; the Bears defeated the New York Giants, 23–21, in Chicago. In 1936 the league conducted its first draft of college players, now the standard procedure for allotting talent.

In 1946 the All-America Football Conference, a rival professional league, was formed. Both leagues bid for key players, and salaries rose accordingly. The Cleveland Browns dominated the new league, winning division and league championships in each of the league's four seasons.

Another major event in 1946 was the ascendance of Bert Bell, owner of the Philadelphia Eagles, to the office of National League commissioner. He held the post until his death in 1959 and was largely responsible for the growth of the professional game.

The war between the leagues cost millions of dollars on both sides. It ended on Dec. 9, 1949, when the All-America Conference disbanded. Three of its best franchises—Cleveland, San Francisco, and Baltimore—were absorbed by the National League, which now had 13 teams.

Growth. Professional football continued to grow. In 1957 a crowd of 102,368, a professional record, saw the Los Angeles Rams defeat the San Francisco Forty-Niners, 37–24, in the Los Angeles Memorial Coliseum.

The American Football League, a new rival of the National League, started play in 1960 with eight teams. Miami started play in 1966 as the ninth team. The new league lost more than $3,000,000 in its first season, but its financial stability was assured when in 1964 it signed a five-year television contract worth $36,000,000.

The two leagues fought bitterly to sign graduating collegians, sometimes paying bonuses that surpassed half a million dollars. The bidding war financially weakened teams in both leagues until the leagues reached a peace agreement on June 8, 1966. Effective in 1970, there would be one league (the National) composed of two conferences under one commissioner (Pete Rozelle, who headed the National League). The agreement also called for a common draft of college players and the Super Bowl game between the two conference champions annually. The

FOOTBALL FUNDAMENTALS

To function well as part of a team, the football player must spend hours on the field to develop the basic skills: passing, blocking, kicking, catching, and running.

PASSING

Passing can be a quick, spectacular means to a score. A passer needs poise and good judgment as well as accuracy.

(1) Delivery of ball begins as player, with arm cocked, begins pivot on ball of right foot to aid in stepping in direction of throw. (2) Left arm and hand extend at shoulder level in direction of target. (3) He begins transfer of weight to left foot. (4) Releasing ball, he has weight on left foot. (5) He follows through with forward, downward sweep of arm.

BLOCKING

Blocking is essential in offensive play. Blockers protect the passer and clear the way for the ball carrier.

(1) Head and shoulder block: player lunges forward and, elbows extended, pins opponent with neck and forearm. (2) Cross-shoulder block: blocker pivots, projecting shoulder into opponent. (3) Reverse body block: player pivots and whips body across front of opponent. (4) Double-team block: "post" man halts opponent, who is driven back by "drive" man's head and shoulder block.

PUNTING

A team failing to make a first down may choose to punt. A well-placed punt can reverse the direction of a game.

(1) Punter receives ball. (2) Holding ball with long axis parallel to ground, he takes short step with kicking foot. (3) He follows with natural step on nonkicking foot. (4) As kicking leg comes forward, ball is released below hips and close to kicking foot. (5) Kicking leg comes forward with knee flexed. (6) Leg snaps upward, and instep hits belly of ball.

PASS CATCHING

(1) Running receiver, fingers spread and palms open toward his face, is in position for ball. (2) After the ball is caught, receiver secures ball in the arm opposite the nearest opponent.

RUNNING

(1) Runner with ball tucked into his arm takes high steps to keep balance and pumps free arm naturally, like a sprinter. (2) When trapped, runner lowers shoulders for greater power.

American League teams agreed to pay indemnities to the National League of $18,000,000 over a 20-year period.

The National Football League gained wide acceptance in the 1960's during the Green Bay (Wis.) Packers' seasons under the celebrated coach, Vince Lombardi. The professional sport created new attention in 1969 when the New

York Jets, champions of the American Football League, upset the Baltimore Colts, champions of the National Football League, in the Super Bowl, a victory the Jets' quarterback, Joe Namath, had "guaranteed."

With that impetus, and with the demise of the American Football League, the National League flourished in the early 1970's. The NFL-AFL merger had created a 26-team National League, and Seattle and Tampa Bay were added for the 1976 season. The three major networks paid $50,000,000 a year to televise games. Advertisers paid $225,000 per minute for commercials during Super Bowl telecasts. Franchises cost $16,000,000, and ticket prices ranged as high as $20.

But there were problems. One was the World Football League, a new major league that started play in 1974 with 12 teams. It signed such National League stars as Larry Csonka, but financing was inadequate and television and the public were not overly interested. The league collapsed midway through the 1975 season after losses estimated at $20,000,000.

Anotner problem arose when federal courts, in separate cases in 1975 and 1976, ruled that the draft of college players and the compensation clause (the so-called Rozelle Rule) violated federal antitrust laws. The NFL and its players association, after three years of negotiations, agreed in 1977 to a contract that modified the draft and compensation clause. In addition, the league agreed to pay $15,875,000 in damages to individual players.

Canadian Game. Canadian football closely resembles the American variety but is a more wide-open game. The sport is popular, especially on the professional and university level. Many outstanding college players from the United States join professional teams in Canada; each professional team of 32 players may carry 15 American players, and play 14 in any one game. Many of the coaches of these teams were born and trained in the United States.

These are the major differences between American and Canadian football. In Canada:

1—Each team has a 12th man, at one time called a flying wing, now usually called a slot back.

2—The field is 30 ft (9.1 m) longer from goal line to goal line and 35 ft (10.7 m) wider.

3—The end zones are 25 yd (22.8 m) deep.

4—The offensive team has three downs, not four, in which to gain 10 yd (9.1 m).

5—A punt that lands behind the goal line must be run out from the end zone or the kicking team scores a rouge, or single, worth one point.

6—On punt returns blocking is allowed above the waist only.

7—There is no fair-catch rule for punt receivers, but opposing tacklers cannot come within 5 yd (4.6 m) of the receiver until he catches or at least touches the ball.

The Canadian Football League has an Eastern Conference (Hamilton, Montreal, Ottawa, and Toronto) and a Western Conference (British Columbia, Edmonton, Saskatchewan, Calgary, and Winnipeg). Conference winners meet each fall to contest for the Grey Cup.

High School. Football is played by thousands of high schools in the United States; hundreds of additional schools play six-man, eight-man, or nine-man varieties. High schools generally use college rules. Ohio, Pennsylvania, and Texas are the hotbeds of high school football.

High school football started in 1876 with a game between Andover Academy of Massachusetts and Exeter Academy of New Hampshire, actually preparatory schools. Since then football has become the major sport in high schools in every state.

Variations

Six-Man. Six-man football was originated by Stephen E. Epler in 1934 while coaching at Chester (Nebr.) High School. His idea was to reduce injuries and to make the game safe for smaller boys. The six-man game is played by many schools having small enrollments, small playing areas, or small budgets.

A six-man team has three backs and three linemen. The field is scaled down to 240 by 120 ft (73 by 36 m). The ball must be passed or kicked on every play. Otherwise the rules of the 11-man game generally are followed.

Eight-Man. Eight-man football is another variation favored by many smaller schools. Five men play in the line and three in the backfield. The field is the same size as that for 11-man football.

Touch. Touch football follows the rules of the 6-man, 8-man, or 11-man games except that tackling is not permitted. A play is ended when the ball carrier is touched by one or two hands (depending on ground rules) of a defender.

Any number of players may be used, and the field may be any size. Touch football is especially popular in intramural and sandlot competition. It gained considerable attention as the favorite participant sport of the family of President John F. Kennedy.

Wide World

O. J. Simpson, celebrated ball-carrier of the Buffalo Bills, cuts sharply to register a gain against the New England Patriots.

UPI

UPI

Coaches in action: Vince Lombardi of the Green Bay Packers observing play while linebacker Ray Nitschke stands alongside; Woody Hayes of Ohio State University uses a sideline phone to receive analysis from aides in the stands.

Association. Association football is the name used in Great Britain for the sport known in the United States as soccer, treated in a separate article in this encyclopedia.

Individual Skills

Blocking. This is planned physical contact with an opponent, designed to obstruct him. It is an offensive weapon used to clear a path for the ball carrier.

The basic blocks are the cross-body block, in which the body is thrown across an opponent's thighs, and the shoulder block, in which the shoulder does the work.

It is permissible to block a player from a position in front of, or to the side of, him, but usually not from a position behind him. A block from behind is called clipping and usually results in a 15-yd (13.7 m) penalty against the offending team. The blocker may not use his hands, but the defensive player may use his to ward off or escape the blocker.

Drop Kicking. In the early days of the game this was the principal method of scoring field goals and extra points; it has become a lost art and is now rarely seen. Instead, the place kick is used. The drop kick is made by dropping the ball and kicking it just after it has struck the ground.

Passing. Passing, which almost always refers to forward rather than lateral passing, is a prime offensive weapon, especially in professional football.

The passer grips the ball behind its middle, lifts it behind his ear, steps in the direction he will pass, and throws the ball with a snap of the wrist. He usually "leads" the receiver; that is, he throws the ball ahead of the man who will attempt to catch it.

Passes can be thrown for short or long distances, and a good passer can throw 40 yd (36.5 m) with accuracy. He normally throws the pass from 5 yd (4.5 m) or more behind the line of scrimmage, protected in a "pocket" of teammates blocking for him. The passer usually has about three seconds to release the ball before the defensive team pours in.

Pass Receiving. A good passer will have only moderate success without capable pass receivers. The players eligible to receive a pass are the backfield men and the men at each end of the line of scrimmage (usually the ends).

The pass should be caught in front of the body and with both hands. The receiver must watch the ball in flight as long as possible. Speed is important for a pass receiver, but deception is more valuable in reaching an unobstructed place in which to catch the ball. In most cases the player passing the ball tries to have several available receivers; if his prime target has not been able to break away from the defense, he will then have other targets.

The receiver's duty is to elude his defender or defenders and get in the clear. If he can get behind his defender and then catch the pass, he may have an unobstructed path to a touchdown.

Place Kicking. The place kick is used for field goals and for one-point conversion attempts after touchdowns. It is also used for kickoffs.

For field goals and conversions the center snaps the ball to the holder who touches one of the ball's pointed ends to the ground. Then the kicker strikes it with his toe, aiming for a point just under the center of the ball. The ball rises in an end-over-end motion.

Place kickers in professional football seldom fail on conversion attempts. From 1959 through 1965, for example, Tommy Davis of the San Francisco Forty-Niners kicked 234 consecutive extra points before missing.

At times the ball is held on a kicking tee, similar to but larger than a golf tee. Kickoffs almost always are made from a tee without the use of a player to hold the ball.

Punting. This is primarily a defensive weapon, although it has a definite but infrequently used value in offense.

The punt is a kick made from the instep of the shoe after the kicker drops the ball and before the ball strikes the ground. The punter stands 10 to 15 yd (9.1 m to 13.8 m) behind the line of scrimmage in punt formation, a special alignment that offers maximum protection against the possibility of the punt being blocked by the defensive team.

A team normally punts when it faces the loss of the ball on downs, except when it is deep in enemy territory. By punting, a team loses possession but usually at a much more advantageous point on the field. The punt commonly is made on fourth down, although college teams sometimes punt earlier when deep in their territory.

There are two types of punts—spiral, in which the ball spins, and end over end, in which the ball rotates on its short axis. The punter strives for distance but also attempts to make the kick high so that his teammates, especially the ends, can race downfield and tackle the punt receiver before he can run back a sizable distance with the ball. When the punting team is close to midfield or in enemy territory, it often tries to punt the ball so that it lands or rolls beyond the side lines of the field. In that case the receiving team puts the ball in play at the point where the ball went out of the playing area; since it is deep in its own territory, the team is at a disadvantage. If the punt goes into the end zone instead of going out of bounds before the ball is touched by any player, the ball is put in play on the receiving team's 20-yd (18.2-m) line.

Running. The main method of advancing the ball is by running, also known as rushing. Each team has many offensive plays for various types of runs, some of which involve the handling of the ball by two or three players.

Good runners combine speed, power, and change of pace. They lift their knees high, making themselves difficult targets for the tackler.

Most plays provide interference for the runner. Interference consists of one or more blockers attempting to clear a path for the ball carrier. The successful runner makes the most of his interference, following it until he has a chance to break away and follow his own course.

When confronted by a tackler, the runner tries to elude him or to run past him. He may accomplish this by straight-arming—extending his arm and using it to push the tackler away.

Tackling. This and blocking are the two fundamental skills of football. Tackling is achieved by using the hands or arms to grasp or encircle the ball carrier. Ideally, the tackler hits the ball carrier with shoulder and body, then grasps him and pulls his legs from under him. Tackling is used only by the defensive team, and only the ball carrier may be tackled.

The purpose of tackling is to bring the ball carrier to the ground, thus ending the play and preventing him from gaining additional yardage. It is best, although often difficult, to tackle below the waist. In that manner the runner's legs are immobilized.

Formations Used in Play

Offensive. Basic offensive formations include the veer, wishbone, single wing, double wing, short punt, and the T with its variations. The T formation gave birth to the split T, wing T, and slot T, among other variations. Standard formations often are varied by the flanking of backs and ends.

Defensive. Standard defensive formations include the 4-3-2-2 (the professional four), 3-4-2-2, 6-2-2-1, 6-3-2, 7-2-2, 7-1-2-1 (diamond), 5-3-2-1, and the 5-2-4. In each case the first figure represents the number of defensive players on the line of scrimmage, the next figure the number of line backers (players backing up the linemen), and the other figure or figures the number of defensive backs. Defenses may be changed from play to play, depending on what type of play the defensive team expects the offensive team to use next. A four-man or five-man defensive line is best when a forward pass is expected. More men play in the line when a running play is anticipated.

Players' Equipment

In the game's early days players wore tight pants and sweaters, later canvas pants and jackets. The modern player is dressed somewhat like an armored warrior. His knees, shoulders, hips, and thighs are protected by pads usually made of plastic. He wears tight knickerbocker pants and a jersey numbered on the front and back. His plastic helmet usually has a nylon nose and face guard. His leather shoes have cleated soles and heels to help provide secure footing.

Outstanding Games

Bowl Games. The first postseason bowl game was the Rose Bowl contest of 1902. Michigan's point-a-minute team routed Stanford, 49–0. The game, one feature of the Tournament of Roses in Pasadena, Calif., was dropped in favor of Roman chariot racing and other diversions until 1916, when it was renewed and retained. A West Coast team always has played in the Rose Bowl game, which attracts a crowd of 100,000 annually.

Other major bowl games are the Orange in Miami and the Sugar in New Orleans (both started in 1935), Cotton in Dallas (1937), and the Gator in Jacksonville, Fla. (1946). About 15 postseason bowl games are played each year, the major ones on or near New Year's Day. There were many more bowl games—47 in the 1946–47 postseason period alone—before the National Collegiate Athletic Association adopted restrictions.

Wide World

Rocky Bleier (No. 20) carries the ball as fellow Pittsburgh Steelers fan out to block the Oakland Raiders.

As two Miami Dolphins bear down on him, quarterback Billy Kilmer (No. 17) of the Washington Redskins lofts a short pass.

UPI

Football Honors

All-America Teams. The first college All-America team was selected by Casper Whitney in 1889. For the first two years he was aided by his close friend Walter Camp. Camp chose the first All-America team under his own name in 1897 and picked a team each year until his death in 1925. His teams were regarded as official. Grantland Rice succeeded Camp as the major All-America selector, although many others started choosing such teams, too. In later years All-America teams were named by about 20 major selectors, notably newspapers, news agencies, magazines, and football publications. This practice continues today.

Hall of Fame. The Football Hall of Fame was begun in 1947. In 1954 it became the National Football Foundation and Hall of Fame with headquarters in New Brunswick, N.J. The foundation's purpose is to promote the values of college football and to keep college football records. The Professional Football Hall of Fame was dedicated in 1963 at Canton, Ohio.

FOXX, JAMES EMORY ("JIMMY") (1907–67), American baseball player, born in Sudlersville, Md. He played for Philadelphia (1925–35) and Boston (1936–42) of the American League, and Chicago (1942, 1944) and Philadelphia (1945) of the National League. He was primarily a first baseman, though he also performed as a catcher and third baseman. One of the most powerful right-handed batters in the sport's history, he hit 58 home runs in 1932 and 534 during his major-league career. He was elected to the National Baseball Hall of Fame in 1951.

FRICK, FORD CHRISTOPHER (1894–), American baseball executive, born in Wawaka, Ind. He was a sports writer for the New York *Journal*, 1921–34, and a radio-news commentator, 1930–34. From 1934 to 1951 he was president of the National League of Professional Baseball Clubs. In 1951 he became national commissioner of baseball. During Frick's reign as commissioner each of the major leagues expanded to the West coast and became a 10-team organization.

FRISCH, FRANK FRANCIS (1898–1973), American baseball player and manager, one of the greatest second basemen, as indicated by his early election (1947) to baseball's Hall of Fame. Known as the Fordham Flash, he went from the Fordham campus to the New York Giants in 1919 to begin a 19-year playing career—eight with the Giants, 11 with the St. Louis Cardinals. He had a .316 lifetime batting average (hitting both left- and right-handed) and was a fiery baserunner. As a playing manager, Frisch imparted his rough-and-tumble style to the Cardinals of 1934, the Gashouse Gang, and they won a world championship. His managerial career served the Cardinals (1933–38), Pittsburgh Pirates (1940–46), and Chicago Cubs (1949–51).

G

GALLORETTE, American race horse, foaled in 1942. She won 21 of 72 races in which she competed in the 1940's, often defeating male horses. Her earnings totaled $445,535. In 1956 the American Trainers' Association named her the best female horse in U.S. turf history.

GAMES, CLASSICAL. The earliest athletic games in Greece were connected with the funeral rites of heroes. Homer gives the first detailed account of such contests in the *Iliad* when he describes the matches in chariot racing, boxing, wrestling, foot racing, discus throwing, spear casting, archery, and armored combat enjoyed by the princely warriors after Patroclus' funeral at Troy. Physical fitness then, as in most periods of Greek history, was a prerequisite for survival in battle.

Early in the 1st millennium B.C. the more settled conditions in cities permitted the establishment of athletic festivals in honor of some god at regular intervals and in fixed locations. The Olympic games were so established very early and remained the most celebrated throughout antiquity. The other great Panhellenic festivals (Pythian, Nemean, Isthmian) likewise included games similar to those described by Homer. At first, entrants were probably self-trained, but by the 7th century B.C., years of formal training lay behind each. Gymnastic exercises and sports with well-formulated rules early became as regular a part of Greek education as reading and music. In Sparta they were compulsory, state financed, and ruthless; in Athens, optional, but customary. There, in special schools (palaestrae) children practiced carefully graded exercises under the teacher, who owned the establishment, and later, if they desired, went for more intensive study to an ex-athlete tutor who prepared them for the festival games. Much ancient pottery still exists which portrays athletes using jumping weights (*halteres*), discuses, boxing thongs for hands, pick-axes, oil flasks, strigils (scrapers), punching bags, and cold-shower arrangements. Under such a system, Greece from 540–440 B.C. reached her highest point of athletic excellence.

Traditionally, Rome held its first games (Ludi) in the reign of Romulus, but its athletic program was restricted to one event: horse racing. Later, Ludi assumed a greater importance when they were held regularly in the Circus Maximus at a fixed annual date, and after chariot races, farces, gladiatorial contests, beast hunts, and other novelties calculated to amuse were introduced from Etruria. From beginning to end these Ludi Magni or Ludi Romani were always spectacles, Romans seldom competing except in equestrian events or occasionally in foot races. In 186 B.C. Greek actors and athletes were introduced. In time the number of Ludi increased, often serving to celebrate military triumphs. Though the Romans as individuals appreciated the value of exercise like running, swimming, riding, hunting, wrestling, and boxing, they never seem to have cared to train themselves professionally for competition. The general impact of the excesses and bestiality of the Ludi under the Roman Empire upon the Roman character was the reverse of the noble, unifying influence of Greek festivals on Greece during the days of its independence.

GARDINER, CHARLES ("CHUCK") (1904–34), hockey player, born in Edinburgh, Scotland. He was reared in Canada and became one of the outstanding goal tenders in the history of hockey. He played for the Chicago Black Hawks of the National Hockey League from 1928 through 1934 and led his team to victory in the Stanley Cup championship competition in his final year. He was named to the league all-star team in 1931, 1932, and 1934, and won the Vezina Trophy, awarded to the leading goal tender, in 1932 and 1934. Gardiner is a member of the National Hockey Hall of Fame.

GARRISON, EDWARD H. ("SNAPPER") (1868–1930), American jockey, born in New Haven, Conn. He was the highest-paid jockey of the 1880's and 1890's and retired in 1897 to become a trainer and racing official.

GEHRIG [*gĕr'ĭg*], **HENRY LOUIS ("LOU")** (1903–41), American baseball player, born in New York. He played first base (1923–39) for New York of the American League. He was a left-handed batter who compiled a lifetime batting average of .340 and hit 493 home runs. He and "Babe" Ruth comprised the most formidable pair of hitters on a single club in the history of the sport. Gehrig won the nickname "Iron Horse" by setting a major-league record for consecutive games played—2,130 from 1925 to 1939. His career was ended when he contracted amyotrophic lateral sclerosis, which eventually proved fatal. He was elected to the National Baseball Hall of Fame in 1939.

GIBSON, ALTHEA (1927–), American tennis player, born in Silver, S.C. In 1950 she became the first Negro to compete in the U.S. women's championship singles competition in Forest Hills, N.Y. In 1957–58 she won that title and the Wimbledon women's singles championship. She also won the U.S. women's clay-court singles championship in 1957; in the same year she was a member of the winning teams in U.S., Australian, French, and English women's championship doubles competition. In 1959 she became a professional, later a golfer.

GLIDING AND SOARING originated well before the advent of powered flight. Pioneers in aviation, including Wilbur and Orville Wright, Samuel Pierpont Langley, and Octave Chanute, used gliders in their experiments in the late 19th century. These machines were launched from hilltops at first, later by various types of launching devices, and they landed in adjacent valleys, being capable only of controlled descent. Early launching was manual, and was accomplished by stretching rubber shock cords attached to the front of the glider. When sufficient tension had been built up in this way, the pilot released the machine and it took off into the wind. It was later replaced by one employing winches with drums to wind launching wires. These devices were operated by automobile engines and similar power plants. In the 1930's, in addition to winches, automobile and airplane towing were used. Regardless of the mode of launching, the range of the early glider was limited, and ways were sought to increase it.

The next phase was the development of the towed glider, which reached its peak during World War II when the Germans used such craft for troop carrying and the U.S. armed forces made frantic attempts to do likewise. Piano manufacturers, furniture makers, and other woodworking companies were quickly mobilized to build hastily designed machines in a series designated CG. The CG series 4, 13, and 15, carrying up to 30 people, were designed by A. Francis Arcier. Thousands of these craft were

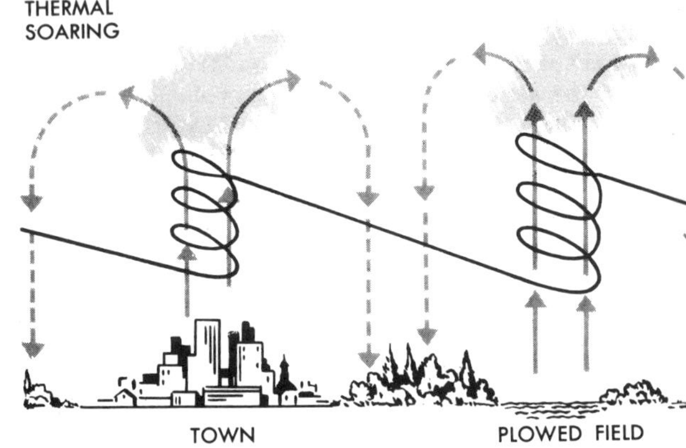

TYPES OF SOARING. In thermal soaring the sailplane utilizes sun-heated air rising in columns above certain areas such as towns, plowed fields, and water. The craft glides from one uplifting current to the next. Ridge soaring is possible when a horizontal moving air mass is deflected by a ridge into upward currents. Wave soaring depends upon air billows, or waves, above hilly country.

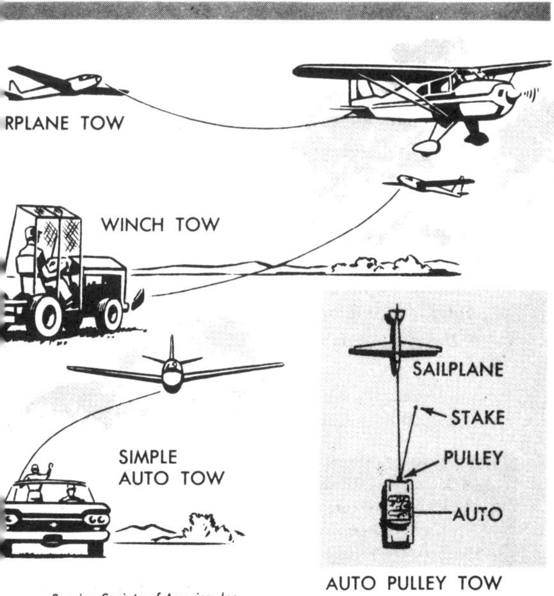

Soaring Society of America, Inc.

METHODS OF LAUNCH: Airplane tow is used to take sailplane to a considerable altitude. Winch tow launches sailplanes from all types of fields, especially those that are rough or slippery. Simple auto tow is used on a large field that has a smooth path for the car. Auto pulley tow is an ideal method for launching from a small field or when wind velocity is low.

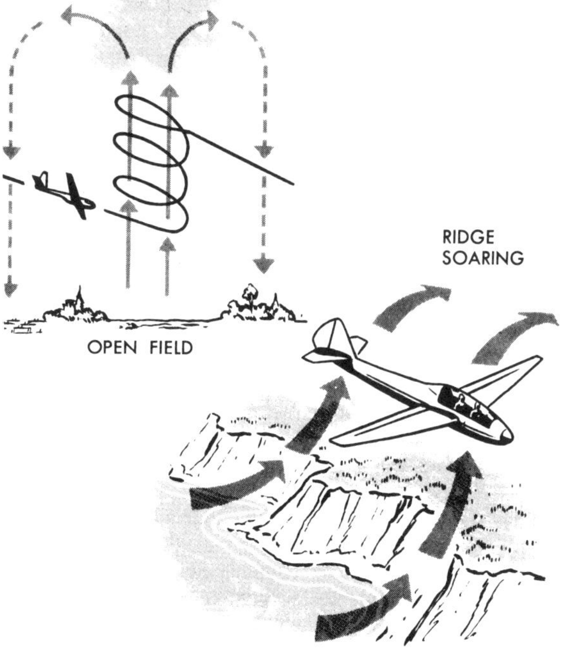

OPEN FIELD

RIDGE SOARING

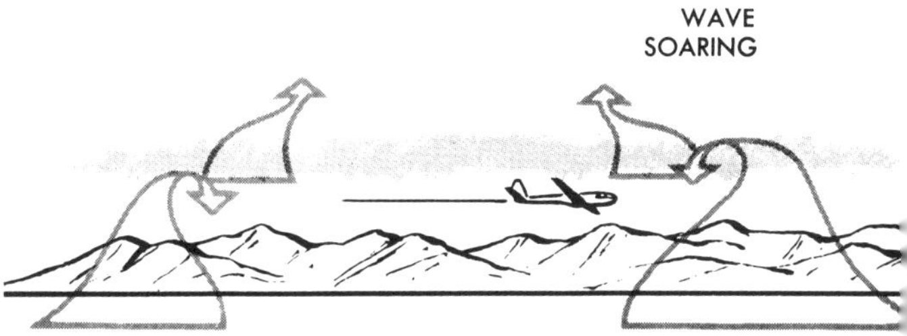

WAVE SOARING

built but few were used, and many were sold as surplus in original crates at prices so low that the wooden cases were used and the gliders discarded. One pilot established a unique record by being towed in a glider across the Atlantic Ocean with devastating effects on his nervous system.

Development of Modern Soaring. In the meantime an advanced type of machine—the sailplane, a refined glider whose wing load is sufficiently small to enable the craft to rise in a upward air current—appeared to further the art of powerless flight. The sailplane is capable of traveling long distances by making skillful use of such currents. With the encouragement of the Soaring Society of America, the sport has developed greatly. There are clubs and soaring contests, and several manufacturers of sailplanes and kits.

Soaring is to powered flight what sailboating is to power boating. With skill and a little knowledge of meteorology, a pilot can travel many miles in a single flight, following the terrain and observing the clouds. Duration records of more than 55 hours have been made, but the Fédération Aéronautique Internationale, the world aviation record keeper, has discontinued competition in this category in the interest of safety, since contests only prove how long the wind blows in certain places and how long a pilot can go without sleep. Altitudes of 20,000 to 30,000 ft. have been attained, and even greater heights have been reached with special oxygen and pressure equipment.

The cost of a new factory-built sailplane ranges from $3,000 to $8,000 but excellent build-it-yourself kits are available at one-third to one-half those prices. The cost of participation can be reduced further by joint or club

N52Y

Soaring Society of America, Inc.

Soaring Society of America, Inc.

At top, restored Detroit Gull primary glider, now considered obsolete. Below, Schweitzer 1–19 utility glider, capable of thermal-soaring flight.

Schweizer Aircraft Corp.

Schweizer 1–23H sailplane, a high-performance craft with sensitive characteristics requiring experienced pilots.

ownership, and there are clubs and soaring sites located throughout the United States.

A student pilot's permit may be obtained at age 14. A private-glider pilot certificate, permitting the applicant to fly nonpaying passengers in sailplanes, is available at age 16, following 100 glider flights or 50 flights that total at least 10 hours. The candidate also must pass a written test and meet the requirements of flight checkout.

GOLF, game in which the player attempts with clubs to propel a small, resilient ball around a course consisting of widely spaced holes, in regular progression and with the smallest possible number of strokes of the clubs. Courses usually consist of 9 or 18 holes.

There are some historians who say that the game originated in the Netherlands and others who say it started in Scotland, but there is agreement on one point: the Scots deserve much of the credit for the popularity the game enjoys today.

History of the Game

The process of hitting a little white ball from a tee into a hole by successive strokes goes back to the early part of the 15th century, when courses were developed on the sand hills, known as "links," along the eastern coast of Scotland. Many were built along high bluffs. Nature, in the form of wind and water, helped design them by forming dunes, ridges, knolls, gullies, and hollows. Even rabbits helped the game. In the process of avoiding becoming the prey of other animals, the rabbits linked their burrows in the dunes by means of runs. These runs were expanded by foxes and hunters. When the early golfers looked for suitable terrain, they found the answer in these rabbit runs, which formed the basis for fairways (the expanses between the tees, from which the ball is hit initially, and the greens where the holes are located). The sheltered oases where the rabbits frolicked provided primitive sites for greens.

One of the most famous golf courses is St. Andrews in Scotland, which was in existence in a rather crude form long before it was formally founded in 1754. A famous pioneer among golfing societies was the Honorable Company of Edinburgh Golfers, which was formed in 1744 and used the Links of Leith, situated near Edinburgh.

The game was played by some of the English royal family during the 15th and 16th centuries, which may account for its designation as the "royal and ancient game." Some of the rulers of that era were not pleased with the growing popularity of the game, however, because they felt the state would be better served if the citizenry spent the same amount of time practicing archery. There was sound reasoning behind this desire because skilled archers would be most helpful in defending the land against invasion. Three attempts by Scottish parliaments to suppress the game in the 15th century proved ineffective, however.

The game was played mostly by affluent club members through the 17th and 18th centuries. The oldest tournament on record is the one that started in Prestwick, Scotland, in 1860, and later became known as the British Open.

Outstanding Early Players. Willie Park, Sr., Tom Morris, Sr., Tom Morris, Jr., and Andrew L. Strath were among the top players in the first 10 years of the British Open. Around 1900 such stars as J. H. Taylor, John Ball, Jr., James Braid, and Harry Vardon appeared. Taylor and Ball were golfers who shunned safe play and never hesitated to hit long brassie (No. 2 wood) shots to the green. They usually were accurate shots, too. Vardon, a master of iron shots, popularized the overlapping grip; he won six British Open titles, the United States Open in 1900, and a total of 62 first-class championships. Ball was an amateur. Vardon, Taylor, and Braid were professionals, known as

GREAT GOLFERS

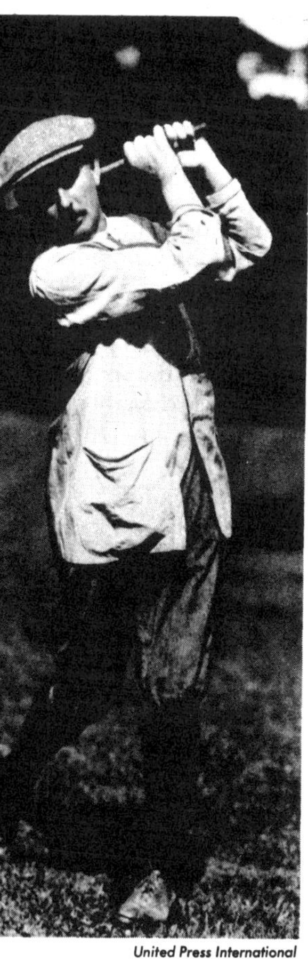

United Press International

English golfer Harry Vardon won the British Open six times.

National Golf Foundation

Walter Hagen, outstanding American golfer from 1914 to 1936.

Golfdom

Bobby Jones, an American, won four major tourneys in 1930.

the "great triumvirate" because they dominated the British championships from 1894 to 1914.

North American Beginnings. The first golf club in North America was founded in 1873 and became the Royal Montreal Golf Club. It is believed that the game was introduced to Canada by sailors from the British Isles.

The honor of being the first golf club in the United States is still in dispute. Though the St. Andrew's Golf Club of Yonkers, N.Y., since moved to Mount Hope, N.Y., has claimed that distinction because of a founding date of Nov. 14, 1888, the Foxburg (Pa.) Country Club has furnished affidavits from elder citizens stating that the club was formed in 1887. These affidavits have been deposited with the United States Golf Association (USGA). One of the affidavits was by Harry R. Harvey, who says he attended the organizational meeting of the club and was its secretary from the date of founding to 1941. The Sarasota (Fla.) Golf Club claims it is even older than Foxburg, listing 1886 as its year of founding by J. Hamilton Gillespie. Both Sarasota and Foxburg are on their original sites.

St. Andrew's moved to its present site in 1897. The first St. Andrew's course in Yonkers was a three-hole layout in a cow pasture belonging to John Reid, one of the founders of the club. Then the club moved to an apple orchard on Palisade Avenue, and it was there that the club members became known as the "Apple Tree Gang." The next move was to Grey Oaks in 1894, where the club remained until its shift to Mount Hope.

A 1798 print depicts Scottish golfers on St. Andrews course, founded formally in 1754, about 30 mi (50 km) northeast of Edinburgh.

The Bettmann Archive

Other early U.S. courses are those of Tuxedo Golf Club, Tuxedo, N.Y. (1889); Newport Golf Club, Newport, R.I. (1890); Middlesboro Golf Club, Middlesboro, Ky. (1890);

National Golf Foundation
Mildred Didrikson Zaharias, three-time winner of the U.S. Women's Open championship.

Sam Snead, American professional golfer who won many major tourneys.
National Golf Foundation

Arnold Palmer, whose fame was spread by the advent of televising tournaments.
Wide World

and Hotel Champlain Golf Course, Bluff Point, N.Y. (1890).

The USGA, governing body of U.S. play, was formed in 1894, with five charter clubs. By 1900 there were more than 1,000 courses in the United States. New York and Massachusetts each had more than 150 at that time.

Shortly after the turn of the century, the first great U.S. amateur, Walter J. Travis, captured many headlines. Travis, who did not take up golf until he was 35, won the United States Amateur tourney (begun in 1895) three times and the British Amateur once. Wherever he played, Travis always had an ample supply of long, black cigars and an aluminum, mallet-head "Schenectady" putter. The putter, which he used with consummate skill, was criticized as being illegal. It was well that he had such talent on the greens because his drives were among the shortest in the game during that period.

Another great amateur player of the period was Jerome D. Travers, who won the United States Amateur four times and the United States Open (originated in 1894) once. Willie Anderson, a professional, won three United States Opens in a row, from 1903 to 1905, a feat that never has been matched. Anderson also had won the Open in 1901. His total of four Open victories later was equaled by Robert Tyre ("Bobby") Jones, Jr., and Ben Hogan.

Growth in the United States. The game in the United States received its greatest impetus in 1913, when a 20-year-old former caddie named Francis D. Ouimet won the United States Open in Brookline, Mass. In achieving his victory, the tall amateur defeated two of Great Britain's greatest players, Harry Vardon and Ted Ray, in a playoff. People who previously had only a casual interest in golf suddenly became anxious to play the game. Ouimet's triumph proved that it was not necessary to be wealthy to become a skilled golfer. Public and private courses increased, and millions took up the game.

In 1914 Walter Hagen won his first United States Open title. From then until 1936 he was one of the dominant figures of American golf. Hagen was a great showman, and his ability to make decisive shots under pressure always ensured a big following wherever he played.

Charles ("Chick") Evans, Jr., of Chicago won the United States Amateur and United States Open titles in 1916. In the Open, which he won with a score of 286, Evans used only seven clubs, all with hickory shafts.

The Professional Golfers' Association (PGA) of America was formed in 1916 and held its first championship that year at the Siwanoy Country Club in Bronxville, N.Y.

The first international amateur competition between the United States and Great Britain, designated later as the Walker Cup matches in honor of George H. Walker, the donor of the cup, was held at Hoylake, England, in 1921. The following year the United States Public Links championship was started for amateur players.

Gene Sarazen, a former caddie, started on the road to fame in 1922 by winning the United States Open and PGA titles. Robert Tyre Jones, Jr., the outstanding golfer during the first half of the 20th century, won his first major title in 1923, the United States Open. Bobby, the boy wonder from Atlanta, subsequently compiled a record of 13 American and British championships and retired at the age of 28. His greatest feat was his grand slam—victories in the United States Amateur, the United States Open, the British Amateur and British Open in 1930. Tommy Armour, one of the game's top instructors, won the United States Open in 1927.

Professional matches between the United States and Great Britain were started in 1926. They became known as the Ryder Cup matches, in honor of Samuel A. Ryder, a Briton who donated the trophy, and are played every two years. The first Curtis Cup matches between women amateur players of the United States and Great Britain were organized in 1932 and played at Wentworth, England. They were named for Harriot and Margaret Curtis, prominent U.S. golfers.

The Masters tournament at Augusta, Ga., was started in 1934. It is played at the Augusta National Golf Club, which was developed by Robert Tyre Jones, Jr., and some associates on the site of a nursery. Its prize money and the fame that accompanies a victory in it make the Masters one of the major competitive events in the sport.

The year 1934 also marked the rise of W. Lawson Little, Jr., to prominence. The long-hitting Little won the United States Amateur and the British Amateur tourneys in 1934 and repeated these victories in 1935. Subsequently he turned professional.

In the 1930's, Ben Hogan, Byron Nelson, and Sam Snead began their rise to fame. Hogan, known as "The Iceman" because of his cool, emotionless attitude under pressure, won the United States Open four times and is regarded as one of the finest tacticians the game has produced. Nelson won 11 consecutive tournaments in one year. Snead is considered the smoothest swinger in the history of golf. Beneath the façade of a hillbilly that made him immensely popular with fans and in great demand as an after-dinner speaker, Snead had an agile mind that brought him wealth.

Then came the era of the Big Three millionaires—Arnold Palmer, Jack Nicklaus, and Gary Player—and Bill Casper Jr. They achieved fame and wealth much sooner than previous champions because of exposure on national television.

While a few champions continued to come out of the caddie ranks, such as Lee Trevino, a different breed of professional started to take over. The new champions were college educated. Most of them attended the Professional Golfers' Association business school to learn pro-shop marketing techniques. If they failed to survive the pro tour, in which the leaders could earn nearly $300,000 a year in purses, they could earn $50,000 a year at many of the wealthy clubs in metropolitan areas.

Though Gary Player of South Africa was the best-known of the foreign contingent, there were others, such as Henry Cotton and Bobby Locke of Great Britain and

PLAYING HOLES

Diagrams show three of the holes of the Masters tournament course at Augusta, Ga. Each hole has its par, or the number of strokes necessary to play it perfectly. Left, 9th hole, 420 yd (384 m), par 4. Normally a long drive down the middle of the fairway is preferable. Playing to left is advantageous only when strong wind is against the player. Hole opens up as drive is played to right, but distance to hole increases. Center, 13th hole, 475 yd (434 m), par 5. Golfer may play ball close to creek and get a more level lie for next shot. Driving farther to right increases distance and gives annoying hillside lie. Right, 16th hole, 190 yd (174 m), par 3. Ball is driven across pond, with two regulation putts for tricky green.

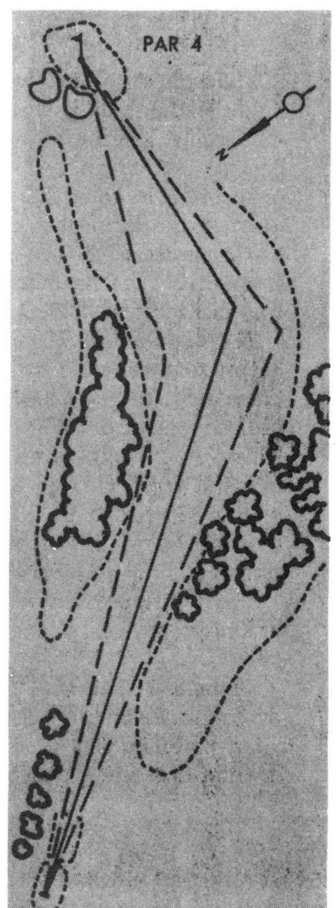

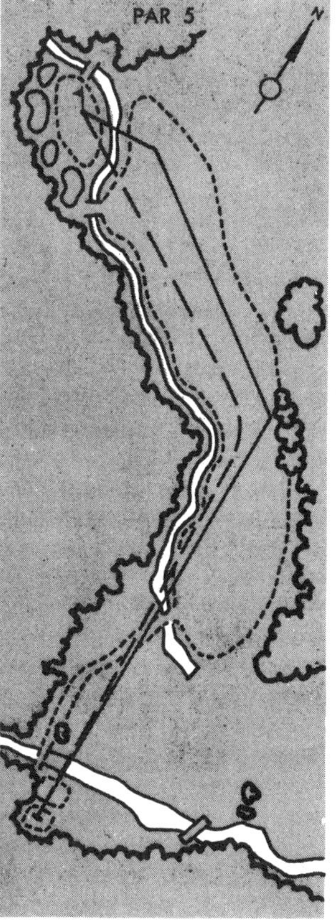

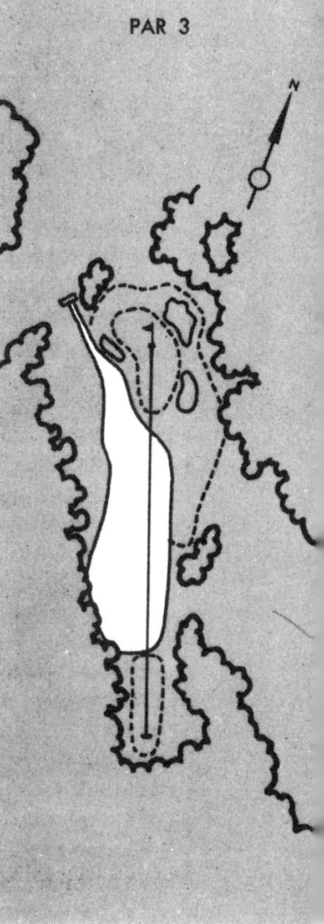

Roberto de Vicenzo of Argentina, who gained worldwide recognition.

Women golfers also came into the television limelight, and although the purses on their tour did not approach the total of the men's tour, they were substantial. Among the stars were Mildred Didrikson Zaharias, Patty Berg, Betty Jameson, Betsy Rawls, and Louise Suggs in the tour's formative years. Later, the big winners included Mickey Wright, Carol Mann, JoAnne Carner, Donna Caponi, Susie Berning, and Sandra Haynie.

Colleges, which had previously awarded most of their scholarships to football, basketball, and baseball players, began to realize that golfers no longer could be ignored. Some, such as the University of Houston, recruited extensively and sent many graduates into the pro ranks. Because of the lure of year-round golf, the Southern areas were highly successful in these efforts.

Golf has helped change the mode of living for many of the affluent in the United States. Huge real estate developments in South Carolina and Georgia, for example, have been financially successful because they could guarantee that their homes would border a golf course built as an integral part of the development.

Wealthy estate owners in major urban areas, hard-pressed to maintain their retreats because of soaring real estate taxes, but acutely conscious of the need to protect the environment, have been the largest source of land for new full-size golf clubs. Many of the estate houses have proved useful as clubhouses.

In many crowded metropolitan areas, the land shortage has been solved by the development of "executive" courses or similar layouts of short, par-3 length.

Rules and Procedure of Play

One of the oldest codes for the game is the first St. Andrews code, formulated in 1754. From its 13 rules have been developed the rules approved by the United States Golf Association and the Royal and Ancient Golf Club of St. Andrews, Scotland. The original code follows:

(1) You must tee your ball within a club length of the hole.

(2) Your tee must be on the ground.

(3) You are not to change the ball which you strike off the tee.

(4) You are not to remove stones, bones, or any breakclub for the sake of playing your ball except upon the fair green and that only within a club length of your ball.

(5) If your ball come upon water, or any watery filth, you are at liberty to take your ball and throw it behind the hazard six yards (5.4 m) at least. You may play it with any club and allow your adversary a stroke for so getting out your ball.

(6) If . . . balls be found anywhere touching one another, you are to lift the first ball till you play the last.

(7) At holeing, you are to play your ball honestly for the hole, but not to play upon your adversary's ball, not lying in your way to the hole.

(8) If you should lose your ball by its being taken up or any other way, you are to go back to the spot where you struck last and drop another ball and allow your adversary a stroke for the misfortune.

(9) No man at holeing his ball is to be allowed to mark his way to the hole with his club or anything else.

(10) If a ball be stopped by any person, horse, dog, or anything else, the ball so stopped must be played where it lies.

(11) If you draw your club, in order to strike, and pressed so far in this stroke as to be bringing down your club, if then your club shall break in any way, it is to be accounted a stroke.

(12) He, whose ball lies furthest from the hole, is obliged to play first.

(13) Neither trench, ditch or dyke made for the preservation of the links, nor the scholars holes or the soldiers lines shall be accounted a hazard, but the ball is to be taken out, teed, and played with any iron club.

The weight of the ball must not be greater than 1.62 oz (45.93 g), and the size not less than 1.68 inch (4.27 cm) in diameter. The velocity of the ball must not be greater than 250 ft (76 m) per second when measured on the USGA's apparatus. In international team competition, however, the size of the ball is not less than 1.62 inch (4.11 cm) in diameter, and the velocity specification does not apply.

A player is allowed a maximum of 14 clubs during a round. The penalty for breach of this rule is the loss of each hole in which a violation occurred in match play and the loss of two strokes for each hole in which a violation occurred in stroke play, or, as it is sometimes called, medal play.

Types of Competition. In match play the game is scored by holes. A hole is won by the player who holes his ball with the fewer strokes. In a handicap match the lower net score wins the hole. A hole is halved if each side holes out in the same number of strokes. A match is won by the side that is leading by a number of holes greater than the number of holes remaining to be played. If A leads B by two holes, with only one hole remaining, he wins by a score of 2 and 1.

In stroke play the winner is the competitor who completes the round or rounds in the fewest strokes. Here any number of players can compete, as individuals, and their total number of strokes for the entire round or rounds comprises their score; in match play, one or more players compete as a team in opposition to another team.

Foursomes play, sometimes known as Scotch foursomes, consists of a match in which two players oppose two others. Each side employs one ball and the partners take alternate shots.

Pinehurst play is similar to foursomes except that both players on a team drive—that is, make the first, or tee, shot—on each hole and then select the ball they will use for the duration of play on that hole. The other ball is removed from play.

In blind bogey play, prior to beginning, a player selects a handicap that, in his judgment, will allow him to have a net score between 70 and 80 for 18 holes. After the round is completed, a tournament committee draws a number in the 70's and the player whose net score is closest to the figure selected is adjudged the winner. In the case of a tie, the winner usually is picked by drawing lots.

When players do not have established handicaps, systems known as Peoria, Callaway, and Horner are used. In Peoria play, six holes are selected for handicap purposes after the players have started their round. The scores of a player on the six holes selected are added. Then they are multiplied by three, and par for the course is subtracted, thus determining the handicap. In Callaway play, a competitor's highest score for a single hole or specified series of holes is deducted from his gross score to determine the net score. For example, if a player scores a total of 90 and the aggregate of his three highest individual scores is 20, his net score is 70.

In the Horner system, for total scores of 100 or less, the player's best nine individual scores are picked. Then the strokes by which he went over par on these holes are totaled to determine an "allowance." Eagles and birdies are counted as pars and no deduction is made for them. The allowance for the nine selected holes is doubled and this amount is subtracted from the actual score for 18 holes to determine the net score. For scores of 100 or more, the same method is used except that the best 10 holes instead of the best 9 are used as the basis for determining the allowance.

A USGA handicap is derived from a golfer's "handicap differential" for the lowest 10 rounds of the last 25 he has played. The handicap differential is the difference between the course's rating and the golfer's score.

Par. Par, the score an expert golfer is expected to make for a given hole, is based on the yardage of the hole measured from the middle of the tee area to the middle of the green, according to the line of play planned by the architect in laying out the hole. The USGA lists the following yardages for guidance:

Score	Men's Par	Women's Par
3	Up to 250 yd (229 m)	Up to 210 yd (192 m)
4	251–470 yd (230–430 m)	211–400 yd (193–366 m)
5	471 yd (431 m) and over	401–575 yd (367–526 m)

Amateur and Professional Status. An amateur golfer is defined as one who plays the game solely as nonremunerative or nonprofit-making sport. An amateur can forfeit his status and be termed a professional for a number of reasons, including the following:

(1) Receiving compensation for serving as a professional golfer or as a teaching or playing assistant to a professional golfer.
(2) Playing for prize money.
(3) Lending one's name or likeness for use in any way for the advertisement or sale of anything, regardless of whether the product is used in, or pertains to, golf.
(4) Because of golfing skill or reputation, accepting compensation for making a personal appearance, whether or not in connection with a golf competition or exhibition.
(5) Taking any action that clearly indicates the intention of becoming a professional golfer.
(6) Ghostwriting—allowing one's name to be advertised or published as the author of golf articles or books of which he is not actually the author.
(7) Serving as a caddie, caddie master, or club maker after one's 21st birthday.

Etiquette of Play. There are a few simple rules that constitute etiquette and make the game safer and more enjoyable for those who play. They form an excellent guide for both the novice and experienced golfer. These rules follow:

(1) No one should move, talk, or stand close to or directly behind the ball or the hole when a player is addressing the ball or making a stroke.
(2) The player who has the honor (lowest score for a hole) should be allowed to drive first (from the tee) in beginning play on the next hole.
(3) No player should hit the ball from the tee until the players ahead are out of range.
(4) Play should be conducted without delay of any sort.
(5) Players searching for a ball should allow other players coming up to pass them by making an appropriate signal and should not continue their play until those players have passed and are out of range.
(6) Before leaving a bunker, a player should carefully fill up all holes made by him therein.
(7) Players should ensure that any turf cut or displaced by them on fairways or greens is replaced at once and pressed down.
(8) Players should ensure that, when dropping golf bags or the flagstick (used to mark the hole), no damage is done to the putting green, and that neither they nor their caddies damage the hole by standing close to the hole or by mishandling the flagstick. The flagstick should be properly replaced in the hole before the players leave the putting green.

Moment of triumph: Tom Watson—and his caddy, too—acknowledge the applause from the gallery on the 18th hole after Watson dropped his last putt to win the Masters at Augusta.

UPI

(9) When the play of a hole has been completed, players should immediately leave the putting green.

Priority on the Course. In the absence of special rules, singles matches, threesomes, or foursomes should have precedence over, and be entitled to pass, any other kind of match. A single player has no standing and should give way to a match of any kind.

Players in any match comprising a whole round are entitled to pass those engaged in a shorter round. If players in a match fail to keep their proper place on the course, by falling more than one clear hole behind the players in front, they should allow players of the match behind them to pass.

Equipment

The earliest golf ball was made of feathers stuffed into a thin leather bag. It was a ball whose distance in flight was largely determined by the tightness with which it was packed. But at best it was not a distance ball, and there is no record of its going 200 yd (183 m). In 1848 an improvement in the form of a gutta-percha ball was adopted. Gutta-percha, a resinous gum, proved to have good tensile strength, but the maximum distance in flight of such a ball was about 225 yd (206 m).

The Modern Ball. The advent of the rubber ball in 1899 has led to remarkable distance. In 1933, during the British Open at St. Andrews, Scotland, Craig Wood, an American professional, made a 430-yd (393 m) drive on the fifth hole. However, it was achieved on a dry course and with the aid of a tail wind. George Bayer, also an American "pro," made a 426-yd (390 m) drive in Tucson, Ariz., in 1955. Tee shots of 300 yd (274 m) are not unusual for some professionals and top amateurs today.

Hard-hitting golfers use high-compression balls; those of limited physical strength usually use low-compression balls.

Clubs and Their Use. Golf sticks also have undergone evolution. From the weird wooden-shaft clubs of yesteryear, matched sets of woods and irons of remarkable beauty, durability, weight distribution, graduation, and utility have been developed. The most significant of the golf club improvements has been the evolution of lightweight shafts of titanium, graphite, and super lightweight steel. The materials enable the player to achieve greater acceleration of the club on the downswing, thus getting longer shots with less effort than needed by carbon steel.

Wood clubs (those with wooden heads), used for hitting the ball from the tee or for long distances in general, are now numbered from one through four or five. The No. 1 wood (formerly called "driver") is used for maximum distance; in decreasing order of achievable distance are others, each having increasingly greater loft, that formerly were called "brassie," "spoon," "baffy," and "cleek."

Irons (iron-headed clubs), used for relatively shorter shots, are numbered from one through nine or ten. They, too, are differentiated by varying loft and are selected according to the length of the shot and the terrain of the course. Formerly they bore such names as "driving iron,"

GOLF SWING

Backswing starts from address. Order of movement is hands, arms, shoulders, and hips, which are activated almost simultaneously. As the hands reach hip level, the shoulders are turning and start pulling the hips around. The turning hips begin pulling the left leg to the right. Left heel should be raised no higher than 1 in. from the ground to avoid imbalance and other complications. When the backswing is completed, the golfer's chin should be touching the left shoulder. Now the golfer should be comfortably poised for the downswing.

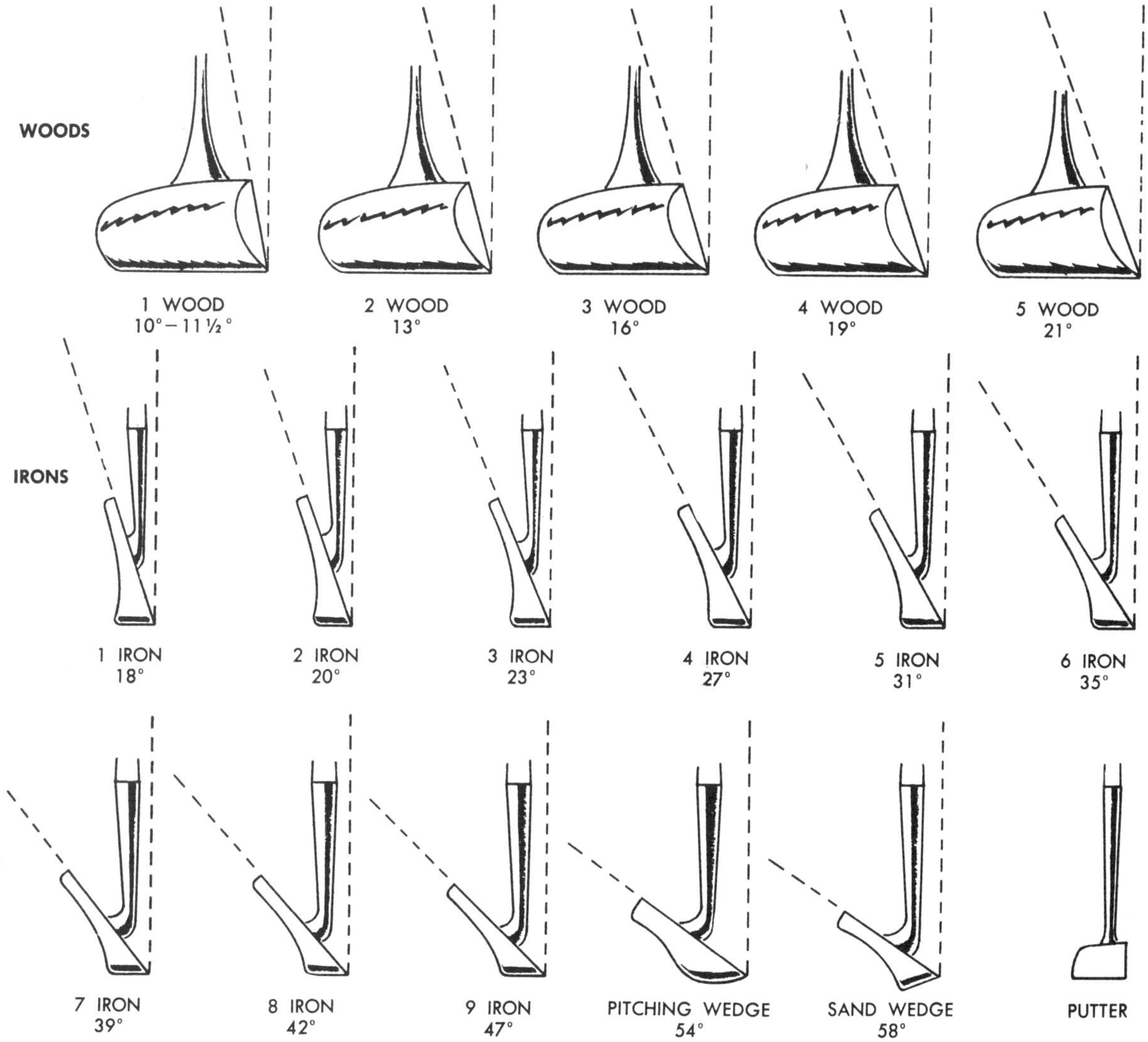

WOODS
1 WOOD
10°–11½°
2 WOOD
13°
3 WOOD
16°
4 WOOD
19°
5 WOOD
21°
IRONS
1 IRON
18°
2 IRON
20°
3 IRON
23°
4 IRON
27°
5 IRON
31°
6 IRON
35°
7 IRON
39°
8 IRON
42°
9 IRON
47°
PITCHING WEDGE
54°
SAND WEDGE
58°
PUTTER

Wood clubs are used for hitting the ball long distances. The 1 wood gives maximum distance. As the loft, or backward slant of the club face, increases, potential distance decreases. Selection of iron clubs with various lofts is determined according to distance and terrain. The putter is straight faced, for rolling the ball on the green.

POTENTIAL DISTANCES OF CLUBS

4
3
2
WOODS
1
9
8
7
6
5
4
3
2
IRONS

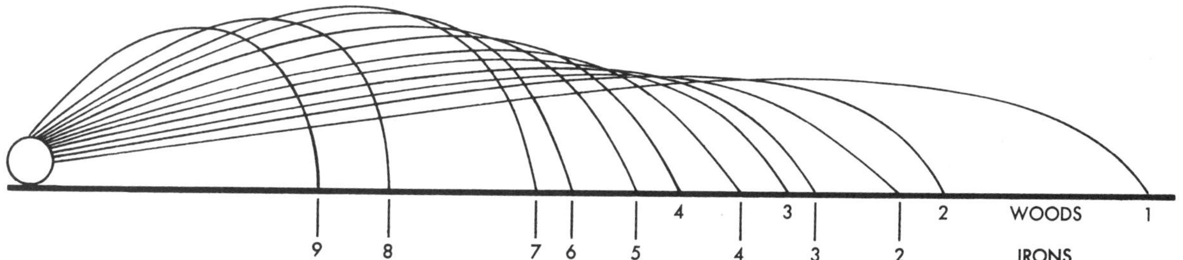

Diagram of potential distances and arcs of ball when an average golfer uses various clubs. Achievable distances of woods are 5, 200 yd (183 m); 4, 210 yd (192 m); 3, 220 yd (201 m); 2, 230 yd (210 m); 1, 240–270 yd (220–247 m). Potentials of irons are 9, 111 yd (102 m); 8, 122 yd (112 m); 7, 133 yd (122 m); 6, 144 yd (132 m); 5, 155 yd (142 m); 4, 166 yd (152 m); 3, 177 yd (162 m); 2, 188 yd (172 m); 1, 200–210 yd (183–192 m).

Golf World

Golf spectators throng to the Masters tournament, held annually at the difficult Augusta (Ga.) National Golf Club, co-designed by Bobby Jones and Alistair MacKenzie.

"midiron," "mashie," and "niblick." The putter, an iron with a straight face, is used for rolling the ball on the green and into the hole.

Play on a hole whose par is four, for example, normally would involve use of a wood club for the initial tee shot; one iron for making the approach to, and landing on, the green, and two strokes with the putter.

Through the years, the "beast of burden" known as the caddie has been gradually disappearing. In his place are caddie carts and electric golf cars, which remove the burden from the golfer's back but unfortunately cannot supply information on yardage or trace an errant drive in the rough.

Glossary

The following are terms commonly used in golf:

Ace, a hole made in one shot, a hole-in-one.

Address, the position a player takes when preparing to hit the ball.

Approach, a stroke that is made when the player is close to the green. Also the portion of the fairway that is close to the green.

Away, the ball that is the greatest distance away from the hole when two or more balls are in play.

Baseball grip, a grip like that used on a baseball bat instead of the standard grip produced by overlapping or interlocking the little finger of the right hand with the forefinger and middle finger of the left hand.

Birdie, a score one stroke under par.

Blast, a shot from a sand trap in which the club head

PUTTING TECHNIQUE

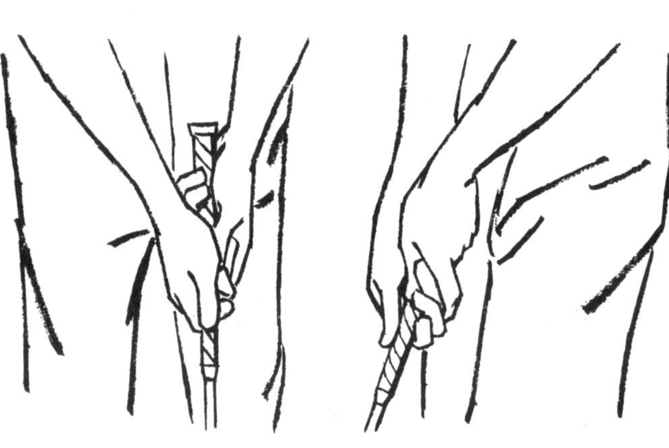

After studying green and lining up putt, golfer grips iron firmly, without squeezing, so that forefinger of left hand overlaps fingers of right hand, with both thumbs straight down shaft. The golfer's eyes are directly over the ball, and his feet are relatively close together with the ball centered in front of them. Only the wrists are used in the backswing with the club kept low and straight. Wrists are stiff in the follow-through as the golfer swings his arms and shoulders straight at the cup.

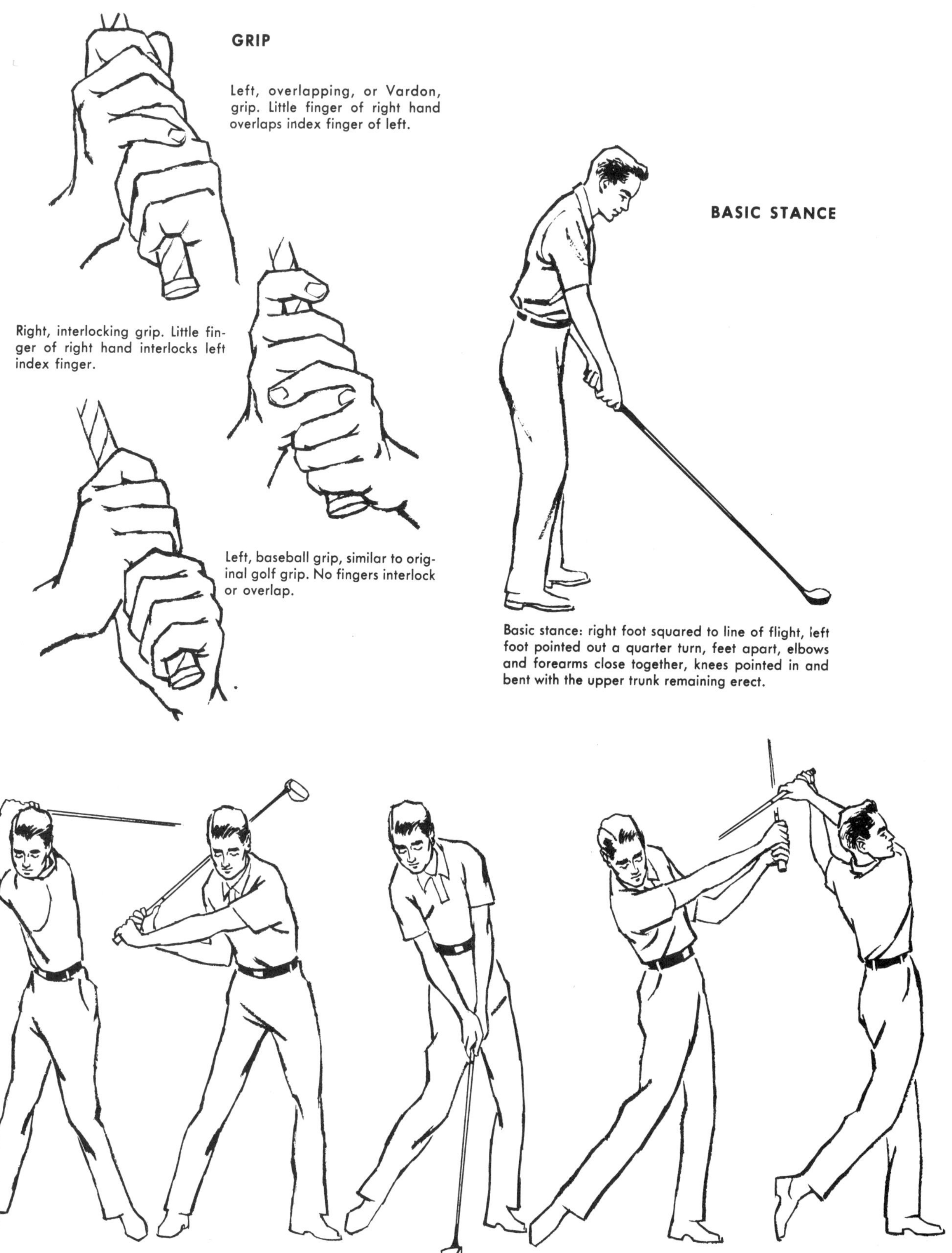

GRIP

Left, overlapping, or Vardon, grip. Little finger of right hand overlaps index finger of left.

Right, interlocking grip. Little finger of right hand interlocks left index finger.

Left, baseball grip, similar to original golf grip. No fingers interlock or overlap.

BASIC STANCE

Basic stance: right foot squared to line of flight, left foot pointed out a quarter turn, feet apart, elbows and forearms close together, knees pointed in and bent with the upper trunk remaining erect.

Downswing is initiated by the hips turning back to the left. As the body unwinds, a chain action of shoulders, arms, and hands multiplies power. At moment of impact right arm is slightly bent, and back of left hand faces toward the target with the wristbone raised and preceding any other part of hand to increase distance and accuracy. In follow-through golfer completes high swing, his hips still leading his shoulders so that at completion his belt buckle points definitely to left of target.

strikes the sand behind the ball instead of hitting the ball directly.

Bogey, par in strict usage. However, the term is commonly used by many golfers to describe a score of one stroke more than par.

Bunker, a trap or hazard, usually with sand in it.

Bye, the position of a player in a tournament who advances without playing a given round.

Carpet, a green; under ideal conditions, greens are very smooth.

Carry, the distance a shot travels in the air before landing.

Chip shot, a low approach shot in which the ball rolls after landing on the green.

Compression, the degree of tension of the rubber threads that are wound around the core of a ball.

Course rating, an evaluation of the degree of difficulty of a golf course, expressed in strokes. The figure is determined by checking other courses that are so rated and making a comparison.

Distance, the number of yards a shot travels in the air and by roll of the ball on landing.

Divot, piece of turf that is removed by the club when a player makes a shot.

Dog-leg, a hole that does not take a straight line from tee to green but turns to the left or right.

Down, the total number of holes or strokes by which a player is behind his rival.

Dub, a poor golfer. As a verb, to make a poor shot.

Eagle, a score of two strokes less than par for any hole but a par-3 hole.

Explosion, a shot from a trap in which the sand behind the ball, rather than the ball itself, is hit by the club head.

Fade, a shot that starts to the left and drops to the right with little roll after it lands.

Fairway, the area between tee and green that is mowed.

Fore, a warning that a ball has been hit or is about to be hit; a request for silence.

Frog hair, short rough around a green.

Green, the short-grass area of a hole used for putting, denoted by a flag. This area immediately surrounds the hole in which the ball eventually drops.

Gross, a golfer's score before his handicap is subtracted.

Ground, to rest the club head on the ground behind the ball when preparing to hit the ball.

Hook, a shot that curves to the left when hit by a right-handed golfer.

Lie, the spot where a ball comes to rest after a shot is made.

Line of flight, the direction in which a ball travels.

Lip, the edge of the cup on the green.

Nassau, a type of scoring in which one point is awarded for winning the first nine holes, one point for the second nine holes, and a third point for victory in over-all match play.

Net, score after the handicap has been deducted from the gross score.

Open, a tournament in which both amateurs and professionals may compete.

Penalty stroke, stroke added to a player's total for infraction of rules.

Pitch, a high shot, usually made near the green, that does not travel far after landing.

Pitch and run, an approach shot that travels in the air for part of its total distance and then "runs," or rolls, after landing.

An intense Jack Nicklaus putts in the Bing Crosby Pro-Am tournament at Pebble Beach, Calif. Nicklaus was acclaimed the best all-around player in the history of the game.

Wide World

Pivot, the rotation of the player's body that occurs during a golf swing.

Preferred lie, improved position of the ball on the fairway, brought about, for example, by removing it from a spot where the turf is not in good condition.

Pull, a straight shot that is pulled to the left of the target by a right-handed golfer.

Push, a shot hit to the right of the target.

Rough, the long-grass area that borders fairways.

Round robin, competition in which all players oppose one another.

Scratch player, a player whose skill is such that he does not require a handicap.

Shank, a shot that goes far to the right of the direction intended because the ball has been hit with the area of the club face that is near the base of the shaft.

Slice, a shot that curves to the right when hit by a right-handed golfer.

Stymie, the situation resulting when another ball is in the way of a putt, between the ball being rolled on the green and the cup.

Tee, the area where the first stroke on a hole is taken; also, the wooden or plastic peg used to elevate the ball before hitting it from that area.

Texas wedge, the putter, when that club is used to roll a ball out of a trap and onto the green.

Top, to hit the ball on top, causing it to roll along the ground instead of achieving flight.

Up, the margin of superiority in strokes or holes held by a player or side in a match with another.

GONZALES [*gŏn-zä'ləs*], **RICHARD ANZALDO ("PANCHO")** (1928–), American tennis player born in Los Angeles. A self-taught player who ranked 16th among U.S. amateurs in 1948, he won the U.S. men's outdoor singles championship that year and continued his meteoric career by retaining the title in 1949. In 1949 he became a professional; during the 1950's he was the outstanding U.S. player in that branch of the sport.

GRAHAM, OTTO EVERETT, JR. (1921–), American football player. He was the quarterback of the Cleveland Browns from 1946 through 1955, when they won 10 consecutive division titles in professional football (All-America Conference, 1946–49; thereafter National Football League). *Sport Magazine* selected him as the best professional football player of that decade. He was a triple-threat halfback at Northwestern University and won All-American rating in 1943. In professional football he was especially noted for his forward passing. In 1959 he became head football coach at the U.S. Coast Guard Academy.

GRANGE, HAROLD EDWARD ("RED") (1903–), American football player, born in Forksville, Pa. As the greatest player of the 1920's, he became a legendary figure in U.S. sports. He was named All-American halfback while playing for the University of Illinois in 1923 and 1924 and All-American quarterback in 1925; in those three years he gained 3,637 yd. by rushing. In 1924, against a powerful University of Michigan team, he scored five touchdowns—four in 12 minutes—and gained 402 yd. by rushing. In 1925, against Pennsylvania, he scored three touchdowns and rushed for 363 yd. on a muddy field in his first Eastern appearance. He lifted professional football from the doldrums when he joined the Chicago Bears in 1925 and popularized the sport through exhibition tours. He retired from the game in 1934 and became a sports broadcaster.

GREENBERG, HENRY BENJAMIN ("HANK") (1911–), American baseball player and executive, born in New York. He spent all but the final year of his major-league career as a player (1933–47) with Detroit of the American League. A right-handed-hitting first baseman, he had a lifetime mark of 331 home runs. In 1938 he led the league in home runs with 58. During the 1950's and early 1960's he was an executive of the Cleveland and Chicago clubs of the American League. He was named to the National Baseball Hall of Fame in 1956.

GREYHOUND RACING. *See* Dog: *Dog Racing.*

GRIFFITH, CLARK CALVIN (1869–1955), American baseball player, manager, and executive, born in Clear Creek, Mo. He pitched for clubs in both the National and American leagues between 1891 and 1914, winning 237 games. He managed Chicago (1901–2), New York (1903–8), and Washington (1912–20) of the American League and Cincinnati (1909–11) of the National League. He was president and co-owner of Washington, 1920–55, and was named to the National Baseball Hall of Fame in 1946.

GROVE, ROBERT MOSES ("LEFTY") (1900–75), American baseball player, born in Lonaconing, Md. A left-handed pitcher, he played for the Philadelphia Athletics (1925–33) and the Boston Redsox (1934–41), both of the American League. His lifetime total of 300 victories and 141 defeats gave him a winning percentage of .680. In 1931, when he won 31 and lost four, he won 16 consecutive games, tying a league record for consecutive victories in a season. His remarkable fast ball was primarily responsible for his 2,271 strike-outs. In 1947 he was elected to the Baseball Hall of Fame.

GYMNASTICS [*jĭm-năs'tĭks*], **sport in which both prescribed and optional physical exercises must be performed in an artistic yet formally correct manner. The sport, organized for national and international competition, is practiced throughout the world.**

A number of experts have ascribed the conception of the sport to man's subconscious impulse toward atavistic activity, such as swinging from trees. The term and sport, however, can be traced to ancient Greece, where *gymnazein* meant "exercising in the nude." In modern gymnastics, participants are clothed. The rising number of gymnasts and gymnastic teams in schools and athletic associations as well as public attendance at gymnastic meets indicate the sport is gaining greater mass popularity than it enjoyed in the past.

History. Modern gymnastics developed in the early 1800's in Sweden, where a series of calisthenic exercises was devised. At about the same time gymnastic apparatus was also developed in Germany and Czechoslovakia. The popularity of the sport in the Scandinavian countries and then throughout Europe was marked by formation of gym-

GYMNASTICS COMPETITION

Photo by John Crosby, courtesy AAU

Larry Banner of the U.S. Olympic team performing a calisthenics exercise.

Annan Photo Features

Albert Asarian of the Soviet Union, an Olympic champion of the stationary rings.

nastic clubs and societies. Also in the 1800's American interest in the sport developed when German immigrants brought their *Turnverein* and Czechs their Sokol programs to the United States.

Gymnastics is now an important international sport. The International Federation of Gymnastics (FIG) conducts world championship contests every four years. The wide international interest in the sport is reflected in the standings of men's teams in the 1960 Olympics in Rome. The first six teams were, in this order: Japan, U.S.S.R., Italy, Czechoslovakia, United States, and Finland.

On another plane, gymnastics is recognized as effective in physical therapy and is called remedial or corrective gymnastics. Certain gymnastic or gymnastically derived exercises have proved of benefit in restoring or rehabilitating muscles atrophied or injured in wars and accidents or from diseases such as poliomyelitis and cerebral palsy.

Types and Conduct of Competition. Competition is divided between the sexes; men and women compete separately. There are seven categories of competition for men in determining international championships: calisthenics (floor exercises), vaulting horse (long horse), pommeled horse (side horse), stationary rings (which hang free but which the competitor should not allow to swing), parallel bars, horizontal bar, and all-around (rated on the basis of the combined score of the first six). Women's categories include vaulting horse, uneven parallel bars, balance beam, floor exercises to music, and all-around.

Each category includes compulsory and optional exercises. All contestants must perform the same series of compulsory exercises chosen for the meet; optional ones are originated by each contestant. Compulsory exercises are rated for perfection of execution, based on mechanical correctness, form, ease, grace, rhythm, balance, continuity, posture, timing, and the execution of each individual part to its highest potential. Optional exercises are judged for originality, difficulty, artistic grace, and integration of the parts. Great agility and strength are needed to perform gymnastic feats with what is considered artistry; if a competitor shows strain or uses strength crudely, the performance is downgraded.

A body of four judges, directed by a superior judge, evaluates the competition. The highest and lowest grades submitted by the judges are eliminated from consideration to insure fairness and avoid personal bias; the two scores remaining are averaged to produce the contestant's final mark. Team honors are won by adding the scores of team members. In determining individual honors, the meet's six highest-scoring contestants in each event compete again in one optional exercise. The scores thus earned are then added to the contestants' previous totals, and a winner is declared for each event.

The International Federation of Gymnastics (FIG) is the sport's ultimate ruling body. It sets the standards for international competition, guides individual nations in the establishment of their standards, supervises the technical

Attar Photographers

A gymnastics performer grasping the parallel bars in a handstand.

Annan Photo Features

The Soviet Union's Larisa Latynina on the uneven parallel bars during Olympic competition.

Attar Photographers

Donald Toney of the University of Massachusetts in a giant cart wheel from a vaulting horse.

aspects of gymnastics in the Olympics, and provides judges for the Olympics.

Competition within each country is administered by a national member body of the FIG, such as the Amateur Athletic Union (AAU) in the United States. Gymnastics is also practiced in schools and colleges, but these programs vary from the standards established for international competition. Compulsory exercises are omitted entirely in U.S. college programs, for example. Although the AAU is striving to bring scholastic gymnastics up to international competitive levels, it includes in its gymnastic program, as noninternational events, such traditional American activities as rope climbing, tumbling, rebound tumbling, and exercises on swinging rings.

Acrobatics v. Gymnastics. Gymnastics has also been linked with acrobatics, although the connoisseurs shudder at the linkage. An acrobat has been defined as one who performs gymnastic feats, but this is not quite correct. Where an acrobat must make even easy tricks look difficult, a gymnast must appear effortless. Where gymnasts have rigidly prescribed routines, acrobats are free to do as they please. Gymnastic training is ideal schooling for an acrobat, but the reverse is not true. And while gymnasts are on an amateur level, the acrobat is a professional.

H

HAGEN [*hä′gən*], **WALTER** (1892–1969), American professional golfer, born in Rochester, N.Y. From 1914, when he won the United States Open tournament, until the early 1930's, he was the game's leading player and did much to popularize golf through his outstanding play under pressure, his showmanship, and his sartorial splendor. He also won the U.S. Open in 1919; the Professional Golfers' Association tourneys in 1921, 1924, 1925, 1926, and 1927; and the British Open in 1922, 1924, 1928, and 1929. In 1926 he defeated the great U.S. amateur "Bobby" Jones, 12 and 11, in a special 72-hole match.

HALAS [*hăl′əs*], **GEORGE STANLEY** (1895–), American football coach, born in Chicago. As founder, owner, president, coach, and player, he made the Chicago Bears one of the outstanding teams in professional football. The Bears, founded in 1920 as the Decatur (Ill.) Staleys and coached by Halas from that date, won the National Football League championship in 1921, 1932, 1933, 1940, 1941, 1943, and 1946. He also played for the Bears, 1920–29. He introduced the modern T formation to the professional game, together with the study of motion pictures of games as a device for scouting and for corrective practice.

HANDBALL, competitive game played indoors or outdoors by two or four players. Four players compete in teams of two. The object is to hit a small ball, with the gloved hand, against a wall or walls so that the opponent or opponents are unable to return the hit before the ball has bounced twice on the floor. There are two versions of the sport: the four-wall (indoor) game, in which all walls and the ceiling are used; and the one-wall game, in which only the front wall is used.

The regulation four-wall court is 46 ft. long, 23 ft. wide, and 23 ft. high; the back wall is 10 ft. high. The service line is 18 ft. from the front wall; and the short line, over which the ball must pass after it hits the front wall on the serve, is 23 ft. from the front wall. The service zone is between the service line and the short line and 18 in. from the side walls. The regulation handball is made of black rubber; when inflated, it is approximately 1⅞ in. in diameter. It weighs about 2.3 oz.

Four-Wall Game. Play begins in the four-wall game with the server standing in the service zone. He must drop the ball and then hit it, as it rebounds from the floor, against the front wall. The ball must have enough force to bounce back from the front wall beyond the short line to the floor before hitting the ceiling, back wall, or side walls. If the ball does not clear the short line, it is called a "short." After two consecutive shorts the right to serve goes to the opposing side. The receiver may return the serve before it strikes the floor or on the first bounce. He may also hit a short on the first service. In all cases the return may strike the ceiling or side walls on its way to the front wall. Play continues until one player cannot make a return. If it is the server, he loses his serve; if it is the receiver, one point is given to the server. Twenty-one points constitute a game.

One-Wall Game. The court is smaller for the one-wall game, measuring 34 ft. long and 20 ft. wide; the front wall is 16 ft. high. The rules are similar except that only the front wall is used.

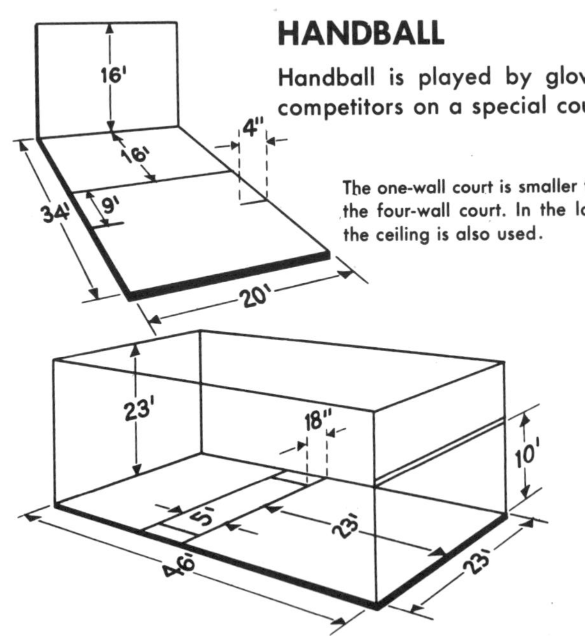

HANDBALL

Handball is played by glove[d] competitors on a special cou[rt]

The one-wall court is smaller th[an] the four-wall court. In the lat[ter] the ceiling is also used.

United Press International

Baseball players Jim Rivera (left) and Sammy Esposito play handball. The game is a good wintertime conditioner for such athletes.

Ireland is credited with originating handball in the 10th century. In the 1870's the game was brought to the United States, where it is under the jurisdiction of the Amateur Athletic Union (AAU).

HARVEY, DOUGLAS NORMAN ("DOUG") (1924–), Canadian hockey player, born in Montreal. He joined the Montreal Canadiens in 1947 and played with them through the season of 1960–61. During that period he was named the National Hockey League's outstanding defense man six times, and to the league all-star team nine times. He was playing coach of the New York Rangers of the NHL in 1961–62 and again won all-star rating.

HEFFELFINGER, WILLIAM WALTER ("PUDGE") (1867–1954), American football player, born in Minneapolis, Minn. While a member of Yale University's early teams, he became one of the great guards and blockers in the history of the sport. He won All-American rating in 1889, 1890, and 1891. From 1893 through 1895 he coached football teams at the University of California, Lehigh University, and the University of Minnesota.

HENIE [*hĕn'ē*], SONJA (1913–69), ice skater and actress, born in Oslo, Norway. She won the world figure-skating championship in 1927 and retained it during nine successive competitions. She won the women's figure-skating championship in three successive Olympic Games (1928, 1932, 1936). In 1936 she became a professional skater and went to the United States; in 1937 she entered films, and in 1938 she became star and coproducer of the first of many ice spectacles.

HIPPODROME [*hĭp'ə-drōm*], in ancient Greece, an oval track for chariot and horse racing, with tiered seats for spectators. A barrier down the middle divided the area in two, and the starting-finish end was slanted, so that the holders of inner positions would travel the same distance as those on the outer. The most famous Greek hippodrome was at Olympia. Later famous hippodromes at Constantinople, Antioch, and Alexandria were actually representatives of the Roman *circus*, translated as "hippodrome" in Greek. In modern times the word has been applied to variety theaters such as the old Hippodrome on Sixth Avenue in New York and the London Hippodrome.

HOGAN [*hō'gən*], BEN (1912–), American professional golfer, born in Dublin, Tex. One of the leading money-winning players in the history of the sport, he won the United States Open title in 1948, 1950, 1951, and 1953; the Professional Golfers' Association tourneys in 1946 and 1948; and the Masters and British Open tourneys in 1953. One of the game's outstanding tacticians, Hogan also won fame for his coolness under pressure and for his competitive spirit, which was instrumental in his comeback following injuries suffered in an automobile accident in 1949.

HORNSBY, ROGERS (1896–1963), American baseball player, born in Winters, Tex. Considered the greatest right-handed batter in the sport's history, he won seven National League batting championships between 1920 and 1928; compiled averages over .400 three times, including .424 in 1924, a modern major league record; and had a career average of .358, second only to Ty Cobb's .367. Between 1915 and 1937 he played, principally at second base, for St. Louis, New York, Boston, and Chicago of the National League and St. Louis of the American League. His blunt, outspoken manner made his career as manager a turbulent one. He managed St. Louis (1925–26); Boston (1928), Chicago (1930–32), and Cincinnati (1952–53) of the National League and St. Louis (1933–37, 1952) of the American. He was elected to the National Baseball Hall of Fame in 1942.

HORSEMANSHIP AND RIDING. Horsemanship, in the form of chariot driving, seems first to have appeared in Asia in Mesopotamia approximately 4,000 years ago. However, the Greeks apparently were the first mounted horsemen, with horse races recorded as part of the 33d Olympiad, which took place in Greece in 648 B.C. The earliest surviving work on horsemanship is the *Hippike* (c.365 B.C.) by Xenophon. Not until the Renaissance was the further development of horsemanship appreciably marked by the appearance of published material. At that time the Italians drew upon Xenophon and extended the latest thought throughout France and England.

Through the 17th, 18th, and 19th centuries the development of horsemanship passed for the most part to France and England. Early in the 20th century, however, Italy again became prominent in the field, with the appearance of Federico Caprilli, a young Italian cavalry officer. Departing radically from the highly formalized, rigidly controlled concept of horsemanship which had preceded him, Caprilli sought and formulated a system of training and riding aimed at offering the horse a degree of freedom and natural balance hitherto unknown. The basis of Caprilli's method in time became known as "the forward seat." This was a system of riding whereby the rider took the weight off the horse's hindquarters, while giving full freedom of action to its neck and head.

The new concept stirred an immediate controversy, meeting with stiff resistance from the proponents of the classical school, who defended stoutly the traditional idea of a rigidly controlled and collected mount. Vindication for Caprilli, however, came with the dazzling success of the Italian army show-jumping team at the Olympia International Horse Show in London in 1908.

Throughout the 1920's and into the 1930's, Caprilli's methods were pursued, chiefly through their interpretation by his principal pupil and advocate, Piero Santini. In 1937 Wilhelm Museler published *Riding Logic* in Germany, a work which further advanced and refined Caprilli's ideas. But Museler went far beyond Caprilli and Santini, stressing the importance to the rider of the proper use of the back and the back muscles as an aid in the control of the horse. The influence of this was extremely strong upon European riders in the post-World War II period and has been nowhere more evident than in the re-emergence of German show-jumping supremacy in recent years.

In the United States, horsemanship originated with the introduction of the modern horse to the North American continent by the Spanish Conquest in 1519. The influence of European thought upon American riding and training has, from the beginning, been profound. The basic elements of the most modern thought on the subject, as propounded early in the 20th century by Caprilli, soon appeared as the result of studies made by U.S. army officers at the cavalry schools of France, Italy, and Germany. However, with the dissolution of the cavalry arm in 1948, influence passed to civilian adherents of the sport. The for-

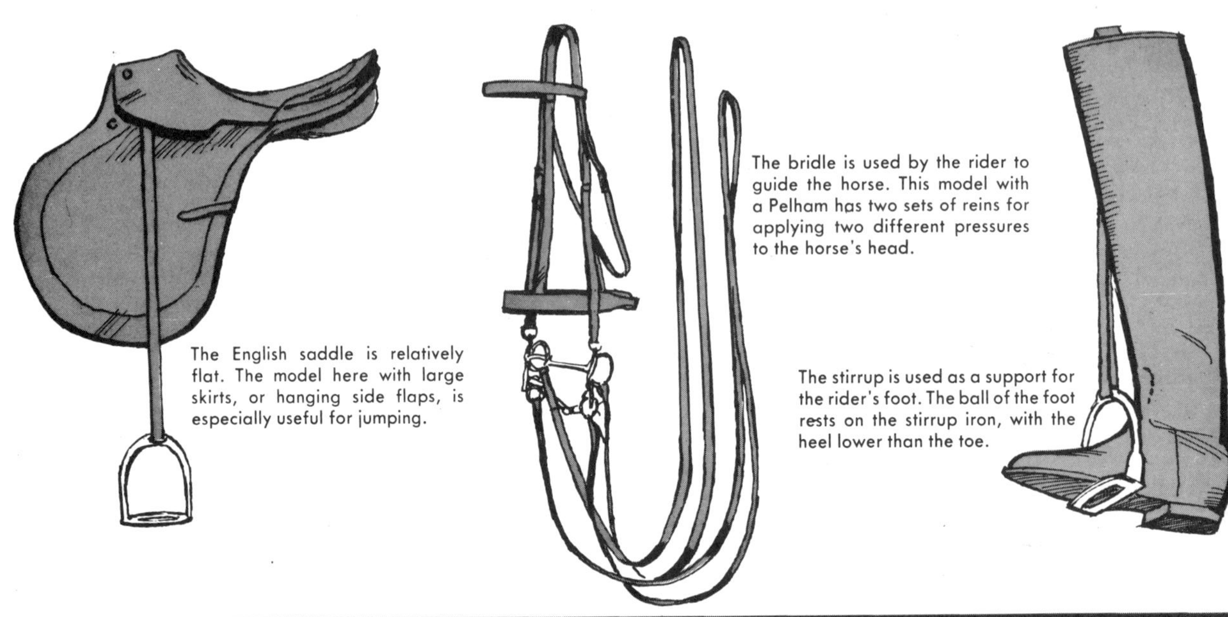

The English saddle is relatively flat. The model here with large skirts, or hanging side flaps, is especially useful for jumping.

The bridle is used by the rider to guide the horse. This model with a Pelham has two sets of reins for applying two different pressures to the horse's head.

The stirrup is used as a support for the rider's foot. The ball of the foot rests on the stirrup iron, with the heel lower than the toe.

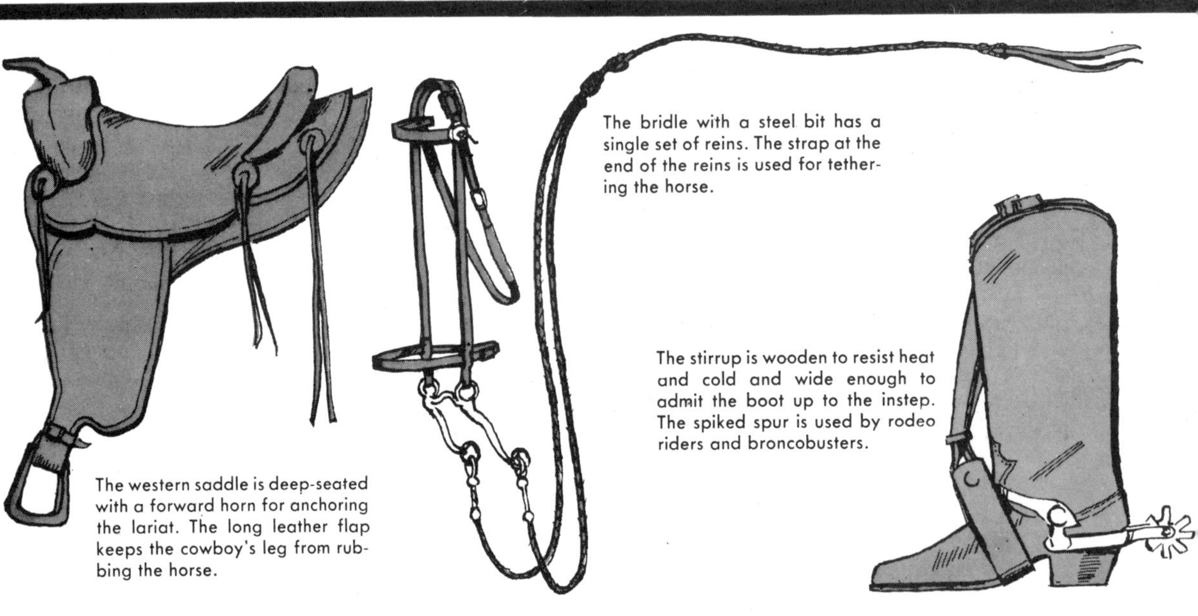

The western saddle is deep-seated with a forward horn for anchoring the lariat. The long leather flap keeps the cowboy's leg from rubbing the horse.

The bridle with a steel bit has a single set of reins. The strap at the end of the reins is used for tethering the horse.

The stirrup is wooden to resist heat and cold and wide enough to admit the boot up to the instep. The spiked spur is used by rodeo riders and broncobusters.

mation of the U.S. Equestrian Team in 1949, to fill the gap left by the disappearance of the U.S. army show-jumping team from international competition, has been of vital importance in continuing and broadening the European influence upon American riding. At the present time, leaders in international riding competition are the teams of Germany, Italy, the United States, and Great Britain, with France frequently a strong contender.

All styles of riding, whatever their ultimate purpose, depend upon basic principles remarkably unchanged since Xenophon first recorded his observations on horsemanship. All have in common certain fundamental requirements. Common to all is the necessity for a firm, deep seat which will afford the rider maximum security and comfort. In addition, there is also the necessity for an efficient method of control of the horse. This method, however pursued, must afford the rider a workable means of communicating his desires to his mount.

The instruments of communication with the horse are referred to as the aids and consist principally of the hands, legs, weight, voice, whip, and spur. The use of these aids in proper combination must be accompanied by a basic understanding of the psychological relationship between rider and mount. Since maximum pleasure in riding derives from the rider's sense of security, his control of the horse, and his ability to manage his mount comfortably and efficiently, the beginner is well advised to seek competent instruction. As in most sports, performance is based

Ray Woolfe, Jr.—Alpha

ENGLISH-STYLE HORSEMANSHIP
This style is used by the majority of riders, including participants in shows, hunts, and races, as well as cavalrymen and pleasure riders. Horsemen don various traditional outfits on different occasions. A gentleman of the hunt, illustrated here, may wear a tweed riding coat, tan riding breeches, black boots, bowler hat, and white stock tie.

Annan Photo Features

WESTERN-STYLE HORSEMANSHIP
This horsemanship style was developed by cowboys in the American West to fulfill the requirements of their cattle-raising tasks. Typical attire for the rider, as illustrated, is heavy-duty work clothes — including blue jeans, matching jacket, solid colored or checked shirt—and neckerchief, ten-gallon felt hat, and leather boots with high heels.

upon a solid foundation of basic principles well understood and applied.

HORSE RACING. Although called the Sport of Kings, it is also the public's sport, and, next to soccer, possibly the most universal sport in the world. The U. S. citizen tends to get as excited about the Kentucky Derby as he does about baseball's World Series. There are few things that make a Briton more proud than a chance to stand in the Royal Box at Ascot, or to be numbered among the thousands watching the Grand National. The yearly running of the Melbourne Cup is a continental holiday in Australia, royalty has traveled across the sea to watch Canada's Queen's Plate, and the Arc de Triomphe is a high point of the social season in France.

Once the horse had been developed to the point where it could be ridden, racing was not far distant. At first, the horse was ridden only by kings and other leaders, but soon others gained the distinction of owning horses. Rivalry entered the picture, and races to determine the speediest horse became prevalent. Crossbreeding and mating horses became a hobby of the aristocratic and wealthy, especially in England. The owning of lithe and supple horses with an abundance of speed became the fashion.

Early in the 18th century in England it was decided that only the records of the horses that stemmed from the sires Matchem, Herod, and Eclipse would be preserved. Because of their racing abilities, these three stallions were believed to have royal blood. When their ancestry was traced it was found that Matchem, foaled in 1748, descended from Godolphin's Arabian. Herod, foaled in 1758, came from Byerly's Turkish stallion known as the Turk. Eclipse, born in 1764, the year of a total eclipse, was traced to Darley's Arabian. It was agreed that all three of the forefathers were thoroughly bred, hence the name of thoroughbred. Thus, every thoroughbred is descended directly in his male line from one of these famous horses.

At first there were no race tracks. The owners merely measured off four miles—possibly because this was the distance of the Olympic chariot races—and competed in matched races for personal satisfaction and whatever side bets that were arranged. In 1174 the first known race track was established. Located in London, it was known as the Smithfield track. In 1512 the Chester Fair, also in England, offered a wooden ball carrying a flower wreath to the winner. It was the first of racing's trophies.

The prize had little value, and soon the various fairs, in an effort to outdo each other, were offering silver balls. In 1609, again at Chester, the sheriff ordered a silversmith to fashion a silver ball of rare beauty. He rejected the first two of the artist's efforts as unworthy, but did accept the third. Now what was to be done with the two rejected balls? Finally, he decided to give the most beautiful ball to the owner of the winning horse, the second

Left, horses break from the starting gate in a race at Garden State Race Track, Camden, N.J. The gate, used at all major U.S. tracks, encloses each horse in a separate stall to facilitate alignment. An elecric mechanism opens the gates simultaneously so that the horses can start together.
(BURT GLINN—MAGNUM)

most beautiful to the second-place owner, and the third most beautiful to the owner of the third-place horse. Thus was established racing's traditional one, two, three of finish. The Sport of Kings now had a well-developed format.

The United States

We have no definite information about the first actual race in the United States. However, it is known that Col. Richard Nicolls, first English governor of New York arrived in 1664, and in Feb., 1665, announced a series of races for Hempstead, Long Island. He called the site Newmarket in honor of a similar establishment in England, but Yale University is custodian of a silver dish which is inscribed that it was "wunn at hanstead planes, 1668." Capt. Sylvester Salisbury, a British army officer, is believed to have been the winning owner of the dish and a huge sports and recreational complex on Long Island known as the Salisbury Club commemorates his triumph.

From the meager beginnings at Hempstead, racing has grown until in 1966 it was rated as a $60,000,000,000 industry by the Thoroughbred Racing Association. The TRA survey of 1966 indicates that in that year 63,689,528 patrons paid their way into race tracks in the 29 states where the sport and its attendant betting is legalized. The fans wagered $4,685,129,670. In turn, the same states were enriched $388,452,125 by a tax on the betting. Additional millions of revenue came from such sources as licenses, fees, and taxes on real estate and other property holdings.

After its hesitant start in New York, racing spread quickly. Virginia had five tracks in operation during the 1680's. That state dominated the young country's racing for the next century, but after the American Revolution Kentucky moved to the front. In many ways the Blue Grass state still maintains this dominant role. Louisville's Churchill Downs annually is the scene of the Kentucky Derby, the most glamorous race of the United States. Many of the country's 1,700 breeding farms are centered around Lexington because of the lush, lime-rich grasses. Modern feeding methods also have raised breeding farms in California, Florida, Virginia, Maryland, and New York to a par with those in Kentucky.

Racing was such a passion in Lexington that owners could not wait for the construction of a park, and raced their horses along what is now South Broadway with such fury that residents complained. The Town Trustees in 1793 made the competition illegal. Not until four years later was Williams Race Track, Kentucky's first, built. It was too small by 1828, and had to be replaced.

Blooded breeding stock, both sires and dams, had been imported from England from the earliest days. Bulle Rock, who arrived in 1730, is honored by many racing historians as the first thoroughbred stallion to stand in the United States. Bay Bolton, who reached the United States in 1738 or 1739, is nominated as the first thoroughbred mare to cross the Atlantic. Both these claims are denied by Southern race followers, who insist that it was not until 1750, when Lord Baltimore presented a stallion named Sparks to Samuel Ogle, governor of Maryland, that the first thoroughbred stallion was imported.

These regional views and debates led to a series of four North-South match races, all held on Long Island, that highlighted racing until it went into decline during the Civil War. The Southern representatives won three of the four encounters, and enriched their followers and backers by an estimated $2,000,000.

Racing, however, did not wait for the Civil War to end. In 1864 John Morrissey, a former bare-knuckle prize fighter who had turned to politics, held a race meeting in Saratoga, N. Y., during the month of August. Prior to that time race meetings lasted only a few days, as is still the vogue in most parts of the world. But Morrissey prevailed upon the wealthy owners, who made Saratoga a health mecca each August, to bring along their thoroughbreds and to while away the long, hot afternoons with a race program each day. The idea was an immediate success, and today U. S. racing is characterized by long seasons. New York City, for instance, begins its season in March and continues until December. California has virtually all-year racing, with San Francisco and Los Angeles alternating. Miami begins its program in November and runs through to mid-April. Six-week meetings have been held in New Jersey, Delaware, Louisiana, and Arkansas.

The aristocratic Travers family of New York City was widely identified with racing in Morrissey's time. To assure their appearance at Saratoga he named his first stake race after the family. The Travers, first raced in 1864, is still run annually and is the oldest stakes race in the country. Not until 1875 was the Kentucky Derby first held.

A horse normally is at his racing peak during his third year, and the fields in the Derby, Preakness, and Belmont are restricted to that age. These three races make up the triple crown, the sport's most sought after distinction. The Belmont Stakes, since 1963 run at Aqueduct in New

Horses are photographed at the finish wire to determine which reached it first. Shown is a two-horse photo finish at the Aqueduct Race Track, N.Y. (THE NEW YORK RACING ASSN., INC.)

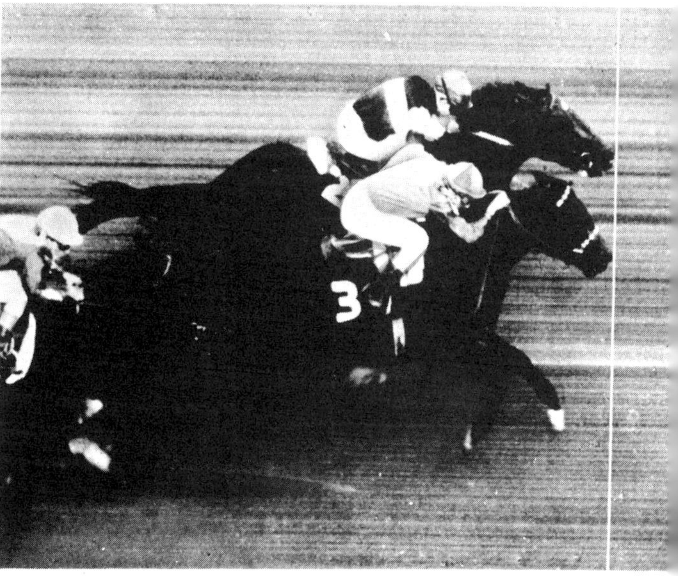

York City, was begun in 1867; the Preakness Stakes at Pimlico, Baltimore, in 1873; and the Derby in 1875. It was not until 1919 that all three were won by the same horse, Sir Barton. Since then only seven others have accomplished the same feat: Gallant Fox in 1930; Omaha, a son of Gallant Fox, in 1935; War Admiral in 1937; Whirlaway in 1941; Count Fleet in 1943; Assault in 1946; and Citation in 1948.

The fallacy of trying to determine the greatest thoroughbred ever to have raced in the United States by using the amount of money won as the measuring stick can be shown by the purses of these three stakes. Sir Barton picked up a total of $57,275 for his trio of triumphs in 1919. A triumph in each of the three in 1967 would approximate $400,000. All three are stakes races, a term applied to events in which owners of the horses pay an original entry fee and another the day before the race. These fees are earmarked for the race, plus an additional sum put up by the sponsoring track. The amount then is divided according to a set formula. Rarely are there two stakes races on one program, the others being overnight affairs in which the owners designate their probable starters 24 hours before a race and the track sets up a purse for distribution. The track gets its money by taking a percentage of the betting handle.

Famous Horses. Just which is the greatest thoroughbred ever to race in America? The arguments to name any specific horse would be endless. On the basis that a great horse is one who does everything asked of him on a race track, the greatest of all could be Kelso, named Horse of the Year five consecutive times from 1960 to 1964. The brown, gelded great grandson of Man o' War, owned by Mrs. Richard C. DuPont, won 39 of 63 starts and amassed winnings of $1,977,896 before being retired. Kelso's bank account is the largest ever collected by a horse.

The sentimental favorite probably would be Man o' War, a chestnut horse foaled in 1917 and winner of 20 races in 21 starts. The lone defeat was by Upset in the 1919 Sanford Memorial stakes at Saratoga. Man o' War, who lived to be 30 years of age, is buried near Lexington, Ky., and is one of few animals to have a monument above his grave. He raced in the colors of the Glen Riddle Farms.

Another thoroughbred to gain the affection of many was Alfred G. Vanderbilt's Native Dancer. This gray beauty's only defeat during a career from 1952 through 1954 was to Dark Star in the 1953 Kentucky Derby. Another of the same era was Nashua, owned by Belair Stud and winner of 22 of 30 starts in a three-year career.

Further back is Sysonby, a bay foaled in 1902, who started only 15 times in a two-year span that ended in 1905 but who won 14 of the races and is rated by many as the fastest horse ever on a U. S. track. Colin, a brown horse who followed Sysonby by three years, captured all 15 of his races.

In contrast to the abbreviated racing careers of both Colin and Sysonby is that of Exterminator, who began at the age of 2 and raced until 9 and won 50 of 100 official starts. He was the winner of the 1918 Kentucky Derby.

The list of candidates also must include Whirlaway and Citation, both triple crown winners. Each was for a time the all-time money-winning horse. Citation's career was interrupted as a four-year-old, but he returned in 1950 and went on to win almost $250,000 in that season and the next. Equipoise, Count Fleet, Swaps, Tom Fool, Buckpasser, Sarazen, Roamer, Hindoo, Domino and Top Flight, a filly, must also be mentioned. Regret is the only filly to win the Kentucky Derby. She triumphed in 1915.

Jockeys. In the early days of racing, the owner usually rode his own steed in any contest involving wagering. As the sport intensified, a rider whose weight would be no burden was sought out. Many of the earliest riders were slaves or serfs. As time went on, men who weighed about 100 lbs. became jockeys-for-hire. One of the first great ones was Tod Sloan, who started his career in the United States and climaxed it with sensational riding in England. Because of his stubby stature, he used exceptionally short stirrups and rode high on the animal's neck. This became known as the monkey crouch in England, and soon was adopted everywhere.

Many regard Isaac Murphy, a Negro, as the greatest of all jockeys. He was dominant between 1880 and 1890 when he won 44% of his races. His record of three Kentucky Derby victories held until 1948. Murphy was especially effective with Salvator and Freeland, two exceptional thoroughbreds of the era. Oliver Lewis, another Negro jockey, won the first running of the Derby aboard Aristides in 1875. Other outstanding early riders were Ed (Snapper) Garrison, famous for his furious finishes; Jimmy McLaughlin, a remarkable judge of a horse's pace; Walter Miller, who rode 388 winners in 1906; and Roscoe Goose, Mark Garner, Laverne Fator, and Frank Robinson.

In the years surrounding World War II, the names of Earl Sande, Jackie Westrope, Basil James, Sonny Workman, Charles Kurtsinger, Donald Meade, and George (The Iceman) Woolf were heard most frequently. Since then Eddie Arcaro, whose 4,779 winners during a 31-year career in the saddle won purses worth $30,039,543; Johnny Longden, the Canadian-born rider whose 6,032 winners is a world's record; William Shoemaker, the biggest threat to Longden's record; and Ted Atkinson, Eric Guerin, and Steve Brooks have been rated among the best.

In recent years, riders from Latin America have invaded the ranks. The top three 1966 riders in North American jockey circles were Avelino Gómez, a Cuban who did most of his riding in Canada; Jorge Velásquez of Panama; and Braulio Baeza, another Panamanian whose 298 winners won purses totalling $2,951,022, a record sum for a single year.

Normally, a jockey contracts to ride for a major owner. As such, he is paid a basic salary plus 10% of all purses won. Arcaro thus earned at least $3,003,954 during his career, while Baeza's pay in 1966 was $295,102.20. Arcaro, helped to the headlines by riding for Calumet Farms, guided Whirlaway in 1941 and Citation in 1948 to triumphs in the Kentucky Derby, Preakness, and Belmont Stakes. Longden was astride Count Fleet when that thoroughbred triumphed in the 1943 triple crown.

Greatest of the European riders probably was Sir Gordon Richards, knighted by Queen Elizabeth II in 1953. He retired in 1954 with 4,870 winners, a world's record that stood until surpassed by Longden on Sept. 3, 1956. Sir Gordon celebrated his knighthood the day after

Horse and jockey clear a hedge in the Grand National at Aintree, England. The world's most famous steeplechase, it covers almost 4½ mi. and has 30 hazardous jumps. (BIRNBACK PUBLISHING SERVICE)

he was elevated by winning the 1953 Epsom Derby for the first time in 28 years of trying.

Trainers. Another vital individual in the success of any thoroughbred is the trainer, usually a person who has spent a lifetime with horses and knows their every need. Among the most famous of these were Ben A. Jones and his son Horace (Jimmy) Jones, who prepared the Calumet Farms representatives for 20 years starting in 1939. The elder Jones saddled six Kentucky Derby winners, starting with Lawrin in 1938. The most successful, in point of triumphs, is Hirsch Jacobs, who started in 1926 and by 1967 had seen more than 22,000 of his charges win.

Another famed trainer was James (Sunny Jim) Fitzsimmons, a former jockey, who supervised the conditioning of the Belair Stud runners and whose Gallant Fox and Omaha won the triple crown. Perhaps the best horse he handled was Nashua. Edward Neloy established a record in 1966 when the Phipps family string in his care won 41 stakes races in a single year. Their earnings were $2,198,370. In all, the Phipps runners banked $2,456,250, the first time any trainer had won more than $2 million in one season.

Other famous trainers were Louis Feustel, who handled Man o' War; Max Hirsch, whose best was Assault; Sam Hildreth; Willie Molter; James Rowe, Sr. and Jr.; John Gaver; Preston Burch; H. J. (Derby Dick) Thompson; Phil Bieber; William F. Mulholland; W. C. (Bill) Winfrey, who prepared Native Dancer; Meshach Tenney; and Jack Price, the owner-trainer of Carry Back.

Outside the United States

England is probably the most race-minded country apart from the United States. The British, who did so much to develop racing in North America, spread the sport to all parts of their vast colonial empire. England's Derby and Grand National have been copied everywhere, and Ascot week marks the height of the British summer social season.

France and Italy have much less racing than England but it all is of the highest order. Italy has produced such great winners and stallions as Nearco, Niccolo Dell'Arca, and Ribot. Just prior to World War II, France was producing horses that won in all parts of the world, especially in the great English classics. The French government controls the breeding industry. Much of the French racing is centered in the beautiful Longchamp course near Paris.

Ireland's breeding stock is of the very best, but the Irish are most famous for having brought the Sweepstakes to the fore. In a Sweepstakes, millions of dollars' worth of tickets are sold. Those who hold tickets on the winning horse get huge rewards, but thousands of dollars also go to charity.

Canada, handicapped by adverse climatic conditions for the breeding and development of thoroughbreds, holds various meetings in the major cities along the U. S. border. Canada's most famous contribution was Northern Dancer, owned and bred by E. P. Taylor, who won the 1964 Kentucky Derby. Among the standardbreds Canada has provided the gelded pacer Winnipeg, one-time holder of the world's record for altered horses over a mile. Included among the many Grand Circuit stars were Lee Hanover, who trotted a mile in 2 min. flat, and Armbro Flight, one of the world's best trotters in the late 1960's. Canada's most glamorous race is the Queen's Plate, started in 1860, 15 years before the Kentucky Derby.

Horse racing prevails throughout Latin America, with Argentina leading the parade both in races and breeding stock. The Argentine polo pony is favored in all parts of the world. Brazil, Uruguay, Paraguay, Chile, and Peru all have outstanding racing programs, and Chile ranks next to Argentina in blood stock. The racing plants at Buenos Aires, Santiago, Rio de Janeiro, and São Paulo are sumptuous.

Some of the world's greatest race horses have been produced in Australia and New Zealand. Phar Lap, the wonderful gelding whose death shortly after his arrival in the United States almost led to an international incident, was foaled in New Zealand, as were Carbine and Cardigan Bay. Carbine added to his fame as a stud in both Australia and England, while Cardigan Bay was one of the favorites in the pacing world during the middle 1960's.

In 1930 Phar Lap won the Melbourne Cup, Australia's major racing event.

Steeplechase

Steeplechasing, or racing over jumps, can be traced to the battlefield and the hunt, where often it was necessary for a horse and rider to clear fences, streams, and boulders in great haste. Steeplechasing derives its name from the time when the hunters raced home from the chase to an agreed point, usually the village church whose steeple could be seen for miles around in all directions. The distances varied, seldom less than 4 mi. and rarely more than 20, and any short cut that would save both time and distance was used.

The most famed attraction in this phase of racing is the Grand National, contested annually since 1839 over the Aintree course outside of Liverpool, England. Two trips around this irregularly shaped triangle makes the distance 4 mi., 856 yd. There are a total of 30 jumps or brooks and some, such as Becher's Brook, are so severe that their names have become a part of the nonracing language to identify a hazard. The U. S. counterpart is the American Grand National, normally held at Belmont Park, N. Y. The only horse to have won both was Battleship, a U. S. thoroughbred who won at Belmont in 1934 while carrying 147 lb. and at Aintree in 1938 while laden with 160 lb.

To this day, many steeplechase riders are amateurs rather than professional jockeys. The weights that the horses carry, to equalize the chance for winning, are much greater than those carried by horses who race on flat tracks. George H. (Pete) Bostwick of Westbury, N. Y., is rated among the greatest amateur riders of all time.

Harness (Standardbred) Racing

Harness racing, in which the horse pulls a vehicle and driver, has made great strides in popularity since World War II. Prior to that time, many of the horses used were farm animals whose major duties were other than racing. But with the advent of night racing on lighted tracks, the sport has made dramatic progress.

Harness horses have either of two gaits, the pace or the trot. In pacing, the horse moves along by thrusting out his right foreleg and his right rear leg at the same time, following with his left foreleg and his left rear leg. In trotting, the horse steps along with the right foreleg and the left rear leg working in unison, as do his left foreleg and his right rear.

Although virtually all the early trotting and pacing records were set under saddle, competition now is restricted to the pulling of the lightweight vehicle known as the sulky. Originally, the sulky was a four-wheeled wagon or family carriage, and the race course a street or a stretch of road. After 1891 two low wheels, separated by an axle on which the driver sits, became the style. The wheels have pneumatic tires and the shafts are fastened to the horse by a light harness. Weight of the equipment has been cut to about 25 lb. This, plus the driver's weight, gives the harness horse a burden of about 200 lb. Yet, topflight trotters and pacers step a mile in 2 min. or less. The average for the same distance by thoroughbreds, whose load of jockey and saddle averages about 120 lb. and rarely exceeds 130, is 1 min. 38 sec.

Harness horses are known as standardbreds but many of them have the same family tree as the thoroughbreds. Generally, the harness horse is slightly smaller than the thoroughbred, a bit heavier and far more sturdy. When the standardbred was used under saddle, the pace was the preferred gait. The trotter, however, was the choice when it came to hauling the family carriage, because of the pacer's rolling style. On the race track one gait is as good as the other when it comes to speed.

The sport was brought to the United States in the 18th century and centered in Rhode Island for many years. Messenger, a gray stallion imported from England as a thoroughbred in 1788 when he was eight years old, generally is regarded as the father of harness racing in North America, although he could neither trot nor pace. He

Right, harness racing at Yonkers Raceway, in New York. The horse, using the trotting gait, moves in unison its left foreleg and right hindleg, and then the other two legs. The driver rides in a light two-wheeled carriage, or sulky. (YONKERS RACEWAY)

Rider holds in her teeth the blue ribbon won by her mount at the National Horse Show of America. (WIDE WORLD)

Horse and rider clear a hurdle in the National Horse Show of America at Madison Square Garden, N.Y. (WIDE WORLD)

produced many progeny, some of which became famous as runners while others did equally well as trotters and pacers. Four of his sons—Wintrop's Messenger, Bishop's Hambletonian, Mambrino, and Coriander—sired outstanding harness horses. His grandson, Rysdyk's Hambletonian, also known as Hambletonian X, born in 1849, ultimately became the foundation of the sport. A survey made in 1950 showed that 90% of all harness racing champions are descended from the Rysdyk stallion, with at least 75% claiming this relationship through their fathers. The Hambletonian, most famous event in trotting, is named for him. It has been held at various sites but has been a fixture at Du Quoin, Ill., since 1957.

Records have been kept since 1845 when Lady Suffolk, an outstanding mare, trotted a mile in 2 min. 29.5 sec. and set what was accepted as the world's record. In the years that have followed it has been lowered through the efforts of such horses as Flora Temple, Dexter, Goldsmith's Maid, The Abbott, Peter Manning, and Greyhound, regarded by many as the greatest trotter of all. His mile record of 1 min. 55.25 sec. was set in 1938, and still stood in 1967. Since 1945 the stars have been Speedy Scott, Ayres, Sumac Lad, Armbro Flight of Canada, and Roquetine of France.

Pacing, for which records have been kept since 1844, has Aggie Down as its first world record holder of the mile with a time of 2 min. 29 sec. The time has been cut to 1 min. 54.8 sec. through the efforts of Pocahontas, Sleepy George, Single G, Little Brown Jug, Winnipeg of Canada, Direct, and the fabulous Dan Patch, one of the most exploited and beloved horses of all time. Since 1940 Bret Hanover, Romeo Hanover, Bullet Hanover, Adious Butler, Overtrick, and Cardigan Bay, a product of New Zealand, have dominated.

For many years harness racing emphasized distance rather than speed. The first trotting race on record was held in Hunting Park in Philadelphia in 1829 with Gallant and Whalebone, two grandsons of Messenger, as the contestants. The winner would be the horse which triumphed in three of the five heats, each heat to be 4 mi. Gallant won three of the first four heats and was declared the winner. The two trotters each had stepped 16 mi. during the long afternoon.

Today the emphasis is on speed. Most races consist of one heat with the distance usually a mile. What this change has done to excite interest can be shown by the growth of the sport. Roosevelt Raceway of Westbury, N. Y., is generally credited with popularizing night races, although afterdark events had been held as early as 1900 in Boston. When Roosevelt held a 27-night inaugural program in 1940, slightly fewer than 75,000 patrons attended and their betting for the entire four weeks came to $1,200,086. But on Aug. 20, 1960, Roosevelt Raceway had a single night's attendance of 51,861 and on Nov. 30, 1962, the patrons at Yonkers Raceway, another New York City suburban track, bet $3,191,020.

In addition to the change to speed, the introduction of the mobile starting gate in 1946 helped spur harness racing into popularity. The fixed starting gates that are universal on thoroughbred tracks are impossible to use with sulkies. Prior to 1946, the standardbreds started far up the track and tried to cross the starting line in a straight row. Often this attempt failed and the contestants had to be recalled. One race established a record with 18 recalls in one hour. When Steve Phillips came to Roosevelt Raceway in 1940 he interested the officials in the idea of two huge folding steel arms fastened to the rear of an automobile. The noses of the horses were close to the extended arms as they sped over the start in a line. The arms folded away as the automobile sped out of the path of the horses. Now a recall is a novelty, and almost all races start on time.

At one time many of the owners did their own driving, but now professionals do it. Among the first of these was the famed Ed (Pops) Geers, who revived the interest in pacers in the early 1900's. Others of that era included Walter Cox; Tom Berry; William Caton, who gained distinction by going to Russia and becoming the regular driver for the Czar; Sep F. Palin; Fred Eagan; Ben White; Dr. H. M. Parshall; and Harry Thomas. Modern drivers include Stanley Dancer, William Haughton, George Sholty, Delmer Insko, John Chapman, Frank Ervin, Joe O'Brien, Ralph Baldwin, John Simpson, Robert Farrington, and Delvin Miller.

With the increase of popularity in harness racing came the breeding farm. There is at least one in every state of the United States. The three most famous are the Hanover Shoe Farms, Hanover, Pa., and Walnut Hall Farm and Castleton Farm, both at Lexington, Ky. Untried yearlings can cost as much as $125,000, but the rewards also are great. By 1967 there were half a dozen races in which the purse exceeded $150,000. The retired Sumac Lad was the top money winner among the trotters with $885,000, while Bret Hanover, also retired, was the richest of the pacers with $922,616.

Various area commissions combined in 1938 to form the United States Trotting Association, which has been in control of all phases of harness racing since then. It has its headquarters in Columbus, Ohio.

See also PARI-MUTUEL; articles on famous horses, jockeys, and trainers.

HORSE SHOWS. Showing horses stems from ancient times, the oldest existing records dating from the Olympic games of the 8th century B.C. The horse show, as it exists currently, is a direct descendant of the agricultural shows and horsefairs of England but evolved in the early 19th century in somewhat different form. Later, as mechanically driven vehicles replaced horsedrawn ones, the number of draft and coach horses was greatly diminished. So-called pleasure horses, either for riding or driving, gradually came to constitute the vast majority of the entries in such shows.

Present-day Extent. Horse shows were mainly confined to the East coast until the 20th century; now they flourish throughout every state and in Canada. The tremendous increase in their popularity is traceable to the shift of urban population to the suburbs, the ease with which exhibitors can move their horses by motorized transport, the social aspect (many shows are held for charity in conjunction with fairs), and the growth in the number of participants, especially among children. In the early 1960's the total number of horses in the United States was decreasing, but the number of horses used for riding or driving was increasing.

Although no exact figure on the number of shows held annually is available, the number is growing rapidly. The American Horse Shows Association, a national organization founded in 1917, lists over 500 shows conducted by its members (perhaps one-fifth of all the shows held) and more than 7,000 individual members. During a single year in the 1960's more than $1,500,000 in prize money was awarded at shows recognized by the association. Aside from encouraging interest in the sport in general and in international competitions in particular, the organization makes and enforces rules of competition, sets standards for the various divisions of competition, settles disputes, assigns show dates, licenses judges, and presents awards to the horses that score the most points in each division in recognized shows during the year. It also rates shows (as A, B, or C events) according to the amount of money awarded and the types of classes held in each division. Many shows conducted by groups that are not members of the association have adopted its rules and norms, thus helping to standardize competition throughout the United States.

Types of Shows. Participants in horse shows include those wishing to sell horses or to improve the value of their breeding stock and those who simply enjoy the sport. Shows range from half-day gymkhanas to national competitions lasting a week or more. Shows such as the American Royal (Kansas City, Mo.), Devon (Devon, Pa.), Royal Agricultural Winter Fair (Toronto, Canada), Pennsylvania National (Harrisburg), Washington International (Washington, D.C.), and the National (New York City) attract exhibitors throughout North and South America. The three last-named shows hold international jumping competitions.

The large shows hold classes in many or all of the recognized divisions of competition. The majority of shows, however, last for one or two days, are held outdoors, and schedule classes only for the types of horses predominant in the area. Hunter trials, with courses particularly suitable to hunters, are popular in fox-hunting districts and are usually associated with the local hunt club. Combined training events, lasting from one to three days and designed to test the versatility, endurance, and soundness of horses, are gaining many supporters.

How Horses Are Judged. Horses are judged on a combination of the following qualifications: appointments (equipment), brilliance, color, conformation (build), handiness, manners, performance, presence, quality, soundness, speed, substance (strength), suitability (of purpose), uniformity (of group), and way of going. For example, a conformation hunter is judged on conformation, performance, manners, and way of going; a cutting horse on cattle work (performance in such tasks as separating a given cow from a herd), rein (handiness), conformation, manners, and appointments; an open jumper on performance and sometimes on speed.

Divisions of Competition. The following divisions among horses and events are recognized by the American Horse Shows Association: Arabian, Combined Training Events, Dressage, Hunting, Saddle and Stock-seat Equitation, Hackney, Harness Pony, Hunter, Jumper, Junior, Morgan, Palomino, Parade Horse, Polo, Roadster, Saddle Horse, Shetland, Walking Horse, Welsh, and Western.

HORSESHOE PITCHING, game of ancient origin, played by two or four players, in which horseshoes are thrown toward an iron stake at each end of a court. The official horseshoe is a U-shaped plate of iron or steel not longer than 7½ in., wider than 7 in., or heavier than 2½ lb. The tips of the open end of the shoe are flanged to form heel calks. The court is 50 ft. long and 10 ft. wide. Two iron stakes are placed 40 ft. apart; they project 12 in. above

A world champion's 1¾-turn grip.

National Horseshoe Pitchers' Assn. of America

HORSESHOE PITCHING

Spinning the horseshoe in the air helps attain greater accuracy. The grip determines the amount of spin.

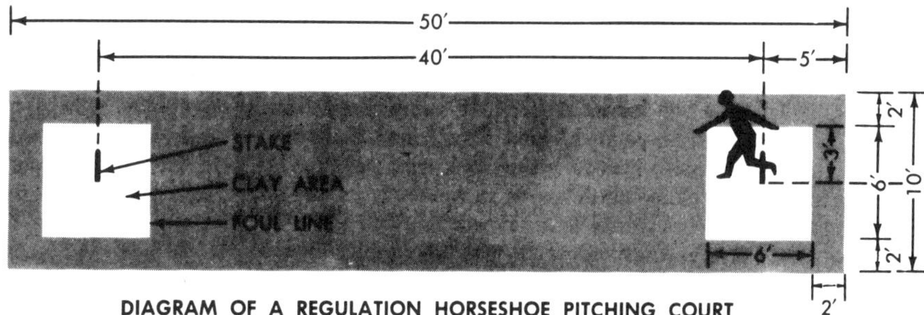

DIAGRAM OF A REGULATION HORSESHOE PITCHING COURT

the ground and have a 3 in. forward tilt. In women's competition the stakes are 30 ft. apart. Each stake is centered in a box that measures 6 ft. on all sides and projects 1 in. above the ground. The box is filled with clay to a depth of 6 in., and the clay is usually dampened for play.

The object of the game is to pitch the horseshoes so that they encircle the stake or land closer to the stake than the opponents'. When a horseshoe encircles the stake far enough to allow the touching of both heel calks with a ruler (without touching the stake), it is called a ringer.

Play begins (in singles competition) with one contestant pitching two horseshoes toward the far stake; then his opponent follows suit. When pitching, the players must stand within the boxed area and at least 18 in. from the stake and must remain there until the shoe has landed. The opponent must remain outside and to the rear of the box until the other player has completed his turn. When each player has thrown two horseshoes, an inning is completed; they then go to the opposite end of the court and tally the score. A ringer counts three points, and a shoe closer to the stake than an opponent's counts one point. Ties have no scoring value for either player. Twenty-one points usually constitute a game, but in tournaments play is for 50 points. In doubles play, two opponents are at one stake, while their partners pitch from the opposite stake.

The National Horseshoe Pitchers' Association of America and the Amateur Athletic Union of the United States publish rules for the sport.

Quoits, a game with basically similar rules, is played with either metal or (more recently) rubber ring-shaped objects instead of horseshoes.

HOWE, GORDON ("GORDIE") (1928–), Canadian hockey player, born in Floral, Saskatchewan. He began his brilliant career as a right wing with the Detroit Red Wings of the National Hockey League in 1946. By the end of the 1962–63 season he had won the Hart Trophy (awarded annually to the league's most valuable player) six times, a record feat; had been named to the league all-star teams eight seasons; and had won league scoring titles during six seasons. When he scored his 627th goal, during the 1964–65 season, he established a new career scoring record in NHL play.

HUBBELL [*hŭb'əl*], **CARL OWEN** (1903–), American baseball player, born in Carthage, Mo. A left-handed pitcher for New York of the National League, 1928–43, he was known as the "Meal Ticket" because of his consistently brilliant performance. Employing the screwball as his most effective pitch, he won 253 games, including 24 in succession during 1936–37. In the 1934 All-Star game, Hubbell struck out Babe Ruth, Lou Gehrig, Jimmy Foxx, Al Simmons, and Joe Cronin in succession. He was named the league's most valuable player in 1933 and 1936, and was elected to the National Baseball Hall of Fame in 1947.

HULL, ROBERT MARVIN ("BOBBY") (1939–), Canadian hockey player, born in Point Anne, Ontario. One of the most precocious players in the sport's history, he was the leading scorer of the National Hockey League at the age of 21; during that season (1959–60), he scored 81 points. A year later he had scored more than 100 goals during his brief career with the Chicago Black Hawks, whom he had joined in 1957. A left wing and one of the strongest men in hockey, he was named to the NHL all-star team during the seasons of 1959–60 and 1961–62. In the 1965–66 season he established NHL records for goals (54), points (97), and powerplay goals (22).

HUNTING, in modern usage, is the chase and capture or killing of wild animals for food and for sport. Though men of past ages lived mostly by the game they could kill, today hunting in the civilized portions of the world and especially in North America is mostly for sporting purposes—for the thrill of pursuit and the deep, age-old satisfaction of outwitting a cunning wild creature in its own element.

In the woods and fields of North America an army of conservation specialists has dedicated itself to the preservation of all wild species. Carefully regulated game laws apportion the amount of game that may be legally killed and insure the perpetuation of all species. The necessity of this is apparent from the growing number of hunters. Between 1940 and 1960 the population of the United States, for example, increased by approximately one-third; the number of hunters by one-half. Every fall—when most hunting seasons are at their peak—more than 15,000,000 hunters purchase licenses. License fees support conservation programs.

Hunting is divided into two kinds: big game and small game. Big game includes the large hoofed animals, cats, and African game, and is usually done with a rifle that shoots a single bullet over long distances with great accuracy. Small game includes birds, rabbits, and squirrels, hunted most often with a shotgun whose many small pellets provide a short-range but wide pattern that can bring down a running or flying animal.

Small Game

Basic Types. Four animals comprise the bulk of small-game types. They are ring-necked pheasants, originally imported in 1881 from China and found roughly north of the Mason-Dixon line across the United States; bobwhites and other quail, generally found south of the Mason-Dixon line; doves, migratory birds whose flights carry them the length of the country; and cottontail rabbits, familiar to every suburban dweller. These animals are hunted by walking through covers—thickets providing cover for game—either alone or with a dog. Hunters shoot when the animal jumps into flight or runs away. Gray and fox squirrels are found in the hardwood forests of the North and East and are sometimes hunted with small rifles, the hunter sitting quietly in the woods until the squirrels appear in the treetops. Ruffed grouse are birds of the dense Northern pine forests, renowned for their explosive burst into fast flight.

Ducks and Geese. Equally important to small-game hunters are waterfowl, the ducks and geese that migrate every year from their nesting sites in Canada to wintering grounds in the southern portions of the continent. These birds follow well-defined sky highways, called flyways, down the East Coast, the Mississippi River system, along the mountain ranges of the Western states, and the West Coast marshes and lakes. The stately Canada geese, flying in their steady V formation, have long been a herald of the change of season and a symbol of the far traveler.

The smaller ducks in their innumerable species also migrate incredible distances from the most northern regions to the tropics. Ducks and geese are hunted from blinds—crude disguises made of branches or grass to hide the hunters. Since all species are attracted to their own kind, hunters use decoys, or wooden imitations of the species hunted, to lure the ducks and geese within range of their fire. Major duck species are the mallard, pintail, black, widgeon, greenwing, broadbill, and canvasback. There are hundreds more, each with its colorful local name. The principal species of geese in hunting are known as Canada, blue, and snow.

Big Game

Deer. Big game starts with deer in any consideration of North American hunting. There are three main species: the white-tailed deer of the thick-forested East; the larger mule deer of the Western plains and mountains; and the black-tailed deer of the Northwest. Deer are altogether capable of sharing their range with man and become garden nuisances in many areas. Only the male, or buck, is antlered. In many states at various times does, or females, are legally killed along with bucks when herds must be reduced. An estimated 1,000,000 white-tailed deer, 700,000 mule deer, and 150,000 black-tailed deer were killed annually in the early 1960's.

Some deer hunters choose a position along a well-traveled trail and wait for the deer to move past them. From this stand the hunter shoots with a rifle quickly as the buck or doe comes racing past. Other hunters, including those who stalk deer or surround areas where they are likely to be found, move about considerably.

Moose, Elk, and Antelope. Other more dramatic big-game species are killed on the North American continent in sufficient numbers to make them an important part of hunting. The huge horse-sized moose with its massive palmated antlers is a creature of the Canadian lake regions and Alaska, Montana, and Wyoming. Some 5,000 are killed annually. In the mountains of the western and

BIG GAME HUNTING

Birnback Publishing Service

Hunting the rhinoceros in Kenya, Africa. Above, a photographer with special camera in hand races to cover the kill. Right, a hunter takes aim at the dangerous animal. Far right, the successful hunter poses with his prey.

Duck hunting in the Louisiana marshes.

A Florida hunter sounds a duck call as his alert retriever poises for action. Hunting with bow and arrow is growing in popularity (*right*).

SMALL GAME HUNTING

Birnback Publishing Service

northwestern states the elk (or, more precisely, the wapiti), another horse-sized antlered animal, is hunted when winter snows drive herds from the inaccessible mountain peaks. The yearly kill exceeds 60,000. On the prairie, the small but fleet and sharp-eyed pronghorn, the so-called American antelope, is the hunter's quarry. Shot at long range, some 60,000 are killed annually.

Bear. The black bear is a common species throughout the United States and Canada. Too cunning to be outwitted by most hunters, it is pursued with dogs in many areas, shot in ambushes employing horsemeat or fish as bait, and most often stumbled upon and shot by astonished but alert deer hunters. The massive grizzly bear, brownish yellow in color and found only in Wyoming, Montana, British Columbia, and Alaska, where it is called the brown bear, is the only truly dangerous North American game. Despite many stories and the capabilities of all large wild creatures to the contrary, the grizzly and to a much lesser extent the moose are the only North American game animals that can be expected to charge and make every effort to kill the hunter when wounded.

Other North American Types. Other North American big-game species of importance in glamour and challenge, if not numbers, are bighorn sheep and mountain goats, found only in the ruggedest of mountain terrain, and caribou, the large, breathtakingly antlered wanderers of the arctic tundra. Even the American buffalo, or bison, has returned to the game list in Canada, where herds, carefully protected since their near extermination in the 1860's and 1870's, have now multiplied beyond the foraging capacity of their range.

The wild turkey, classified as big game although a fowl and by no means big, is another important American game animal whose restoration throughout many states has been an astounding accomplishment of modern conservation and game management. Crafty and majestic, the wild turkey affords both an impressive trophy and a source of fine eating. Thousands are killed by hunters in Arizona, New Mexico, Texas, Alabama, Florida, Georgia, Mississippi, Pennsylvania, North and South Carolina, West Virginia, and Virginia.

African Game. These courageous and dangerous qualities are not lacking in the legendary big game of Africa. Although the many antelope and fowl of Africa are harmless enough, hunters on even an expensive and well-organized safari can expect trouble from any of the so-called African Big Five—rhinoceros, elephant, lion, leopard, and Cape buffalo. Heavy rifles firing a bullet with a diameter about that of a 25-cent piece are used for hunting such large game.

Hunting with Hounds

Another important and colorful facet of North American hunting involves the use of hounds in locating and pursuing game. In such hunting, immortalized in song and story, packs of well-trained dogs are used to run fox, raccoon, bears, and, in the West, mountain lions. The baying of the hounds locates the course of the hunt, which may extend many miles. The men follow on foot or horseback to reach the spot where the quarry is treed or turns to battle the pack. Since most of these animals are nocturnal, moving about at night, such hunts usually take place at night, and storytelling around the campfire is an integral part of their charm.

Hunting with Bow and Arrow

One of the fastest-growing new hunting sports employs the bow and arrow. In this case hunting techniques are the same but hunters use as a weapon the traditional longbow developed by medieval English archers. Then, as now, it was a fearfully capable weapon in the hands of an expert. However, its short range and the ease with which an arrow can be deflected by a bush or tree limb make it a hard weapon to kill with in the thick covers of North America. Consequently, conservation authorities have allowed long open seasons in which archers can enjoy themselves hunting mostly for deer. Just enough deer are killed to keep the bow hunters enthusiastic and the deer

fairly safe. Nevertheless, the popularity of the sport reveals a significant change in what participants consider as the rewards of modern-day hunting. These go far beyond the traditional "bringing home the bacon" and include a full appreciation of the beauty and retreat of the outdoors, a welcome change from the pressure and intensity of modern living. The "bacon" can stay in the woods and still fulfill its age-old function if the hunter returns to his home refreshed, happily weary, and restored from the pursuit of it.
See also ARCHERY; FIELD TRIALS.

HURLING, traditional Irish game similar to field hockey but far more vigorous. Along with Gaelic football and soccer, it is one of the most popular sports in Ireland. An all-Ireland championship has been held since 1887 and has attracted crowds of up to 80,000 in recent years. The governing body for the game is the Gaelic Athletic Association, Dublin, founded in 1884. The sport is also popular in the United States with persons of Irish ancestry, especially in New York City. An annual competition is held there for the St. Brendan Cup between teams from New York and Ireland.

Hurling is played on a turf field, measuring 140–160 yd (128–146 m) in length and 84–100 yd (77–91 m) in width, with goals at each end. A team consists of 15 players. The playing stick, or hurley, resembles a field-hockey stick and has a broad curved blade; the stick is about 3 ft (1 m) long, and the widest part of the blade measures 4 in (10 cm). The ball is 9–10 in (23–25 cm) in circumference, weighs $3\frac{1}{4}$–4 oz (100–125 g), and usually has a cork center and a leather cover. Each team seeks to hurl the ball into the opponents' goal. The ball may not be lifted off the ground with the hand when in play, but when off the ground, it may be struck with the hand or kicked. Players may catch the ball or pick it off the ground with the side of the stick, balance it thereon, and run with it or hurl it from the stick into the goal. The goal posts are 16 ft. high, 21 ft. apart, and have a crossbar 8 ft. above the ground. If the ball is hurled from the stick into the net strung between the goal posts under the crossbar, three points are scored; if the ball is hurled in the same manner over the crossbar and between the posts, one point results.

Irish Tourist Office

Hurling, popular game of Ireland, played in Croke Park, Dublin.

I

ICEBOATING. *See* WINTER SPORTS.

ICE HOCKEY, game played by two teams of six players each. The playing surface is usually an enclosed area, or rink, though it may also be an outdoor expanse of natural ice. The players are equipped with skates and wooden sticks. The object of each team is to score points by propelling a disk (puck) of vulcanized rubber into the opponent's goal while preventing the opponents from driving the puck into the goal the team is defending at the opposite end of the playing area. Unlike most games, hockey permits the substitution of players without halting play; this and the high speed attained by the players have caused it to be called "the fastest sport on earth."

Professional hockey ranks as one of the most popular spectator sports in Canada and the United States, attracting large crowds to arenas and reaching additional millions of persons through television.

Origin and History

Ice hockey developed in Canada during the latter part of the 19th century. There is no general agreement among historians about the exact nature of its origin, however. According to some accounts, the game was first played in 1855 by soldiers of the Royal Canadian Rifles in Kingston, Ontario, who adapted field hockey to ice. Some historians claim that it began in the Victoria Skating Club in Montreal; others list Halifax, Nova Scotia, as the birthplace. About 1875 a code of rules was formulated by students of McGill University in Montreal. The first league is believed to have been formed in 1885 in Kingston. By 1891 the Ontario Hockey Association, composed of amateur teams, was organized as the forerunner of present-day professional leagues.

Amateur Competition. The game spread to Europe in 1907 and has flourished there in more recent years on an amateur basis. After World War II the Soviet Union made quick strides to challenge Canada's supremacy in amateur hockey, which still exists side by side with the professional version. And despite the game's spread from Canada, where it continues as the national winter pastime, Canada has remained virtually the only source of professional players, including those on teams representing U.S. cities. In addition to climatic advantages, Canada has an abundance of rinks where boys are exposed to the game at an early age.

UPI

Furious action erupts around the goal in hockey, "the fastest sport on earth." The Chicago Black Hawks' goalie, Tony Esposito, falls flat on his back as the puck, shot by the New York Rangers' Bill Fairborn (10), bounces off a post of the goal in a Stanley Cup playoff game.

Stanley Cup. The most prized possession in ice hockey is the Stanley Cup, awarded to the National Hockey League team that wins a postseason playoff series among division leaders. This cup was first put in competition among Canadian amateur teams during the 1893–94 season by Lord Stanley of Preston, Governor-General of Canada. Its importance stimulated the growth of professionalism, somewhat surreptitiously at first, as communities vied in building strong teams, an effort that took the form of importing the best players from other localities and paying them fees. The first professional league was organized in northern Michigan in 1903, but most of the best players remained in Canada on so-called amateur teams in two leagues, the Eastern Canadian Hockey Association (ECHA) and the Federal League, until 1909.

The National Hockey Association (NHA), first major professional league, was formed in that year with five teams: two in Montreal and others in the Ontario cities of Renfrew, Cobalt, and Haileybury. In 1910 the NHA absorbed two teams, in Montreal and Ottawa, from the rival Canadian Hockey Association, an outgrowth of the ECHA. The National Hockey Association thus became a seven-team league with over-the-table professional salaries. Renfrew, nicknamed the Millionaires, had signed the Patrick brothers, Lester and Frank, pioneers in the game, for the unheard-of-salaries of $3,000 each during the eight-game season. The Montreal Wanderers, however, won the first NHA championship.

In 1911 the Patrick brothers went to western Canada to form the Pacific Coast Hockey League (PCHL) that later included U.S. franchises in Seattle, Wash., and Portland, Ore. The PCHL challenged the NHA's exclusive right to the Stanley Cup; in 1913 Victoria, British Columbia, of the PCHL defeated Quebec of the NHA in a championship series, but Quebec refused to put up the trophy as a prize for this competition. In 1914, however, the NHA accepted the challenge without reservation, and Toronto defeated Victoria in hockey's first "world series." In 1917 Seattle became the first U.S.-based team to win the Stanley Cup.

National Hockey League. In the same year, 1917, the National Hockey Association disbanded and the present-day major league, the National Hockey League, was formed with teams in Montreal (two), Toronto, Ottawa, and Quebec (although the last-named city did not enter competition until 1919). At the time of its formal inception, Toronto was the only team with an artificial-ice rink. Frank Calder, who had been secretary of the old NHA, was the NHL's first president.

During the next 10 years the league experienced growing pains. In 1924 Boston became the first U.S. city in the NHL; a year later the Hamilton, Ontario, club (which had been transferred from Quebec) became the New York Americans, and a new team was formed in Pittsburgh. In 1926 three more U.S. teams were added—New York Rangers, Chicago, and Detroit—to form a 10-team league with two sections. In the Canadian division there were two Montreal teams (Les Canadiens and Maroons), Toronto, Ottawa, and the New York Americans; in the American division, New York Rangers, Boston, Chicago, Detroit, and Pittsburgh. With many of the PCHL players joining the new NHL teams, the Stanley Cup henceforth became the exclusive possession of the NHL.

In 1930 the Pittsburgh franchise was shifted to Philadelphia, but a year later this team and the Ottawa team withdrew. In 1932 Ottawa resumed competition; in 1934 its franchise was transferred to St. Louis, where it re-

STANLEY CUP WINNERS

1893-94	Montreal A.A.A.
1894-95	Montreal Victorias
1895-96	Winnipeg Victorias
1896-97	Montreal Victorias
1897-98	Montreal Victorias
1898-99	Montreal Victorias (February)
1898-99	Montreal Shamrocks (March)
1899-1900	Montreal Shamrocks
1900-01	Winnipeg Victorias
1901-02	Montreal A.A.A.
1902-03	Ottawa Silver Seven
1903-04	Ottawa Silver Seven
1904-05	Ottawa Silver Seven
1905-06	Montreal Wanderers
1906-07	Kenora Thistles (January)
1906-07	Montreal Wanderers (March)
1907-08	Montreal Wanderers
1908-09	Ottawa Senators
1909-10	Montreal Wanderers
1910-11	Ottawa Senators
1911-12	Quebec Bulldogs
1912-13	Quebec Bulldogs†
1913-14	Toronto Arenas
1914-15	Vancouver Millionaires
1915-16	Montreal Canadiens
1916-17	Seattle Metropolitans
1917-18	Toronto Arenas
1918-19	No decision.*
1919-20	Ottawa Senators
1920-21	Ottawa Senators
1921-22	Toronto St. Pats
1922-23	Ottawa Senators
1923-24	Montreal Canadiens
1924-25	Victoria Cougars
1925-26	Montreal Maroons
1926-27	Ottawa Senators
1927-28	New York Rangers
1928-29	Boston Bruins
1929-30	Montreal Canadiens
1930-31	Montreal Canadiens
1931-32	Toronto Maple Leafs
1932-33	New York Rangers
1933-34	Chicago Black Hawks
1934-35	Montreal Maroons
1935-36	Detroit Red Wings
1936-37	Detroit Red Wings
1937-38	Chicago Black Hawks
1938-39	Boston Bruins
1939-40	New York Rangers
1940-41	Boston Bruins
1941-42	Toronto Maple Leafs
1942-43	Detroit Red Wings
1943-44	Montreal Canadiens
1944-45	Toronto Maple Leafs
1945-46	Montreal Canadiens
1946-47	Toronto Maple Leafs
1947-48	Toronto Maple Leafs
1948-49	Toronto Maple Leafs
1949-50	Detroit Red Wings
1950-51	Toronto Maple Leafs
1951-52	Detroit Red Wings
1952-53	Montreal Canadiens
1953-54	Detroit Red Wings
1954-55	Detroit Red Wings
1955-56	Montreal Canadiens
1956-57	Montreal Canadiens
1957-58	Montreal Canadiens
1958-59	Montreal Canadiens
1959-60	Montreal Canadiens
1960-61	Chicago Black Hawks
1961-62	Toronto Maple Leafs
1962-63	Toronto Maple Leafs
1963-64	Toronto Maple Leafs
1964-65	Montreal Canadiens
1965-66	Montreal Canadiens
1966-67	Toronto Maple Leafs
1967-68	Montreal Canadiens
1968-69	Montreal Canadiens
1969-70	Boston Bruins
1970-71	Montreal Canadiens
1971-72	Boston Bruins
1972-73	Montreal Canadiens
1973-74	Philadelphia Flyers
1974-75	Philadelphia Flyers
1975-76	Montreal Canadiens
1976-77	Montreal Canadiens

** In the spring of 1919 the Montreal Canadiens traveled to Seattle to meet Seattle, PCHL champions. After five games had been played—teams were tied at two wins each and one tie—the series was called off by the local department of health because of the influenza epidemic and the death from influenza of Joe Hall.*

† Victoria defeated Quebec in challenge series. No official recognition.

mained for one season, prior to being dissolved. When the Montreal Maroons disbanded in 1938, the seven-team NHL abandoned its two-division setup. In 1941 the New York Americans changed their name to Brooklyn Americans, but a year later they disbanded. That left six teams—the Montreal Canadiens, Toronto Maple Leafs, New York Rangers, Boston Bruins, Chicago Black Hawks, and Detroit Red Wings. In 1967 they formed the East Division when six new franchises formed a West Division—the Philadelphia Flyers, Pittsburgh Penguins, Minnesota North Stars, St. Louis Blues, Los Angeles Kings, and California Seals. Expansion continued, with the Buffalo Sabers and Vancouver Canucks added in 1970, the New York Islanders and Atlanta Falcons in 1972. Franchises were awarded to Washington, D.C., and Kansas City for the 1974–75 season when the 18 teams were split into four divisions.

The NHL's popularity led to the organization of another league, the World Hockey Association, in 1972, with 12 franchises representing New York, New England, Philadelphia, Cleveland, Chicago, Minnesota, Houston, Los Angeles, Quebec, Ottawa, Winnipeg, and Alberta. The credibility of the WHA was enhanced when the Winnipeg Jets persuaded Bobby Hull, a star goal scorer for the Chicago Black Hawks,, to sign a long-term contract reported to be worth $2.5 million, including a $1 million bonus. Several other NHL players followed Hull to WHA teams as salaries skyrocketed in both leagues.

In 1972 the international aspect of ice hockey increased when an eight-game series was arranged between Team Canada, an all-star group of NHL players, and a Soviet Union squad. To the embarrassment of Canada, which believed that NHL players were without equal, the Soviet team won two and tied one of the four games in Canadian cities. Team Canada, however, rallied to win the last three games of the four in Moscow for a one-game edge.

In the early years of the NHL no team ever won the Stanley Cup more than two years in succession. Following World War II three "dynasties" appeared: Toronto won the cup in 1947, 1948, 1949, and 1951; Detroit finished in first place in regular-season play seven consecutive years, 1949–55, setting a record, and won the Stanley Cup four times in that period (1950, 1952, 1954, 1955); and Montreal set a record by winning the Stanley Cup five times in succession, 1956–60.

Equipment and Conduct of Play

Although rinks vary in dimensions, the regulation measurements are 200 ft. by 85 ft. (61 m by 25.9 m) This rectangular surface is divided into three zones by two blue

UPI

The Boston Bruins' Bobby Orr, a Hart Trophy winner, keeping the puck away from the Philadelphia Flyers' Jim Johnson.

lines, each 60 ft. (18.29 m) from, and parallel to, the goal lines. At each end of the rink, centered on these goal lines, are the goal cages, which are 6 ft. wide, 4 ft. high (1.83 m by 1.22 m) and backed with netting.

Each team consists of a goal tender, whose job is to guard his team's goal and block the entry of the puck as opposition players attempt to score; two defense men, who are stationed near their team's goal and who seek to impede the progress of opposing players seeking to score; a center; and two wings, who, like the defense men, are assigned to right and left sides of the rink and who, together with the center, comprise the offensive (scoring) unit of the team.

The puck is a disk 3 in. (7.62 cm) in diameter and 1 in. (2.54 cm) thick. Players control and propel the puck with wooden sticks whose length, from top of handle to heel, may not exceed 53 in. (129.62 cm), and whose blades may not be more than 14.75 in. (37.465 cm) long. The maximum height of the blade is 3 in., except in the case of the goal tender's stick, which has a maximum of 3.5 in. (8.89 cm). To safeguard themselves from the severe bodily contact involved in the game, players wear protective equipment under their uniforms.

The game consists of three 20-minute periods. In Stanley Cup competition, if the score is tied at the end of regulation play, the teams begin an additional 20-minute period, and then additional ones, if necessary. However, in overtime the game ends immediately when a goal is scored. A goal, counting one point, is scored when the puck crosses the opponents' goal line.

Play begins with a face-off. In a circle in the center of the rink, the referee drops the puck between the opposing centers, who attempt to pass it to their respective wings. The team that gains possession of the puck then tries to score by a combination of passing and shooting (propelling the puck toward the goal with the stick, largely through action of the wrists). As it approaches the opponents' goal, none of its players may precede the puck in crossing the blue line nearest that goal.

The principal defensive skill employed by the opposing team is known as checking, whereby an offensive player is knocked down or thrown off balance so that he loses control of the puck. Such checking is accomplished by blocking the offensive player through bodily contact or by using the stick to take from him possession of the puck.

Common infractions of rules include holding an opponent, tripping him, slashing him with the stick, and practicing unnecessary roughness in other ways. These result in penalties 2 and 5 minutes in duration, during which time the offender leaves the ice and enters a penalty box at the side of the rink. No substitution is permitted for a penalized player, except in the case of the goal tender. More serious penalties are 10 minutes long; match penalties (forefeiture of the game caused by an act such as striking an official) or disqualification of players rarely are invoked by the principal official, the referee, who is assisted by two linesmen.

Wide World

Bobby Hull (9) of the Winnipeg Jets and goalie Pete Donnelly (23), right, of the New York Golden Blades watch a deflected puck in World Hockey Association action.

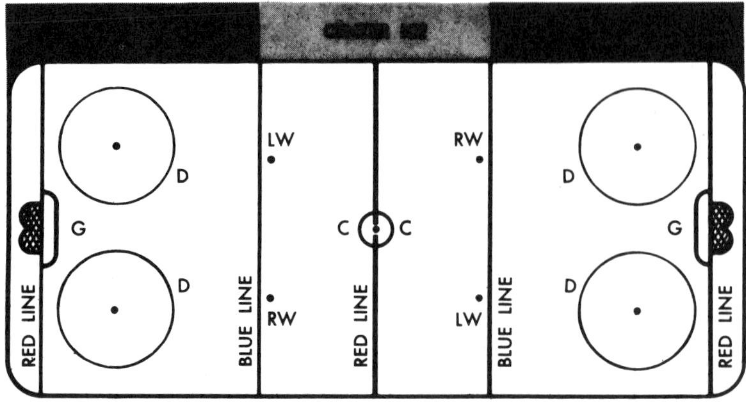

Diagram illustrating team positions at the beginning of a hockey match. Each team has two defense men (D), who stand forward of and flank their goal tender (G) and support him against the opponent's scoring threats. In the center zone are the team's offensive players, the right-wing (RW) and left-wing (LW) men, who stand behind and flank their center (C).

Basic equipment used in a regulation hockey game.

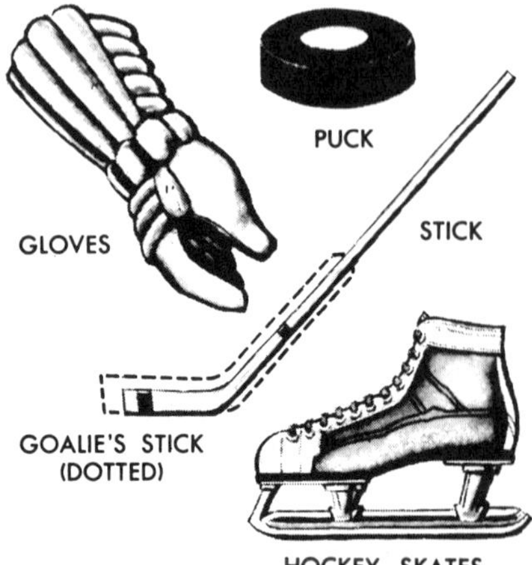

Famous Players

Hall of Fame. The National Hockey Hall of Fame is divided into players and "builders of hockey." Among the game's all-time stars are Howie Morenz, Eddie Shore, Lester Patrick, Georges Vézina, Charles ("Chuck") Gardiner, Frank Nighbor, Aurèle Joliat, Frank ("Cyclone") Taylor, Art Ross, Édouard ("Newsy") Lalonde, Joe Malone, Bill Cook, Frank Boucher, Nelson ("Nels") Stewart, Frank ("King") Clancy, Mervyn ("Red") Dutton, J. D. ("Dick") Irvin, and Ivan ("Ching") Johnson. Among the builders are Lord Stanley, Frank Calder, Frank Patrick, and Conn Smythe.

Perhaps the most famous hockey players of all time are Maurice ("Rocket") Richard of Montreal and Gordon ("Gordie") Howe of Detroit. Richard scored a record total of 626 goals between 1942 and 1960, when he retired. Howe shattered that record, scoring 786 goals before his first retirement in 1971. Two years later, at age 45, he and his two oldest sons, Marty and Mark, signed with the Houston Aeros of the WHA in a $2 million deal. But the legends of Richard and Howe were challenged by Bobby Orr of Boston, a defenseman. Beginning in 1970, Orr was voted the Hart Trophy, emblematic of the NHL's most valuable player award, an unprecedented three seasons.

ICE SKATING. *See* SKATING.

J

JACOBS [*jā'kəbz*], **HELEN HULL (1908–)**, American tennis player, born in Globe, Ariz. A long-time rival of Helen Wills Moody, she was the U.S. girls' singles champion (1924–25); U.S. women's singles champion (1932–35); and a member of the U.S. women's doubles championship team in 1932, 1934, and 1935 and of the U.S. mixed doubles championship team in 1934. In 1936 she won the All-England women's singles title. In 1953 she achieved the rank of commander in the U.S. Naval Reserve. Miss Jacobs also wrote books on tennis.

JACOBS, HIRSCH (1904–70), American trainer of thoroughbred horses, born in New York. In the early 1960's he became the leading trainer in U.S. racing history, having saddled more than 3,000 winners. His most famous horse was Stymie, which he claimed for $1,500 in 1943 and which eventually earned $918,485.

JAI-ALAI [*hī'ə-lī'*], game played somewhat like handball. It is known as *pelota* (ball) in Spain. Since it was always played at fiestas, the Cubans adopted the name *jai-alai* (merry festival) after the game was imported in 1900. There is some dispute over its origin. Some historians say it was discovered among the Aztecs by Hernándo Cortés in Mexico in the 16th century and brought to Spain. Others say it was a variation of handball developed in the Basque country of Spain. At first the bare hand was used, then a flat bat, next a short basket, and finally, the long, curved wicker basket, or *cesta*, now employed. Today jai-alai is played in at least six countries—the United States, Mexico, Spain, Italy, France, and the Philippines. It has also been played in Egypt, Belgium, and China. As a professional sport it has reached its highest peaks in Mexico and in the United States, where it was introduced at the World's Fair in 1904.

Only two pieces of equipment are used in the game, the *cesta* and the *pelota*. The *cesta* consists of a glove that fits over the hand, a wooden frame, and a basket handwoven from reeds grown on the mountaintops of northern Spain. The reeds are very light but extremely strong. Each player is given a preference as to the size of his basket. The *pelota*, or ball, is handwound from strips of virgin Para rubber, grown in Brazil. A layer of linen thread is added, then two coats of goatskin. About two-thirds the size of a baseball, it is harder and heavier than a golf ball and has been clocked at speeds of more than 150 mph. This makes the *pelota* the fastest ball in any sport. When the cover is scratched it must be replaced.

JAI ALAI

JAI ALAI—a very fast game—involves catching the very hard ball (pelota) in the wicker racket (*cesta*) and hurling it against a wall. At right, in Tijuana, Mexico, a player has just returned the ball, and his opponents await the rebound. (EDWARD SIEVERS—BIRNBACK)

Wire screens protect spectators or persons waiting to play. (BIRNBACK PUBLISHING SERVICE)

Basically a form of three-walled handball, jai-alai is played in indoor arenas called *frontons*. The court is 176 ft. long and 55 ft. wide. The height of the walls (front, back, and side) is usually 40 ft. The rules of the game, which is played in singles or doubles (like tennis), call for the server to bounce the ball once and then, using his *cesta*, to hurl it against the front wall. Provided it rebounds within the confines of the court, his opponent must return the ball to the front wall before it bounces twice, catching and throwing in one motion. In doing so, he may play the ball off the side or back wall.

As played in Florida today, jai-alai matches six to eight singles or doubles teams, two of which play at one time. When a point is scored, the player losing the point retires and another takes his place. The elimination continues until one player has reached the required number of points to win the game. Normally, a six-man game will be played to five points, an eight-man game to seven.

JEFFRIES, JAMES J. ("JIM") (1875–1953), American boxer, born in Carroll, Ohio. He won the heavyweight title in 1899 by knocking out Bob Fitzsimmons in 11 rounds. He retired undefeated in 1905. In 1910, at the urging of his followers, Jeffries opposed Jack Johnson, who knocked him out in 15 rounds and thus won the heavyweight title. This defeat in Jeffries' last bout was the only one of his career, during which he won 18 of 21 matches (11 by knockouts, 2 ending in draws).

JOHNSON, BYRON BANCROFT ("BAN") (1864–1931), American baseball executive, born in Norwalk, Ohio. He became president of the Western League in 1893; in 1900 he organized it into the American League, and served until 1927 as its first president. Johnson was the dominant member of the three-man National Commission, which ruled U.S. professional baseball, 1903–21.

JOHNSON, JOHN A. ("JACK") (1878–1946), American boxer, born in Galveston, Tex. He was the first American Negro to hold the heavyweight championship. Johnson claimed the title after defeating Tommy Burns by a technical knockout in 1908, and he won recognition as undisputed champion by knocking out James J. Jeffries in 1910. He lost the championship in 1915 by a knockout in the 26th round of his match with Jess Willard.

JOHNSON, WALTER PERRY (1887–1946), American baseball player and manager, born in Humboldt, Kan. A right-handed pitcher who was regarded by many as having the most overpowering fast-ball delivery in the sport's history, he won 416 games for Washington of the American League from 1907 to 1927. He struck out 3,497 opposing batters during his career, a record major-league total, as are his 113 shutouts and 56 consecutive innings of shutout pitching (1913). In 1913 he won 36 games and had an earned-run average of 1.09 per game. He was named the league's most valuable player in 1913 and 1924, and became a charter member of the National Baseball Hall of Fame in 1936. Johnson, who was also known as Barney and The Big Train, managed Washington (1929–32) and Cleveland (1933–35) of the American League.

JUDO. *See* JUJITSU.

JUJITSU [*jōō-jĭt'sōō*], a system of weaponless combat and self-defense. It is based on the principle of first apparently giving way to the attacking force, then adding one's own force so that the sum of both forces is applied against the attacker. Thus a physically weaker opponent can gain victory over the stronger. Broadly, the techniques used are:

1) Throwing the opponent to the ground.
2) Immobilizing the opponent on the ground.
3) Applying painful reverse pressure to the opponent's joints.
4) Rendering the opponent unconscious by choking.
5) Striking the opponent in a sensitive or vital point.

There is evidence that the art is of Japanese origin,

Judo, Inc.

Left, a multiple exposure photograph showing a contestant on the ground flipping his standing opponent. This maneuver is called Tomoe Nage, or stomach throw.

Jujitsu, Oriental in origin, is the forerunner of modern judo.

Jujitsu or judo is valuable training for both military and police.

though some historians believe it came from China; certainly jujitsu had its major development in Japan. References to it appeared as early as the 8th century in the *Kojiki* (Record of Ancient Matters).

Judo. The modern renaissance of the art began at the close of the 19th century. In 1882 Jigoro Kano, a master of jujitsu, established a new school, known at its present site in Tokyo as the famed Kodokan Institute of Judo. Kano chose the name *judo* ("gentle," or "soft way") to distinguish his revitalized concepts from those of the ancient art, which had fallen into disrepute. He selectively reformed its methods; dangerous techniques were reserved for practice in form only, thereby permitting the development of judo as a competitive sport. Above all, the greatest stress is given to the mental and spiritual (or philosophical) basis underlying the physical dynamics. The black belt, awarded to masters of the art, symbolizes various higher degrees of attainment of these aims.

The metamorphosis of jujitsu into judo made it accessible to young and old and kindled a world-wide interest. In 1902 Kodokan judo was introduced in the United States by invitation of President Theodore Roosevelt, who studied the art. In 1952 representatives of twenty nations formed an International Judo Federation. The National Judo Black Belt Federation of the United States, organized in 1955, is the official judo body of the United States. It is affiliated with the Amateur Athletic Union of the United States, which conducts annual national championship tournaments, and with the International Judo Federation, which conducts biennial world championship tournaments. Judo's importance in international competition was signified when it was added to the program of the 1964 Olympic Games.

K

KARATE [*kə-rä'tä*], system of self-defense that originated in China and spread to Okinawa and other parts of the Orient It is a form of kenpo, an ancient Chinese mode of combat that utilizes the hands, arms, feet, legs, and other parts of the body as the sole weapons. The present literal definition of karate, "empty hand," derives from Japanese usage and dates from 1923.

Many of the original elements of kenpo were taken from the movements of mammals, fowls, and reptiles. These elements, which became known by such names as "panther punch" and "butterfly kick," were devised and developed by individuals who divulged their findings only to their immediate families. It was during the Ming Dynasty (1368–1644) that the technique of kenpo became widely known.

There are many present-day styles of karate. In China they number well over 300; the five principal Okinawan styles are Kobayashi-ryu, Shito-ryu, Uechi-ryu, Shoreiji-ryu, and Goju-ryu. Japan in turn modified the adopted styles of Okinawa and derived its own, including Shotokan and Waddo-ryu. Korea and Hawaii have also evolved styles. A recent development has been the practice of karate as a sport in Japan, and, to a lesser degree, in the United States.

Karate opponents demonstrate a kick. The defender extends his leg so that the ball of his foot strikes the aggressor's jaw. The leg has more power and reach than the arm. (ED PARKER)

KARATE

Below, defense against an overhand club attack. The defender blocks the attacker's right arm with his own left arm. His right hand is ready to strike.

The basic movements in karate as a method of self-defense and counterattack include use of the hands and arms in punching, thrusting, or clawing, and employment of the legs and feet in kicking. As in jujitsu, a basic factor is knowledge of certain vulnerable portions of the antagonist's anatomy and of the most effective means of attacking those areas. The portions most often attacked are the eyes, throat, and groin.

Many people have associated karate with judo, but they are not closely related. Karate is similar to boxing; judo can be compared with wrestling.

Methods of training in karate are numerous, but the more common are hardening the bodily weapons by punching padded posts, thrusting the fingers into sand, and kicking sandbags. Shadowboxing is also used in developing offensive and defensive movements stressing agility, balance, and co-ordination. Sparring without actual bodily contact also has been introduced by the Japanese in the practice of karate as a sport.

KEELER, WILLIAM HENRY ("WILLIE") (1872–1923), American baseball player, born in Brooklyn, N.Y. Famed as a scientific batter who aimed his hits at areas beyond the reach of opposing fielders ("I hit 'em where they ain't"), he compiled a .345 batting average while playing the outfield and third base for New York (1892–93, 1910), Brooklyn (1893, 1899–1902), and Baltimore (1894–98) of the National League and New York (1903–9) of the American League. He was a left-handed hitter and thrower. In 1897 when he batted .432, Keeler hit safely in 44 consecutive games, a major-league record for 44 years.

KELLY, LEONARD PATRICK ("RED") (1927–), Canadian hockey player, born in Simcoe, Ontario. One of the most versatile players in the sport, he was named to the National Hockey League all-star team six times, as a defense man, between 1951 and 1957, and also performed at center and left wing. He played for the Detroit Red Wings of the NHL from 1947 to 1960, when he was traded to Toronto. He scored more goals than any defense man in league history. He won the Lady Byng Trophy, awarded to the player who combines the highest degree of sportsmanship, gentlemanly conduct, and ability, in 1951, 1953, 1954, and 1961.

KENDO, Japanese sport of fencing with staves, used by military forces in training for hand-to-hand combat.

KETCH. *See* SAILING.

KETCHEL, STANLEY (1886–1910), American boxer, born in Grand Rapids, Mich. One of the most devastating punchers in the sport, he won the middleweight title in 1908 by knocking out Jack Sullivan. He lost it to Billy Papke in the same year, but regained it later that year by knocking out Papke. Ketchel's attempt to dethrone Jack Johnson as heavyweight champion in 1909 resulted in his being knocked out. Ketchel, nicknamed the Michigan Assassin, was shot and killed in 1910.

KITE FLYING. The kite in its commonest form is an aerial toy, consisting of a framework of two or more sticks cov-

KITES AND KITE FLYING

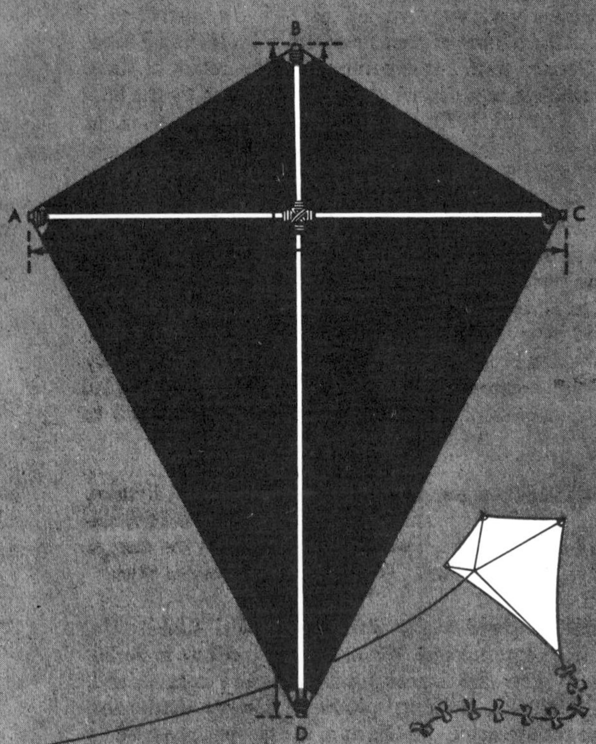

Measurements should be exact. Kites may be made larger or smaller than the pattern calls for, but the proportions must be kept the same. Never use nails or wire for making or flying kites.

ENDS OR CENTERS NOTCHED 1/32″ DEEP

CENTER LASHING

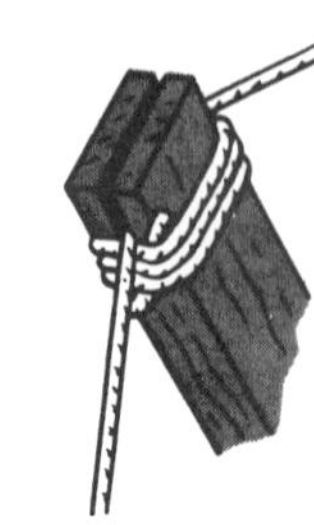

NOTCHED AND LASHED TIP

MAKING A KITE

Cut thin sticks of spruce or pine to size and notch them, horizontally where they intersect, vertically at the tips. Glue the center notches together and lash the joint with string. Run a string frame through the tip notches A, B, C, D, securing it with lashing and glue at each point. Lay the frame on a large piece of unglazed paper and cut around it, leaving a margin of 2 in. Fold this margin over the string frame, fitting it around the tips with circular cuts, and paste it down. Turn the kite over so the paper cover is on top. With a piece of string, measure off the distance AB-BC, cut the string, and tie it at A and C. Tie another string at B and D, with enough slack so that it just meets the A-C string when pulled up at the center. Knot the strings at this center point to form the bridle, to which the flying string is attached. For the tail, tie a string of paper or cloth bows to D. The performance of the individual kite determines how long the tail should be.

KITE VARIETIES

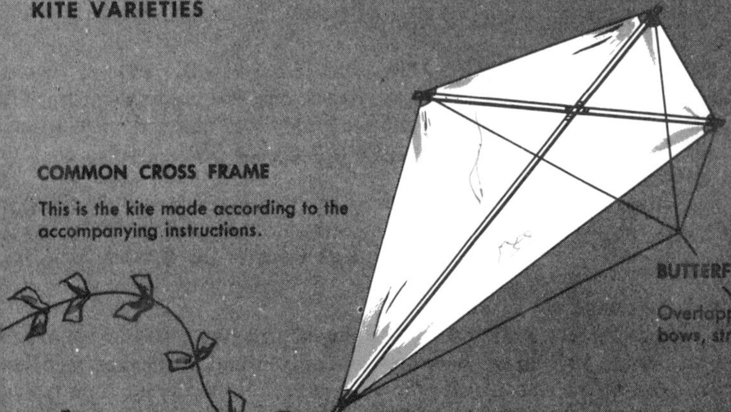

COMMON CROSS FRAME

This is the kite made according to the accompanying instructions.

BUTTERFLY

Overlapping curved sticks form the bows, string forms the straight edges.

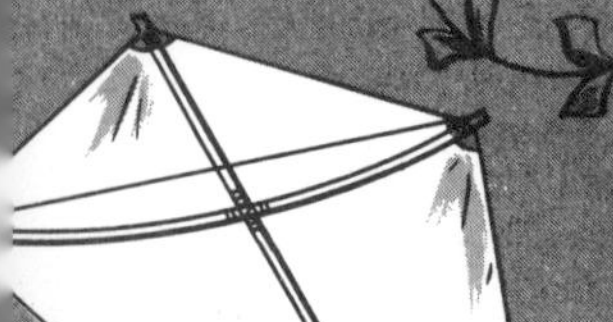

EDDY BOW

No tail is needed. Reduced air pressure behind the kite stabilizes it.

BOX

The Wright brothers used box kites to study the lift power of air currents.

COYNE WINGED

A triangular box kite with wings, it has considerable lift capacity.

ered with paper or cloth, and flown at the end of a string. Kites, shaped like birds, bats, other animals and idols, have been flown since the beginning of recorded history for fun, as part of festivals, in forms of worship, for scientific purposes (such as carrying meteorological instruments), and even to hoist men aloft as observers in directing artillery in warfare. In the mid-20th century kites have taken new shapes with the introduction of the Rogallo nonrigid type, which uses shroud lines instead of sticks, and the Aerokite, which functions at the outset as a balloon and then as a traditional kite, when its wings take over in a current of air.

Methods of flying kites remain basically the same, regardless of the type of kite used. Representative varieties of kites include the familiar box kite, Malayan diamond type, and French military kite (a flat kite with two vanes). A wind of at least 4 mph is required, which can be created if necessary by casting the kite into the air in a manner similar to casting with a fishing rod. The traditional means of raising a kite—by leading it into the wind—is still the best. The direction of the wind can often be determined by observing the flight of smoke from chimneys. Kites should not be flown in the vicinity of high-tension wires, nor should they be flown in the rain, despite Benjamin Franklin's example of using a kite in studying the electrical nature of lightning.

Although the United States is an acknowledged leader in kite production, the glazed string used in kite fighting to cut an opponent's kite string is not available to U.S. followers of the sport. It is India's secret weapon in this form of competition; nevertheless, Indian kites are much more handsome than practical in actual use.

KOUFAX [*kō'făks*], **SANFORD ("SANDY")** (1935–), American baseball player, born in Brooklyn, N. Y. Koufax, a left-handed pitcher, was signed by the Brooklyn Dodgers in 1955, and he remained with the team when it went to Los Angeles. When he announced his retirement from active baseball in 1966, because of an arthritic left arm, his achievements included four no-hit games (one a perfect game), the most pitched by one man; 382 strike-outs in one season (1965), a major league record; leading the National League in earned-run average for five consecutive seasons (1962–66), a record; and an average of more than one strike-out per inning pitched. He won the Cy Young Award for baseball's outstanding pitcher three times, and he was the National League's Most Valuable Player in 1963.

KRAMER [*krā'mər*], **JOHN ALBERT ("JACK")** (1921–), American tennis player, born in Las Vegas, Nev. After winning the U.S. boys' singles title in 1936, he won the U.S. men's singles championship, 1946 and 1947, and the British men's singles title at Wimbledon, 1947; he was a member of the teams that won the U.S. men's doubles title, 1940, 1941, 1943, and 1947, and of the team that won the U.S. mixed doubles title, 1941. He also was on the team that won the British men's doubles title, 1946 and 1947. He became a professional in 1947 and a promoter of professional tennis in the 1950's.

See also TENNIS.

L

LACROSSE [*lə-krôs'*], game played by two teams of 10 persons each on a turf field 110 yd. long and 60 to 70 yd. wide. (In Canada the number of players is 12 or—especially in an indoor version—6.) Each team defends a goal at one end of the field and attempts to score points by causing the ball to enter the goal defended by the opponent at the opposite end. Each such act of scoring counts one point. A game consists of four 15-minute periods.

The ball, made of India sponge rubber, weighs 5 to 5¼ oz. and measures not less than 7¾ in. in circumference. Each player is equipped with a stick, or crosse, having an adjustable meshwork head. The ball is kept in play by being carried, passed, or batted with the crosse, or rolled or kicked. Scoring is accomplished by batting or kicking the ball into the goal. The ball may not be touched with the hands except by the goalkeeper when he is trying to prevent scoring.

In addition to the goalkeeper, each team comprises three attack players, stationed closest to the opponent's goal; three players at mid-field, who function on both attack and defense; and three, stationed close to their own goal, whose function is defensive. Defensive play, as in hockey, consists basically in impeding the progress of the attacking player by means of body-checking (using the body to block the attacker) and by taking the ball from the attacker's crosse with the aid of the defensive player's own crosse.

Fouls are classified as personal, expulsion, or technical. Personal fouls include illegal body-checking, illegal checking with the crosse, tripping, unnecessary roughness, and unsportsmanlike conduct; the offending player is forced to leave the game for from one to three minutes, depending on the severity of the violation. Expulsion fouls, resulting in suspension of the player for the remainder of the game, are called when the player deliberately strikes, or attempts to strike, an opponent with hand, crosse, or ball. Expulsion also results when a player commits five personal fouls. Technical fouls, resulting either in the suspension of the offending player for 30 seconds (if his team does not have possession of the ball) or loss of possession of the ball by his team, are called for such violations of the rules as interference, holding, pushing, touching the ball with the hands, illegal offensive blocking, withholding the ball from play, illegal procedure, and being off side.

History. Lacrosse, the oldest game played in North America, was called bagataway by the Indians of Canada, who originated it long before the arrival of the white man. Bagataway did not limit the size of the field or of the teams, which sometimes numbered as many as 1,500 men. In later years, when French Canadians adapted this primitive sport, they referred to it as *la crosse* because the netted stick used by the Indians resembled a bishop's crosier.

In 1867 the Canadian William George Beers was in-

Hy Peskin—Alpha

LACROSSE

A goalkeeper and his teammate lunge to protect the nets as an opponent presses a scoring attempt. Adapted by early French settlers from an ancient Indian game, lacrosse was standardized in 1867 and subsequently introduced abroad by touring Canadian teams.

DIAGRAM OF LACROSSE FIELD

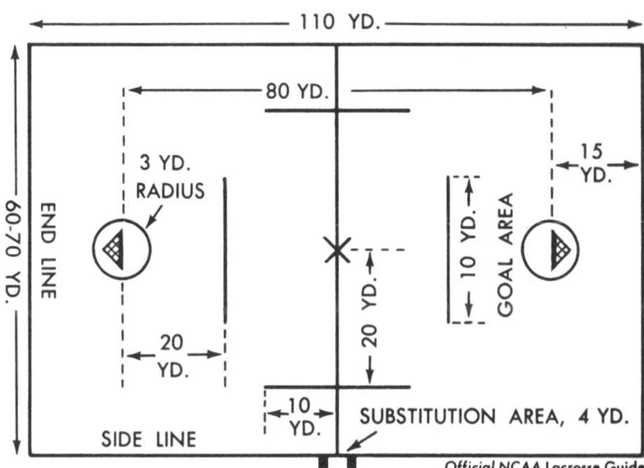

Official NCAA Lacrosse Guide

strumental in framing the first rules of modern lacrosse. He successfully advocated that lacrosse be made Canada's national game, and arranged tours of Great Britain by Canadian teams. The game is still played in England and Australia. In Canada it is controlled by the Canadian Lacrosse Association; in the United States, where it is under the jurisdiction of the United States Intercollegiate Lacrosse Association, the game has achieved its greatest popularity in Eastern colleges.

LADEWIG, MARION (1915–), American bowler, born in Grand Rapids, Mich. Often called the "bowling grandmother," she was considered by many the greatest feminine competitor in the sport's history. Between 1949 and 1963 she won eight women's championships in the annual all-star tournament of the Bowling Proprietors' Association of America. In 1962 she won the women's title in the world invitational tournament for the third time.

LAJOIE [*lăzh'ō-wā*], **NAPOLEON ("LARRY")** (1875–1959), American baseball player, born in Woonsocket, R.I. He played, primarily as a second baseman, for Philadelphia (1896–1900) of the National League and Philadelphia (1901, 1915–16) and Cleveland (1902–14) of the American. Lajoie, who compiled a lifetime batting average of .339, led the American League in batting three times. His average of .422 in 1901 is the highest ever registered in that league. He managed Cleveland, 1905–9. He was named to the National Baseball Hall of Fame in 1937.

LANDIS [*lăn'dĭs*], **KENESAW MOUNTAIN** (1866–1944), American jurist and baseball commissioner. He was born in Millville, Ohio, educated at the University of Cincinnati and Union Law School in Chicago, and practiced law in Chicago from 1891 to 1905. For the next 17 years he was U.S. district judge for the northern district of Illinois. He presided during the trial of the Standard Oil Company of Indiana rebate cases (1907) and imposed a record-breaking fine of $29,240,000, but the decision was reversed on appeal. In 1918 he heard the government's case against the Industrial Workers of the World for antiwar activities. After the Black Sox baseball scandal of 1919, a conspiracy to "fix" the World Series, Landis became the first commissioner for the American and National Leagues of professional baseball. In that position he ruled the sport for 23 years (1921–44) and did much to restore its reputation for honesty.

LATROBE, borough of southwestern Pennsylvania, about 34 mi. southeast of Pittsburgh. It has manufactures of steel and textiles. Professional football originated here in 1895. Inc., 1854; pop., 11,749.

LAWN TENNIS. *See* TENNIS.

LEAHY [*lā'hē*], **FRANK** (1908–), American football coach, born in O'Neill, Neb. Except for Knute Rockne, under whom he played tackle at the University of Notre Dame, Leahy was the most distinguished football coach in the history of that school. After serving as head coach at Boston College, 1939–40, he was head coach at Notre Dame, 1941–53. His teams there recorded 89 victories, 11 losses, and 9 ties; six of those teams were undefeated and five won national championships. Upon retiring from coaching Leahy became a corporation executive.

LENGLEN [*lĕng'lən*], **SUZANNE** (1899–1938), French tennis player. Between 1919 and 1926 she won the French women's singles championship six times and the British women's singles title an equal number of times. She also was a member of many championship teams in doubles competition. She turned professional in 1926.

LEONARD, BENJAMIN ("BENNY") (1896–1947), American boxer, born in New York. A master of his craft, he fought in more than 200 bouts and won 64 by knockouts. He won the world lightweight title in 1917 by knocking out Freddie Welsh and retired in 1925 after successfully defending the championship against all comers. His attempted comeback as a welterweight in 1931 was unsuccessful. He was fatally stricken by a heart attack while refereeing a match in New York.

LITTLE, (WILLIAM) LAWSON, JR. (1910–68), American golfer, born in Newport, R.I. During the height of his competitive career, he was noted for his long drives. He won the United States Amateur and British Amateur championships in 1934 and 1935. Little became a professional in 1936; in 1940 he won the United States Open by defeating Gene Sarazen in a spectacular play-off.

LITTLE LEAGUE BASEBALL is an international youth program consisting of five divisions for boys and girls between the ages of 9 and 18. It provides organized recreation through family and community participation.

Launched in 1939 with three teams in a relatively small community—Williamsport, Pa.—Little League Baseball has mushroomed to become a worldwide youth sports movement. Its early growth was confined largely to rural areas in Pennsylvania. However, in 1947 it began spreading, and today it is active in every state of the United States and in 30 other countries.

In 1961, in response to a demand for an extension-type program for boys 13 to 15, Senior League play was introduced. In 1968, with the number of Little League and Senior League graduates growing, a Big League program for young men 16 to 18 was initiated. Little League Softball and Senior League Softball were innovations in 1974.

Each league schedules and conducts its own program. At the close of the season, each local league is entitled to select an all-star team for entry in tournament play that can ultimately lead to World Series competition. Regional eliminations determine the final participants for the series. The Little League World Series is held in Williamsport, Pa., Senior League in Gary, Ind., and Big League in Fort Lauderdale, Fla.

Rules of play are basically those of conventional baseball. The major difference involves use of a smaller field in Little League competition: the distance between bases is 60 ft (18.3 m); the distance between the pitcher and the batter is 46 ft (14 m). In Senior League and Big League play, the distance is 90 ft (27.4 m) between bases and the pitching distance is 60 ft (18.3 m). In Little League Softball the 60-ft base path prevails and the pitching distance is 40 ft (12.2 m).

Little League Baseball is a federally-chartered nonprofit organization administered by a 15-member board of directors. Headquarters and administrative offices are located in Williamsport. Regional and state centers are located in St. Petersburg, Fla.; Waco, Texas; Lisle, Ill.; San Bernardino, Calif.; and Ottawa, Ontario, Canada. Liaison between headquarters and the local league is maintained through some 450 volunteer district administrators.

Each local league is autonomous to the extent of selecting its own officers, providing facilities, and financing the activity. However, each league must apply to headquarters annually for a charter. Little League derives its primary financial support from annual charter fees of local leagues and from contributions.

In a playing season, Little League Baseball has more

An overflow crowd watches the Little League World Series in Williamsport, Pa., headquarters of the global program.

Vanucci Foto-Services—Little League Baseball

than 10,000 leagues involving some 2,500,000 to 3,000,000 youngsters around the world and a corresponding number of adult volunteers.

LONGDEN, JOHN ERIC ("JOHNNY") (1910–), American jockey, born in England and raised in Canada. He rode more winners than any other jockey in the history of horse racing. As a 51-year-old grandfather, he rode his 5,500th winning mount early in 1961. His record was achieved principally in the United States, though he also competed in England, Australia, and Canada.

LOTT, GEORGE M., JR. (1906–), American tennis player, born in Springfield, Ill. Never an outstanding singles player, he was one of the greatest in doubles competition. He was a member of championship teams in the following categories: U.S. men's doubles, 1928–30, 1933; U.S. mixed doubles, 1929, 1931, 1934; U.S. men's indoor doubles, 1932, 1934; Wimbledon men's doubles, 1931, 1934; Wimbledon mixed doubles, 1931. He became a professional in 1935; in that year and 1937 he was a member of championship teams in men's doubles.

LOUIS [*lo͞o'ĭs*], **JOE,** professional name of Joseph Louis Barrow (1914–), American boxer known as the "Brown Bomber," born in Lexington, Ala. He won the world heavyweight title in 1937 from James J. Braddock by an eighth-round knockout. He retired as undefeated champion in 1949 after defending his title 25 times. His attempt to regain the title in 1950 failed. Prior to that, Max Schmeling had been the only man to defeat Louis, scoring a 12th-round knockout in 1936; in 1938 Louis had knocked out Schmeling in the first round. A deadly puncher with great speed, Louis was one of the few heavyweights following Jack Dempsey to capture the public fancy in the manner of earlier fighters.

LUCKMAN, SIDNEY ("SID") (1916–), American football player, born in New York. He was one of professional football's most astute and talented quarterbacks. After an outstanding athletic career at Columbia University, he played professionally (1939–49) for the Chicago Bears, whom he led to four National Football League championships. He threw 139 touchdown passes as a professional; in one game he passed for seven touchdowns and 433 yd. He was named to NFL all-star teams five times.

LUISETTI [*lo͞o-sĕt'ē*], **ANGELO ("HANK")** (1916–), American basketball player, born in San Francisco. He won All-American rating, 1936–38, at Stanford University where he had a career total of 1,596 points, then an all-time high. In a single game against Duquesne in 1937, he scored 50 points, a remarkable total in an era not marked by present-day astronomical scores. Luisetti did much to popularize the one-hand jump shot.

LUJACK [*lo͞o'jăk*], **JOHN ("JOHNNY")** (1925–), American football player. One of the greatest of all quarterbacks in collegiate play, he won All-American rating at Notre Dame in 1946 and 1947; he was awarded the Heisman Trophy in 1947 as the nation's best college player. Lujack ran, passed, and punted with exceptional skill, and had few equals on pass defense. Later (1948–52) he distinguished himself in professional play as a member of the Chicago Bears of the National Football League.

M

McCARTHY, JOSEPH VINCENT ("MARSE JOE") (1887–), American baseball manager, born in Philadelphia. Although he never reached the major leagues as a player, he was one of the sport's outstanding managers. He led Chicago of the National League, 1926–30; and New York, 1931–46, and Boston, 1948–50, of the American. His Chicago Cubs won a league title in 1929; his New York Yankees won eight league titles and seven World Series.

McCOY [*mə-koi'*], **KID,** professional name of Norman Selby (1873–1940), American boxer, born in Rush County, Ind. He dethroned Tommy Ryan as world welterweight champion in 1896; in 1897 he was among three boxers who claimed the middleweight title, and still later he fought as a light heavyweight. McCoy was rated the best light heavyweight in the sport's history by the boxing authority Nat Fleischer in 1959. He was the inspiration for the expression "the real McCoy," the description once given him by an admiring newspaperman.

McGRAW [*mə-grô'*], **JOHN JOSEPH** (1873–1934), American baseball player and manager, born in Truxton, N.Y. As a third baseman for Baltimore of the National League (1892–99) he helped to establish that team's legendary reputation for Spartan play. He managed the team in 1899, and also the Baltimore club of the newly formed American League (1901–2). McGraw's greatest fame was gained as manager of New York of the National League (1902–32). A dynamic, fiery figure, often called "Little Napoleon," he led his New York teams to 10 league championships and 3 World Series victories.

MACK, CONNIE, professional name of Cornelius McGilli-

Connie Mack, a pioneer in the creation of the American League, was active in baseball for 68 years in many capacities.

United Press International

cuddy (1862–1956), American baseball player, manager, and executive, born in East Brookfield, Mass. He began as a catcher with Washington of the National League in 1886 and later managed Pittsburgh of that league and Milwaukee of the Western League. One of the pioneers in organizing the American League, he founded its Philadelphia team in 1901, and managed it, 1901–50; during that time his teams won nine league championships and five World Series. He was president of the team, 1936–54. One of the sport's most revered figures, Mack personified the scholarly tactician among baseball men. He was elected to the National Baseball Hall of Fame in 1937.

MAHAN [*mə-hăn'*], **EDWARD W.** (1892–1975), American football player and coach, born in Natick, Mass. Few fullbacks in history could approach him in running ability. Playing for Harvard, he won All-American rating in 1913, 1914, and 1915. He was the school's finest player in Percy Haughton's era as coach; during Mahan's three years of competition, Harvard lost only once. He coached football at Harvard, the University of California, and Eastern prep schools. Still later, beginning in 1924, he served as Harvard baseball coach.

MAN O' WAR, American Thoroughbred race horse, foaled in 1917 and nicknamed "Big Red." In winning 20 of 21 races during 1919 and 1920, he earned $249,465, a remarkable sum in an era of relatively small purses. In his second and last year of competition, he set five American records in events ranging from 1 mi. to 1⅝ mi. Turf experts voted him the greatest racer in the first half of the 20th century.

MANTLE [*măn'təl*], **MICKEY CHARLES** (1931–), American baseball player, born in Spavinaw, Okla. A switch-hitting outfielder, he joined New York of the American League in 1951 and won fame for his great power at bat and his speed afoot, despite recurrent injuries to his legs. A high point in his brilliant but rather erratic career was reached in 1956 when he was the league leader in batting (.353), home runs (52), and runs batted in (130). He was voted the league's most valuable player in 1956, 1957, and 1962. In 1967 he shifted from center field to first base. The same year he hit his 500th home run, the sixth major league hitter to achieve this record.

MARATHON. *See* TRACK AND FIELD.

MARCIANO [*mär-sē-ăn'ō*], **ROCKY,** professional name of Rocco Francis Marchegiano (1924–69), American boxer, born in Brockton, Mass. He won the world heavyweight championship by knocking out "Jersey Joe" Walcott in 13 rounds in 1952; he held the title until 1956 when he retired, after having won all 49 bouts of his professional career. Marciano, who had an aggressive, bruising style, was a powerful puncher despite his stocky frame and short arms.

MARIS [*măr'ĭs*], **ROGER EUGENE** (1934–), American baseball player, who became the first man to hit 61 home runs in a major league season. An outfielder for the New York Yankees, the left-handed slugger hit his 61st homer

Roger Maris hitting his record-setting 61st home run on the last day of the 1961 major league baseball season. (WIDE WORLD)

on Oct. 1, 1961, the last day of a 162-game season. (Babe Ruth, also a Yankee, had set the previous record: 60 homers in 154 games in 1927.) Maris, a native of Hibbing, Minn., was voted the most valuable player in the American League in 1960 and again in 1961. A major leaguer from 1957 through 1968, he had a lifetime total of 275 home runs.

MATHEWSON, CHRISTOPHER ("CHRISTY") (1880–1925), American baseball player, born in Factoryville, Pa. He was one of the sport's greatest pitchers. In 17 seasons (1900–16) in the National League—all but half of the last with New York—the right-hander won 373 games. This figure was matched by one other player in the league's history. Mathewson struck out 2,499 batters, a league career record. He won more than 30 games in a single season four times, achieving 37 victories in 1908. He pitched two no-hit games, and in the World Series of 1905 pitched three shutouts. He managed Cincinnati of the National League (1916–18) and was president of the Boston team of that league (1923–25). In 1936 Mathewson became a charter member of the National Baseball Hall of Fame.

MAYS, WILLIE HOWARD (1931–), American baseball player, born in Fairfield, Ala. An outfielder, he joined the New York Giants in 1951, and remained with the team when it went to San Francisco in 1958. An exciting, colorful player, he combined great batting power with daring base running and spectacular defensive play. He completed the 1966 season with a total of 542 home runs, a record second only to Babe Ruth's. He led the National League in home runs for the season in 1955, 1962, 1964, and 1965, in 1965 hitting 52 runs and topping his own previous league record of 1955 for most runs in a season. He was named Most Valuable Player of the National League in 1954 and again in 1965.

MIDDLECOFF, CARY (1921–), American golfer, born in Halls, Tenn. He was a dentist before becoming a professional golfer in 1947. From that year through 1966 he earned $294,168.33 in tournaments sanctioned by the Professional Golfers' Association. His notable victories were the United States Open tournaments in 1949 and 1956, and the Masters tournament in 1955.

MOODY, HELEN NEWINGTON WILLS (1906–), American tennis player, born in Centerville, Calif. She is generally considered the greatest woman player in the sport's history. Gaining national recognition as a mere girl, she won the U.S. women's singles championship, 1923–25, 1927–29, 1931; the Wimbledon women's singles title, 1927–30, 1932–33, 1935, and 1938; and the French women's singles crown, 1928–30, 1932. She was a member of the championship team in U.S. women's doubles, 1922, 1924–25, 1928, and of the championship mixed-doubles team in 1924 and 1928. A strong, seemingly tireless player, she gained the nickname "Little Poker Face."

MORENZ [*môr-ĕnz'*] **HOWARTH ("HOWIE")** (1902–37), Canadian hockey player, born in Mitchell, Ont. Considered by many the greatest center in the sport's history, he played for the Montreal Canadiens of the National Hockey League, 1923–34, and for Chicago and the New York Rangers before returning to the Canadiens in 1936; an injury suffered during play led to his untimely death. Exceedingly fast, he scored 270 goals in NHL competition and was named the league's most valuable player three times. He is a member of the National Hockey Hall of Fame.

MOTORBOATING, as a leisure-time pursuit, involves a wide range of activities, competitive and noncompetitive. The types of motorboats in wide use in the United States are almost as varied as the manner in which they are used. Owners of small craft use their boats primarily for fishing, hunting, cruising, water skiing, camping, skin diving, and racing. Most boats are designed for specific uses; many are adaptable in design and fulfill several different functions.

Motorboats are generally described, in terms of power, as of two types: inboard and outboard. An inboard boat is one whose engine is mounted inside the boat as a permanent installation. A drive shaft serves as the link between the boat's engine and its propeller. The shaft extends down, at an angle, through the boat's hull; it remains in a fixed position and is supported, underneath the hull, by a strut made fast to the bottom of the boat.

An outboard boat is one whose engine is generally mounted on the transom of the boat and is considered portable; that is, the engine can be removed at will since it is not a fixed installation. The shaft of an outboard engine extends downward, in an almost vertical position. Virtually all outboard engines are equipped with a pivot, or hingelike device, which permits them to tilt upward if the lower unit of the motor strikes an underwater object.

The tilting characteristic of an outboard engine allows an outboard boat to be beached more readily than an inboard boat; it also permits an outboard boat to be operated more easily in shallow water than an inboard.

Engineers are constantly striving to improve the type of power used in small craft. A recent development is the "inboard-outboard" engine, which combines the better features of both the inboard and the outboard. In effect, the engine is an inboard installation, mounted inside the hull, at a point with a low center of gravity, near the bottom of the boat. The engine makes use of an outboard drive, or lower unit. The outboard drive is coupled to the engine through a cut-out in the transom of the boat. The "inboard-outboard," on certain hulls, shows an economy of operation, usually inherent in an inboard engine, yet has the versatility of the outboard with its tilting characteristics.

The engines described in the foregoing are powered with gasoline. Some small craft are powered with diesel engines. A diesel engine burns oil, has fewer moving parts than a gasoline engine, and is more economical to operate. However, the initial cost of a diesel engine is considerably

Evinrude

The sturdy outboard day cruiser has sufficient room for family outings. As its name implies, it is not equipped with bunks or facilities for long nonstop trips.

Glasspar Co.

The 10-ft. fiber-glass boat uses a low-horsepower outboard motor. Lightweight and easy to handle, it accommodates two people comfortably and safely.

The high-speed outboard runabout is the most popular type of boat. Safety factors restrict its use to inland or protected ocean waterways. (EVINRUDE)

more than that of a gasoline engine. For this reason, relatively few small craft are diesel-powered. Diesel engines have their greatest use among work boats and on the largest of pleasure craft. Engine manufacturers are constantly experimenting with new types of propulsion, including various types of jet and turbine power in motorboating.

The horsepower of engines covers a wide range. Present-day outboards range from 1½ to 100 hp. Many inboard engines deliver several hundred horsepower. Among the factors that determine the type of engine to be used with a given boat are the design of the hull and the purpose for which the boat is used.

Types of Boats

All boats, sail or power, fall into two broad classifications of hull design. They are either displacement types or planing types. A displacement boat is one that is generally wide, or beamy, and has considerable draft, or depth, below its waterline. This type has a tendency to settle into the water; it literally displaces the water through which it runs.

A planing boat is generally one of shallow draft. Its hull is usually lighter than that of a displacement boat of comparable size; a planing boat has a tendency to ride on the surface of the water. A planing hull is considered faster than a displacement hull. Most boats used for racing are of the planing type.

The length of a boat is considered as a straight-line measurement from bow to stern. The measurement is referred to as "over-all length." Length is never considered as a gunwale measurement along the edge of the deck. The gunwale, or rail, is curved and does not give an accurate measure of footage from bow to stern.

Small Outboard Craft. The smallest boats adaptable to power are rowboats, dinghies, and prams. These range from 8 to 12 ft. in length. Some are used as tenders for larger craft. Many, in their original design, were meant to be propelled by sail or oar. However, small, lightweight outboard motors, in the 3-, 5-, and 10-hp range, are frequently used on boats of this type.

Some of these boats are referred to as "car-toppers." These are lightweight, made of wood, aluminum, or fiber glass, and can be carried conveniently, lashed to a rack atop an automobile. This type finds favor among fishermen, hunters, and campers.

Runabouts. Outboard runabouts are usually 14 to 18 ft. in over-all length. Runabouts are frequently highly styled, borrowing the concept of sports-car design from the automotive field. Inboard runabouts are seldom less than 18 ft. long. The inboard runabout is usually beamier than its outboard counterpart and has more freeboard, or measurement from its waterline to deck.

Outboards for Fishing. Outboards used for fishing span a wide range of hull types. Some, in the 12- to 16-ft. class, are used primarily in protected waters. Others are 18 to 21 ft. in over-all length. Few outboard boats are recommended for use in offshore ocean waters. Those that do venture offshore, and are skippered by knowledgeable seamen, are usually outfitted with twin engines.

Outboard Cruisers. Outboard cruisers are generally about 21 ft. in over-all length. Most have compact cabins with two bunks, a small marine toilet, and a stainless-steel galley consisting of a combination sink and drainboard. Some, called "day cruisers," are for day use; they are not outfitted with bunks, nor do their accommodations encourage lengthy nonstop trips. Some outboard cruisers are fitted with built-in gas tanks which hold up to 30 gal. of fuel. Many of these boats make use of portable 6-gal. tanks. The portable tank is convenient when a skipper is cruising in an area where there are no gas docks; the tank can be taken ashore and the fuel replenished at a filling station.

Outboard Houseboats. Outboard houseboats generally range from 20 to 40 ft. in length and are usually powered by one or more engines. Most houseboats are boxlike in structure. Their hulls are usually rectangular in shape. A houseboat is considered an extremely functional design. Because of its wide beam and flat bottom, a houseboat is more stable than a conventional hull, which has either a rounded or "V" bottom.

The rectangular shape of the houseboat also allows for more efficient use of interior space. Bunks, lockers, and closets are easily built into a houseboat; they are not so easily built into a conventional hull with its many curves and rounded surfaces.

The upper deck of a houseboat is generally a large, flat plane. Because of its size, it easily accommodates deck chairs and mattresses, making it an ideal sun lounge. Compared to other craft, houseboats are usually slow in speed. However, they are extremely comfortable, and many families use them as water-borne vacation or week-end "cottages."

Small Inboard Craft. The smallest inboard boats are usually about 18 ft. in length. They are as varied as outboards and include fishing boats, runabouts, and "utilities," or all-purpose boats. Utilities frequently serve as tenders for larger craft. They are often found at clubs where they render ferry service for club members.

Inboard Cruisers. Inboard cruisers range up to 50 ft. in length. Their appointments depend entirely upon the extent to which their builders go beyond providing essentials. Some are luxurious, including individual staterooms for the owner, captain, and guests. Boats of this sort are frequently fitted with stall showers, lounges, numerous wardrobe lockers, large galleys, and deep-freeze units for preserving food during lengthy trips.

Some inboard cruisers, called "fishermen," are designed specifically for sport fishing. Those used in the pursuit of game fish, such as marlin or swordfish, are often equipped with aluminum towers which serve as lookout posts. Boats of this type usually have one or two "fighting chairs" made fast to the floor of the cockpit. A fighting chair looks somewhat like a large barber chair. Sockets, which hold fishing rods, are attached to its arms.

Water-Skiing and Skin-Diving Boats. Within recent years, special boats, both inboard and outboard, have been designed for water skiing and skin diving. Water-ski boats have light, fast planing hulls. They are equipped with special speedometers and carry a minimum of hardware such as cleats, or chocks, which might foul a skier's towline.

Skin-diving boats are of a utility type. They have large, open cockpits which allow ample room to bring aboard gear and to move about in preparation for a dive. On some, a portion of the boat's bottom is cut out, allowing for installation of a glass-bottom well. The well serves as a window, permitting a view of activity beneath the boat. A compact folding ladder, which generally fits to the boat's coaming, is considered essential equipment on small craft used for skin diving.

Safety Requirements

All motorboats, no matter what their size and power, are required by law to carry at least one life preserver for each person aboard. Every motorboat, according to size, must have one or more fire extinguishers aboard. The U.S. Coast Guard defines the equipment required by law. The Coast Guard also recommends the use of certain equipment which, if not legally required, should be aboard a boat in the interest of safety.

Racing

Types of Competition. The American Power Boat Association and the National Outboard Association are the two national organizations that sanction and supervise motorboat competition in the United States. Competition is open to a wide variety of craft. It includes closed-course racing for inboard and outboard boats; long-distance, or marathon, racing; drag racing; and predicted-log contests for cruisers. In the last-named, the skippers estimate the times at which their craft will pass designated markers along the course, taking into account such factors as engine speed and tidal currents. The victor is the one whose estimates come closest to the actual times recorded in the running of the race.

Types of Craft. Motorboats used for racing are divided into classes determined by such factors as piston displacement of the boat's engine, measured in cubic inches; the maximum cost of the engine; and the design and construction of the boat's hull.

Many races are for "stock" boats, hydroplanes, or runabouts. A stock boat is one that adheres to the builder's original specifications and has not been modified. Many stock runabouts are typical family boats which, when not racing, might be used for fishing or water skiing. A hydroplane is a basic racing hull; its bottom usually has a "step," or break, in its surface plane which allows the boat to ride slightly airborne over the water.

The American Power Boat Association currently lists more than 60 different classes of motorboats as eligible for competition in sanctioned regattas. Some classes are more popular in one part of the country than in another.

The "heavyweights" in racing are commonly called Gold Cup boats. These are unlimited hydroplanes, so designated because there is no limit to the horsepower they may carry. Many of these boats are equipped with aircraft engines, sometimes delivering more than 2,000 hp. They may have one or more engines. The boats must measure more than 25 ft. and less than 40 ft. in over-all length. The unlimited hydroplanes are those that race for the Gold Cup.

Famous Races. In recent years, the Gold Cup, the most coveted prize in U.S. motorboat racing, has been competed for on the Detroit River, Detroit; Lake Washington, Seattle; and on Lake Mead, Nevada. The Gold Cup, a 90-mi. race comprising three 30-mi. heats, was first run in 1904. It is not unusual for a Gold Cup boat to average better than 100 mph in competition. Recent winners of

This hydroplane is equipped with a modified V-8 automobile engine, and can attain speeds of more than 100 mph. Hydroplanes in general are shallow-draft inboard motorboats. (CHAMPION SPARK PLUG)

A stock racing outboard runabout takes to the air in the Race of Paris, a highly competitive marathon on the Seine River. (UPI)

The inboard runabout is a long-time favorite. This 6-passenger 18-footer is powered by a 185-hp V-8 marine engine. (CHRIS-CRAFT)

the Gold Cup have been Jack Regas, William M. Stead, Bill Muncey, and Ron Musson. Musson won three consecutive years, in 1963, 1964, and 1965.

The Harmsworth Trophy, the outstanding prize in international competition, was first placed in competition by the British newspaper publisher Sir Edward Harmsworth in 1903. The Gold Cup was put up by the American Power Boat Association. Other leading races involving U.S. boats are the President's Cup, Silver Cup, and Detroit Memorial Trophy.

Speed Records. World speed records are usually made in time trials, over a straight, measured course which has been cleared, rather than in competition with other boats. The speeds have increased dramatically over the past years. Roy Duby became the first to officially exceed 200 mph. in other than jet craft when he was clocked at 200.419 in 1962. The 200-mph. mark had been broken in a jet-propelled boat in 1955 by the Englishman Donald Campbell, and he later far exceeded that record.

Other Outstanding Individuals. Each year, the American Power Boat Association names outstanding drivers, boat owners, or race officials to its Honor Squadron in acknowledgment of their contributions to the sport. Among the members are Stanley S. Sayres, Seattle, Wash., whose boats, *Slo-Mo-Shun IV* and *Slo-Mo-Shun V*, driven by different pilots, won the Gold Cup for five consecutive years, 1950–54; W. Melvin Crook, Montclair, N.J., a prominent racing driver in the 1930's, but more recently a regatta official who served as referee in the Gold Cup competition; Paul B. Sawyer, Jr., Rochester, N.Y., who dominated amateur outboard and intercollegiate racing in the 1930's; and George W. Sutton, Jr., New York City, an official of the American Power Boat Association who furthered international competition by establishing liaison with the Union of International Motorboating, Brussels, Belgium.

Scope of Motorboating

Motorboating is primarily a family participant sport. Only a fraction of the motorboats throughout the country are used for racing. The vast majority are used for cruising, fishing, camping, water skiing, and skin diving.

It is difficult to determine, with accuracy, the total

The flying bridge of this 31-ft. sea-going inboard cruiser serves as a lookout post for sighting game fish. (BERTRAM YACHT CO.)

PARTS OF A TYPICAL OUTBOARD MOTOR

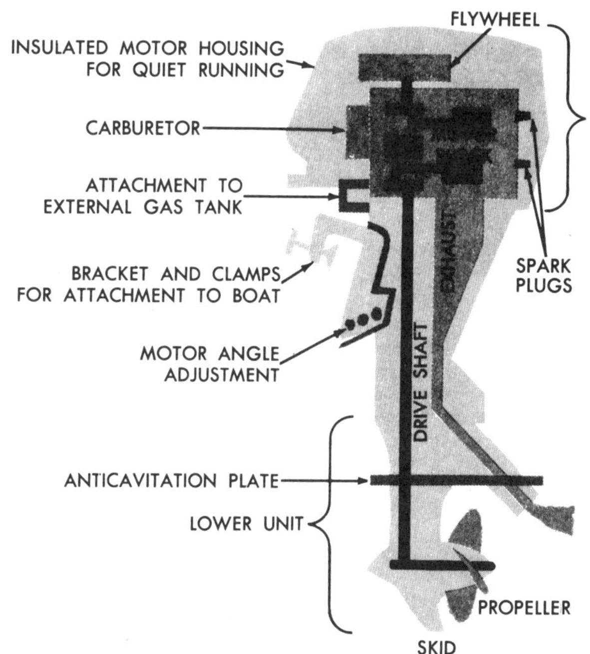

TWO NEW POWER SYSTEMS

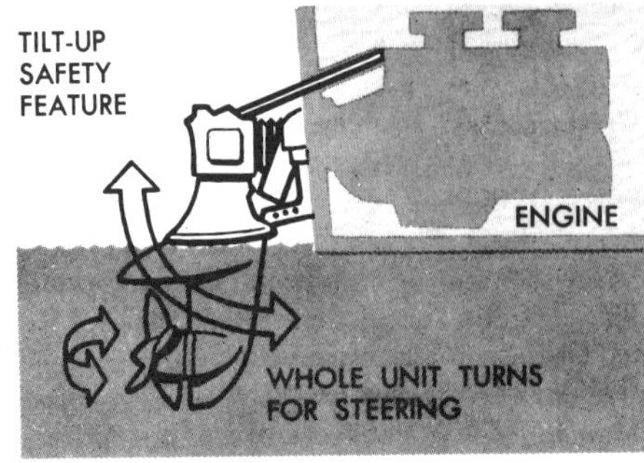

INBOARD-OUTBOARD
This system offers the economy, power, and reliability of the inboard plus the outboard advantages of shallow-water operation and ease of transport.

Bertram Yacht Co.

Buehler Corp.

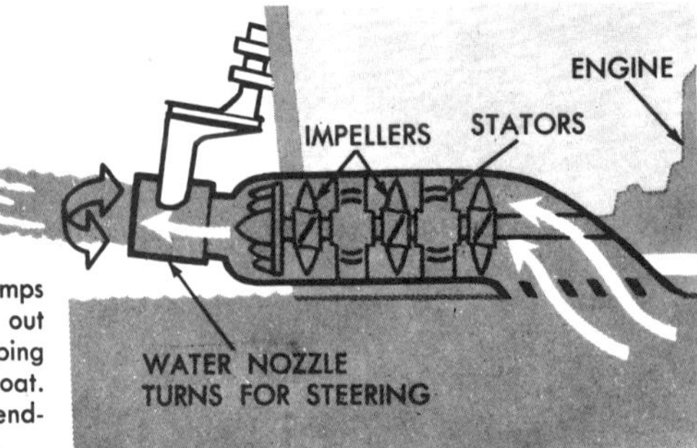

WATER JET
The engine-driven turbine pumps water in through the grill, out through the nozzle, developing thrust, which propels the boat. There are no underwater appendages to foul or create drag.

number of boats in use. Under the Federal Boating Act of 1958, the federal and state governments began conducting a "census" to tally the number of boats powered with engines. Meanwhile, industry estimates in the early 1960's placed the count at some 850,000 inboard boats and from 4,000,000 to 6,000,000 outboard craft, all of varying size.

The reasons for the recent growth of boating in the United States and Canada are both social and economic. Economic prosperity has meant increased wages, a shorter working week, and more leisure time. Boating, like many sports, has benefited from such a combination of factors. In addition, boating appeals to many since it is a sport in which all members of the family can participate, regardless of age. Also, boating is not limited to one section of a country, nor to tidewater areas. Man-made lakes, the result of hydroelectric projects, exist in many areas, including the Tennessee Valley, the Ozarks, and the Texas-Oklahoma border. The creation of these lakes has opened vast inland seas, now used by the owners of small craft.

The introduction of the boat trailer has given new dimension to the sport. Many boatmen, not living near the water, now trail their craft to distant rivers, lakes, and harbors. Interest in camping has brought many families into boating; one activity complements the other. Many states are presently expanding campsites to include fuel docks, launching ramps, and berthing facilities for owners of small craft.

Programs for Beginners. Two organizations, the United States Coast Guard Auxiliary and the United States Power Squadrons, conduct extensive educational programs for beginners in boating. The Coast Guard Auxiliary is a voluntary civilian body. The Auxiliary frequently assists the Coast Guard in the patrol of regattas and special events held on the water. The Auxiliary also conducts "courtesy examinations" of small craft, advising boat owners on equipment required by law and recommended in the interest of greater safety.

The United States Power Squadrons is comprised of 52,000 members representing more than 300 squadrons throughout the nation. Its courses include piloting, seamanship, small-boat handling, engine maintenance, and navigation. Information concerning its classes may be obtained from the national headquarters of the United States Power Squadrons, Englewood, N.J.

See also SAILING; SKIN DIVING; SURFBOARDING; WATER SKIING.

MOTORCYCLING. The motorcycle, like most vehicles of mechanical propulsion, became an instrument of competitive sport soon after its invention late in the 19th century. Manufacturers of these early motorcycles pitted their machines against those of other manufacturers as a means of proving the worth of their products to the buying public. Thus was born the forerunner of modern competition among riders.

Types of Competitive Events. The five categories of present-day competition include:

Flat-track Racing. This occurs on a dirt-surfaced oval measuring a mile, half mile, or quarter mile in length. Use of brakes is not permitted; instead the rider employs engine compression in slowing down.

Road Racing. A road-racing course is a hard-surfaced, closed course, part or all of which may be a public road. In these events, which are of longer duration than those conducted on flat, dirt tracks, brakes are used.

T. T. (Tourist Trophy) Racing. Such events are conducted on specially prepared dirt courses whose paths are not straight, and which include ascents and dips. Brakes are used.

Hill Climbs. In these, contestants in a given event run

REAR BRAKE
DIMMER AND HORN
CLUTCH
HEADLIGHT
FOOT REST
SEAT
GAS TANK
INSTRUMENTS
GEAR SHIFT
KICK-STARTER
FRONT BRAKE
TWIST THROTTLE

CARBURETOR
SEAT
FRAME
EXHAUST
DRIVE CHAIN
KICK-STARTER
GEAR SHIFT

Triumph Engineering Co., Ltd.

torcyclist wears a helmet and heavy leather suit for protection.

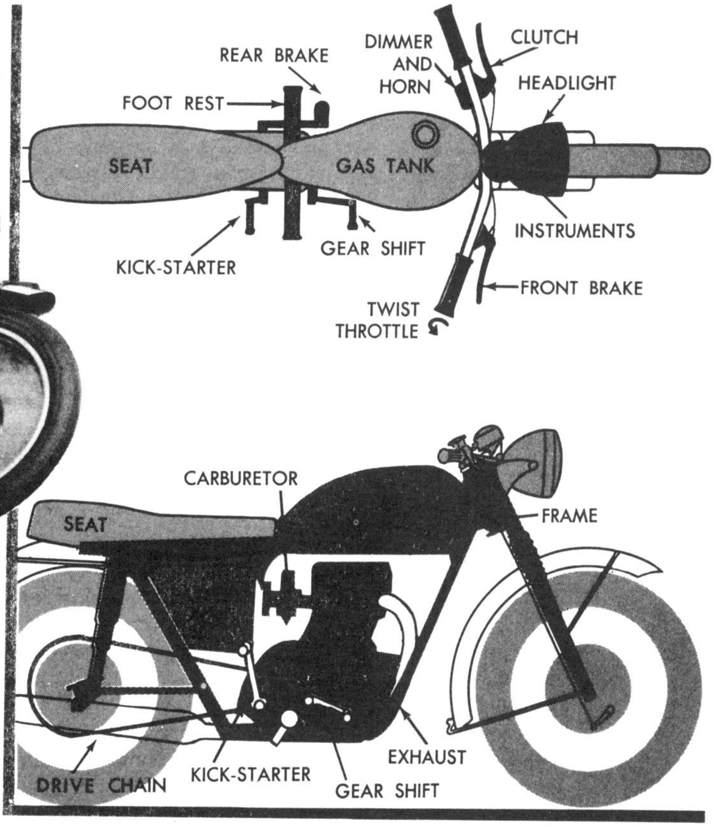

MAJOR PARTS OF A MOTORCYCLE

usual arrangement of motorcycle parts is pictured, but variations st. The standard modern machine has a gasoline engine to gene- e power, transmitted to the rear wheel by a drive chain. Separate kes are provided for front and rear wheels. The clutch is located the left handlebar and the throttle on the right.

MOTORCYCLES FOR SPORT

A motorcycle makes a turn in a Grand Prix race. This competition attracts outstanding drivers and machines. Sometimes with five forward speeds and traveling over 150 mph, the motorcycles race on paved highways or tracks. The circuit is closed so that machines make repeated laps on one course. Some streamlining of the machines is permitted. Almost every major motorcycle manufacturer enters Grand Prix events. (HONDA MOTOR CO.)

their machines up a steep, specially prepared hill, competing against time.

Sportsmen Events. Unlike the other categories, these events are not conducted for prize money. Instead, trophies are awarded to winners of such competitions sanctioned by the American Motorcycle Association, the governing body in U.S. competitive motorcycling. Sportsmen events include scrambles (conducted over rough terrain, frequently on hillsides), road runs (road events conducted against time), endurance runs (events in which the driver travels over both surfaced roads and rough terrain, and competes against time), hill climbs, economy runs (in which drivers strive for maximum distance on a specified amount of fuel), field meets (involving trick racing), and drag (acceleration) races.

U.S. Competition. In the early 1960's the American Motorcycle Association annually sponsored more than 3,000 competitive events. Prize money was paid in about 10% of that total. Approximately 1,250 riders competed in the over-all total; about 2,000,000 spectators witnessed the events. The national championship events in Daytona Beach, Fla., annually attracted great interest.

International Competition. On the international level, the sport is governed by the Fédération Internationale Motocycliste. It enjoys wide popularity in virtually every country. The most famous event is the Isle of Man T. T. spectacle, conducted annually and involving competition for machines of various motor sizes. Another noteworthy event, the International Six-Day Trials held regularly in different countries, provides a severe six-day test of men and machines.

MOUNTAINEERING, the technique of climbing earth's high places, may be variously described as an art, a science, a sport, and a form of exploration. In scope it includes all mountain activity from the scaling of a small cliff to an assault on a giant peak. Its basic aspect is the physical one of reaching high points difficult of access. But it embraces many other elements as well, among them aesthetic pleasures, the thrill of discovery, the avoidance of dangers, and the sustaining of life in remote and inhospitable places.

History. As a sport and a craft, mountaineering has a comparatively brief history. The first ascents of major peaks were made in the late 18th century, and in the mid-19th century came the so-called golden age of European mountaineering, during which almost every peak in the Alps was successfully scaled. This period culminated in 1865 in the conquest of the Matterhorn by the Englishman Edward Whymper and six companions, four of whom were killed in the descent.

Using holes cut in the ice by the leadman, a climber makes an almost vertical ascent on Mount McKinley. Climbers are tied together with nylon rope as a safeguard against falling. The ice ax and crampons, the framework of steel spikes on boots, help prevent slips and falls. Other essential equipment includes oxygen for high-altitude breathing and dark glasses to prevent snow blindness.

Sam Silverstein

From Europe, activity spread out across the world. There were expeditions, many successful, in the North American Rockies, the South American Andes, and to the great peaks of Alaska, Africa, and Asia. With the beginning of the 20th century, the prize goal of climbers became the Himalayas, on the frontier of India and Tibet —the highest mountains on earth. In attempt after attempt, men struggled toward their summits, notably that of Mount Everest, which, at 29,141 ft., is the highest of all. But although there were many near-misses, there were for years few successes.

Then, following World War II, came the second golden age of mountaineering. Before 1950 not one of the earth's 13 highest peaks (all in the Himalayas) had been climbed to the top. By 1961 all had been climbed. Most notable of the ascents was that of Everest itself in 1953 by a British expedition. Among other outstanding climbs, by teams of various nationalities, were those of K2, Kanchenjunga, Makalu, and Dhaulagiri.

Largely, these recent successes have been due to vast improvements in the physical paraphernalia of mountaineering: to concentrated foods, warmer yet lighter clothing and shelter, and above all to effective oxygen equipment. But there have been psychological factors as well. For with each successive venture there has been greater knowledge, greater confidence, less fear of the untrodden and unknown.

Present-day Extent. Mountaineering activity, however, is by no means confined to large expeditions to major peaks. By far the greater part of it is carried on by small groups of climbers on lesser mountains that have been scaled many times before. The immediate goal is usually a summit or high point, but it is the climbing itself, the means rather than the end, that is the important thing. The exercise of physical skills, the overcoming of obstacles, the beauties of nature, the lure of the unknown—these, for most climbers, are the essence of mountaineering.

The Alps of Europe are still the most popular mountain area in the world. In the United States various sections of the Appalachians, Rockies, Sierras, and Cascades have, year by year, attracted increasing numbers of climbers. That danger exists in the mountains is undeniable. But it can be enormously reduced—on lesser ones almost eliminated—by knowledge, care, and sound judgment. Among the organizations in the United States devoted both to the pleasures and safety of mountaineering are the American Alpine Club, New York; the Appalachian Mountain Club, Boston; the Colorado Mountain Club, Denver; the Sierra Club, San Francisco; the Mazamas, Portland, Oreg.; and the Mountaineers, Seattle, Wash.

MUSIAL [*mū'zē-əl*], **STANLEY FRANK ("STAN THE MAN")** (1920–), American baseball player, born in Donora, Pa. A left-handed batter and thrower, he played the outfield and first base for St. Louis of the National League, beginning in 1941. Though he began his career as a pitcher, he changed positions because of a shoulder injury and became one of the greatest hitters in the history of the sport, despite a highly unorthodox batting stance.

Between 1941 and 1958, his most productive period, he compiled a career batting average of .340, led the league in batting seven times, and was voted its most valuable player three times. In the early 1960's he held 17 major league career records, including those for total bases and extra-base hits, and 30 National League records. He retired as a player at the end of the 1963 season.

N

NATIONAL ASSOCIATION OF COLLEGIATE COMMISSIONERS, organization composed of the chief administrative executive officers of 11 of the major U.S. collegiate athletic conferences. It was formed in 1940 as the National Association of Football Commissioners; it took its present name in 1948. National headquarters are in Kansas City, Mo.

NATIONAL ASSOCIATION OF INTERCOLLEGIATE ATHLETICS (NAIA), organization devoted to administration of sports programs of U.S. colleges and universities of moderate enrollment. It was formed in 1940 as an outgrowth of the National Association of Intercollegiate Basketball, which was organized in 1937 to stage a national basketball tournament for smaller colleges; it took its present name in 1952. Though the NAIA widened its functions after 1952, it continued to serve its original goal of furthering intersectional and national competition for fully accredited four-year colleges and universities below the "major" classification. In the early 1960's the NAIA comprised approximately 460 schools whose average enrollment was about 1,500. The membership is divided into 32 districts throughout the entire United States. National headquarters are in Kansas City, Mo. The governing body is the executive committee, composed of representatives of member schools.

NATIONAL COLLEGIATE ATHLETIC ASSOCIATION (NCAA), major administrative organization of U.S. intercollegiate athletics. It was formed in 1905 to bring about reforms in playing rules of intercollegiate football with specific regard to tactics that then caused a rising tide of injuries and deaths. Originally called the Intercollegiate Athletic Association, it took its present name in 1910 and steadily broadened its functions. In the 1960's the NCAA had a membership of nearly 600 colleges and universities, athletic conferences, and coaches' organizations. Its headquarters are in Kansas City, Mo.

The NCAA conducts meets or tournaments in the following sports: baseball, basketball, cross-country, fencing, golf, gymnastics, ice hockey, skiing, soccer, swimming, tennis, track and field, and wrestling. Separate competitions for college and university divisions (according to sizes of member schools) are held in basketball, cross-country, golf, tennis, track and field, and wrestling. Each winning team is designated National Collegiate Champion.

Since 1952 the NCAA has provided enforcement machinery to implement the organization's legislation, which all members are obligated to observe. NCAA committees formulate and publish rules of play for baseball, basketball, boxing, fencing, football, gymnastics, ice hockey, lacrosse, skiing, soccer, swimming, track and field, and wrestling.

The NCAA compiles and distributes statistics and records of its participant groups in football, basketball, and track and field; maintains an extensive film library; administers group insurance programs whereby member schools can provide catastrophe and medical coverage for athletes injured in practice, play, or transport; and participates in Olympic and Pan American Games by serving as an administrative agency in fund raising and sports organization and by providing coaches and athletes for U.S. teams.

See also NATIONAL ASSOCIATION OF INTERCOLLEGIATE ATHLETICS (NAIA).

OAKLEY [ōk'lē], **ANNIE,** original name Phoebe Anne Oakley Mozee (1860–1926), American sharpshooter. Born in Darke County, Ohio, she was reared in poverty and paid off the family mortgage between her 9th and 15th years by shipping game she had killed to Cincinnati. When a vaudeville show with a remarkable marksman named Frank E. Butler came to Cincinnati, she was matched against him and won by one point. Butler fell in love with the young girl, corresponded with her for a number of years, and then returned to marry her and add her to his act. Recognizing the appeal of her girlish innocence coupled with her deadly shooting eye, Butler showed the good sense and modesty, then rare among performers, to make her the feature of the show while he concentrated on being her manager. In New Orleans in 1885 the couple joined Buffalo Bill's Wild West Show, where she continued to be a star performer.

Some of Annie Oakley's exploits with a gun, fully authenticated, are almost unbelievable for accuracy, speed of firing, and endurance. A favorite of Queen Victoria and of European royalty, she even had the "honor" of shooting a cigarette from the lips of the future Kaiser Wilhelm II of Germany. She was partially paralyzed after 1901 but continued to break shooting records into the 1920's. Complimentary tickets with punch holes in them have come to be called "Annie Oakleys" because of her reputation for

Culver Pictures
Annie Oakley displaying some of her many marksmanship awards.

riddling a playing card with a half-dozen bullets during the time it took to float from a man's hand to the ground.

OLDFIELD, BERNER ELI ("BARNEY") (1878–1946), American pioneer automobile racer, born in Wauseon, Ohio. In 1902 he won his first major race, a 5-mi (8 km) event near Detroit, by driving the famous 999 racer, designed by Henry Ford; his time was 5 minutes, 28 seconds. In 1903 he became the first man to drive a racing car on a curved course at 60 mph (97 kmph) under officially sanctioned conditions. Oldfield set an official speed mark, 131.724 mph (211.98 kmph), in 1910. After his retirement from racing in 1918, he headed his own tire-manufacturing firm.

OLYMPIC GAMES, series of competitive sports events, were originally held in ancient Greece. Revived in 1896 as a worldwide athletic contest, the modern Olympic Games are held every four years and are considered the ultimate competition among amateur athletes. The Winter Games—contests held on snow and ice—were added in 1924.

Ancient Games

The Olympic Games, the most celebrated of the ancient Panhellenic athletic festivals, were held every four years in late August or early September at Olympia in connection with rites honoring Zeus. In earliest times, funeral games had taken place at Zeus's oracle, and in legend the foundation of the games was attributed to Hercules.

Supposedly half-forgotten during the troubled centuries after the Trojan War, the Olympic Games were renewed about the 9th century B.C. as a peace move. A truce was established which demanded safe conduct for all Greeks traveling to and from the Olympic festival and forbade wars during that season. This remained an unalterable law throughout Olympia's existence.

No reliable victor lists were kept for the first 27 celebrations (108 years) after the renewal. These began officially with the games in which Coroebus won the foot race (776 B.C. by modern chronology). These games were thus erroneously called Olympiad I by ancient compilers. Already in the 7th century B.C. the games were immensely popular throughout the Greek world and embodied a mixture of business, social, religious, and athletic events. By 472 B.C. the new city of Elis, 34 mi (55 km) from Olympia, became the administrative center of the festival.

The date, duration, and athletic events of the Olympic Games were altered from time to time, but by the early 5th century B.C. the festival probably required five days. Aspiring athletes had to arrive in advance for a month's pitiless training under special Olympic rules and under trainers quick with the punishing stick. Events were open only to men of strictly Greek parentage and of proven ages: 17–20 for junior events, 20-plus for senior events. After a colorful procession of all participants from Elis to Olympia, the athletes took part in religious rites and lot-drawing for positions. They then swore before Zeus regarding their Greek parentage, unblemished character, and adherence to training rules for the previous 10 months. This was followed by the swearing of the umpires.

Athletic contests in the 5th century B.C. included foot racing for 200 yd (183 m), 400 yd (366 m), and 3 mi (4.8 km) or more; the pentathlon (foot race, jumping, discus throwing, javelin throwing, and wrestling); wrestling; boxing; the *pancratium* (ground wrestling with no holds barred); racing in armor for 400 yd (366 m), and chariot and horse racing.

Victors were awarded wild olive wreaths at Olympia in the temple of Zeus. Sacrifices, parades, and singing of traditional triumph songs followed and culminated in a complimentary dinner for victors in the public hall. Champions received, in addition, valuable gifts and privileges upon their return home.

The Olympic Games, after a history of almost 1,200 years of recorded victor lists, ceased about 400 A.D. as a result of Christian edicts against the Zeus temple at Olympia and of chaotic conditions throughout Greece.

Modern Olympic Games

The first modern Olympic games took place in Athens, Greece, in 1896, when about 300 male athletes, representing 13 countries, participated in nine sports. The revival of the games is generally credited to a French educator and sportsman, Baron Pierre de Coubertin, but a team of archeologists also played an important role. In the 1870's they had unearthed most of the Olympia complex near the Temple of Zeus in Athens, prompting Coubertin's effort.

Coubertin, believing that a restoration would be good for the youth of the world, brought together in Paris in 1894 an international group which enthusiastically greeted his suggestion. The original plan was to hold the first modern games in Paris in 1900—to coincide with the Paris International Exposition—but Greek delegates were persuasive that the renewal should take place in Athens.

Setup of the Games. The governing committee of the Olympic Games is the International Olympic Committee, consisting of between 60 and 80 officials from national Olympic committees of member countries. It controls every aspect of the games, holds regular meetings and conferences, and is headed by an executive board consisting of a president, three vice presidents and five selected members.

The IOC elects its own members, who must be free from political, sectarian, or commercial influence. Each member must be able to speak either French or English.

One duty of the IOC is continually to update rules and regulations concerning participating athletes, particularly with regard to amateurism. The cardinal rule is that an athlete must not have been, must not be, and must not be under contract to be a professional athlete, coach, or trainer in any sport. Other rules require conformity to drug regulations and medical control, and submission to examinations when ordered by the IOC's medical commission. For example, competitors in sports restricted to women must comply with prescribed tests for femininity. There is no age limit for competitors, but only citizens of a country can represent that country in the games.

Any amateur sport widely practiced by men in at least 40 countries and on at least three continents may be included in the program for the summer games. But each program of games must include at least 15 of the following sports: archery, athletics (track and field), basketball, boxing, canoeing, cycling, equestrian sports, fencing, football, gymnastics, handball, field hockey, judo, modern pentathlon, rowing, shooting, swimming and diving, water polo, volleyball, weightlifting, wrestling, and yachting.

Women's sports are restricted to those practiced in at least 20 countries or on at least two continents.

Each country is permitted to enter at least one athlete or one team in each event.

Any athlete who has been found guilty of violating the eligibility rules of the games is stripped of his medal or medals.

The ritual of an Olympic oath dates back to the ancient games, but it did not become a regular practice in the modern games until the 1920 Olympics in Antwerp, Belgium. There Victor Bolin, a Belgian fencer, recited the oath on behalf of all participating athletes.

The medal ceremonies are kept simple. Three medal winners—or three medal-winning teams—mount the dais to receive their awards (first place, gold; second place, silver; third place, bronze). They then turn to face the flags of their respective countries and stand at attention while the anthem of the country winning the gold medal is played. Its flag is raised higher than the other two.

The games are held in the first year of an Olympiad, a period of four years beginning in a year divisible by four. It is a rule that the games cannot be postponed. However, World War I forced cancellation of the scheduled 1916 games in Berlin. World War II wiped out the 1940 games originally scheduled for Tokyo—later reassigned to Helsinki—as well as the 1944 games in London.

The IOC selects a host city six years before the games. Whenever there is a cancellation, the number of the Olympiad progresses as if the games had been held. So the Montreal Olympics of 1976 were the XXI Olympiad, even though actually the 18th of the modern era.

Winter Olympics. The Winter Games were first held in Chamonix, France, in 1924 when 16 nations competed for 14 gold medals in the following sports: bobsleigh, ice hockey, Nordic skiing, figure skating, and speed skating. Winter Olympics were discontinued after the 1936 games—which included Alpine skiing for the first time—but resumed in St. Moritz, Switzerland, in 1948. They are held in the same year as the summer games.

One ironic footnote to the first Winter Olympics was the last-place finish in a field of eight by an 11-year-old Norwegian schoolgirl in the figure-skating competition. Her name was Sonja Henie, and she went on to win three Olympic and 10 world championships while blossoming into one of the greatest sports personalities.

Politics and the Olympics. The attention focused on so publicized an international event made it certain that someone would endeavor to turn the gathering into a political arena. Hitler had injected a political note into the 1936 Berlin Olympics when he credited Aryan supremacy with Germany's victories. In more recent times politicizing the games has intensified. In Mexico, which was host to the 1968 games, clashes between high school students in July grew into massive student protests against the government. One student contention was that the money spent preparing for the games should have been used to combat poverty. Before the games took place in October the town-gown confrontation became a student-army battle that left 200 dead, hundreds wounded, and other hundreds in jail.

Violence moved into the Olympic games proper in 1972, when Munich was host city. There, eight Palestinian terrorists carrying machine guns and hand grenades in athletic equipment bags, invaded the Israeli athletes' headquarters in Olympic Village. They took 9 Israelis hostage and demanded the release of 200 Arab political prisoners held by Israel. Subsequent events cost the lives of 11 Israeli athletes, 5 terrorists, and one West German policeman. The games, which had all but stopped, went on to completion, after a moving ceremony as a memorial to the slain.

In the much more security-conscious Montreal setting in 1976 violence was avoided, but politics persisted. Many African nations refused to participate when the IOC did not act against New Zealand, whose rugby team had toured South Africa, which had been excluded from the Olympics because of its racism.

Another political struggle involved the athletes sent as representatives of the Republic of China. When the ICC ruled that they represented Taiwan only, the athletes withdrew.

Olympic Highlights

1896, Athens—Americans won nine of 12 track and field events while dominating the overall competition that opened on the 75th anniversary of Greece's independence from Turkey. But a victory by Spiridon Louis, a Greek shepherd, in the 40-km (nearly 25-mi) race was by far the

Spiridon Louis, a Greek shepherd, won the 40-km race and provided the most dramatic moment as the Olympic Games were revived in Athens in 1896. In the last lap Greek royalty—Prince George and Crown Prince Constantine—ran with the shepherd.

The Bettmann Archive

most dramatic single event. Louis trailed until the final four kilometers, then took the lead and was well in front when he entered Panathenaic Stadium. Some 80,000 spectators roared their delight and Greece's Prince George and Crown Prince Constantine jogged beside him during his final lap.

The first Olympic gold medal went to an American. James Connolly of the Boston Athletic Association won the "hop, step, and jump" after paying all his own expenses to make the trip to Greece.

1900, Paris—An American trackman, Alvin Kraenzlein of Pennsylvania, provided most of the heroics by capturing four gold medals: the 60-m dash, the 110-m hurdles, the 200-m hurdles, and the long jump. The United States won 17 of the 30 gold medals awarded.

Unusual events included a tug-of-war, won by a joint team from Denmark and Sweden; an underwater swim, and a 200-m obstacle race during which competitors had to swim through barrels spaced along the course.

1904, St. Louis—The gold medal domination by the American team was awesome as it finished first in 22 of the 23 events Archie Hahn, James Lightbody, and Ray Ewry, all trackmen, registered three victories each. The only non-U.S. winner was Etienne Desmarteau of Canada, who took the 56-lb (25-kg) weight throw.

The first life suspension of an Olympic performer excluded Fred Lorz of the United States, who dropped out of the marathon race but then accepted a ride of several miles in a car and ran into the stadium to be proclaimed the winner. The incident was soon brought to light, and Thomas Hicks of the United States was awarded the gold medal.

1908, London—A British runner, Wyndham Halswelle, won the gold medal in the 400-m race without competitors. A foul had been ruled during the championship race; J. C. Carpenter, an American, was disqualified, and the race was ordered rerun. But the two other Americans in the final refused to take part in protest against the judge's decision, so that Halswelle became the only participant.

The end of the 1908 marathon race is one of the games' most heart-touching stories. Italy's Dorando Pietri, exhausted by the grueling ordeal on an extremely hot day, arrived at Shepherd's Bush Stadium but collapsed before reaching the finish line. Officials got him back on his feet and directed him to the finish line. However, this assistance resulted in his disqualification, and an American, John Hayes, was awarded the gold medal. Pietri was presented with a special gold cup for his performance.

1912, Stockholm—Jim Thorpe, an American Indian, was the sensation of the games, winning two gold medals—the decathlon and the modern pentathlon, which was being held for the first time. In the following year it was revealed that Thorpe had participated in semiprofessional baseball earlier in his career and, because he had received several dollars in payment, was in fact not an amateur according to the rules and therefore disqualified.

1916—No Olympiad (World War I).

1920, Antwerp—Finland's track and field team stole the show even though the Americans won 41 of the 150 gold medals. The Finns won nine of their 15 medals in track and field, thus breaking the dominance of the United States in its specialty. One of the Finnish standouts was Paavo Nurmi—known as one of the games' legendary performers—who won the 10,000-m run and cross-country race.

Hannes Kolehmainen, who had won three gold medals for Finland four years earlier, captured the marathon by finishing just 13 seconds ahead of the runner-up.

1924, Paris—Nurmi, by this time nicknamed "The Flying Finn," was far and away the sensation. He won the 1,500-m run, the 5,000-m run, and the 10,000-m cross-country race and led the Finns to victories in the 3,000-m and crosscountry team events.

Johnny Weissmuller, who would later become world-famous as Tarzan in the movies, won the 100-m and 400-m individual freestyle swimming events and sparked a U.S. victory in the 800-meter freestyle team event.

1928, Amsterdam—Women participated in track and field for the first time. Canada won two of the five medals as Ethel Catherwood finished first in the high jump and ran as a member of the victorious 400-m relay team.

1932, Los Angeles—For the first time, athletes were

quartered in an "Olympic Village" that was specially constructed. It housed some 1,300 male athletes. About 300 women competitors lived in a hotel during the games.

The most memorable event may have been the 3,000-m steeplechase, won by Finland's Volmari Iso-Hollo, who couldn't believe his time of 10 minutes 33.4 seconds because he had won a qualifying heat in 9 minutes 14.6 seconds. Later it was learned an official's mistake meant Iso-Hollo had run an extra lap—a total of 3,460 m.

1936, Berlin—The torch relay was held for the first time in the modern games. Athletes took turns carrying the flame from Greece to Grunewald Stadium. (Now the torch relay is standard procedure.)

Although host Germany dominated the competition by capturing 33 gold medals to America's 24, the individual star was U.S. trackman Jesse Owens, who won three championships on his own—the 100- and 200-m dashes and the long jump—and assisted the U.S. victory in the sprint relay. Owen's winning leap in the long jump—26 feet 5¼ inches (about 7.75 m)—broke the previous Olympic record by more than 12 inches (30 cm).

1940 and 1944—No Olympiads (World War II).

1948, London—Fifty-nine countries were represented by 4,468 athletes. The United States, with a sweep of eight gold medals in men's swimming and 11 in track and field, dominated.

1952, Helsinki—Emil Zatopek of Czechoslovakia, who had captured the 10,000-m run in 1948, won gold medals in the 5,000-m and 10,000-m races and in the marathon, all in record times. Two eventual world professional heavyweight boxing champions—Floyd Patterson of the United States and Ingemar Johansson of Sweden—competed. Patterson won the middleweight crown but Johansson was disqualified in the heavyweight division for "not trying."

1956, Melbourne—The emergence of the Soviet Union as a world power in amateur sports was evident in the first Olympics held in the Southern Hemisphere. However, the Soviets were denied a chance to play for the gold medal in water polo when beaten by Hungary, which eventually captured the championship. The Hungarian team had left Budapest just after Soviet Union armed forces had quelled the Hungarian uprising and the contest was extremely emotional.

1960, Rome—Australian Herb Elliott's victory in the 1,500-m race was one of the highlights, as Elliott and the five men who finished behind him eclipsed the previous Olympic record for the event. Another highlight was the close victory by Rafer Johnson of the United States in the two-day decathlon, edging Yang Chuan-kwang of Taiwan.

1964, Tokyo—Australia's Dawn Fraser and America's Don Schollander were standouts. Fraser became the first woman to win gold medals in the same event in three straight Olympics (100-m freestyle swimming), while Schollander became the first swimmer to win four gold medals in one Olympics.

1968, Mexico City—The award presentation of the 200-m race, won by Tommie Smith of the United States, left an unpleasant memory of the games. While the American anthem was played Smith and runner-up John Carlos, also a black American, lifted gloved hands in a "black power" salute, which resulted in the U.S. officials immediately ordering them home.

Brown Brothers

Jesse Owens winning a dash at Berlin in 1936.

1972, Munich—U.S. swimmer Mark Spitz shattered four individual world records and helped the American team break three in team events. His capture of seven gold medals itself set a record.

Perhaps the most controversial competitive event in Olympic history was the 1972 gold-medal final in basketball when the Soviet Union defeated the United States, 51–50. Confusion over the time remaining in the game—three seconds—permitted the Russians to put the ball in play under their own basket three different times before Alexandre Belov, a Soviet forward, scored a field goal as the buzzer sounded. The U.S. coach, Hank Iba, filed a protest that was disallowed. The Americans refused to accept the silver medal for second place. It was their first loss in basketball in Olympic history.

1976, Montreal—Nadia Comaneci, a 14-year-old Rumanian gymnast, stole the hearts of the onlookers with a spectacular performance that included seven perfect scores and earned her three gold medals. No gymnast had compiled a perfect score in previous Olympics.

Lasse Viren of Finland and Vasili Alekseyev of the Soviet Union also were memorable. Viren became the first man in Olympic history to win the 5,000-m and 10,000-m in back-to-back games. Alekseyev won the gold medal in heavyweight weightlifting by hoisting 255 kg (561 lb) over his head in the clean and jerk, a world record—98 kg (217 lb) more than his own body weight.

OTT, MELVIN THOMAS (1909–58), American baseball player, born in Gretna, La. Joining New York of the National League in 1926, at 17, "Master Melvin" quickly established himself as one of the sport's great left-handed hitters and one of the team's most popular players. His entire playing career (1926–47) was spent as an outfielder with New York, and he also managed the team (1942–48). His career total of 511 home runs stood as a league record in the early 1960's. Ott later served as a baseball broadcaster. He was elected to the National Baseball Hall of Fame in 1951.

OUIMET [*wē'mĕt*], **FRANCIS** (1893–1967), American golfer, born in Brookline, Mass. As a 20-year-old former caddy in 1913, he defeated two noted British players, Harry Vardon and Ted Ray, in a play-off for the United States Open championship. Ouimet was the first amateur to win the Open, and his victory was credited with creating the first widespread interest in the game in the United States. He won the United States Amateur championship in 1914 and 1931, and was the runner-up in 1920.

OWENS, JESSE (1913–), American athlete, born in Decatur, Ala. During a single afternoon in 1935, as a member of the Ohio State University track and field team, he set world records, since surpassed, in the 220-yd. dash (20.3 seconds), 220-yd. low hurdles (22.6 seconds), and broad jump (26 ft., 8¼ in.), and equaled the record in the 100-yd. dash (9.4 seconds). In the Olympic Games of 1936 he further distinguished himself by winning the 100-meter run, 200-meter run, and broad jump. Beginning in the 1950's he was active in social work for the Illinois Youth Commission. In 1955 he made a good-will tour of India for the U.S. State Department.

P

PADDLE TENNIS, game similar to lawn tennis. It is played by two or four persons using wooden or plastic paddles instead of standard tennis rackets. The regulation paddle is between 15 and 17 in. long and weighs 12 to 14 oz.; it has a short handle but a striking area the same size as that of a tennis racket. The regulation ball is a tennis ball slightly deadened to compensate for the smaller playing area. Until the late 1950's the ball was made of sponge rubber, and in some areas rubber balls are still employed. The regulation court is 44 ft. by 20 ft. The game can be played indoors or outdoors. The court surface is usually clay, grass, wood, or asphalt. The net is 2 ft. 7 in. from the surface at the posts.

Most of the rules of lawn tennis apply, including those for scoring. In the adult game, however, the underhand serve was made compulsory in 1959; in such play only one serve is allowed on each point, and the entire area of the court is in bounds in both singles and doubles. These exceptions do not apply to paddle tennis for children; in children's singles, the playing area is 44 ft. by 16 ft. In 1961 the court was modified to provide an additional playing area on each side of the net, between the base line and a line parallel to the base line and 3 ft. behind it. Lobs (ball returned in a high curve) are in bounds if they land within such an area; drives still must fall within the base line.

Paddle tennis was originated in 1897 by an American, Frank Peer Beal, as a game in which children could be taught the fundamentals of lawn tennis. Play soon spread to adults also. In the 1960's there were about 8,400 courts in the United States. The United States Paddle Tennis Association, with headquarters in New York, has standardized playing rules.

See also TABLE TENNIS; TENNIS.

PADDOCK, CHARLES WILLIAM (1900–43), American athlete, born in Gainesville, Tex. Representing the University of Southern California and later the Los Angeles Athletic Club, he was one of the outstanding sprinters in U.S. and Olympic track competition between 1920 and 1928. He died in an airplane crash near Sitka, Alaska, while serving in the Marine Corps.

PALMER, ARNOLD (1929–), American golfer, born in Youngstown, Pa. He was the sport's outstanding performer in the early 1960's. The son of a professional golfer, he scored his first major victory in 1954 by winning the United States Amateur tournament. After turning professional in 1954, he won the Canadian Open, 1955; Masters tournament, 1958, 1960, 1962, and 1964; United States Open, 1960; and British Open, 1961, and 1962. By 1965 he had won $586,211 in play sanctioned by the Professional Golfers' Association, a record total. His earnings of $128,230 in 1963 bettered his previous PGA records for a single year. Many of his victories were accomplished by thrilling last-minute rallies.

PAN AMERICAN GAMES, a series of sports events for amateur athletes of the Western Hemisphere, held every four years. The first competition took place in 1951 in Buenos Aires; subsequently the games were scheduled in Mexico City (1955), Chicago (1959), and São Paulo, Brazil (1963).

The games are modeled on the Olympic Games, the rules of which, in general, apply. The technical rules of competition are those of the international sports federations that govern the various sports represented, as in the Olympics. Over-all administration and regulation of the games is provided by the Pan American Sports Organization, which is made up of the Olympic Games committees of the 25 participating countries.

The program includes all sports of the Olympic Games (except judo, canoeing, and field hockey) plus four non-Olympic sports; men's baseball, girls' basketball, girls' volleyball, and synchronized swimming. The United States Olympic Committee performs the same functions in Pan American competition that it does in the Olympic Games. Selection of U.S. teams also follows the procedure for picking Olympic competitors. Many athletes compete in both sets of games.

See also OLYMPIC GAMES.

PARACHUTE JUMPING, as a sport (popularly known as sky diving), is a comparatively recent but fast-growing activity. At the Pulitzer Air Races in Philadelphia in 1926

Above, the sky diver has just left the plane at 6,000 ft.

Below, the parachutist is in position for landing.

Right, a late-afternoon jumper has the setting sun for background.

Below, a sport parachutist collapses a chute on the ground.

United Press International

Stuart Davis—Birnback

a young American named Joe Crane suggested a spot-jumping contest (one measured by accuracy in landing) between the handful of parachutists present. A target was set out in the center of the field for what was probably the first parachuting competition anywhere.

In 1932, 46 contestants competed in what had become known as a precision-landing contest at the National Air Races. Thereafter the National Aeronautic Association formed a parachute committee that became the National Parachute Jumpers' Association prior to World War II, under Crane's leadership. During the war, the association's name was changed to the National Parachute Jumpers-Riggers Association.

International Competition. In 1948 the sport became international in scope when the Fédération Aéronautique Internationale (FAI) formed a parachuting commission. Rules for competitive parachuting were formulated and the first world-championship meet was held under that organization's sponsorship in 1951 in Tivat, Yugoslavia. France won the competition, which was based solely on precision landing (accuracy in landing on a target). A similar criterion was employed in the second meet, in 1954, in St. Yan, France, which was won easily by Russian jumpers. In that meet Fred Mason, an American soldier in Europe, became the first U.S. representative in world-championship competition.

In the 1956 meet in Moscow, won by the Czech team, the second present-day criterion for judging competition was added to accuracy in landing. This was body control, or grace and precision in aerobatic maneuvers during free fall (the period between leaving the aircraft and the opening of the parachute). For the first time the United States was represented by a team, which was assembled, trained, and captained by Jacques André Istel, and which finished sixth in a field of 10. A unique, new steerable parachute, employed by Soviet entrants, made accuracy in landing a fine art. The distances between the target center and the point where the parachutist reached earth soon diminished from several meters to a few centimeters.

The U.S. team, captained by Lewis Sanborn, finished sixth among 14 entries in the fourth world-championship meet in 1958 in Czechoslovakia. Speed in executing aerobatic maneuvers in free fall became a criterion, along with style in body control; high-power optical instruments were used by judges to sight each maneuver. The Soviet team won that meet and the 1960 meet held in Sofia, Bulgaria, in which the United States finished fourth. A U.S. women's team participated for the first time in the 1960 event; with one exception, U.S. representatives were Army male and female parachutists. One of them, James Arender, became the first American to win a gold medal in world-championship competition. Another, Richard Fortenberry, placed second in over-all individual rating.

In the 1962 meet at Orange, Mass., won by the Czech team, five events were arranged for men and the same number for women. These included two precision-landing tests for groups of jumpers, two for individual competitors, and a competition judged on the basis of style in maneuvers. The last-named involved the rapid and precise execution of two figures of eight and two backward loops within 20 seconds of a 30-second free-fall period. In this part of the competition the parachutists were informed of the order of the maneuvers by signals flashed from the ground, after they had made their exits from the aircraft.

Another major international competition, the Adriatic Cup Meet, was first held in Yugloslavia, in 1957. The steady emergence of the United States as a leading contender in sport parachuting was emphasized in 1961 when its team won every event in a special invitational meet in France.

World Records. In the 1960's the sport listed 82 world records in the categories of altitude and precision landing. These were further divided according to competition for men and women, individuals and groups, night and day jumping, and jumps with and without delay. (A jump without delay is one in which the white of the pilot, or extraction, chute must show within three seconds of the jumper's leaving the aircraft.) Prior to Nov., 1961, the Soviet Union and its satellites held all world records. In that month four Americans led by Jacques Istel established new group-of-four daytime and nighttime precision-landing records for jumps with delay from 1,500 meters. Both jumps resulted in group averages of just over 4 meters from the target center. The average distance from the target center in daylight was 4.145 meters (13 ft., 7 in.); the average for the night jump was 4.229 meters (13 ft., 10½ in.).

In June, 1960, a Soviet parachutist established a record for altitude in jumping: 48,671.2 ft. Another Soviet jumper set a world record for precision landing, .29 ft. (representing the average of two consecutive jumps), in May, 1961.

Extent in the United States. The present-day successor to the Parachute Jumpers-Riggers Association, the Parachute Club of America, had a membership of several thousand in the early 1960's. Its members compete in local and regional meets, all governed by the FAI, and there also is an intercollegiate league. Safety and skill have become the goals of a well-regulated sport that once had only the status of a barnstorming attraction.

PARI-MUTUEL [pär'ē-mū'chōō-əl], a form of betting in which the total amount wagered, less a share for the state and management, is divided among the winning betters in proportion to the amount wagered. In effect, the betters themselves set the odds. The system was devised in Paris about 1870 by Pierre Oller. Several attempts were made to popularize it in the United States later in the same decade. These were unsuccessful, but early in the 20th century the states that legalized betting on horse racing at the tracks gradually replaced track bookmakers with the new system. (Much off-track betting is also conducted by bookmakers operating outside the scope of the system—and of the law.) In the mid-1960's there were 25 states with legalized pari-mutuel betting on horse racing. This form of wagering is also employed to a lesser extent in American dog racing and *jai alai*.

In the United States and Canada the operation of pari-mutuel betting in horse racing involves three pools, into which all money wagered on a given race goes. These are known as "straight" (all the money bet on horses to win), "place" (money bet on horses to finish second or better), and "show" (money bet on horses to finish third or better). A complex calculating machine known as a totaliza-

Wide World

Officials at Aqueduct Race Track in New York City watch as a totalizator figures the payoff money for each horse. Below, on the long "tote" board behind the track are indicated the amount of the win, place, and show pools for the race, the odds for each horse, and the return on a $2 bet if the horse finishes "in the money."

Annan Photo Features

tor automatically records every bet made in each pool and indicates the odds for each horse to win as the wagering proceeds up to a short time before the race begins. Holders of straight tickets collect only if the horse of their choice wins; those holding place tickets collect only if their choice finishes first or second; holders of show tickets collect if their choice finishes first, second, or third.

In determining returns to successful betters holding straight tickets, the total amount in the pool is first decreased by statutory deductions (usually 15%, representing the state tax and the share of the track management); the remainder is returned to holders of such tickets. The betters have determined the odds through the total amount they bet; a successful horse heavily favored in the wagering returns a relatively small amount to his backers because there are many of them to share the proceeds of the straight pool, unlike the situation in which a less heavily favored entrant wins. In determining the return to successful holders of place tickets, the total amount in that pool is decreased by 15% and then by the money bet on the winning entrant and the one finishing second. The remainder is divided by two and each part is added to the amount of the place bets on the winner and runner-up. Division of the show pool is identical in detail except that the remainder is divided into three equal parts. Most European countries employ only the straight and place pools.

In the United States payment of "breakage" (odd cents per dollar usually in excess of a multiple of 10, in the calculation of the return) varies from state to state; frequently such money is kept as additional revenue for track and state. Entirely separate pools are employed for such forms of combination wagering as the "daily double," involving the selection of the winners of two successive races, and *quiniela*, the selection of the winner and runner-up in a given race.

See also Dog Racing; Horse Racing.

PATRICK, LESTER ("The Silver Fox), **(1883–1960),** Canadian hockey executive and player, born in Drummondville, Quebec. He is known for developing ice hockey into Canada's national pastime. Patrick began his playing career with the Montreal AAA team in 1901. He developed the power rush that gave hockey its slogan as the fastest game in the world. He was paid the then unheard-of sum of $3,000 for a 12-game season with the

Renfrew, Ontario, Millionaires in 1909 and his experience there led him to British Columbia, where the Coast League was formed.

Patrick went to New York in 1926 after selling his holdings in the Pacific Coast Hockey League, and became manager of the New York Rangers, the team being organized by Madison Square Garden. He retired from the Rangers in 1946. Patrick and his brother, Frank, and Patrick's two sons, Lynn and Murray, form the most famous family in hockey. Lynn and Murray played with the Rangers and served as coaches in the National Hockey League.

PATTERSON, FLOYD (1935–), American boxer, born in Waco, N.C. In 1956, at the age of 21, he became the youngest world heavyweight champion in history when he knocked out Archie Moore to take the title vacated by the retirement of Rocky Marciano. Patterson had turned professional four years earlier, shortly after winning the Olympic middleweight championship in the games at Helsinki, Finland. In 1959 he lost the heavyweight title to Ingemar Johansson of Sweden by a third-round knockout. In 1960 Patterson became the first man to regain that title when he knocked out Johansson in the fifth round. In 1962 he was dethroned by Charles ("Sonny") Liston, who knocked him out in the first round.

PETTIT [*pĕt'ĭt*], **ROBERT ("BOB")** (1932–), American basketball player, born in Baton Rouge, La. He won All-American rating at Louisiana State University in 1954. In the same year he began an outstanding career as a professional in the National Basketball Association; he played during the 1954–55 season with Milwaukee and then with St. Louis, after the Milwaukee franchise was shifted to St. Louis. The 6 ft., 9 in. forward, noted for the accuracy of his long-distance, one-hand jump shots, retired after the 1964–65 season. In his 11 seasons he was named to the NBA all-star team each season. At the time of his retirement he held the all-time NBA career record for scoring—more than 20,000 points.

PHYSICAL EDUCATION, one of the oldest forms of education, yet relatively new in the American school and college curriculum. Undoubtedly the first physical educator was a parent who taught his son to climb, throw a spear, or chase a deer. Throughout history, physical education, like all formal education, has been changed to serve the needs and will of a given culture. Consequently, at various times learning and participation in physical skills have stressed movement as a means of survival, as a medium of communication and expression, a means of exploring and learning, a system of disciplining, and a fundamental form of leisure and play.

A sound program of physical education draws on physiology, sociology, and psychology to understand, interpret, and improve all of man's physical activity. The content of the instructional program is determined by the kinds of activities deemed important by a culture; the conduct of the program is dictated by the outcomes sought.

The objectives of physical education in American schools are based upon the developmental needs of school- and college-age youth. It is the area of instruction primarily concerned with the development and maintenance of the human body and with the most effective and efficient use of the body in work and play. Physical education strives to develop capacities and desires to maintain good health, to afford opportunities to solve problems by careful thought, to increase capability for making moral choices, and to encourage emotional expression.

The Ends and Means of Physical Education. The specific objectives and methods of physical education are: (1) to develop and maintain organic power: activities in the program are designed to develop muscular strength, physical endurance, speed, and cardiovascular efficiency; the needs and methods of physical and emotional relaxation are taught; (2) to aid neuromuscular development; coordination, rhythmic sense, and efficiency and grace of movement result from participation in selected activities; (3) to aid in the development of sound personal and social attitudes and behavior: sports and games are employed to encourage initiative, self-direction, and decision making, and at the same time develop sociability and a feeling of belonging; (4) to aid in development of intellectual and interpretive ability: activities within physical education are designed to encourage students to analyze, plan, and make decisions; and (5) to develop physical skills and attitudes that encourage pleasurable physical participation in, and observation of, recreational and related activity: a good base of skills and appreciation of play are important to future recreation and aesthetic appreciation of movement as in dance.

To achieve the five objectives for all students requires a broad program with specific activities selected on the basis of the maturity and ability of each instructional group. These activities, or tools, include fundamental movements and skills; quiet and active games; activities specifically linked with physical fitness; individual and dual games and sports; team games and sports; combative activities; rhythm and dance; stunts, tumbling, and other gymnastic activities; aquatics; and adaptive activities for the handicapped. Many of these activities take place indoors in playrooms, classrooms, gymnasiums, or swimming pools; others occur outdoors on tennis courts, play fields, and tracks; some are appropriate in a variety of settings.

What a Physical-Education Program Includes. For clarity of administration, the total program is organized into three categories: instructional, voluntary, and adaptive.

Instructional Program. This encompasses the activities that take place during the regular school day. Emphasis is placed on developing fitness, physical skills and techniques, and strategy in games as all of them relate to the objectives of the school program. The overall program of physical education, from kindergarten through college, should be graded and progressive, in keeping with the students' varying levels of growth, development, skill, and knowledge. Such a program constantly affords new challenges, but meeting them successfully also involves use of knowledge based on previous experiences.

Voluntary Program. This refers to those phases of physical education in which a person participates because he chooses to do so. Such activities, when appropriate to maturity and needs, serve to provide additional opportunities for students to participate beyond the instructional pro-

The healthful and social values of physical education classes are recognized by many school systems.

Palmer—Monkmeyer

gram and apply the skills, knowledge, and behavior learned in the instructional program. Included in the voluntary program are: (1) recreational activities—noncompetitive or with informal competition during available free time, (2) intramurals—competitive events between individuals or teams within a single institution, (3) play days—inter-institutional events in which many participate in a variety of sports activities without being organized into school teams, (4) sports days and festivals—inter-institutional events in which the many competing groups maintain school identity, (5) extramurals—competition between a group from one institution and an outside group, and (6) interscholastic and intercollegiate activities—competition between two selected groups of a given level that are trained and coached to play a series of games in a single sport. In all of these activities the spirit of fun should prevail; ideally, the focus is on education in leisure activity.

Adaptive Program. This is designed for those who, for reasons of health, should not participate in the regular instructional program. Some students remain in the adaptive program throughout their school life because of permanent disabilities; others, who are convalescing from an illness or temporary disability, may stay only a short time. Activity is prescribed in the adaptive program on the basis of medical analysis of each individual and not according to a predetermined general standard. The activities do not necessarily vary from those offered in the instructional program. Adaptations may be made to suit individual needs.

See also GYMNASTICS; articles on individual sports.

PING-PONG. *See* TABLE TENNIS.

PLANTE, JACQUES (1929–), Canadian hockey player, born in Mount Carmel, Quebec. He joined Montreal of the National Hockey League in 1952 and became the team's regular goal tender in 1954. In winning the Vézina Trophy (awarded annually to the goalie of the league's least scored-on team) for the sixth time, during the 1961-62 season, he performed a feat accomplished only once previously in league history, by Bill Durnan of Montreal in the 1940's. Plante was named to the NHL all-star teams for 1955–56, 1958–59, and 1961–62. He won the Hart Trophy as the league's most valuable player during the 1961–62 season. Prior to the 1963–64 season he was traded to the New York team.

POLICE ATHLETIC LEAGUE (PAL), recreational adjunct of police departments. Organized in the 1930's as part of the juvenile aid bureaus, police recreational programs have become dissociated from such specialized agencies. PAL's are private, nonprofit organizations supported by the membership fees of adult associate members, private donations, and the proceeds from benefits and campaigns. The program aims at providing recreational facilities in areas with a high rate of delinquency and seeks to give children in such neighborhoods a more favorable image of the police.

POLO, a game in which two teams of players on horseback attempt to drive a ball through goals set up at each end of a turf field. According to most accounts, the sport existed in ancient Persia and spread to Tibet, China, Japan, and India. The only authentic data on modern-day polo dates from the early 1860's, when the early form of the modern game began to take shape in India. A short time later polo was brought to England and thence to the United States.

The Americans' fondness for this thrilling sport, which places great stress on team play, soon brought about international competition. The famed Westchester Cup series, dating from 1886, matched teams from Great Britain and the United States. After 1939, however, play between Britons and Americans consisted only of informal matches in England. Another noted series, for the Cup of the Americas, involved the United States and Argentina. The last matches in this competition were played in 1950.

The chief U.S. championships are decided in the National Open and National 20-Goal competitions. In the 1960's there were more than 80 well-known clubs represented by teams in the Northeastern, Central, Southeastern, Northwestern, Pacific Coast, and Southwestern circuits. The game, which can be played outdoors or indoors, expanded notably in postwar years in its outdoor form in the Northwest and southern California. The indoor game is played in New York and Chicago.

How the Game is Played. The outdoor game, involving four men on each side, is played on a field 300 by 160 yds. in dimension. The ball, which measures not more than 3¼ in. in diameter and is made of willow or bamboo root, is propelled by means of mallets wielded by each player. The mallets, which are flexible, are made of cane.

Indoor (arena-type) polo is played by teams comprising three men each. The field, though not standardized, is much smaller than in outdoor play. In each case the object is to score goals (points). American players are rated according to ability by the United States Polo Association. These ratings—from 0 to 10 goals—are indications of a player's potential, as based on performance in championship or tournament competition, and do not signify that he will score that number of goals in any given game.

The game is divided into six chukkers, or periods, each

Outdoor polo is played by two teams of four men each. The players, mounted on horseback, attempt to propel the ball, not more than 3¼ in. in diameter, between goal posts by striking it with long-handled mallets. Indoor polo is played on a smaller field with three men on each team.

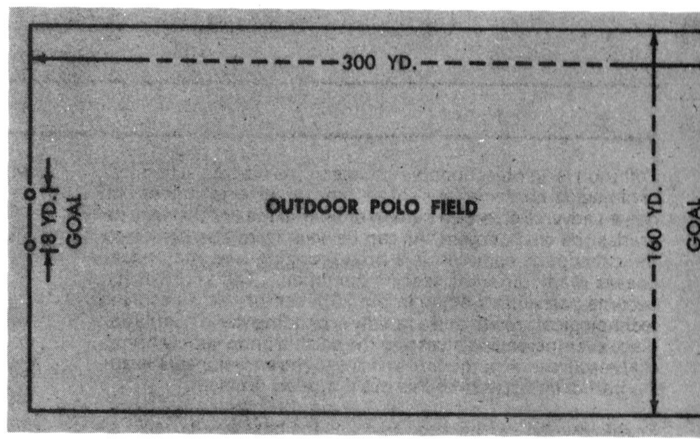

The regulation outdoor polo field is 300 yd. long and 160 yd. wide. Distance between goal posts at both ends of the field is 8 yd.

Players of the Argentine (in light shirts) and British teams during the Polo Coronation Cup match in Sussex, England.

United Press International

7½ minutes in length. Penalties are assessed for illegal hooking of a player's mallet, dangerous riding, illegal bumping of another player, and crossing in front of a player riding downfield. A severe foul, such as dangerous riding, results in the award to the offended team of an automatic goal and a free shot from a point 40 yd. from the goal.

PYTHIAN [pĭth'ē-ən] **GAMES,** in ancient Greece, national festival held at Apollo's shrine in Delphi every fourth August to commemorate Apollo's slaying of the Python. Originally held every eight years, the festival at first included a one-day musical competition for the best hymn to the god composed with a lyre accompaniment. Reorganized c.582 B.C. under the direction of the Amphictyonic Council, the festival added games on the Olympic plan to the music contests. The brilliance of the chariot races and equestrian events soon almost eclipsed Olympia. Victors received laurel wreaths. The Pythian Games were still held as late as 361 A.D.

Q

QUOITS. *See* HORSESHOE PITCHING.

R

RACING CARS. SEE AUTOMOBILE RACING.

RACKET GAMES, sometimes racquet games, group of indoor racket-and-ball games played in walled enclosures, or courts, having surfaces of cement or boards. They include court tennis (so called to distinguish it from the more familiar lawn tennis), rackets (often called hard rackets to distinguish it from squash rackets), squash rackets, and squash tennis. Most play takes place during the winter season under artificial lights. Professionals are employed as instructors or coaches, but except for exhibition purposes, organized competition is almost entirely on an amateur basis.

Although the games differ considerably in courts, equipment, and rules, the common object is to strike a ball against a wall so that the ball rebounds out of reach of an opponent. In rackets, squash rackets, and squash tennis, contestants play to the front wall as in handball. In court tennis, however, they play to the floor and walls across a center net which separates them as in lawn tennis. The court, instead of being rectangular, as in the other racket games, is polyhedral and simulates the structure of a medieval hall or yard.

All of the racket games are played between two persons (singles) or, except in squash tennis, between two pairs (doubles). Squash-rackets doubles is played in larger courts than those used for singles. Only squash rackets is played to any extent between women or as mixed doubles (between teams each composed of a male and female player).

Court Tennis. This is the oldest of the racket games. References to it appear in 14th-century literature. By 1415 it was enjoying royal patronage in England and France; the language of the game still includes Norman French. In the 19th century there was a revival of interest after the game had been out of favor for about 100 years. As a sport associated with status, like polo, it was imported to the United States along with professional racket masters. About 15 courts were built in the eastern United States as features of private clubs and country estates. In the early 1960's about eight were still in use. No new court had been built since 1915 because of the cost and the growth of indoor and outdoor lawn tennis and squash rackets. There is, however, a sufficient following of players and sponsors of this complex game in the United States and abroad for its traditional annual competitions to be reported in local newspapers.

Most of the remaining courts are patterned after the one at Hampton Court built for Henry VIII. A typical court is 110 ft. long and 38 ft. wide, with walls rising 30 ft. to a skylight ceiling. The playing surfaces are a special slatelike cement. A net 5 ft. high at the ends and 3 ft. at the center is strung across the middle of the court to divide the service side from the receiving, or hazard, side. A projecting shedlike construction with a slanted roof, known as the penthouse, forms the lower parts of the two end walls and, looking from the service side, the lower part of the left wall. The right wall slants out near the hazard end to form a buttress known as the tambour. Below the penthouse roof there is a line of windows, or galleries, along the left wall. A window, or grille, is situated in the hazard end wall next to the tambour, and a long window, or dedans, extends across the service end wall. These openings are screened to protect spectators behind them. Points may

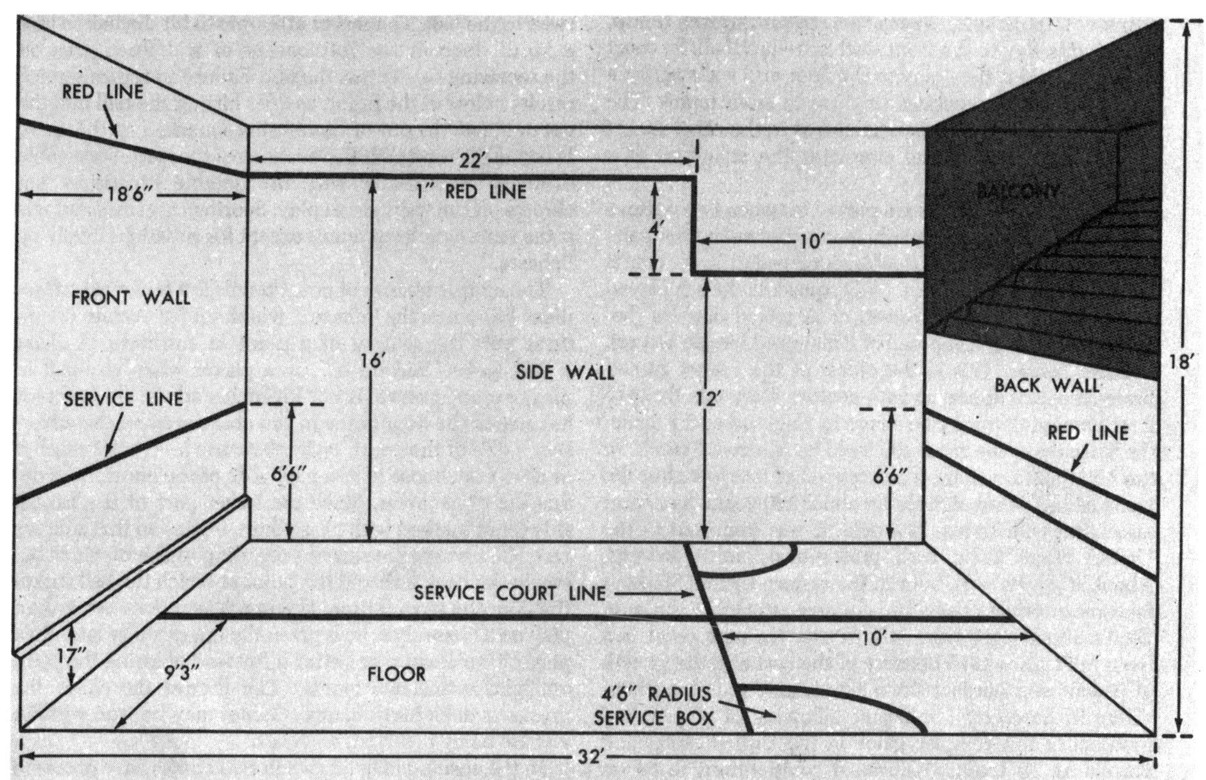

DIAGRAM OF A SQUASH RACKETS COURT

This is the singles court used in the United States. Different measurements are required in doubles and in England. Balls hitting above the top red line on the four walls are out of court. The balcony is for spectators.

be won outright by hitting the ball into the dedans, the grille, or the last gallery on the hazard side.

The game is usually played as doubles. The rackets are 27 in. long, of sturdy construction with slightly crooked heads. They are gripped short, instead of near the butt of the handle, and the stroke is a chopping motion rather than a long swing. The balls are made of tightly wound string and layers of cloth covered with white felt, and are somewhat smaller than ordinary tennis balls. It is customary to leave balls in quantity on the dedans sill, for convenience in play.

The game begins with service, which is always from the same end of the court. The right to the advantage of serving is determined by the spin of a racket or a coin. Service is delivered underhand or overhand and by imparting twist to the ball. The server attempts to hit the ball so that it lands deep in the left corner of a defined area on the receiving side across the net. Failure to return service results in loss of the point, as does hitting the ball into the net or above the out-of-bounds lines marked on the walls. If service is returned, the exchanges thereafter resemble ordinary lawn tennis with the notable exception that caroms off the walls are in play. Scoring by games and sets is the same as in lawn tennis except for situations involving "chases."

The unique feature of court tennis is a technical refinement known as the "chase," which under certain conditions puts the scoring of a point in suspense. A chase is said to be "laid down" by a player when any ball in play, except a serve, is not hit by his adversary before it has struck the floor twice in the chase area on the adversary's side of the court, either because he cannot reach it or does not choose to. On each side of the court, lines define the chase areas. Since the larger part of the hazard side is not marked with chase lines, chases on that side are rare. Chases are measured according to the distance between the back wall and the point at which the ball strikes the floor the second time. When a player does not make a play on a chase shot, he is given the opportunity later (in a play-off) to equal it or better it (instead of losing the point outright, as in lawn tennis). The shorter the chase, the greater will be his difficulty. Games may be won without a chase being involved, however.

In the ensuing play-off (when two chases have occurred on one side) to determine the winner of the points at issue, the players change sides of the court. The player who has allowed the chases to be laid down must put a ball out of reach of his opponent and within the opponent's chase area. This ball must be closer to the back wall than the chase with which he is contending in order for the player to win the point. He wins it if he succeeds in this, or if his opponent miscues.

In the play-off, as otherwise, a shot into the grille, or dedans, or into the last gallery on the hazard side automatically wins the point. An error, such as hitting the ball into the net, automatically loses it. In the play-off, if the chase laid down is equal in length to the chase being played off, no point is scored and that chase is called off. If a game is within one point of completion, a single chase causes a change of sides and a play-off. Service changes hands at the end of each set, but otherwise only when there is a chase to be played off. A scorekeeper, or marker, posted in the penthouse at the net, calls out the chase lengths and the score after each point.

Judgment is an important element in court tennis—specifically, knowing when not to play in a chase situation. Having a chase, called "half a yard," laid down against a player is a disadvantage to him, since it will be hard to equal in a play-off. One called "chase three yards" would probably be invited.

Rackets. Although this game follows court tennis in order of antiquity, it is of comparatively modern origin and bears as much resemblance to *jai alai* as to court tennis. Rackets as known today is reputed to have had its beginnings early in the 19th century against a wall at Debtors Prison in London. It probably derived from a form of fives, or paddle handball, which was already a traditional pastime at some English schools. The standard rackets ball is still made of cloth tightly wound with twine and covered with leather or tape, and 1½ in. in diameter. As the ball's symmetry is affected by impact with the cement walls of the court, dozens may be used in one match. The rackets, which are 30 in. long, have long, slender shafts and round, gut-strung heads. A typical court is 50 ft. long, 30 ft. wide, and has a correspondingly high ceiling. A padded board, or telltale, extends across the base of the front wall to a height of 24 in. above the floor. Balls must strike above this board to be in play.

Play begins with the contestants stationed behind a line at the rear of the court. The server hits the ball to the front wall so that it rebounds diagonally to the receiver's half of the court behind the service line. In American play only one serve is allowed but aces (points scored when the serve is not returned) are frequent. As in handball, the players alternately try to drive the ball back to the front wall before it has bounced twice on the floor. It is permissible to hit the ball on the volley or before it has struck the floor. The hitting is severe and the ball glances at great speed off the floor and walls. If the receiver fails to return the ball, the server scores a point and repeats service from the other side of the court. When the server misses, the receiver becomes the server but does not score. Fifteen points constitute a game, and three of five games a match victory.

Squash Rackets. This is the most popular of the racket games and almost as world-wide as lawn tennis. Pakistanis and Egyptians are among the leading players. With the aid of sponsorship by schools and organizations, its following is increasing, especially in the United States, where it is played from coast to coast. By about 1874 squash rackets had become a game in its own right as a combination of rackets and fives. The word "squash" in the name remains unexplained. It was probably attached by English schoolboys, who are credited with devising the game. Today the word is often used alone to refer to squash rackets rather than squash tennis.

The 27-in. wooden racket is shorter than that used in rackets but otherwise the same. The ball, 1¾ in. in diameter, is hollow and made of black rubber. Perhaps because the game was taken up in North America before standards were set in England, differences between the American and English versions became sufficiently fixed to handicap international competition on even terms. The American singles court is 32 ft. long, 18½ ft. wide, and 16

he 27-in. racket is gripped short and handled with a chopping notion. The ball is made of string and cloth and covered with felt.

ound-headed and strung with gut, the 27-in. racket is used to it the hollow black rubber ball, 1 ¾ in. in diameter.

ft. high at the front wall. A metal strip, or telltale, extends across the base of the front wall as in rackets. In the middle 1920's the telltale was officially lowered from 24 in. to 17 in. with a view to improving the game by increasing the difficulty of reaching the ball on the first bounce. The best courts are constructed of maple boards after the manner of bowling alleys.

The principles of the game are identical with those of rackets. However, on account of the different properties of the ball and the smaller court, the emphasis is on retrieving and stamina, although form is also important. The advantage generally lies with the player achieving a position between his opponent and the front wall. Interference between the players, calling for the point to be replayed, is not unusual, since the rules grant each player unimpeded access to the ball. The server is given two opportunities on each point to make a proper serve—one that hits the front wall above the service line (a line parallel to the floor and 6½ ft. above it) and rebounds into the opposite half of the court behind the line from which the ball is served. Both the server and receiver may score points, and the game is won by the first to score 15. In cases of even scores at 13 or 14 points, the player who has been equaled sets the final total, which may extend to 18. Matches are decided on the basis of three of five games.

English courts are 2½ ft. wider than the American and Canadian, the ball is smaller and softer, the rackets are lighter, and playable rebounds off the back wall are less frequent. The game total is 9 points, and scoring is limited to the server. Doubles are not played in England.

Squash Tennis. American in origin, this game dates from the last years of the 19th century. Its principles are the same as in squash rackets. The technique of play differs, however, on account of the larger, livelier ball used in squash tennis, the lower back-wall line (over which the ball may not travel on the fly from the front wall), and the requirement that serves drop short of the service line in rebounding. The fast caroms of the ball off the walls put a greater premium on position than on pursuit.

The game did not become a recognized sport in schools or colleges or outside the United States. However, it paralleled squash rackets in popularity and organized activity among business and professional men in New York City and several other metropolitan centers until the mid-1930's. Specially made light-weight lawn-tennis rackets and mesh-covered, high-pressure balls were its distinguishing equipment. Numerous mahogany-stained courts, slightly narrower and longer than standard for squash rackets, were installed in hotels and athletic clubs. In recent years squash tennis has yielded to the growth of squash rackets and is played in white courts that were either built for the latter game or converted to its specifications. Ordinary lawn-tennis rackets are acceptable in squash tennis; the ball is green in color and resembles a lawn-tennis ball, though it is slightly smaller. Under rules revised from the original ones, both receiver and server may score points instead of only the server. Fifteen points still constitute a game, but matches are now decided on the basis of three of five games instead of two of three.

See also BADMINTON; JAI ALAI; PADDLE TENNIS; TABLE TENNIS; TENNIS.

RICHARD, MAURICE ("ROCKET") (1921–), Canadian hockey player, born in Montreal. One of the greatest performers in the history of the National Hockey League, he played for the Montreal Canadiens from 1942 to 1960. When he retired at the close of the 1959–60 season, after leading the team to a record fifth consecutive victory in Stanley Cup competition, Richard had scored 544 goals, a record NHL career total until Gordie Howe surpassed it in 1963. His feat of scoring 50 goals in a single 50-game season (1944–45) also stood as a record, though others subsequently scored 50 in 70-game seasons. A fiery competitor, Richard was named to eight NHL all-star teams, as a right wing, and was voted the league's most valuable player in 1946–47. In 1961 he was elected to membership in the National Hockey Hall of Fame.

RICKEY, BRANCH WESLEY (1881–1965), American baseball executive, born in Lucasville, Ohio. Rickey entered baseball as a catcher with the St. Louis Browns in 1905. His playing career was brief, 119 games in four seasons. He began a half century as manager and executive with the Browns in 1913. Rickey's longest association was with the St. Louis Cardinals (1917–42), but he was also president of the Brooklyn Dodgers (1942–50), general manager of the Pittsburgh Pirates (1950–55), and consultant to the Cardinals (1962–64).

It was during his term with the Browns that Rickey originated the farm system, but he developed it fully with the Cardinals. The major league team bought some minor league franchises outright and entered working agreements with others. This system developed the players who brought the Cardinals nine pennants and six World Series titles between 1926 and 1946. By the latter year, Rickey was with Brooklyn. That season, Jackie Robinson played with the Montreal Royals, the Dodgers' chief farm club. Robinson joined the Dodgers in 1947 and, with other Negro stars, helped them win six pennants between 1947 and 1956. In 1967 Rickey was posthumously elected to baseball's Hall of Fame.

RIFLE, SPORTING, rifle designed for one of two forms of recreation: hunting or target shooting. While some rifles are adaptable to both, there are basic differences which are dictated by their respective uses. The hunting rifle is carried afield on foot, sometimes for considerable distances in rough terrain. It cannot be excessively long or heavy. The target rifle, by contrast, is fired from a stationary position. Its length and weight therefore can, and usually do, exceed those of hunting arms.

Hunting Rifles. Generally, the characteristics of hunting rifles depend upon the species and size of the game to be hunted, and thus in some measure upon wild-life habitat or geography. A rifle adequate to cope with the relatively small black bear of the eastern Appalachians, for example, could prove dangerously feeble against an infuriated Rocky Mountain grizzly or an Alaskan Kodiak.

Since World War II, hunting rifles have become shorter and lighter. Two developments have made this possible: lighter metals and plastics, which substitute for steel and wood, and more powerful compact ammunition. Whereas most bolt-action game rifles weighed 8 lb. or more and had 24-in. barrels before World War II, most now have barrels about 22 in. long and seldom weigh above 7 lb. Carbines with 18- to 20-in. barrels, and weighing 5½ to 6½ lb., are increasingly popular. This trend has influenced military shoulder arms.

Target Rifles. The characteristics of target rifles are governed largely by the type of competition to be entered. The mammoths are the bench-rest types whose weights of 20 to 30 lb. and up are borne by benches, rather than by the rifleman. Even the smallest target pieces customarily outweigh the .22 caliber rifles of squirrel-hunters. (Caliber is the diameter of the bullet expressed in hundredths of an inch, in this case .22 in.) Where ordinary .22's run 4 to 5 lb. and have barrels of

SPORTING RIFLE SELECTION GUIDE

Game	Caliber Rifle	Bullet (weight in grains)	Muzzle Velocity (approx. feet per second)	Muzzle Energy (approx. ft.-lb.)
VERMIN RABBIT SQUIRREL RACCOON	.22 .22 Hornet .220 Swift .257 Roberts	40 46 48 117	1,335 2,690 4,110 2,650	158 740 1,800 1,820
DEER BEAR PUMA MOOSE ANTELOPE WOLF COYOTE GOAT	7 mm. Mauser 30-30 30-40 Krag 30-06 .300 Savage 8 mm. Mauser .35 Remington	175 170 180 180 150 200 200	2,490 2,220 2,470 2,700 2,670 2,320 2,100	2,410 1,860 2,440 2,910 2,370 2,390 1,950
BEAR BUFFALO MOOSE LION TIGER CROCODILE	.300 H&H Magnum .375 H&H Magnum 45-70 .458 Winchester	220 270 405 500	2,620 2,740 1,320 2,125	3,350 4,500 1,570 5,010
ELEPHANT RHINOCEROS TIGER	450-400 .375 Weatherby .460 Weatherby Magnum	400 300 500	2,150 2,800 2,725	4,110 5,223 8,245

18 to 20 in., the target model .22 used to win most championships in recent years weighs approximately 15½ lb. and has a 27½ in. barrel. High-power target rifles, usually about .30 caliber, feature 24- to 28-in. barrels and often weigh 10 lb. or more.

Like many hunting rifles, especially those intended for use at 100 yd. or more, target rifles are fitted with telescopic sights unless rules of specific matches forbid them. The field or area taken in by the target rifle's scope, however, is usually less wide and more intensified than that of the hunting scope, for an obvious reason. The target is fixed, the game generally is moving. Small-bore (.22 caliber) target rifles are invariably single-shot, accommodating only one cartridge at a loading. High-power rifles usually, but not always, have a magazine capacity of several rounds.

Sporting Rifle Calibers. Except for the .22 rimfire cartridges with their little 25- to 40-grain lead bullets, virtually all sporting-rifle ammunition is centerfire rather than rimfire. This means that the primer, or ignition, is in the center of the base of the cartridge rather than at the side. It makes possible a more powerful cartridge. The trend has been to smaller-diameter bullets in a necked-in case of relatively large powder capacity. Reducing the bullet size cuts wind resistance and results in bullets that travel at higher speeds with flatter trajectories, or more nearly in a straight line from muzzle to target. An increasing number of the modern cartridges, especially for "varmint" or small-game hunting, are .22 caliber in bullet diameter but have 45- to 55-grain bullets that are longer than those of the rimfires.

The largest American sporting-rifle cartridges, such as the Winchester .458 Magnum and Weatherby .460 Magnum, propel bullets weighing 500 grains. These giants travel with a muzzle velocity two or three times that of a .22-caliber, long rifle bullet, continue much farther and, of course, hit far harder. They are essentially big-game calibers and are considered capable of taking the largest game in the world. British sporting rifles as large as .600 caliber continue in limited use but are fast disappearing.

Sporting Rifle Actions. The British double-barrelled rifle, beloved of generations of big-game hunters in Africa and Asia, is almost never seen afield in North America. The four leading types of actions, all capable of being manufactured to fire more than two shots without reloading, are the bolt, lever, pump or slide, and semiautomatic.

The bolt-action still dominates the field, although semiautomatic rifles have come into increased sporting use. In the bolt-action rifle, a knob or handle retracts and closes the bolt in such a way that a cartridge enters the chamber at the rear of the barrel, is locked in, and fired by the firing pin enclosed in the bolt. Lever-action rifles, made famous by Winchester, have a lever whose working thrusts the cartridge up and forward into the chamber and cocks the rifle so that the firing pin is ready to strike. In the pump- or slide-action rifle, sometimes nicknamed "trombone," loading is achieved by pumping an arm or mechanism under the barrel forward and back. The semiautomatic, loaded manually for the first shot, requires no further manual effort to reload, energy being furnished by the discharge of each previous cartridge.

ROBERTSON, OSCAR (1938–), American basketball player, born in Charlotte, Tenn. He won All-American rating at the University of Cincinnati in 1958, 1959, and 1960 and established a National Collegiate Athletic Association scoring record, 2,973 points in 88 games, during that period. Known as "the Big O," Robertson had a remarkable professional career. He was a guard for the Cincinnati Royals and the Milwaukee Bucks of the National Basketball Association. Acknowledged as the game's great playmaker, "the Big O" retired in 1974.

ROBINSON, JACK ROOSEVELT (JACKIE) (1919–72), U.S. baseball player, who in 1947 became the first black man to play in the major leagues. Born in Cairo, Ga., Robinson starred in football, basketball, and track at the University of California at Los Angeles and played one season (1945) with a black baseball team, the Kansas City Monarchs. Then Branch Rickey, president of the Brooklyn Dodgers organization, signed him to the Montreal Royals, a Dodger farm club in the International League. But first Rickey had outlined a plan to break the color barrier: the fiercely competitive Robinson was to endure taunts by intolerant players and fans without fighting back. After leading the International League in batting in 1946, Jackie moved up to the Dodgers in 1947. There, in 10 seasons, his timely hitting, daring base running, and aggressive play helped the Dodgers win six National League pennants and one World Series. In his peak season (1949), he led the league in batting and stolen bases and was voted its most valuable player. His lifetime batting average was .311. Primarily a second baseman, he also played first and third and the outfield. He was elected to the Baseball Hall of Fame in 1962.

ROCKNE [*rŏk'nē*], **KNUTE KENNETH** (1888–1931), American football coach, born in Voss, Norway. He went to the United States at the age of five with his parents and

Knute Rockne (*left*), football coach of Notre Dame from 1918 until 1931, with John Smith, team captain in 1927. (CULVER PICTURES, INC.)

was raised and educated in Chicago. When he received his B.S. from Notre Dame in 1914 he had built a reputation as one of the most brilliant college football players of his day. He remained at Notre Dame as a chemistry instructor and football coach. In his 13 years there his teams won 105 games, lost 12, and tied 5. His coaching exerted a great influence on college football as we see it today.

Rockne originated little in football strategy, but he perfected techniques of the forward pass, hard tackling, a new style of blocking, diagonal charging, and the shift play. He was the first coach to play his teams from coast to coast and the first to use "shock troops," or substitutes, to soften up opponents for a fresh onslaught by the first team. He was one of the first to emphasize working players in separate groups rather than in mass drills. Among his great players were George Gipp, Frank Leahy, and the celebrated Four Horsemen—Harry Stuhldreher, Elmer Layden, Don Miller, and Jim Crowley.

RODEO, the public performance of the competitive games and skills of the cowboy, which has become a major sport in the United States and Canada. Widespread use of the term "rodeo" in this sense dates from the early 1920's. However, such cowboy contests got their start in western North America shortly after the Civil War in connection with cattle roundups, where they served both as an outlet for traditional skills and as a source of entertainment.

In a single year in the early 1960's there were 562 North American professional rodeos sanctioned by the sport's governing body, the Rodeo Cowboys Association, which has its headquarters in Denver, Colo. In the United States these were distributed among 37 states. Texas, with 66, was the leader. The over-all total also included 50 Canadian rodeos in four provinces. Alberta, with 34, had the greatest number. Almost 8,000,000 spectators attended these North American programs. There also were many amateur rodeos, some involving high school and college students, for which no records were kept. Outside North America, rodeos are prevalent only in Australia, where about 80 per year took place in the early 1960's.

Most rodeos are held in outdoor arenas. In a typical arena the performance area is surrounded on three sides by spectators. The fourth side consists of chutes from which the animals and cowboys enter.

Standard Events. The standard program comprises five events, and they are held in the order in which they are discussed in this article.

RODEO EVENTS

SADDLE BRONC
With one hand on a braided rein and the other hand free in the air, the cowboy attempts to remain in a standard bronc saddle for 10 seconds.

CALF ROPING
In this timed event the rider lassoes the calf. He then dismounts, and ties any three of its legs.

BULLDOGGING
The rider leaps from his horse, grabs and twists the steer's horns until the animal is brought to the ground.

BAREBACK RIDING
Bareback riding is similar to saddle bronc riding, except that the mount has only a leather surcingle.

BRAHMA BULL RIDING
The cowboy rides the Brahma bull, holding a rope with one hand while keeping the other hand free. Rodeo clowns lure the vicious bull away from a rider who has been thrown and is in danger of being trampled.

Bareback bronc riding involves riding a mount equipped only with a leather surcingle, or rigging, around its middle. The rider's mount is selected by the drawing of lots. The horses are chosen for their bucking ability. The rider mounts his horse in a stall behind a chute, which is flung open to allow horse and rider to enter the arena. The rider is permitted to grasp the surcingle with one hand. The other must be held free in the air as the rider applies his spurs high in the horse's neck during the specified period of competition, usually 10 seconds. Points are awarded by judges according to the skill of the rider, the degree to which he spurs the horse, and the bucking ability of the horse.

Calf roping is judged according to the time that elapses between the mounted cowboy's departure from the starting box, in pursuit of a calf released through a chute, and his final securing of the calf. In the interval he throws a lariat over the calf's head. The other end of the lariat is tied to his saddle before the start of the event. After dismounting he ties together any three legs of the calf with a pigging string. Mounts used in this event are usually of quarter-horse breeding and quite valuable.

Saddle bronc riding is a direct outgrowth of the cowboy's task of horse breaking. A standard bronc saddle is employed, together with one braided rein, and the rider must keep one hand free in the air during the period of competition following his release from the chute. He also is equipped with dull spurs which he must apply high in the mount's neck. As in all riding events, judging is conducted on the basis of the rider's skill and the horse's resistance.

Steer wrestling, or bulldogging, is a distinct outgrowth of the rodeo, and does not stem from the cowboy's daily work. In this event the mounted contestant pursues a steer with the assistance of a second rider known as the hazer. The latter's principal job is known as "lining the steer"—keeping the animal on a straight course by riding alongside it, on the side opposite that of the contestant. When the contestant has reached the steer, he leaps from his horse, grabs the steer by the horns, and throws the steer to its side by twisting the animal's neck. The performance is judged according to the time that elapses between the contestant's leaving the starting box and the moment when the field judge drops his flag to signify that the steer is down with all four legs extending straight out.

Brahma bull riding, another event not directly related to the cowboy's life outside rodeos, is an outgrowth of riding native steers or wild cows. The procedure and judging follow that of other riding competitions. This is the most exciting and dangerous of all rodeo events. Many of the humpbacked Brahmas are almost impossible to ride, and many are vicious animals prone to hook and trample a fallen rider.

In some areas additional events are scheduled. One prominent event among these is team roping, in which two mounted cowboys compete as a team, one roping a steer's head or horns, and the other roping the animal's hind legs. Another is steer roping, in which a single contestant ropes a steer, trips the animal with the aid of his lariat, and then dismounts and ties together any three of the steer's legs. Both events are judged according to the time required to complete the assigned task. Side attractions include exhibitions of trick roping and trick riding, acts by trained horses and dogs, and cutting-horse contests, in which the cowboy rides into a herd of cattle and separates one animal from the others. Such a contest is judged on the horse's ability (without guidance from the rider) to keep the animal from getting back into the herd.

Contestants' Earnings. Contestants pay entry fees in each event in which they compete, and their remuneration consists solely of money won in the distribution of prizes. The top four performers are awarded prize money in each event. At the end of each year the contestant who has won the most money in a given event is named champion of that event. The contestant who has won the most money in a number of events is designated champion cowboy or all-round champion. In the early 1960's the record for earnings in a single year was held by Jim Shoulders of Henryetta, Okla., winner of $43,381 in 1954. The record for career earnings was $426,869, held by Bill Linderman of Red Lodge, Mont.

ROLLER SKATING, a competitive and recreational pastime that has grown to one of America's primary mass-participant sports for children and adults. It is a means of self-propelled locomotion on wheeled skates attached to the bottom of shoes.

History. The earliest recorded roller skate was made in the Netherlands in the 17th century by an anonymous Dutch ice skater, who attempted to transfer the sport to the ground. He fastened some large wooden spools to wood strips, which he attached to his shoes. In 1763 Joseph Merlin, a Belgian mechanic and musical instrument maker, devised a pair of skates that ran on small metal wheels. But these, like the Dutchmen's invention, did not catch the public's fancy because they permitted the user to travel only in a straight line. It was not until James Leonard Plimpton's invention of the "rocking skate," which he patented in 1863, that roller skating became a practical year-round pastime. Plimpton, called the father of modern roller skating, devised a skate that could be guided easily at the skater's will, by leaning the foot or body to one side or the other.

Roller skating became a big boom, and entertainment and sports entrepreneurs began building rinks throughout America, England, Europe, and Australia. But a few years later its popularity waned because many rinks were mismanaged or improperly regulated. Also, skating became boring once a skater had attained a certain peak of proficiency. In 1879 the National Skating Association of Great Britain was formed to promote, regulate, and reward figure skating and hockey in an effort to maintain the sport's popularity.

The introduction of the ball-bearing skate in the 1880's caused a second surge of skating enthusiasm, which lasted into the 1890's. Rink operators hired professional instructors, presented skating exhibitions, and encouraged figure skating. In large cities new and bigger rinks were built.

Another roller skating boom came shortly after the turn of the century, when it took a stronghold in show business. Broadway producers followed earlier entrepreneurs of opera, ballet, and vaudeville by staging musical comedies, in which chorus girls wore roller skates with rubber-tire wheels. Speed skating was also popular at this time, and

International Roller Derby League

Action gets rough as a high-scoring skater, left, tries to pass a defensive star on a banked track.

so were trick, fancy, and novelty skating. The use of roller skating rinks by the government for military purposes during World War I caused many to close down. Rising rents and supply costs also caused a decline in the sport.

In 1937 the Roller Skating Rink Operators Association (RSROA) was organized, with the primary objective of advancing amateur roller skating. It made rules for competition in both random skating and dance routines. The organization set up national championships in figure, dance, and speed skating for all age groups.

Equipment. To get the most from roller skating one uses shoe skates (skates built onto the shoe). Even better are shoes adapted and fitted for the user's own skills and capabilities. Generally, there are two major types of skates. One is the standard skate, made sturdily and mounted on loose ball-bearing wheels, which is relatively inexpensive. The other is the custom-built precision skate for those who want the best product for dance, figure, or race skating. For indoor skating the shoe skate is usually used. It may have wood, fiber, or plastic wheels, mounted on rubber cushions. For outdoor skating most people wear the type with steel wheels that clamp to the shoe with a strap around the ankle.

Roller rinks were once not standardized, but today the average rink figures 12 laps to the mile. The floors of most indoor rinks are made of maple or other hardwood. Many are made of asphalt. The surface of the floor is covered with a thin layer of plastic, which is replaced every few months. This protects the floor and reduces slipping.

Competition. There are two main types of competitive roller skating: artistic and speed. What is broadly called artistic skating may be divided into various divisions, namely, school figures, dancing, and free skating, as in ice skating. In school figures the skater follows a series of painted lines on the floor in which he does a prescribed number of maneuvers (usually 64). In free skating the skater performs his own creations. Contestants sometimes compete as individuals, as partners, or in teams of four persons. Judgment is based on originality, beauty, and technical skill. Dance skating is done with a partner and judged on skill, grace, and physical motion, with music. The dances are usually standardized in competition.

The roller derby is a form of speed skating. It involves two teams each of five men and five women. The two-hour game consists of four 15-minute periods in the first and second halves. Men skate against men for 15 minutes, and the women take over on a similar basis. It is such a rough game that the skaters usually wear crash helmets and padded tights. A team scores points when a team member, called a jammer, laps (passes) opposing players. Players are allowed to block, but as in hockey, there are penalties for unnecessary roughness, illegal blocking, or kicking.

ROWING AND SCULLING. Although rowing and sculling have a history dating back to early civilization, less strenuous and faster modes of transportation eventually confined them to the area of sports and recreation. In the field of sports, rowing differs from sculling in the number of oars employed by each oarsman. When rowing, the oarsmen pull one oar apiece. When sculling, each man pulls two somewhat shorter and lighter oars, often called sculls.

History. Rowing and sculling, as competitive sports, had their origin in England. The earliest annual race was one initiated by Thomas Doggett, a famous comedian of the London stage. In 1715 he donated a coat and a badge to be competed for annually by the Thames River watermen. Doggett's Coat and Badge Race is even today an important event for English professional scullers.

During the next 200 years English oarsmen and their coaches were regarded as being without peer throughout the world. Foreign crews traveled to England to test their prowess at the Henley Royal Regatta. This regatta, started in 1839 on a straight 1 5/16-mi. stretch of water at Henley-on-Thames, eventually became the mecca of all oarsmen. It is still the most famous and colorful of all rowing regattas.

In the United States two historic regattas that have maintained their fame and importance through the years are the Harvard-Yale race, started in 1852, and the Intercollegiate Rowing Association regatta. Both were originally 4-mi. races. However, the latter has been shortened to 3 mi. and is now rowed on Lake Onondaga, Syracuse, N.Y., after having been held for many years on the Hudson River at Poughkeepsie, N.Y.

Types of Races. There is no standard distance for crew races. The shortest races are the ¼-mi. dashes involving single scullers. The longest modern-day race of major importance is the annual 4¼-mi. Oxford-Cambridge race, rowed from Putney to Mortlake on the Thames River. This race dates from 1829. The sprint distance, used in the Olympic Games and in most European races, is 2,000

DIFFERENCES BETWEEN ROWING AND SCULLING

ROWING

Rowing is a team sport. Crews number 2, 4, 6, or 8 men, usually 8 plus a coxswain, who commands. Each crewman operates one oar, or sweep, which measures 12 ft. Timing and co-ordination for balance are of utmost importance.

SCULLING

Sculling is generally considered an individual sport, although shells are made for doubles and quads. Each man handles a pair of carefully matched oars, or sculls. These are shorter (9 ft. 8 in.) and lighter than rowing sweeps, and have narrower blades.

BASIC ROWING TECHNIQUES

POSITION AT START

With his hands slightly apart on the handle and his feet braced, the oarsman bends forward between his open knees, squares the blade to the water, dips it just under the surface, and pulls.

POSITION AT MIDWAY

The oarsman's arms are bent at the elbows, which are tucked in close to his nearly upright body. His knees are together to get the maximum push with his legs.

POSITION AT FINISH

The oarsman pulls on through, leaning back and bringing his hands up to his chest until the bases of his thumbs just touch. He raises the blade and bends forward to begin the next stroke.

BASIC SCULLING TECHNIQUES

POSITION AT START

The sculler does not open his knees but doubles up over them as far forward as he comfortably can. He raises his hands slightly to dip the blades into the water, keeping them level at all times.

POSITION AT MIDWAY

Halfway through the stroke, the sculls overlap. The sculler passes one hand over the other, keeping them as close together as possible so that the blades remain parallel and the pull even.

POSITION AT FINISH

The sculler leans farther back than the oarsman and may raise his body to meet his hands as he finishes the stroke. Lifting the blades, he continues this forward motion for the next stroke.

meters. Intercollegiate eight-oared races in the United States vary in length from 2,000 meters to 4 mi. Many of the older, traditional competitions are conducted at 1¾ mi. and 2 mi.

Most rowing races are conducted with the crews rowing abreast on parallel courses. A notable exception, the "bumping race," involves intercollege rivalries at Oxford and at Cambridge. Both these universities are situated along streams so narrow and winding that racing abreast is impossible. This has brought about a special type of competition in which the crews are aligned single file at the start, a specified distance apart. In such a race the object of the crew of each boat other than the lead one is to touch the stern of the boat ahead before the finish line is reached.

Rowing and sculling competitions are conducted in boats of several sizes. In the rowing events there are races for eights, fours, pairs, and occasionally sixes. The eights have eight oarsmen and a coxswain who steers and shouts the necessary commands. The fours and pairs may be either with or without a coxswain, and there are separate events for each of these. In addition to these rowing events, there are sculling races for singles (one man), doubles (two men), and quads (four men).

Equipment. There are no regulations governing the size and weight of boats. However, a century of experimentation has resulted in their being very similar. All racing boats have sliding seats that permit the oarsmen to push with their legs and thereby attain additional power and length in their stroke. Another unique feature is the outrigger, consisting of lightweight metal tubing to which the oarlock is attached. It enables the oarsmen to use long oars without necessitating a wide boat.

The racing boats, usually called shells, are made of thin cedar or mahogany planking, $\frac{5}{32}$ in. (3.8 mm) thick. They are about 61 ft (18.6 m) in length and have a beam of 24 in. (609.6 mm) at the widest point. The size and weight depend upon the weight of the crew that the shell must carry. Most eight-oared shells weigh about 280 lb (127 kg). Racing oars are of spruce, 12 ft (3.6 m) in length and hollow throughout the shaft. They weigh approximately 8 lb (3.6 kg) and have curved, spoon-shaped blades.

A good eight-oared crew is capable of a speed of 15 mph (24 kph) for a short distance. Strength and endurance are required of oarsmen, and the speed of a crew is also heavily dependent on perfect timing. The oarsmen must be so adept in the use of their sliding seats that the shell progresses swiftly, yet with an almost complete absence of retardation between strokes.

RUGBY, game of the football family. It is played by two teams, each of which attempts to score points by carrying the ball over the opponent's goal line or by kicking it over a crossbar and between uprights situated on the goal line. Rugby is an offspring of association football—known in the United States as soccer—and the father of American football. It is popular in Great Britain, Australia, New Zealand, South Africa, and France and on the East and West coasts of the United States. Some American college football players play Rugby in the spring to stay in condition, but Rugby itself is greatly overshadowed in the United States by American football.

Origin and Growth. Early in the 19th century soccer was the only sport in the football family. It permitted movement of the ball principally by kicking. Then, in 1823, Rugby was born by accident. William Webb Ellis, piqued at his failure to kick the ball in an interclass soccer game at Rugby School in England, picked up the ball and ran with it across the goal line. This shocking and controversial move created a new game, though its rules were not codified until 1848. In 1863 the London Football Association, which advocated the kicking-only game, wrote rules for soccer. In 1871 the Rugby Football Union, comprising 21 amateur clubs, was created for the "Rugby-type game" and named it Rugby.

The new sport was introduced in 1875 to the United States, where it has remained largely on an amateur basis. In Great Britain, however, some of the players became professionals. In 1895 Britain's first professional Rugby organization, the Northern Rugby Union, was formed. In 1922 its name was changed to the Rugby Football League.

How the Game Is Played. Rugby is played on a turf field no more than 110 yd (100.6 m) long (from goal line to goal line) and 75 yd (68.6 m) wide—somewhat larger than an American football field. The oval, leather-covered ball is inflated. It is the same length as an American football but wider and less pointed, which makes it easier to drop-kick but more difficult to throw.

Since 1875 there have been 15 players on an amateur team—8 forwards (defensive men) and 7 backs (attackers). Professional teams use 13 men. A game consists of 40-minute halves. Play is virtually continuous, as in soccer, and no substitutions are allowed. The ball may be carried or kicked. It may be passed laterally or backward, but not forward. The players wear uniforms much like those of soccer players. Padding is not used and is unnecessary because interference and blocking are illegal. The defense uses tackling to halt the ball carrier, who then must release the ball. Immediately thereafter the ball is put in play through a kick by the first player of either side to reach it.

The scoring system puts a high reward on kicking. A try, or act of crossing the opponent's goal line and touching the ball to the ground (the equivalent of American football's touchdown), is worth three points. A successful conversion after try, by a place kick, counts two points. A goal on a free kick or penalty kick counts three points. A free kick (by place kick, drop kick, or punt) is made by a player who has made a fair catch. A penalty kick by any of these methods is awarded to a player when the opponents have violated the rules of play. A successful drop kick, when the kicker has the option to run or pass, is worth three points.

See also FOOTBALL; SOCCER.

RUSSELL, WILLIAM ("BILL") FELTON (1934–), U.S. Negro basketball player and coach. Born in Monroe, La., he attended the University of San Francisco and was an outstanding college player. Russell was a member of the

The British Travel Assn.

A Rugby player tries to gain ground by carrying the ball in a match at Rosslyn Park, England.

1956 U.S. Olympic basketball team that won a gold medal. He joined the Boston Celtics in 1956, winning the National Basketball Association Most Valuable Player award in 1958, 1961, 1962, 1963, and 1964. In 1966 he was named coach of the Boston Celtics, becoming the first Negro ever to coach a major professional sports team.

RUTH, GEORGE HERMAN ("BABE") (1895–1948), American baseball player, born in Baltimore, Md. Ruth was the greatest batter in baseball history, hitting 60 home runs in one season (1927) and 714 in his career (1914–35). His lifetime batting average was .342.

Ruth began as a left-handed pitcher with the Baltimore Orioles of the International League. He was purchased by the Boston Red Sox in 1914, winning 89 games in six seasons. Ruth's most famous pitching feat was his 29 consecutive scoreless innings in the 1916 and 1918 World Series. By 1918 Red Sox manager Ed Barrow was using Ruth in the outfield because of his hitting. In 1919 Ruth hit .378 and set a major league record with 29 home runs. That winter he was sold to the New York Yankees for $125,000, plus $350,000 that paid off debts of the Boston club.

With New York, Ruth hit 54 home runs in 1920 and 59 in 1921 to bring the Yankees their first American League pennant. The team also won the pennant in 1922 and 1923, then won three more from 1926 to 1928 with Ruth hitting 161 home runs in those seasons. Babe played on his last pennant-winning team in 1932. Ruth left the Yankees in 1935 to become a playing vice president for the Boston Braves. He hit three home runs in his final game early that season at Forbes Field, Pittsburgh. Ruth had only brief connections with organized baseball after that, until his death from cancer. The beloved "Bambino" still remains unchallenged in popularity.

George Herman "Babe" Ruth, American baseball player who became famous as a home run hitter. (UNITED PRESS INTERNATIONAL)

S

SAILING. A sailing craft is, by definition, one that is propelled by a sail or sails. More exactly, the sailing craft uses its sails to extract power from the wind and to apply the resulting forces, as effectively as possible, to make the craft travel in a desired path.

History. It is probable that the earliest "sails" were simply branches or large leaves held up by the occupants of some crude craft in prehistoric times. Eventually hides, woven mats, and finally woven cloth were made into sails. With increasing refinement of sail material it became possible to design more efficient sails, which, in turn, required more sophisticated rigging and hull designs. A thousand years or more before the birth of Christ, sailing had become sufficiently reliable to allow commercial and military traffic throughout the Mediterranean Sea and voyages of exploration in the Atlantic Ocean along the coasts of Africa and Europe.

The designing, building, and handling of early sailing vessels represented the acme of mechanical skill until Roman times. The superior development of sailing craft is easily understood when one considers that they were the only means of access to all civilized centers of the known world. The wind was the only known power source, and it was inexhaustible.

The widespread use of sailing vessels in commerce depended on their ability to sail to a given point and return with the available winds. War vessels could use slave-

Bill Robinson

Pier of a U.S. yacht club. Such clubs provide a meeting place for the growing number of pleasure-boating enthusiasts.

pulled oars to gain their objectives against adverse conditions, but this form of power was too expensive for commercial vessels. The captains of such craft needed sailing skill. Probably it was possible from early times to sail vessels at least with the wind abeam, that is, with the wind direction at 90° to the center line of the craft. Before 1000 A.D. the Vikings were apparently able to sail their finely formed "long ships" somewhat to windward, that is, on a course less than 90° to the direction of the wind. The ability to sail to windward became increasingly important as man laid out his voyages according to commercial demand rather than the vagaries of wind and weather. Skill is required to design, build, and rig a vessel which will sail close-hauled to an upwind destination, and there is also a premium on the skill of the sailor himself. These factors have held true throughout the history of sailing, right up to the present.

Why a Boat Sails

There are three main factors in sailing a boat: the wind in the sails, the water which the boat is sailing over, and the turbulence created by the boat's passage.

The boat is driven by the power extracted from the wind by the sails in the same manner that a glider or airplane is supported by the lift of the wings. The size, height, number, and shape of the sails determine the amount of available power.

Working against the forward drive of the sails are two forms of drag, or resistance. One of these derives from the viscosity, or "stickiness," of the water acting on the craft's submerged surface. The smoother the hull surface, the less is the drag contributed by viscosity. The other is a result of the loss of energy expended in making waves in the wake, as well as the eddies around such appendages as rudder, keel, and propeller. This wave and eddy drag is practically nonexistent at very low speeds, but accounts for about half the total drag at normal cruising speeds.

Sailing skill is a matter of using the wind in the sails to overcome the water and waves. A skilled sailor knows the water that he is sailing through, but it is primarily in his use of sails that his superiority comes to the fore.

Wind-Sail Relationship. The three main points of sailing are based on understanding of the action of the wind on the sails. These points are defined as running free, reaching, and close-hauled.

A boat *running free* is headed directly before the wind or nearly so. It is pushed along its course very much as a motorboat is pushed by its underwater propellers. The difference is that the point of application of the push in the sailboat is high, thus imparting a slight tendency for the boat to nose down. As the course of the boat is brought more into the wind from the running-free point of sailing, the wind force pushes the boat more and more from the side. The boat then approaches the *reaching* point, at which the center line of the craft is at about a 90° angle to the wind. A boat sailing *close-hauled* is sailing as closely as possible into the wind. In this position the driving force decreases, and the boat tends to head into the wind.

The yacht running free receives assistance from the waves and the wind acting on its rigging. When the craft is reaching, the effects of wind and waves on forward progress are negligible. But when the craft is close-hauled, the wind and wave forces tend to hold the boat back. Since the boat's speed can be influenced by the velocity of the waves, much attention is paid in the design of the sailboat to its performance when sailing to windward.

An example of sailing close-hauled may be observed in a modern sloop. The course of the boat lies approximately 45° from the wind direction. As the wind flows around and between the sails, pressure behind the sails builds up while it diminishes ahead of the sails. The result is a force that pushes the boat ahead and to one side. Part of this force tends to heel, or tip, the boat to one side and the other part pushes the boat ahead. In an efficient modern rig the heeling force is approximately one-third of the driving force when sailing close-hauled.

In order for the boat to sail better to windward, the driving force should be as great as possible relative to the heeling force. Unfortunately, other things being equal, the only way to improve this ratio is by lengthening the leading edges of the sails. This can be accomplished only by increasing the height of the mast. But, if the mast is given more height, the heeling force is applied higher up, and creates a greater tendency for the boat to heel. Counteracting this calls for increased stability derived from a wider hull, or additional ballast, or both.

Balance. Another important aspect of a sailboat is good balance. Balance gives a boat a tendency to hold its course with a minimum rudder angle. The dynamic forces from air and water acting on the boat change their points of application, directions, and magnitudes as the wind decreases or increases or changes direction with respect to the boat. To keep a boat sailing a straight course requires an equilibrium achieved by adjustment of the settings of the sails and the rudder angles. A boat so unbalanced that even the maximu rudder angle is not sufficient to hold it on course requires shortening of sail if the course is to be maintained.

Speed-Length Ratio. It is possible to estimate the maximum speed of a sailing vessel by using the speed-length ratio. The maximum ratio to be expected from normal sailing craft is about 1.4 or 1.5. The ratio is expressed in terms of $V/\sqrt{L}$, V being the speed in knots and L the length in feet (the mean of the over-all length and the water-line length). In other words, a craft with an L of 25 ft. may be expected to have a maximum speed of $1.5 \times \sqrt{25}$, or 7.5 knots.

Small boats frequently exceed the speed-length ratio of 1.5. This characteristic is partly due to the phenomenon of planing, which is the tendency of the boat to lift itself out of the water and skim across the surface. Thus a lightly built, stable boat with a fairly large rig may attain a ratio of 3.0 or so. Heavier boats with cruising accommodations are known to attain ratios approaching 2.0 under favorable conditions. But, as a general rule, the larger sailing vessels rarely attain a ratio higher than 1.5.

Rig: Spars and Rigging

The rig of a sailboat comprises *spars*, *rigging*, and the *sails* themselves. The spars include masts, booms, and spreaders. The rigging is divided into *standing rigging* for the support of the spars and *running rigging* for the ma-

WIND-SAIL RELATIONSHIP

DIRECTION OF WIND DIRECTION OF WIND

RUNNING FREE

REACHING

CLOSE-HAULED

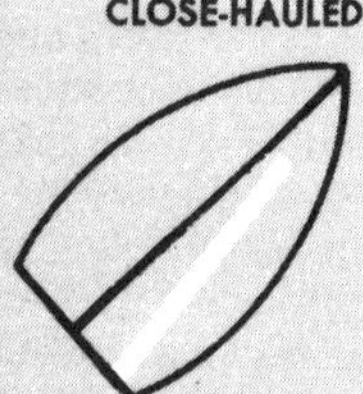

The boat is headed directly or almost directly before the wind.

The angle between the centerline of the boat and the wind direction is about 90°.

The boat is sailing as close as possible into the wind.

Ken Ollar

Bill Robinson

Birnback Publishing Service

nipulation of sails. The entire rig must be strong and adequately fastened to the hull. It must be able to withstand the forces and shocks imposed by wind and rough water.

Development. The history of rigs may be described as a struggle with inadequate materials. The advent of the lateen sail at an early date gave man a remarkably efficient airfoil, sufficiently so that it is still used in some high-speed sailboats. Application of the lateen sail to sailboats was, however, hampered by the heavy spars, the elasticity of the fiber ropes, and the weight and dimensional instability of the sail fabrics. But in the past hundred years three developments have revolutionized rigs. Ironically they came too late to benefit vanishing commercial vessels, but they were fully used in pleasure sailboats. These developments were the use of hollow, metal masts, yards, and booms; the invention of iron and steel wire rope, together with end fittings equal in strength to the rope itself; and the invention of synthetic fibers useful in running rigging and sail fabrics.

These and minor improvements resulted in lofty rigs with slender masts delicately supporting a tracery of fine wire ropes and gleaming sails. The modern rig has an efficiency undreamed of 50 years ago. For example, the Class-J yacht *Reliance*, which successfully defended the America's Cup in 1903, carried 16,160 sq. ft. of sail. In contrast, the last of the J yachts, the *Ranger*, in 1937 carried only 7,500 ft. of working sail, but its average speed for sailing the series of Cup races was 7.8 knots against 7.3 knots for *Reliance*.

The spars and rigging support and extend the sails so that they efficiently extract power from the wind to produce forward motion in the hull. Generally this process requires a structure of great rigidity, and in some cases, carefully controlled flexibility to assure that the sails assume the desired shape and position. At the same time weight must be kept low since excess weight at the masthead reduces stability. Further complicating the picture are many imponderable factors involved in a successful rig, such as the optimum juxtaposition of the sails and the effects of the boat's motion. Much rig design depends on intuition based on experience.

Spars. The main spars, or masts, are the foundations of rigs. Invariably hollow nowadays, masts must withstand strong compression, or "buckling," forces and remain straight.

The traditional material for modern wooden masts is Sitka spruce from the Pacific Northwest. Sitka spruce is strong, lightweight, and available in straight-grained lengths to 40 ft. or more. Spruce masts are made generally by gluing several pieces together and reinforcing them at points of maximum stress. Some masts are in a teardrop shape, which reduces wind resistance, but larger boats have masts that are either oval or rectangular in cross section. The oval shape is more expensive but offers a smoother air flow to the sail. There is little difference between the two shapes in either weight or strength.

Aluminum masts are generally of drawn or extruded tubing in teardrop or elliptic shape, although some are made of round tubing squeezed into the desired oval shape in large presses. For equal strength and somewhat greater stiffness aluminum masts are approximately 25% lighter in weight than wooden masts. Small aluminum masts are usually much less expensive than wooden ones because of the saving obtained in quantity extruding of the metal, but even large aluminum masts can be less expensive than wood. Booms, spreaders, and spinnaker poles are generally aluminum on small boats with aluminum masts, but in larger boats wood is still the popular material.

Standing Rigging. Standing rigging serves to hold the mast in position. Those pieces of standing rigging leading down from the mast to the hull abreast the mast, usually in pairs, are called shrouds, and those leading fore and aft are called stays. Not long ago all standing rigging was simply secured by an eye splice passing around the mast. But splices tended to deteriorate with time and had an elasticity that made it difficult to hold masts straight. Sometimes the location of the splices interfered with the placement of other fittings about the mast.

For these reasons it is almost universal practice now with both wood and aluminum spars to fasten the standing rigging to the masts with metal clips, known as tangs. The tangs are securely bolted and screwed to the spars to withstand the downward pull of the rigging. Tangs and other wrought mast fittings are generally of bronze on wooden spars and of stainless steel or aluminum on aluminum spars.

The standing rigging leads down to turnbuckles at the deck, which are shackled or pinned to the chain plates. Chain plates are among the most important fittings on a sailing boat and must be strong enough to withstand the pull of the rigging with an ample margin of safety. They must be attached to the hull in a manner that distributes the rigging strains over the hull without placing undue stress on a small area or allowing the hull to be pulled out of shape.

In some special cases solid rod, either round or streamlined, is used for standing rigging. But the expense of forging terminals on each end to the exact length required and the susceptibility of the rod to damage have so far discouraged any widespread use of rod rigging.

Running Rigging. Running rigging is the rope used to manipulate and control the movements and positions of the sails and movable spars. In small boats running rigging may be entirely of fiber rope. In larger boats the halyard and some sheets are either all wire rope or wire rope spliced into fiber rope.

Most of the fiber rope used now is Dacron because of its high strength, resistance to deterioration, and lack of stiffness when wet. Dacron is so strong that its widespread use has to some extent required that rigs be designed with greater strength. For some purposes nylon rope is preferred because of its greater elasticity. Of the natural fiber ropes, low cost is combined with good strength and lasting quality in Manila, but both cotton and linen rope are still preferred by some.

Wire rope comes in many different constructions and materials, each having particular advantages. Either double-galvanized, improved plow steel or 18–8 stainless steel is preferred for yacht work.

The standing part of running rigging (that end which is secured to the sail or spar controlled by it) may be made fast by means of snap hooks, shackles, splices, or knots. The line is led through the appropriate pulleys or fair-leads to the point where the hauling part is made fast either to fixed cleats or to cam-operated jam cleats. Lines are often led around winches, similar to the old-fashioned windlasses, to increase the power of the men doing the hauling by as much as 40 times.

Rig: Sails

Sails. The sails, along with the hull, share the responsibility for the performance characteristics of a sailing vessel. Minor flaws, not apparent to the inexpert, may have decisive effects.

Sails are generally made from strips of cloth sewn perpendicularly to the edges not attached to spars. The edges are reinforced with tape or rope of the same material as the sail or with wire rope. Corners and other strain points are reinforced with the cloth. Sails are attached to wire stays with snap hooks for quick removal and to spars with metal slides sewn to the sail and sliding on a spar track. Sometimes the rope on the edge of the sail slides in a groove on the mast.

Aerodynamics. Much mystery still surrounds the aerodynamics of sails because their "softness" makes it difficult to define their shape clearly at any given instant of time. Much of this difficulty was due to the dimensional instability of the sailcloths made of vegetable fibers (first flax and then cotton) under varying conditions of wind and humidity. It is little wonder that sailmaking has become an occult art, each sailmaker jealously guarding his secrets. Even so, the best sail can be easily ruined during the breaking-in process by hauling it out too hard when first set or by setting the new sail in damp weather or heavy winds.

Synthetic Fabrics. The use of synthetic fabrics, beginning with nylon after World War II and followed by Dacron (Terylene, in England) had a notable effect on the sailmaker's art. Although nylon was first looked upon as the ultimate sailmaking material, experience showed it was unsuitable for working sails. Nylon could not resist harmful sun rays and had a high elasticity. However, precisely the same elasticity and light weight made it an ex-

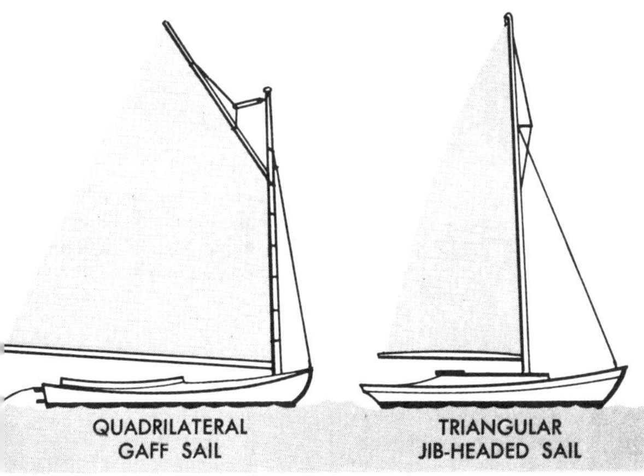

cellent material for such light-weather sails as spinnakers and mizzen staysails.

Since 1950 Dacron has almost entirely supplanted natural fibers in sails. Properly woven and treated, Dacron cloth has practically no drawbacks. It has negligible stretch, an imperviousness to sunlight, low water absorption, and strength. Sailmakers devised sewing techniques to avoid the rapid chafing of the stitches and to bind the edges with webbing tape of the same material (instead of the traditional boltropes).

Dacron became what the sailmaking industry had never had before. Sailmakers could make sails of Dacron to precise sizes instead of allowing for the 6% to 8% of stretch required by the old cotton sails. This characteristic led to scientific experiments in sailmaking and the construction of at least one wind tunnel for testing sails. As yet, however, there is no appreciable body of definitive literature on optimum sail forms.

Sail Shape. Traditionally the ideal shape for a sail to assume is to have most of the draft, or curvature, in the forward third of the sail, with the after two-thirds sweeping back in a fairly flat curve. With headsails this form does indeed seem to be the most desirable as it delivers the air from the leech, or trailing edge, onto the lee side of the mainsail in a straight and efficient flow. The best shape for the mainsail, and other boomed sails, is much less certain. There seems to be some evidence that the shape could be a circular arc, with constant curvature, and even, in some cases, with the maximum curvature along the leech. Until systematic testing of sails is done, these questions will remain unsolved.

The majority of yacht sails are in two main categories: *staysails* (called "stays'ls" by seamen) and *spar sails*. Staysails are snapped onto stays, the fore-and-aft pieces of standing rigging. Although some staysails are set flying (not snapped to any stay), and others have a light club or boom extending all or part of the way along the foot, it is not difficult to separate these from the spar sails. Staysails are invariably triangular except for some sails between the masts of schooners.

Spar sails are those sails, other than staysails, that are attached directly to the masts and are extended out from the mast by approximately horizontal spars. These sails may be triangular, or jib headed, with a boom along the foot and the third side flying free. They may also be quadrilateral with a spar, called the gaff, along the head in addition to the boom along the foot.

The quadrilateral gaff sail is easier to handle in some ways but is more costly and is not quite as efficient, on the average. The jib-headed mainsail is almost universal among modern yachts.

Spinnaker. Light sails are used only on certain points of sailing when the wind is not too heavy. The most noteworthy is the *spinnaker*. At one time spinnakers were rather flat, but in recent years the so-called parachute spinnaker has become standard. The parachute spinnaker is cut full with a high "bosom" and is a powerful sail. The weather lower corner, or tack, is extended by the spinnaker pole, a light spar rigged especially for the purpose. The spinnaker cannot be carried if the apparent wind is forward of the beam. Being rather a nuisance to set and difficult to control under some conditions, the spinnaker is not widely used in cruising but is essential for success in racing.

Sail Area. A rule of thumb for estimating sail area is to square the water-line length of the hull. Light displacement boats and those with short overhangs have somewhat less sail area. Racing boats and those with long overhangs have somewhat more. It is considered that a reasonably able man can handle 400 sq. ft. of a single sail under almost all conditions, and an unusually able or strong man can handle 600 sq. ft.

Shortening Sail. Shortening sail is done when the wind blows too hard. It can sometimes be done by lowering one small sail, although in many boats this change causes an imbalance that makes control impossible. The other way to shorten sail is to reef. Reefing can be done in two ways depending on the equipment on the boat. If the boat has roller reefing gear, the desired amount of sail is rolled up around the boom. If not, a band of the sail is furled down on the boom with light lines, called reef points, sewn to the sail.

Types of Rigs

Catboat. The catboat, with its single jib-headed or quadrilateral gaff sail, is the simplest of all rigs. It is not the easiest to sail, however, because of the lack of second sail to provide balance. In addition, the mast is forward where it is difficult to fix securely into the hull and almost impossible to stay adequately. For these two reasons the catboat rig is rarely seen on boats over 20 ft. Originally devised by Cape Cod fishermen, it is used almost exclusively on centerboard boats, of which the great beam (width) may equal one-half the length. Traditionally, large catboats are gaff rigged and small catboats jib headed. Although the catboat is often used by beginners learning to sail because of its apparent simplicity, many authorities feel that a small sloop provides better basic training.

Sloop and Cutter. These two rigs are basically the same by virtue of having a single mast. The difference is generally considered to be placement of the mast. A cutter has the mast one-third or more of the water-line length aft of the forward end of the water line and usually has two or more working headsails. A sloop's mast is farther forward, and the sloop generally carries a single headsail. The sloop

TYPES OF RIGS

CATBOAT

In this rig, used mostly on centerboard boats of wide beam, there is a single jib-headed or quadrilateral gaff sail, and the mast is stepped well forward.

Morris Rosenfeld

Morris Rosenfeld

SLOOP

The sloop's mast is substantially farther aft than the catboat's. Two sails are carried—a mainsail, which may be gaff or jib-headed, and a headsail. When gaff-rigged, the sloop may carry a triangular topsail.

CUTTER

The mast is stepped one-third or more of the water-line length aft of the forward end of the water line. As a general rule, the cutter carries two or more headsails as well as a mainsail and, like the sloop, a topsail when it is gaff-rigged.

Bill Robinson

SCHOONER

The schooner has at least two masts—a foremast and a mainmast. The foremast may be, but seldom is, as high as the mainmast. Traditionally, the rig includes a gaff-headed foresail.

Morris Rosenfeld

KETCH

The after, or mizzen, mast is shorter than the mainmast and is forward of the rudder post. The ketch can maintain headway in blowy weather under headsails and mizzen alone.

Morris Rosenfeld

YAWL

The mizzenmast is aft of the rudder post. The yawl's mizzen has less area than the ketch's, and mainsail and headsails are correspondingly larger; but, like the ketch, the yawl balances well with furled mainsail.

Morris Rosenfeld

is somewhat more efficient for racing but is slightly more difficult to handle because of its larger jib. Mainsails may be gaff or jib headed. If gaff rigged, the cutter, and often the sloop, carries a topsail, a triangular sail above the mainsail. In the cutter the foremost stay invariably attaches to the mast at the head. In the sloop the foremost stay may attach to the mast at the head or somewhat below. Perhaps the most popular rig in American waters is the jib-headed sloop.

Yawl and Ketch. Like the sloop and cutter the difference between a yawl and ketch is one of degree. The most commonly accepted distinction is the location of the after, or mizzen, mast, which in either case is shorter than the forward, or main, mast. In the yawl the aftermast is aft of the rudder post. In the ketch it is forward of the rudder post. Although the ketch was at one time in vogue, it is rather an inefficient rig sailing to windward because the mainsail backwinds the aftersail, rendering it nearly useless. The chief advantages of the ketch over the yawl are that the mainsail and headsails are smaller and hence easier to handle. The aftermast of a ketch is in a deeper and wider portion of the boat and can be more securely stayed than that of a yawl. Both the yawl and ketch, if properly designed, balance well with the mainsail furled, and sails can be shortened quickly in the event of a sudden blow. The aftersail can be effectively used to adjust the balance of the boat so that little effort is required to steer. Yawls and ketches are more expensive than sloops and cutters, and their rigs are not considered worthwhile for boats less than 32 to 35 ft. in length. However, they are popular in larger boats.

Schooner. The schooner has two or more masts (the commercial schooner *Thomas W. Lawson* had seven), all masts being approximately equally high, or higher moving aft. The schooner rig is generally considered to be an American invention, dating from the 18th century. Originally the schooner was rigged with quadrilateral gaff sails. The yachtsman soon applied the advantages of the triangular jib-headed sail to the aftermost mainsail. In 1925 appeared the staysail schooner, in which the gaff foresail was replaced by a system of staysails between the masts. The schooner is perhaps the most expensive of the rigs described here and is little used now except for really large sailing yachts. Of the two types of schooner the staysail schooner is the more efficient, allowing the setting of the largest number of different sails but requiring more work to man.

Sailing Vessel Construction

The first watercraft were undoubtedly logs, eventually hollowed out to become dugout canoes. As water navigation spread to larger bodies of water, the demands of seaworthiness prompted the addition of planks around the top of the dugouts to increase the width and height. The dugout canoe evolved into the built-up wooden vessel, which has remained fundamentally the same in construction for 5,000 years. With minor variations wooden craft are made up of hull and deck planking fastened to a framework consisting of the keel, stem, sternpost, closely spaced ribs or frames passing over the keel and firmly fastened to it, and deck beams tying the upper ends of the frames together. Depending on the size of the craft, various stringers, bulkheads, ceiling (which might be called auxiliary planking secured to the inboard faces of the frames), and knees are incorporated to provide the necessary strength and rigidity.

Until World War II all except the largest sailing yachts had been built in this same manner. Improvements make the modern yacht built by this method quite a different boat from its ancestors. Among these improvements are better metal fastenings, such as wood screws and through bolts; light, strong, steam-bent frames in place of the essentially weak, heavy, built-up frames of the past; and greater diaphragm strength in bulkheads, decking, and other flat surfaces through the use of flat sheets of plywood.

There has been considerable exploitation of new building methods and materials since the war. These include glued-strip construction, molded plywood, fiber glass-reinforced plastic, and aluminum. All of these methods and materials have in common the *monocoque*, or stressed skin, principle, that is, the use of the skin as the major strength member. In conventional wooden construction the primary purpose of the planking, or skin, is to keep the water out. Structural strength is largely obtained from the framing. In stressed-skin construction framing is largely limited to sufficient bulkheads to assure shape retention and to reinforce areas of concentrated stress.

Glued-Strip. The glued-strip hull consists of square strips of a suitable wood, edge-nailed together and glued with a waterproof glue. Glued-strip construction is simple for either professional or amateur builders. It requires little maintenance and is next to aluminum in strength and stiffness in relation to weight. Glued-strip construction shares with molded-plywood construction the advantages of wood, such as heat and sound insulation, a familiar and pleasant appearance and texture, and high resistance to fatigue.

Molded Plywood. Molded-plywood boats are made of three or more layers of thin veneer, laid at 90° to each other and glued together under heat and pressure. Although boats up to about 40 ft. in length have been built of molded plywood, its use is restricted mostly to small boats 20 ft. and under. The high cost of the mold and the necessary heat and pressure equipment makes the method practical only in quantity production. Molded-plywood boats are somewhat lighter in weight than conventional wooden boats and about equal in weight to fiber glass.

Plastic. Fiber glass-reinforced plastic boats are built of layers of a glass-fiber cloth impregnated with a hard-drying synthetic resin, usually a polyester. The cloth is in a variety of forms, as a woven fabric or as a feltlike mat of glass fibers, the selection depending on the characteristics desired in the finished material. Size is generally limited to about 45 ft. because competitive prices can be obtained only through quantity production. A well-designed and well-built plastic hull is a strong, one-piece structure, unaffected by rot or worms but subject to deterioration from aging and some chemicals. Polyester resins support combustion, but an additive to the resin—or protective paints—can reduce or eliminate this characteristic.

Aluminum. Aluminum is increasingly popular for boat

construction as improved alloys and welding techniques are developed. Vessels of sizes up to about 100 ft. are built of aluminum, and it is extensively used in superstructures of larger passenger and military vessels. Riveting, especially in the thinner gages, and shielded arc welding are used for fastening sheets. Aluminum is about half the weight of steel for equal strength. It is nontoxic, easy to fabricate, and highly resistant to corrosion from marine atmosphere but is sensitive to electrolytic corrosion. Cost is generally somewhat above that of other materials.

Outlook. It is very likely that yachts will continue to be built of wood, aluminum, steel, and fiber glass-reinforced plastic in the foreseeable future, each material being steadily improved and each offering its own advantages and disadvantages. Standardization in yacht design and construction has become increasingly evident since the turn of the century. The multitude of different functions to which vessels are put, however, suggests that mass production as practiced by the automobile industry will never be attained in sailboat building.

Building Costs. Cost was a relatively minor factor in years past when 150-ft. schooner yachts might be built with accommodations for only four or six in the owner's party. With the popularity of sailing, particularly family cruising, the cost factor has become of great importance. Initial and continuing costs of ownership are closely related to the weight of the boat, the cost per unit weight decreasing somewhat with increasing size. Boat costs increased about 3% to 5% annually from 1945 to about 1958, after which the rise has been slight. In 1960 cruising sailboats could be expected to cost from $1.50 to $3.00 per pound, depending somewhat on size but more on quality of material and workmanship and amount and kind of equipment. Annual cost of ownership, including off-season storage, maintenance, operating expenses, depreciation, and loss of income through not investing, has been variously estimated at from 15% to 25% of the replacement cost of the boat, on the basis of all work done professionally.

Sailing

There appears to have been some pleasure boating in all historical ages, but sailing was not organized as a sport until Charles II of England had a fleet of Dutch *jachts* built in the mid-17th century. (The word "yacht" derives from Dutch *jacht,* meaning "small, fast boat.") These were later raced on the Thames River at London, probably the first instance of organized class racing.

A few boating clubs were started in the mid-18th century, but pleasure boating remained a limited sport until developments consequent on the industrial revolution created the middle class and made possible increased leisure time.

The popularity of pleasure boating increased rapidly in the United States in the 20th century. Pleasure boats numbered about 15,000 in 1904, some 2,440,000 in 1947, and about 7,800,000 in the early 1960's. Although power boats have accounted for most of the dramatic increase since World War II, it has been estimated that the last figure includes about 45,000 auxiliary powered sailboats and about 500,000 sailboats without inboard power. The proportion of sailboats to power boats seems to be increasing. Sailing provides an extra dimension of pleasure that power boats do not have, that is, greater self-reliance and contact with nature, since the wind provides the motive power. In a civilization which is becoming more and more mechanized, automated, and plastic-coated, some people may feel a strong need for the simple realities of nature and its demands upon their self-reliance. Sailing, whether in a small day sailer or a large ocean-going yacht, often fulfills this need admirably.

Sailing takes many forms, depending upon size of the pocketbook, geographical location, available time, and inclination. Although the gamut runs all the way from sailing small skiffs on ponds to racing across the Atlantic Ocean in yachts costing hundreds of thousand of dollars, a common denominator is the pleasure and absorption of the participants.

Sailing has always tended to be an international sport. The cruiser finds familiar scenes and sounds halfway around the world from home. And the top skippers in some of the racing classes travel all over the world to championship meets. Even the time and expense of getting large yachts to the scene do not stop the United States from being represented in about all major ocean races, and at least six countries take part in every Bermuda or Fastnet race.

The most international of all sailing events are undoubtedly those held at the quadrennial Olympic Games. In the 1960 games, held in Italy, there were sailing events in five classes, 5.5-Meter, Dragon, Star, Flying Dutchman, and Finn, and entries from 46 countries.

Sailing yachts may be divided into three groups: day sailors, cruisers, and racing craft.

Day Sailers. Boats used for day sailing are generally fairly small but comfortable and roomy. Their prime purpose is to provide safe and pleasant boating for families, although the boats are frequently raced. They range in length to about 20 ft., are open or partially decked, and are generally centerboarders, with large cockpits for family use.

Cruisers. Cruising boats perform somewhat the same function as days sailers, but they are fitted with accommodations permitting the crew to live aboard in reasonable comfort. Although these boats may be divided into ocean racers and out-and-out cruisers, they have in common cruising accommodations, such as berths, galley, toilet facilities, and so forth, and, as a rule, auxiliary power. They still bear in varying degrees the stamp of the commercial craft from which they are descended. Cruisers range in length from 16 ft. with accommodations for two up to large seagoing vessels of 150 ft. or more with accommodations for 20 to 30 persons. The majority are from about 25 to 40 ft., accommodating 4 to 8 persons.

The cruising boats that compete in ocean races are largely functional in concept with hull form, rig configuration, construction, and details of gear largely decided on the basis of their value in winning races. Despite this bias in design, most ocean racers are extremely able sea boats and quite comfortable but fairly expensive cruising boats.

Two very important factors affect the design of the straight cruiser: aesthetic appeal and what might be called romance, tradition, or nostalgia. Aesthetic appeal is a subjective judgment and thus difficult to define, but certain

James B. Allen

This cruising yacht is a skipjack, a type employed in the Chesapeake Bay oyster fishery. Distinguished by its clipper bow and raking mast, the skipjack, along with its close cousin, the bugeye, is the last of America's sailing work boats.

Morris Rosenfeld

The blue jay, a centerboarder 13½ ft. in length, belongs to a one-design racing class.

Descended from a South Sea craft, the catamaran is a shoal-draft, sloop-rigged vessel with two similar hulls, about half their length apart. It can sail very fast, particularly on a reach.

Bill Robinson

curves, angles, shapes, and so forth have come to have more appeal for sailors than others have. Although most of these characteristics of appearance were developed for functional reasons long ago, they are still maintained as the standard of beauty even though their original reason has long since disappeared.

The romantic appeal of sailing is generally expressed in cruising yachts in several ways. They may have an old-fashioned flavor, such as the replica Baltimore clipper *Swift;* or represent fairly recent work-boat types, such as the Friendship sloop or the Chesapeake Bay skipjack; or be designed, built, and rigged in a manner suitable for a cruise around the world even though it is unlikely that they will leave coastal waters. Boats of the romantic type are seaworthy, but are apt to be more expensive for equal accommodations and frequently are not as good sailers as the more functionally designed craft. But the romantic appeal is sufficient to overcome these drawbacks for many people.

Cruising may consist of harbor-hopping in short runs as well as sailing around the world. Since World War II small cruising boats have been developed which can be trailed behind an automobile but which can also be taken on extended ocean cruises.

Racing Craft. The racing yacht is designed for one purpose: to win races. This does not mean that other types of yachts do not race among themselves. Nearly every sailboat has raced at one time or another. In the pure racing yacht, comfort is secondary, if considered at all. The speed of the boat and facility in its handling and operation are of primary importance.

Racing boats are divided into classes, ranging from the small 11-ft. Moth class to the large Class-J yachts, 120 ft. in over-all length. Classes of the larger and more spectacular racing yachts number their members in the tens or hundreds, but some of the smaller class boats number thousands in fleets scattered all over the world. Examples of some of the most popular classes, with approximate size of fleets, are Snipe (15 ft. 6 in.), 13,400; Lightning (19 ft.), 8,800; Enterprise (13 ft. 3 in.), 7,600; Penguin (11 ft. 6 in.), 6,000; Star (22 ft. 9 in.), 4,400; and Comet (16 ft.), 3,600.

Nearly all the smaller racing boats belong to one-design classes. This means that the official design for that class must be closely adhered to in building and rigging each boat. One-design classes provide exciting racing since the

RACING SAILBOAT CLASSES

Class	Restricted (R) or One Design (OD)	Keel (K) or Centerboard (CB)	Length Water Line (ft.-in.)	Length Over All (ft.-in.)	Beam (ft.-in.)	Draft (ft.-in.)	Sail Area (sq. ft.)
BLUE JAY	OD	CB	11-5	13-6	5-2	0-5	90
COMET	OD	CB	14-6	16-0	5-0	0-6	136
DRAGON	OD	K	18-8	29-3	6-5	3-11	235
ENTERPRISE	OD	CB	12-2	13-3	5-3	0-7	113
FINN MONOTYPE	OD	CB	14-1	14-9	4-8	0-6	114
FLYING DUTCHMAN	OD	CB	18-0	19-10	5-11	0-6	162
INLAND LAKE SCOWS							
CLASS A	R			38-0	8-9	0-5	550
CLASS M	R			16-0	5-7	0-3	150
INTERNATIONAL ONE DESIGN	OD	K	21-5	33-5	6-10	5-4	433
INTERNATIONAL 14	R	CB	14-0	14-0	4-8* 5-6**	4-6	175
LIGHTNING	OD	CB	15-3	19-0	6-6	0-5	177
MOTH	R	CB	10-9	11-0	4-7	0-5	72
PENGUIN	OD	CB	11-0	11-6	4-8	1-6***	72
SNIPE	OD	CB	13-0	15-6	5-0	0-6	105
STAR	OD	K	15-6	22-9	5-8	3-4	280
12-METER	R	K	45-0	70-0	12-0	9-0	2,000
5.5-METER	R	K	23-0	35-0	6.23*	4.43**	285* 312**

*Minimum **Maximum ***Rudder Depth

outcome depends almost entirely on the sailor's skill and very little on differences between boats.

Other racing boats belong to restricted classes, with varying degrees of freedom in their design, construction, and rigging. An example is the Moth class, that limits only over-all length and sail area so that a wide latitude in hull and rig is encouraged. The International Meter classes are governed by fairly complex formulas which, though allowing boats of each class to race together without handicaps, permit variations in dimensions, weight, sail area, and so forth.

Multihulled Craft. A completely different variety of sailing craft which has enjoyed steadily increasing popularity since 1945 is the multihulled boat. These are the catamaran, with two similar hulls set side by side and about half their length apart, and the trimaran, an outrigger configuration with a large central hull and a smaller hull on each side set out about one-quarter the length of the main hull. The appeal of multihulled craft lies in their high speed, sail-carrying ability, small angle of heel, and light weight.

Yacht Racing

Competitive racing all over the world ranges from short courses (1 or 2 mi.) in length "around the buoys" in sheltered bays and lakes to transoceanic races across 2,000 to 3,000 mi. of open water. Racing provides an excitement, variety, and dependence on individual skill as well as teamwork perhaps unmatched in any other sport. Racing in those classes of boats that number in the thousands is especially keen, culminating in many series of national and international championships.

Ocean Racing. Ocean racers are a refinement and development of the straight cruising boat. These boats, built, rigged, and equipped to the highest specifications with the latest gear, compete in the multitude of races, lasting a few hours or several days, scheduled wherever boats gather. Although fitted with comfortable cruising accommodations and very seaworthy, the ocean-racing boat is apt to be considerably more expensive and difficult to sail than the out-and-out cruising boat.

Long-distance ocean racing is an excellent teacher of

Morris Rosenfeld

With spinnakers billowing, two yachts vie in an America's Cup Race, considered the blue-ribbon competition of international yacht racing. The contest was established under its present name in 1857.

all phases of seamanship. Sailing day and night at maximum speed irrespective of weather requires a high order of sailing skill. One must also have the ability to carry out continuing maintenance and repair programs at sea and must be able to navigate with a high degree of accuracy under the most difficult conditions. One must cook meals on time, "keep house," and be ready for instant action in case of emergencies, such as gear parting or a crew member going overboard. Perhaps because of these requirements, long-distance ocean racing has a particularly strong appeal and is increasing in popularity at such a rate that some races have a limited number of entrants. Not only does long-distance ocean racing improve the caliber of a yachtsman's seamanship, but it is an excellent proving ground for design, construction, and equipment. The strain and wear and tear on equipment in a long ocean race, resulting from the continuous motion and chafing, is the equivalent of many seasons of normal cruising.

Although racing is generally not considered a spectator sport, there are some notable exceptions. The glamour

Birnback Publishing Service

Two craft are neck and neck in a sailboat competition in Denmark.

Sailboats of the Lightning class at the starting line of a one-design event. The officials' boat is at the left.

Morris Rosenfeld

and thrill of the America's Cup Races have traditionally attracted a large seagoing audience. In recent times such character-filled races as the Retired Skipper's Race and Friendship Sloop Race in Maine, the Out Island Regatta in the Bahamas, and the Thames barge matches in England have attracted considerable audiences both afloat and ashore.

Class Racing. In this category, a fleet of boats sails a predetermined course established by buoys, landmarks, stake boats, or other objects. These courses are usually laid out so that they provide a variety of points of sailing. Boats belonging to the same class race on a boat-for-boat basis, as do restricted classes, in which rigid dimensional specifications (with, however, some freedom of design) are set up to make this possible.

Handicap Racing. Handicapping heterogeneous yachts, such as a group of cruising boats, so they may race against each other is done by establishing a theoretical speed which should be attained by each yacht. This is represented by a number called the "rating," arrived at by one of several formulas in use. In judging the placing of the competing boats, the elapsed time for each race is corrected for the theoretical time.

Handicapping formulas used in various countries are becoming more alike. These formulas take into account length, displacement (or weight), and sail area, as well as many less important factors. Much of the credit for the increasing equity of handicapping rules goes to the Davidson Laboratory, Stevens Institute of Technology, in Hoboken, N.J., which has notably expanded insight into sailboat performance through the hundreds of models tested in its towing tanks.

Early British handicapping was based on an empirical tonnage measurement, which encouraged boats with very narrow beam and deep draft. In the United States handicapping was based largely on length, leading to very beamy shallow boats with large sail plans. The influences of these two approaches are still evident in the design of modern boats, the British tending toward narrow boats, the Americans toward wider boats. Major rating rules in use today are those of the Cruising Club of America and the Storm Trysail Club in the United States and the Royal Ocean Racing Club in England.

A handicapping system developed by the author to enhance the spectator interest has been used for several years in the Retired Skipper's and Friendship Sloop races held in Maine. By this system the handicaps are assigned in terms of distance rather than time, the yachts with larger ratings sailing proportionally farther than those with lower ratings. The extra distance is obtained by a handicap leg so that each boat must round a particular buoy laid out according to the distance it must sail. In such a race there is no need to wait for the handicaps to be figured before knowing the results. The boats place in the order of crossing the finish line. All boats encounter the same weather conditions since the elapsed times are the same, and on the return legs the smaller boats may have the pleasure and excitement of leading the larger.

Yacht Clubs

The oldest-known yacht club is the Cork Harbour Water Club in Ireland, established in 1720. Lloyd's Register of American Yachts for 1961 lists 937 current yacht clubs and boating associations in the United States. Of these 12 are noted as being established prior to 1870 and 171 prior to 1900.

The Detroit Boat Club (1839) is the oldest U.S. club listed, but the New York Yacht Club (1844) has had perhaps the greatest over-all influence of any single club. The schooner yacht *America*, which in 1851 brought home from England the America's Cup, then known as the Hundred Guinea Cup, flew the NYYC burgee. All races for that Cup since then have been arranged and managed by this club.

Yacht clubs serve the functions of bringing together people of similar boating interests, conducting races and group cruises, promoting skill and safety afloat, and providing shoreside facilities for members. Among the most important national organizations are the Cruising Club of America (CCA), noted for its measurement rule for handicapping, and the North American Yacht Racing Union (NAYRU). The latter is the control center for organized racing and represents the United States in the International Yacht Racing Union. Another national organization is the Midget Ocean Racing Club (MORC), devoted to fostering ocean racing among boats under 30 ft. in length.

Long Voyages

Long voyages in small craft have captured many imaginations. The popularizer of this kind of sailing for pleasure was Capt. Joshua Slocum. Capt. Slocum, a master mariner temporarily on the beach, was given an old hulk lying in a field in Fairhaven, Mass. In this 37- by 14-ft. vessel, rebuilt by him and rigged as a sloop and named the *Spray*, Capt. Slocum left Newport, R.I., in Apr., 1895, and returned in June, 1898. He had completed, via the Straits of Magellan and the Cape of Good Hope, the first single-handed circumnavigation of the world. In the years since Capt. Slocum's feat there have been at least 14 circumnavigations of the world with crews of three or less. The average size of the boats was about 38 ft.

A record of small sailing boats which made transatlantic crossings between 1866 and 1952, published in *Atlantic Adventurers* (1953), lists 83, 15 prior to 1900. They ranged in size from 14½ to 43 ft., averaging about 27 ft. Of these boats 16 were 20 ft. or under, and 31 crossings were single-handed. There have been many crossings since 1952, including a single-handed race in 1961 from England to New York with five boats starting and finishing.

From the safe record of so many little ships it can be seen that transoceanic cruises and races are practical. The greatest dangers facing the lone ocean traveler are probably not the sea itself, but the chance of being run down by a larger vessel, going overboard while the boat is steering itself, or the failure of vital parts of the hull, equipment, or rigging.

See also MOTORBOATING.

SANDE [*săn'dē*], **EARL** (**1898–1968**), American jockey. As the leading U.S. stakes-winning rider of the 1920's and early 1930's, he inspired the Damon Runyon poem "A Handy Guy Like Sande." His 972 winning mounts earned more than $3,000,000. In 1930 Sande rode Gallant Fox to the Triple Crown (victories in the Kentucky Derby and Preakness and Belmont stakes). In the mid-1930's he became a trainer of thoroughbred racers, including Stagehand.

SARAZEN [*săr'ə-zən*], **GENE** (1901–), American golfer, born in Rye, N.Y. The first high point in his long career came in 1922, when he won the U.S. Open title. He won the same tournament in 1932, when he also won the British Open. Sarazen won the Professional Golfers' Association tournaments in 1922, 1923, and 1933, and the Masters tournament in 1935. A colorful competitor with a fondness for knickers, he won the PGA Senior tournaments in 1954 and 1958.

SCHAYES [*shāz*], **ADOLPH ("DOLPH")** (1928–), American basketball player, born in New York. In the early 1960's he was the leading scorer in the history of modern professional basketball. After playing for New York University, he joined Syracuse of the National Basketball League for the 1948–49 season. The following season, that professional league and the Basketball Association of America merged to form the present-day National Basketball Association. During the 1957–58 season, as a member of Syracuse, Schayes broke George Mikan's career scoring record of 11,764 points. Two seasons later he became the first player in NBA history to achieve a career total of 15,000 points. The durable star, famous for his arching, two-hand set shots, became coach of his team in 1963 when it was moved from Syracuse to Philadelphia.

SCUBA. *See* Skin Diving.

SEABISCUIT, American thoroughbred race horse. He was foaled in 1933 and died in 1947. Purchased by Charles S. Howard for $8,000 in 1936, the horse was the greatest money winner in racing history at the time he was retired in 1940. From 1935 to 1940 Seabiscuit won 33 of 89 races, including the 1940 Santa Anita Handicap. His record earnings, $437,730, have since been surpassed.

SECULAR GAMES, Roman centennial celebration comprising games, dramatizations, and sacrifices. The purifying rites were intended to sweep away the accumulated evils of the last hundred years. They were introduced in 249 B.C. during the First Punic War to calm the frightened populace. The revival of the games by Augustus in 17 B.C., celebrated in Horace's *Carmen saeculare*, symbolized the beginning of the Imperial era.

SEDGMAN [*sĕj'mən*], **FRANK** (1927–), Australian tennis player. He won the Australian men's singles championship in 1949 and 1950. He was a member of the championship teams in Australian mixed doubles in 1949 and 1950 and in men's doubles in 1951 and 1952. Sedgman was the U.S. men's singles champion in 1951 and 1952 and a member of the championship teams in men's doubles, 1950 and 1951, and mixed doubles, 1951 and 1952. At Wimbledon, England, he won the men's singles title in 1952 and was on the team that won the men's doubles championships in 1948, 1951, and 1952 and the mixed doubles titles in 1951 and 1952. He also competed successfully in French national competition and as a member of Australia's Davis Cup teams before becoming a professional in 1953.

SHOEMAKER, WILLIAM LEE ("WILLIE THE SHOE") (1931–), American jockey, born in Fabens, Tex. He was the leading stakes-winning rider following the retirement of Eddie Arcaro in 1961. In 1964 Shoemaker rode his 5,000th winning mount, a figure reached by only one other jockey —Johnny Longden—up to that time. In 1953, only four years after beginning his career as a jockey, Shoemaker established a record total of winners for a single year: 485. He rode Swaps (1955), Tony Lee (1959), and Lucky Debonair (1965) to victories in the Kentucky Derby.

SHOOTING, sport in which small arms—both rifles and pistols—are fired for accuracy at stationary targets. It is generally competitive and is practiced both indoors and outdoors.

Rifle Shooting

History. Target shooting dates back virtually to the development of firearms in Europe. It is known that a military shooting club existed in Geneva, Switzerland, in 1474. Nevertheless the present-day type of shooting did not develop until after World War I. At the present time this modern form exists throughout the world.

In the United States the colonists and frontiersmen are traditionally pictured as expert riflemen. Although target shooting existed in their day, it was not until the early 19th century, with the immigration of thousands of rifle-conscious German and Swiss mechanics, merchants, and farmers, that the rifle club became a recreation center in many American communities. There was no nationwide organization of such clubs, however. Since rifle shooting was an expensive pastime, these clubs generally attracted the reasonably well-to-do professional men and businessmen of the larger cities. Many of them were officers in the local militia, forerunner of National Guard organizations.

The efforts of such men, and of one in particular, provided the impetus for the founding of a national governing body for the sport. In1871 Col. William C. Church of New York, editor of the *Army and Navy Journal*, campaigned editorially for such an organization. In the same year the National Rifle Association of America (NRA) was organized. It became the governing body of all competitive rifle and pistol target shooting in the United States, and also carries on promotional activities on behalf of the sport throughout all North America. In the early 1960's the organization had about 480,000 individual members and more than 10,000 affiliated clubs, which were classified "senior" and "junior" according to the age of members. Headquarters of the NRA are in Washington, D.C.

Stimulated by this organization, interest in the sport grew steadily. In 1903 the first truly national rifle matches in the United States were held in Sea Girt, N.J. A year

earlier the U.S. Congress had appropriated funds for these national championship events. Since 1907 they have been held annually at Camp Perry, Ohio, interrupted only by World War I and II and the depression of the 1930's. They are sponsored jointly by the U.S. Department of the Army and the NRA. Shooting (both rifle and pistol) is also a part of the Olympic Games. The NRA is affiliated with the U.S. Olympic Committee.

Classes. Present-day rifle shooting includes activity in two classes.

Small-bore. Shooters in this category fire .22-caliber rifles at targets ranging up to 100 yd. distant. For the most part they comprise the civilian—and larger—element of the sport's participants. National small-bore championship competition dates from 1919.

The small-bore shooter's sport depends to a large extent on the quality of the equipment. Good equipment, which is expensive, is also a necessity if a tournament contestant is to make a strong bid for victory. In the early 1960's the average serious contestant paid about $170 for his rifle and an additional $25 for special metallic sights. The latter are employed in one type of rifle shooting in both small-bore and big-bore competition. In the other basic type, weapons with optical, or telescopic, sights are used. (These sights are called telescopic because a small telescope, an integral part of the sight, provides a magnified view of the target. In contrast, metallic sights provide no such aid.) Telescopic sights cost from $75 to $125, approximately the price of another item of equipment, the spotting scope, used for checking the value of a contestant's hits in the target area.

The typical small-bore shooter in the United States is a member of one of some 6,000 senior clubs affiliated with the NRA. The average club has a small-bore indoor range. In all indoor firing, a distance of 50 ft. separates the shooter and target. The standard indoor gallery target has a bull's-eye measuring .150 in. in diameter. The value of a bull's-eye is 10 points. A hit in the circle immediately surrounding the bull's-eye is worth nine points. One in the circle just beyond that is worth eight, and the value decreases correspondingly as the distance from the center of the target increases. Matches are fired in any of four positions: prone, kneeling, sitting, and standing. As an incentive to the indoor sport, local, state, and regional tournaments are held throughout the United States.

Outdoor shooting begins with the arrival of spring. Firing is conducted on courses measuring either 50 yd. (with a bull's-eye measuring .719 in. in diameter), 50 meters (with a .787-in. bull's-eye), or 100 yd. (with a 2-in. bull's-eye). With one notable exception, scoring is the same as in indoor matches. The outdoor target has a small ring within the bull's-eye. This "X-ring" is used to break ties in matches ending with identical scores. If two contestants fire perfect scores of 300 points in a 30-shot match, the

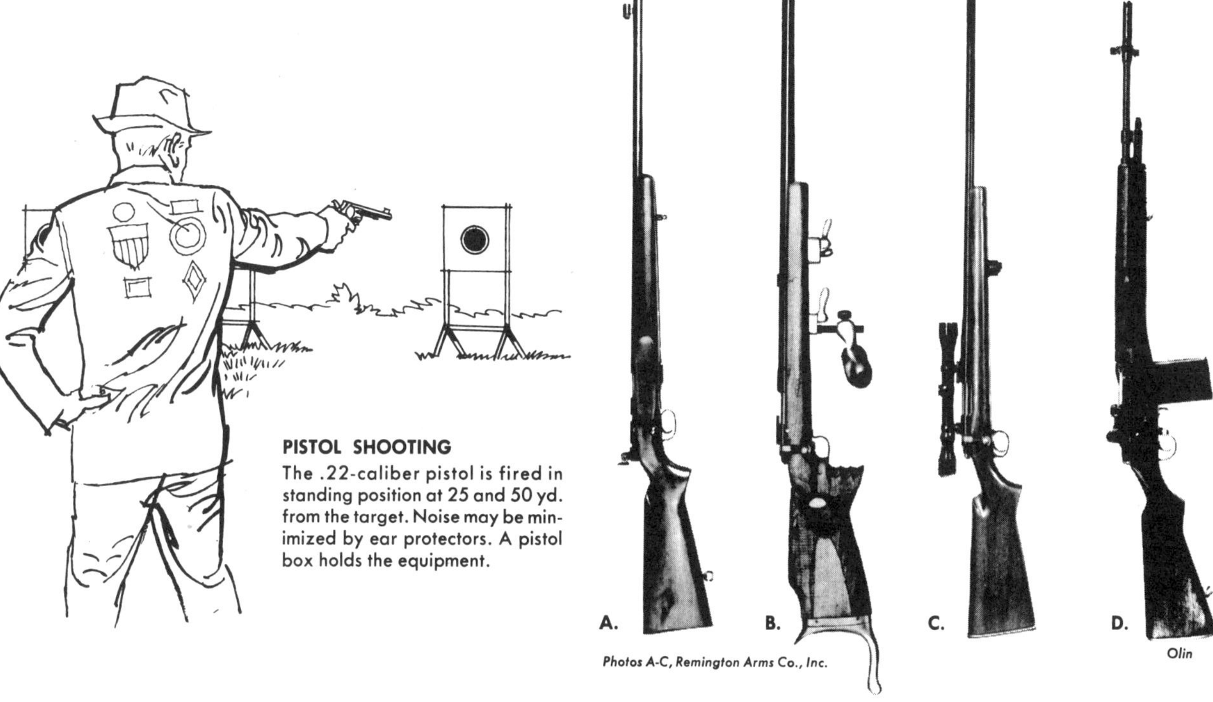

PISTOL SHOOTING
The .22-caliber pistol is fired in standing position at 25 and 50 yd. from the target. Noise may be minimized by ear protectors. A pistol box holds the equipment.

Photos A-C, Remington Arms Co., Inc. *Olin*

RIFLES FOR TARGET SHOOTING
A. NRA-competition .22-caliber rifle. B. Olympic-competition free rifle. C. Big-bore target rifle, scope mounted. D. M-14, big bore.

5 6 7 8 9

Target shown above is actual size of official NRA 50 ft. target for .22-caliber rifles.

A. B. C.

Colt Patent Fire Arms Mfg. Co., Inc.

PISTOLS FOR TARGET SHOOTING
A. National-match .45-caliber pistol. B. Target revolver, .38-caliber. C. Match target .22-caliber pistol.

winner is the one with the greater number of hits in the X-ring. If contestant *A* has 25 such hits among his bull's-eyes, and his opponent has 24, *A* is the winner, and his score is designated 300–25. Outdoor shooting is done almost exclusively from the prone position.

All small-bore events are slow-fire matches in which the shooter is given one minute per shot. The winner of a tournament is determined by the highest aggregate score, which may range from a maximum of 1,600 to one of 6,400, depending on the number of matches included in the competition. Competition is usually divided equally between events employing metallic sights and those specifying telescopic ones.

Big-bore. This category of high-power shooting is practiced mostly by members of the regular armed forces and reserve and National Guard units. The principal piece employed is the .30-caliber U.S. Army service rifle (the M-1 Garand or, since the early 1960's, the M-14). A minority fire the .30-caliber bolt-action rifle. In this branch of competition, the contestant usually fires the rifle as it is issued, without the addition of special sights. In both small- and big-bore events, the rifles are considerably heavier than standard hunting pieces. With greater weight, there is less vibration of the barrel and therefore greater accuracy in firing.

Big-bore matches are conducted outdoors at distances of 200, 300, 600, and (less frequently) 1,000 yd. Firing over the two shorter distances is usually conducted from sitting, standing, or kneeling positions, and either slow-fire or rapid-fire procedure is employed. Slow fire is at the rate of one shot per minute. A typical specification in rapid fire from a standing position is 10 shots per minute. At 600 and 1,000 yd., firing is slow, and such competition employs the prone position.

Bull's-eyes are valued at five points. Standard targets have the following diameters: 4 in. (for a 200-yd. range), 6 in. (300 yd.), and 12 in. (600 yd.). The general procedure of scoring is the same as in small-bore competition. An inner circle (within the bull's-eye), known as the "V-ring," is used in breaking ties. As in small-bore competition, tournaments comprise a specified number of matches, and the winner is determined on the basis of aggregate scores.

Pistol Shooting

Target shooting involving pistols and revolvers developed substantially later than the corresponding sport involving rifles. In the United States this was principally because the real potential of the revolver was not appreciated by a large number of persons outside the armed forces and law-enforcement agencies until after World War II. Interest was stimulated somewhat earlier when the National Rifle Association began to promote this branch of the sport. After the middle of the 20th century interest in it challenged that in rifle shooting. The cleanliness and speed that characterize pistol and revolver shooting account in part for this growing popularity.

In outdoor competition the .22-caliber pistol, .38-caliber revolver, and .45-caliber pistol are fired at distances of 25 and 50 yd. In indoor competition all shooting is done at 50 ft. and only the .22-caliber pistol is used. Both outdoors and indoors the shooter fires in three time sequences: slow fire, timed fire, and rapid fire. Except in special competition involving police personnel, all firing is done from a standing position.

In slow-fire procedure the shooter is given one minute per shot. When practiced outdoors, it is always at a distance of 50 yd. In timed fire the shooter is given 20 seconds for 5 rounds (shots). In rapid fire the time limit is 10 seconds for 5 rounds. Outdoors the timed-fire and rapid-fire sequences are always at 25 yd.

In outdoor competition the contestant can achieve an aggregate of 2,700 points. This figure, representing a perfect score, includes 900 points for each of the three weapons fired. Competition includes 30 shots at slow fire, 30 at timed fire, and 30 at rapid fire. The value of each bull's-eye is 10 points. The bull's-eyes of targets vary according to the length of the course and the rate of fire. For example, at 50-yd. slow fire, the diameter of the bull's-eye is 2.39 in.; at 25-yd. rapid fire and timed fire, the diameter is 3.39 in.; and at 50-ft. slow fire, the diameter is .90 in. In indoor competition, where only the .22-caliber pistol is fired, the highest possible score is 900 points. Otherwise the procedure follows that of outdoor shooting.

Pistol shooting is also a part of the annual national championship matches held at Camp Perry, Ohio. In both rifle and pistol competition there, separate categories involve men and women, and the matches attract outstanding civilian and military shooters. More than 2,000 registered North American rifle and pistol tournaments are held in addition to the national championship matches. *See also* Skeet and Trapshooting.

SIMMONS [sĭm'ənz], **ALOYSIUS HARRY ("AL")** (1903–56), American baseball player, born in Milwaukee, Wis. A right-handed-hitting outfielder, he played for Philadelphia of the American League from 1924 to 1932. In 1929 he was named the AL's most valuable player, and in 1930 and 1931 he won AL batting titles. In each of those three seasons he was a major contributor in his team's successful drives for league championships. Later in his career, which extended through 1944, he also played for Chicago, Detroit, Washington, and Boston of the AL and Boston and Cincinnati of the National League. Simmons finished with a career batting average of .334 and 307 home runs. His success as a hitter was achieved despite a highly unorthodox batting stance. He was elected to the National Baseball Hall of Fame in 1953.

SKATING. In the present-day world, skating on ice is primarily a recreational activity, related only indirectly to its former role as an important means of transportation in northern countries. Through refinement, skating also exists at present as a form of artistic expression, in ice shows and ice ballets, and as a sport in the form of ice hockey (which is covered in a separate article in this Encyclopedia), speed skating (racing), and figure skating. Roller skating is discussed under that heading.

For the most part, ice skating has been confined to countries of the Northern Hemisphere where natural ice is available during a significant part of each year. Such areas include Canada, a large part of the United States, and many sections of Europe. However, since World War II there has been a vast increase in artificially refrigerated rinks. As a result, skating has made significant

inroads in areas where it had been virtually unknown. Such rinks date from the 1870's. They now exist in every part of the world and are especially numerous in the United States (where they exist in each of the states) and Canada. Mechanical refrigeration has not only widened the geographical boundaries of skating but made it a year-round activity.

History of Skating

The history of skating dates from the Middle Ages. Evidence of such activity exists in Scandinavian literature and in the physical record provided by primitive skates made of bone and found in Siberia, China, and northern Europe. The record is continued in 13th- and 14th-century paintings, particularly of the Dutch school. By the mid-17th century skating had become popular throughout northern and central Europe, from which it spread to North America. An entry (1662) in Samuel Pepys's diary refers to it as a "very pretty art."

Prior to its evolution as an important recreational activity and then as a sport, skating was primarily a useful means of transportation during market sessions and fairs. These gatherings in turn provided an opportunity for games and races on skates. Some of the early games took the form of jumping over various objects, with the winner determined on the basis of the highest jump or longest leap. Eventually an interest developed in the marks left on the ice by skates. That in turn gave way to an interest in the drawing of various figures on ice—the forerunner of modern figure skating.

The next major development in ice skating came in the 1860's, when an American dancing master, Jackson Haines, developed the concept of putting ballet on ice by combining skating and dancing. Though he was not well received in his native country, Haines won great acclaim on the Continent and did much to further modern figure skating. Early in the following century his "international style of skating," as it was then called, returned to North America and gradually found an audience. Both figure skating and modern ice shows received great impetus through the feats of Sonja Henie. She won three Olympic figure-skating titles, beginning in 1928, and 10 years later as a professional skater began a lengthy career as the star of her own ice spectacles. Other popular ice shows that combined the elements of ballet and figure skating, together with comedy and vaudeville, were the *Ice Follies*, *Ice Capades*, and *Holiday on Ice*. By 1924 both figure and speed skating had become part of the program of the Olympic Games, and ice hockey had become an established sport in Canada.

The universal appeal of ice skating is due partly to its availability in most countries of the present-day world and partly to the fact that persons of all ages may participate. Children of three, for example, can be found skating with grandparents in their seventies. Besides providing recreation and, for some, lucrative careers, skating is also an excellent form of exercise. In the United States alone in the 1960's the number of ice skaters was estimated at about 30,000,000, and the number of artificially frozen rinks at 500. In the same country the number of new ice skates sold annually was approximately 2,500,000, a figure exceeded many times by the exchange and sale of used skates. The availability of group instruction provided by professionally trained teachers, rather than by skaters without teaching experience, has been a recent stimulus to skating.

Skating also is a leading spectator activity. In the United States approximately 45,000,000 persons pay admissions to ice shows annually. Such spectacles also are well known in Canada and throughout most parts of the world. Ice hockey has its own large following. In addition, through motion pictures and television the audience for various forms of skating has been vastly broadened in the 20th century.

Equipment

Skates. The basic element of modern ice skates is a nondetachable metal blade, usually steel, attached directly to a leather boot by means of screws or rivets. The earliest bone skates were replaced by those made of wood, which in turn gave way to skates made of iron. By the mid-19th century steel skates were in use, but they were attached to regular street shoes by means of straps and then by means of metal clamps. Such a practice led to frequent complaints about "weak ankles," since the low shoes to which the blades were attached did not provide proper

OUTSIDE FORWARD EIGHT

Diameter of each circle is about three times skater's height. At the starting point with your back to the circle you are about to skate, bend your knees, put your weight on your left foot, and push off from that foot. **(1)** Shift your weight to the right foot, and as the left foot rises above the ice a few inches, straighten the left leg and point the toe so that the left skate is carried above the print, or blade mark on the ice. **(2)** Steadily hold this position until at half circle you begin to straighten the bent skating knee and to pass the free foot forward with a compensating backward lean of the body. **(3)** This second position is completed at three-quarters circle so that the free leg is forward. **(4)** Hold this position until **(5)** about 2 ft. from the starting point you bring the skates together and bend your legs for the second circle push-off from the right foot at the starting point. In the second circle the positions followed in executing the first circle are reversed. **(7)** Put your weight on your left skating leg and extend your right a few inches above the ice. Hold this position until **(8)** you begin to swing your free leg forward at half circle. **(9)** The right leg movement continues until **(10)** you have it forward and your body is leaning somewhat backward. **(11)** Maintain this second position until the halting point.

support for the ankles. The same shortcoming was found in some of the earliest modern skates with nondetachable blades. Now skates properly fitted and laced provide sufficient support to enable even the beginner to maintain his balance.

For purely recreational (noncompetitive) skating and figure skating, skates with high boots are generally employed. The blade is approximately ⅛ in. wide and slightly longer than the boot. This type of skate is the most widely used. However, in the front of the blade of skates used for figure skating there are sharp points, or teeth, which act both as brakes and pivotal points for sharp turns and other maneuvers. The next most popular skates are those used in ice hockey. The boots of these are slightly lower, and are reinforced with protective leather and metal. This is to enable the skates to withstand the blows of hockey sticks and pucks. The blades are thinner than those used in figure skating, to permit greater speed and facilitate fast turns, and are reinforced with hollow tubes. To obtain still greater speed, skaters in racing events use blades that are usually twice as long as those on hockey skates. The blades range up to 18 in. in length and are as thin as 1/32 in. The boots of racing skates are made of the lightest possible leather.

Skating Areas. The ice used in skating varies in area, texture, and thickness according to the type of skating being pursued. Most skating instruction is conducted in relatively small areas where teachers can control their groups readily. Areas for speed skating are much larger. Ideally these should provide ¼-mi. courses. In most indoor rinks, however, 12 or 14 laps are required to complete a 1-mi. course. For a description of hockey rinks, see ICE HOCKEY.

The degree of hardness of the ice can be controlled in refrigerated rinks. Hockey usually requires a harder surface than that used in speed skating and figure skating. In competitive skating, in particular, the ice must be level and smooth, since even the smallest piece of foreign matter can cause a serious fall.

Types of Skating

Recreational. In this category is included noncompetitive skating pursued purely for recreation, though all types have a high recreational potential. The largest number of skaters come within this category. In indoor rinks, such skating is usually done to music.

Speed Skating. This is the most popular type of competitive skating. The distances parallel those employed by runners in track meets. In the Olympic Games, for example, there are separate divisions for men and women, with events ranging from 500 to 10,000 meters. Separate competitions to determine Canadian and U.S. speed-skating championships date from the late 19th century. Competition to decide North American championships also began in the same period, as did the annual world-championship events conducted under the jurisdiction of the International Skating Union.

The procedure of speed skating varies in different parts of the world. In North American competition, virtually all speed skating is conducted after the manner of a standard race. All entrants compete at the same time over the same course and the winner is the first to cross the finish line. In European and Olympic competition, contestants race against time, and in the events over long distances only two skate at any given time, each in a separate lane of a double track.

Figure Skating. Because of its inherent difficulty and the restrictive regulations of figure-skating associations, activity in this category is relatively small. It is one of the most appealing and glamorous forms of all athletics,

SOME OF THE WORLD'S OUTSTANDING ICE SKATERS

The U.S.S.R.'s figure-skating pair, Lyudmila Belusova and Oleg Protopopov, a married couple, were gold-medal winners in the IX Winter Olympics, 1964.

A.F.P.—Pictorial

Aigner—Monkmeyer

Sonja Henie, a championship figure skater of the 1920's and 1930's.

Wide World

Barbara Ann Scott, Olympic figure-skating champion.

United Press International

Stan Urban and Sally Schantz, winners of the U.S. national figure-skating finals.

Champion skater Hayes Jenkins performing a flying leap with a sitting spin.

Wide World

however. Treatises on figure skating date from the early 19th century. Although it has been greatly influenced by the ideas of Jackson Haines (d.1875) and Sonja Henie, this branch of skating still has as its cornerstone the drawing of basic figures on ice.

In modern practice, competition is divided into two categories, in each of which contestants (either singly or in pairs) must engage. The first category includes compulsory figures—some 80 established variations of the figure eight, determined by the International Skating Union and internationally recognized in world competition, including the Olympic Games. The compulsory figures to be skated in any given meet are decided in advance by the jurors and officials who determine the winner. Each figure must be executed three times on each foot. This first category counts 60% in the over-all scoring. The remaining 40% of the point value, as determined by the votes of the jurors, is based on free-style, or free skating. This is a type of artistic expression performed to music. Contestants execute variations on basic figures in the form of jumps, turns, spirals, and dance steps.

Separate competition for men and women, together with competition for pairs (one male and one female skater), is included in programs that determine national championships in many countries of the world, including Canada and the United States. These divisions are further broken down into classes according to age and degree of skill. Separate competitions to decide North American, European, world, and Olympic championships follow the same pattern. In addition to Haines and Miss Henie, outstanding modern figure skaters have included Richard T. ("Dick") Button of the United States and Barbara Ann Scott and Donald Jackson of Canada.

Regulatory Organizations. The International Skating Union, with headquarters in Switzerland, is the recognized governing body of skating on a world level. In the United States, the following organizations also help develop and control the sport: Ice Skating Institute of America (an organization of rink operators), Amateur Skating Union of the United States, and United States Figure Skating Association.

See also ICE HOCKEY; ROLLER SKATING; WINTER SPORTS.

SKEET AND TRAPSHOOTING, the two major sports devoted to the shotgun. Of the two, skeet is much the younger, and was deliberately invented. Modern trapshooting developed over a period of many years as an outgrowth of hunting. Because it is the older sport and the one from which skeet derived, trapshooting is treated in detail first in this article. Both have in common shooting at moving targets sprung into the air from traps. The participants may be likened to hunters firing shotguns at birds in flight, whereas small-arms shooters fire at stationary targets with rifles and pistols.

Trapshooting

In the standard installation for singles competition, five shooting positions, or firing stations, are set up on a line 16 yd. behind the single trap from which all targets are catapulted into the air. (In another type of competition, explained later in the article, contestants may be more than 16 yd. from the trap.) The trap is placed equidistant from the extremities of this line. Each contestant fires 25 shots during a round, 5 from each position, or station. Twelve-gauge shotguns with barrels at least 30 in. long are employed. The long barrel is helpful in pointing out targets and also reduces muzzle blast. The latter factor is important in lessening the distraction suffered by the contestant on either side of a given shooter when he fires.

The targets, known as "clay pigeons," are saucer-shaped objects of silt and pitch, 4½ in. in diameter. Upon a signal from the contestant, the target is sprung into the air, traveling away from the firing line with the convex side up. The targets are thrown hard enough to sail 50 yd. from the trap. Since the contestant is at least 16 yd. behind the trap, the minimum possible distance from contestant to the point where the target falls (if it is not hit in flight) is 66 yd. Since the maximum efficient range of a shotgun is 30 to 35 yd., however, the shooter attempts to break the target at that distance. Scoring is on the basis of the number of targets broken.

To equalize competition in registered matches, a system of handicapping was instituted in 1924. Consequently, the modern installation contains a series of shooting stations located directly behind each of the five basic stations. The basic stations are 16 yd. behind the trap. Behind each are stations ranging from 17 to 27 yd. behind the trap. In handicap matches each contestant is assigned a station on the basis of his skill as reflected in his competitive record. This record in turn is based on the results of 750 shots. Under this system, a relatively unskilled contestant might fire from the basic station 16 yd. behind the trap. A highly skilled entrant would be assigned a position farther back on the course, where he would be farther from the targets and consequently have a more difficult task. This system of handicapping makes it possible even for persons with physical disabilities to compete with the physically normal.

Types of Competition. There are three types of trapshooting events. In singles competition contestants fire at single targets from positions 16 yd. behind the trap. Handicap events also involve single targets, but the distance behind the trap from which the individual fires depends upon his handicap, as determined by his past record. Doubles is a form of competition in which the contestant fires at two targets, sprung into the air simultaneously in different directions. Contestants are all 16 yd. behind the trap.

History. Trapshooting came to North America from England, where it developed in the 18th century as a sport employing live pigeons. In the 19th century it was introduced to U.S. and Canadian shooters. The first U.S. national championship tournament was held in New Orleans in 1885. The Amateur Trapshooting Association (ATA), with headquarters in Vandalia, Ohio, is the controlling body for formal U.S. and Canadian competition. It has about 17,500 members. In addition, there are many participants in the sport who do not compete in registered matches. In the United States in the early 1960's the number of installations for the sport was about 3,000.

Annual championship competition is conducted by the ATA in Vandalia. About 2,000 shooters take part in these events, attracted by the opportunity to win as much as $10,000. The big event of this competition, the Grand American Handicap, is contested in divisions for men

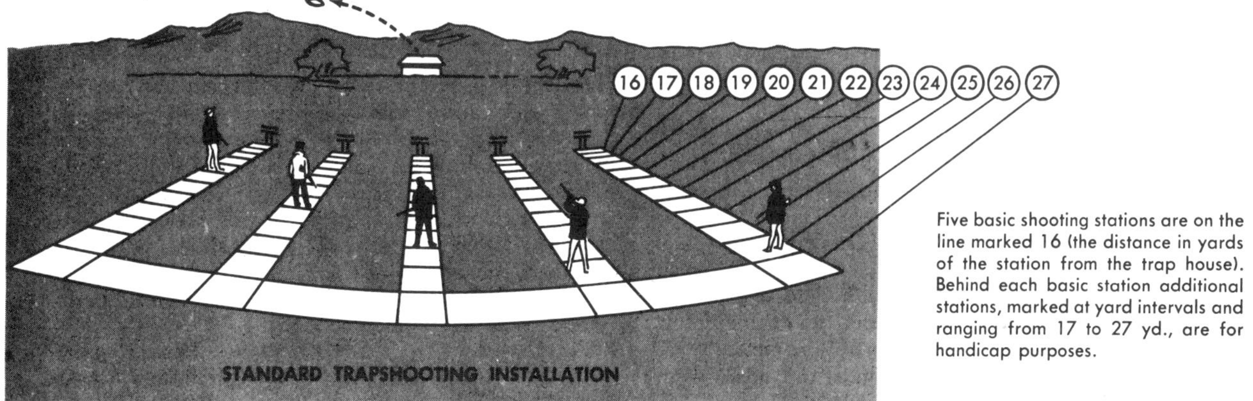

Five basic shooting stations are on the line marked 16 (the distance in yards of the station from the trap house). Behind each basic station additional stations, marked at yard intervals and ranging from 17 to 27 yd., are for handicap purposes.

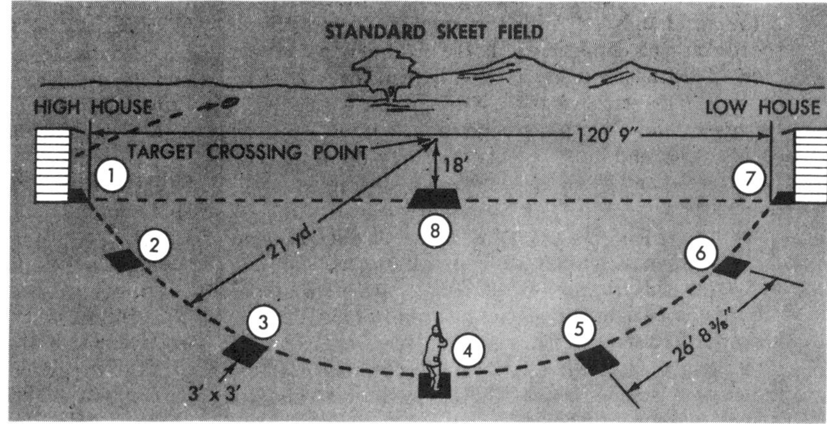

Seven shooting stations are spaced 26 ft. 8 3/8 in. apart on an arc. The eighth station is midway between stations one and seven, which are 120 ft. 9 in. apart. The point where targets from the high and low houses cross is 18 ft. from station eight and 21 yd. from other stations.

and women. A distinguishing characteristic of that event is the frequency with which it is won by little-known contestants, unhindered by the severe handicaps assigned to more illustrious entrants.

Skeet

Skeet is a form of trapshooting whose basic principle is duplicating all the varied angles of flight encountered in shooting birds on the wing. Clay targets are employed, however. In general, trapshooting appeals to wild-fowl hunters, and skeet to the hunters of fast-flushing upland game birds. The wild-fowl hunter has more time to track and groove his shots, which is the basic skill involved in trapshooting.

Evolution of Modern Sport. Skeet was invented early in the 20th century by a group of Massachusetts hunters, of whom William Harnden Foster made the foremost contribution. In its original form it was known as Round the Clock because of the various positions assumed by the gunners. The installation consisted of a circle, with a radius of 25 yd., in the form of a clockface. A trap was placed at 12 o'clock (the point on the circumference corresponding to 12 on a clockface). This trap threw its clay targets directly over 6 o'clock. The contestant fired two shots from each of the 12 stations (corresponding to the hour markings on a clockface). Then he fired the 25th shot from the center of the circle at an incoming target. The object then, as in modern skeet, was to score the greatest number of hits.

One serious drawback was the extent of the danger zone, since shots were fired in every direction. Changes were urged, and by 1926 the modern skeet layout had been devised. This layout is roughly semicircular. At each extremity of the arc along which contestants fire, there are single traps that catapult their targets either consecutively or simultaneously. The traps are enclosed in stations known as "houses." The trap on the left side of the course is elevated to provide high, flat-flying targets. Because of this elevation the house at the left is designated "high," and the one at the right "low." There are eight shooting stations on the field, each carrying a number from one to eight. The first and seventh are located next to each of the houses, and five are along the arc running between the first and seventh. The eighth is midway between the first and seventh and is 20 yd. distant from both.

A round in skeet consists of 25 shots for each competitor. Starting at the first station the shooter fires one shot at the target sprung from the left trap, then one at the target sprung from the right. In this case the targets are sprung consecutively. This procedure is followed at each station, which accounts for 16 shots. Then he returns to stations one, two, six, and seven and at each shoots twice as targets are thrown simultaneously from the two traps. The 25th shot, at a single target, is taken at the point where the contestant had his first miss during the round. If he has had no misses, he may take the shot from any station and at either target. This is known as an optional shot. The great majority of skeet shooters choose the seventh station and the outgoing target (sprung from the low house) because of the relative ease of making such a shot.

Unlike trapshooting, skeet competition is divided according to the gauge of the shotgun employed. "All-gauge" matches are fired with weapons that are 12-gauge or smaller, though the great majority employ the first category. Separate competitions employ 20- and 28-gauge and 410-caliber shotguns.

To provide equality in competition, shooters are classified according to their scores in registered matches. For contestants other than young adults there is further classification according to age. These categories include veteran (for contestants 70 and older), senior (ages 60 to 69), subsenior (50 to 59), junior (13 to 16), and subjunior (under 13).

There were approximately 35,000 skeet shooters in the United States in the early 1960's, and about 1,000 skeet installations. The parent organization of the sport, the National Skeet Shooting Association, has headquarters in Dallas, Tex. Founded in 1935, it conducts national championship competition annually.

See also SHOOTING.

SKIING [*skē'ĭng*] may be a competitive sport or a noncompetitive recreational activity. In either case the skier pits his courage and skill against the natural force of gravity and the difficulties of terrain. Formally defined, skiing is the art of gliding over a snow-covered surface on narrow strips of wood or metal, one on each foot. For its devotees, however, it is virtually a way of life.

History

Skiing originally was a part of everyday living, a means of locomotion through the snowy wastes of the Scandinavian countries. The word "ski" comes from Norway, the cradle of the sport, and skiing itself dates back to the Stone Age. This is evidenced in a rock carving in Rødøy, in northern Norway, and in the discovery of the famous Hoting ski, which scientists have proven to be over 2,500 years old. This antique wooden ski, found perfectly preserved in a bog, shows a proper groove for guiding on its underside, not too different from the modern ski. The superstitious Stone Age skiers even had their own god and goddess, Ullr and Skade, to watch over them, and some modern skiers still observe such ancient rites by carrying Ullr medals in their pockets.

Origin as a Sport. Although skiing was necessary for survival to the early Norsemen, and still is an important means of transportation in mountain warfare, in the course of time man's natural competitive spirit prevailed. As a result, the earliest ski race, the *langlauf* ("long run"), developed in the second half of the 19th century. This cross-country race over rolling hills, together with the more artificially developed ski jumping, forms two events —known as Nordics—in modern competitive skiing.

The Scandinavians, world travelers, took skiing with them. In 1855 they introduced the sport in Australia. They skied in Canada in the 1870's, and were lured by gold fever to Alaska—on skis—in the 1890's. Although reports of skiing in Wisconsin date back to 1840, the earliest recorded skiing in the United States took place in California in 1856. There the celebrated John A. ("Snowshoe") Thompson, a Norwegian by birth, carried the mail across the high Sierras to the miners of Placerville. Thompson's success brought skiing to the fore as a means of transportation for snow-choked communities. The miners, eager for excitement, took to racing straight down the mountains—a primitive form of the downhill race as it presently exists.

Ironically, it was an Englishman who introduced skiing to the Alpine countries of Europe. In 1888 Col. Napier brought skis to Davos, Switzerland, and was immediately looked upon as mad by the natives. The following year his noted compatriot, Arthur Conan Doyle, joined him in a cross-country tour of the Alps, and the sport slowly began to gain favor. At present the Alps are covered with ski lifts. Skiing, in fact, is practiced throughout the world —even in such unlikely places as Morocco, Hawaii, Lebanon, Korea, Japan, and New Zealand. Ski resorts stretch across Canada, and the United States boasts more than 500 ski hills, some as far south of the Mason-Dixon Line as North Carolina and Tennessee. In North America skiing was the fastest-growing sport in the early 1960's. At that time it was practiced by more than 3,000,000 persons; in the mid-1950's the number was less than 1,000,000.

Equipment

As with skiing itself, the earliest technique originated in Norway, and is named for the town of Telemark. The Telemark turn was produced by an awkward bending of one knee—awkward because the equipment used was quite rustic. Slabs of ash 12 ft. long were attached to the feet by a loose leather harness, and a single heavy pole was held between the skis for steering and balance.

Today both technique and equipment are highly refined. Ski boots are constructed on a unique double-boot principle. A complete inner boot and a complete outer boot of stiff leather give maximum support to the all-important ankle joints. Skis are of scientific design, of laminated hickory or flexible metal, with sharp steel edges offset to cut into and hold onto the snow. Special plastic bases, which reduce friction and make turning easier, give added downhill speed. The metal binding that attaches boot to ski now serves a dual purpose. It holds the foot firmly to the ski in the course of skiing but releases the ski from the boot in a severe fall, thus reducing injuries to the point where they are a minute statistic (.01 per 1,000 skiers in the early 1960's). The old alpenstock (a long, iron-pointed staff) has been replaced by lightweight aluminum poles with molded hand grips.

Modern Technique

Like the equipment employed, modern ski technique has a scientific basis. It is an integral series of steps designed to guide a beginning skier down gentle slopes, at slow speed, then on to the steeper, more advanced runs as he becomes more expert in controlling his equipment. Fundamentally, the skis are controlled by turning. The more turns the skier makes away from the "fall line" (the

United Press International

Two contestants during the 15-km. race of the Salpausselkä Games, a major cross-country event held in Finland. Such cross-country races are called Nordic events.

imaginary line marking the shortest route down the hill), the slower the speed.

Types of Turns. Turns in skiing are classified according to the ability of the skier.

(1) Slow-speed, "steered" turns, such as the snowplow turn, are made by placing the skis in an inverted V, or half-turn, position, with tips together, tails apart. The wider the V, or "plow," the slower the speed. The actual turn is accomplished by placing body weight on one ski, the right ski for a left turn, and vice versa.

(2) Intermediate turns all carry the word "christie" (or "christy"), short for Christiania, former name of Oslo, the Norwegian capital. In any form of christie the skis must be in a parallel position as the turn is completed. An uphill christie, used to stop the skis completely, is accomplished by skidding the tails of both skis downhill and the tips uphill. In a stem christie one ski is pushed out (stemmed) at the beginning of the turn, but the turn is completed with the skis parallel.

(3) Advanced maneuvers include the pure (parallel) christie, a long-radius, high-speed turn in which the skis remain parallel throughout the entire execution, and the Wedeln, a series of short, parallel turns made at high speed in the fall line of the hill. This latter maneuver is the ultimate goal of most skiers.

(4) Aerial turns (*Sprünge*), used by experts, include a variety of aerial turning maneuvers, accomplished with the aid of the poles. These are designed to avoid obstacles or bumps in the terrain.

Competitive Events

There is little difference between the expert skier and the racer, since all racers must be experts if they are to exert the greatest control over their skis at high speed. Yet racing is a thing apart from recreational skiing. Youngsters in competitive skiing begin training as early as five years of age. At 18 they progress from junior to senior competition. At 24 they are eligible to join the International Professional Ski Racing Association (IPSRA), whose prizes are money rather than medals.

Competition in skiing is divided into two categories: Nordic events and Alpine events. The Nordics consist of cross-country racing, jumping, and Nordic combined.

Cross-Country Racing. In cross-country competition, racers are equipped with special narrow, lightweight skis and loose bindings, which permit freedom of heel movement. Contestants traverse a prescribed course of natural terrain, including uphill, level, and downhill areas, to the finish line. The length of a race can vary from 10 km. for women to 50 km., in major competition, for men. The racer who completes the course in the least time is the winner.

Jumping. In contrast, jumping is a more contrived and spectacular competition. Specialized equipment includes long, heavy skis with multigrooved bottoms that facilitate tracking, or maintaining a course. A scaffolding houses the inrun, the long, steep chute that the jumper descends to reach the necessary speed for flight. The course also includes the outrun, the long hill upon which he lands and gradually loses speed as it levels at the bottom. The jumper is scored on the basis of distance and form, which have assigned point values. As many as five judges score the jumper's form after observing his position at the take-off, in the air, and on landing.

Nordic-combined competition requires the skier to enter both the cross-country and jumping events. Combined scores, expressed in points, determine the winner.

Alpine competition takes three forms: downhill racing, slalom, and giant slalom. In all three, contestants race against time, starting down the course at one-minute intervals.

Downhill Racing. Of the three Alpine categories of rac-

Ski Magazine—*Del Mulkey*

Sun Valley News Bureau

Left, a skier in a slalom event of the Fédération Internationale de Ski, composed of national skiing organizations. The federation conducts world championship meets every four years. Above, a racer in the Harriman Cup downhill event, held annually at Sun Valley, Idaho. Both slalom and downhill racing are Alpine events.

ing, downhill is the most exciting and dangerous—a test of speed and endurance. The course, which must be 1¾ mi. long with a vertical drop of 2,500 ft. in international competition, usually follows the natural terrain of the steepest trail on the mountain, with but a few control flags to limit the racers' speed. In international competition speeds of 60 to 70 mph are not uncommon.

Slalom. Slalom is downhill racing on a twisting course. Each contestant must run a course designated by a series of gates set in various combinations. Each gate is a pair of identically colored flags or markers. Ability to make rhythmic, rapid turns is the key to success here, since a slalom course in international competition can consist of as many as 75 gates. Each racer takes two runs down the course. The lowest total time determines the winner.

Giant Slalom. Giant slalom combines the elements of slalom and downhill racing. The speed attained is greater than in a slalom, since the gates are fewer and set farther apart, yet such competition is more controlled than downhill racing. As in downhill competition, a single run determines the victor. Alpine-combined competition comprises slalom and downhill racing.

Major Competitions. The two most important events in competitive skiing are the world championships and the Olympic Games, held two years apart on even years. The world championships are sponsored by the Fédération Internationale de Ski (FIS). It controls all international events except the Olympics. By a point system encompassing each international race, it determines the world's best skiers each year.

Sun Valley News Bureau

A skier at Sun Valley, Idaho, has left the inrun, or chute, and sails through the air for a 110-ft. jump, a Nordic event.

But for sheer spectacle and excitement, the pinnacle of championships is the Olympic Winter Games. To capture a medal—gold, silver, and bronze for the first three finishers in each event—is to reach the summit of a racing career. In total performance the Scandinavians have been strongest in the Nordic events, and the Austrians and French have dominated the Alpine races. The most glittering single performance was the winning of three gold medals in the 1956 games by Toni Sailer of Austria, who finished first in each of the Alpine events: downhill, slalom, and giant slalom.

See also WINTER SPORTS.

SKIN DIVING, a form of underwater activity in which the diver remains below the surface of the water for extended periods of time, often through the use of a special device for breathing. It differs from diving with standard gear in that there are no connections between the diver and the surface. Skin diving makes possible numerous pursuits, among them spear fishing, treasure hunting, underwater photography, the exploration of sunken ships, the collection of animal and plant life, and the search for artifacts of historical significance.

Types

Skin diving takes several forms: surface diving, "snorkel" diving, and aqualung diving. In each, the diver wears a face mask with an oval or elongated window which permits him to see under water without distortion.

Surface Diving. The term "surface diving" generally applies to activity in which a diver wears only a face mask and does not use any type of breathing device. A surface diver simply takes a deep breath of air before submerging and holds it while under water. He may expel air while under water, but when he needs to refill his lungs he must resurface and breathe again before making his next dive.

Snorkel Diving. A snorkel diver makes use of a simple breathing device which gives him slightly more latitude than that of the surface diver. The device is a snorkel, a rubber or plastic tube. The most popular type of snorkel is shaped like the letter J. The straight portion of the tube is about 12 in. long. The curved end of the tube is fitted with a mouthpiece through which the diver breathes. The straight end is open to admit and to expel air. A diver can swim just below the surface of the water for lengthy periods so long as the open end of his snorkel juts above the water somewhat in the manner of a periscope. The snorkel permits the diver to swim in shallow water, keeping his head below the surface for a better view of the bottom. He can also dive to a depth beyond the length of his snorkel provided he takes care not to swallow the water that fills the tube.

In making a dive that takes his snorkel beneath the surface, the swimmer sucks air through the mouthpiece before going under. He then holds his breath, makes his dive, and resurfaces when he needs more air. As soon as his snorkel breaks the surface, he rids it of water by blowing through the mouthpiece.

Aqualung Diving (SCUBA). This form makes use of a compressed-air breathing device, the aqualung. Compressed air is contained in a cylinder strapped to the diver's back. The diver breathes through a mouthpiece connected to a tube which feeds from an air chamber linked to the cylinder. The diver also exhales through the mouthpiece. In

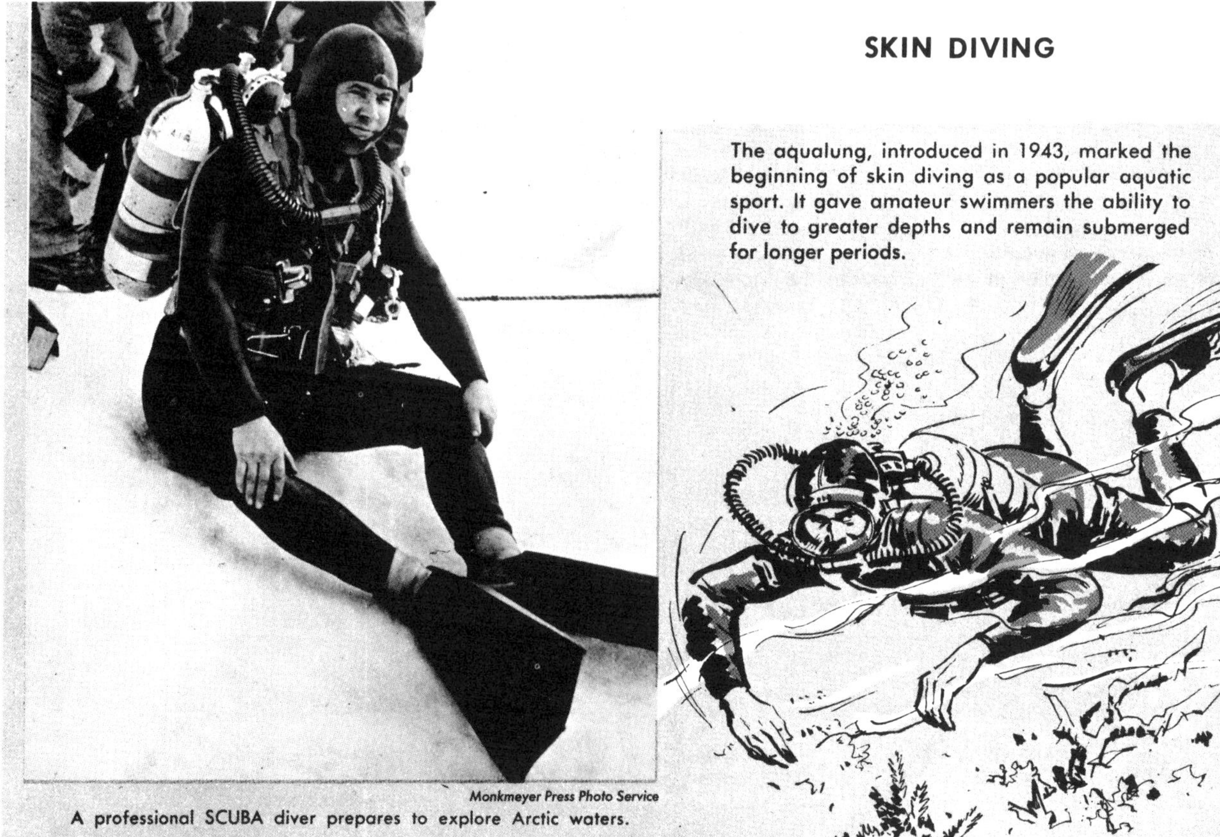

The aqualung, introduced in 1943, marked the beginning of skin diving as a popular aquatic sport. It gave amateur swimmers the ability to dive to greater depths and remain submerged for longer periods.

Monkmeyer Press Photo Service

A professional SCUBA diver prepares to explore Arctic waters.

A swimmer using a snorkel can swim or float on the surface of the water with his face submerged. Although snorkels can be made longer, at depths of even a few feet, water pressure makes it difficult for the diver to expand his lungs.

Below, a surface diver firing an underwater spear gun. Such equipment increases the need for strictly observing the rules of safety.

Roy Pinney—Monkmeyer

American Youth Magazine

Teen-age SCUBA enthusiasts carefully checking equipment before skin diving in Huntington Bay, New York.

the process of exhaling, a small valve prevents the exhaled air from entering the inhalation breathing tube. Instead, the stale air passes through a second tube, and is diverted into the water through exhaust vents.

The present-day aqualung is a form of SCUBA, a device whose name is the sum of its initials: self-contained underwater breathing apparatus. The aqualung is an open circuit SCUBA, that is, the air used by the diver passes in an open circuit from the cylinder, through a tube, into the diver's lungs, and, when exhaled, into the water. The diver using an aqualung breathes compressed atmospheric air.

The original SCUBA, which differs from the present-day aqualung, was a closed-circuit breathing device whose cylinder contained pure oxygen. The oxygen breathed by the diver traveled in a closed circuit, that is, the air, when exhaled, remained in the breathing apparatus instead of being diverted into the water. As the diver exhaled, the stale air was directed into a canister containing soda lime, which filtered out carbon dioxide and moisture. In effect, the diver's exhaled air was reprocessed, to be used again with fresh oxygen fed from the cylinder strapped to the diver's chest. This type of SCUBA is called a rebreather. It is still in use and finds its most practical application among such professional divers as Navy frogmen. Most expert skin divers recommend that the beginner or sports diver limit himself to use of the aqualung rather than the rebreather type. They maintain that use of the rebreather requires considerable training. Its hazards for the novice range from the improper use of oxygen to the chance accumulation of carbon dioxide, either of which can cause physical discomfort or illness.

Equipment

The basic equipment of the skin diver depends upon the type of activity in which he is engaged. In addition to his breathing device and face mask, the diver is generally outfitted with flippers, exposure suit, diving knife, weight belt, pressurized wrist watch, and depth gage.

Flippers are rubber fins, shaped like a duck's webbed feet. Flippers are worn on the feet of the diver, giving him greater thrust and mobility as he swims under water. Flippers also help the diver conserve the energy that would be expended in swimming barefoot.

Exposure suits are tight-fitting sheaths made of rubber or a rubber-base plastic. These are recommended for use in water that is colder than 70° F. A "dry" suit is one under which the diver wears a heavy undergarment to retain his body heat. A "wet" suit is made from foam neoprene and is worn without an undergarment. Neoprene is an elastomer; in its foam form it permits water to seep through its layers of cells in the manner of capillary action. The diver's body heat warms the water in the inner layer of cells, forming a liquid insulation against the cold water outside the suit.

Lead weights, worn on a belt, offset the buoyancy of a diver's body when he is under water. A diving knife is a basic working tool, allowing the diver to chip and cut underwater objects or to free himself if he becomes entangled in line. A pressurized wrist watch enables the diver to record the time spent beneath the surface. Most depth gages are about the size of a wrist watch, and are worn in the same manner, permitting the diver to determine easily his distance beneath the surface.

Maximum Depths and Safety Precautions

The depth that can be attained in skin diving depends largely upon the skill of the individual diver and the proper use of his equipment. Descents of more than 300 ft. have been made by divers using aqualungs employing a mixture of oxygen and helium. According to Elgin Ciampi, a leading U.S. skin diver who is also a marine biologist and an underwater photographer, a depth of 60 ft. is the safe limit when a snorkel is employed. A diver with an aqualung, breathing compressed air, should not exceed a depth of 130 ft., according to Ciampi. All experts are in agreement that skin diving is a dangerous undertaking for the person without proper guidance, and should be attempted only upon completion of proper training.

The origin of skin diving has never been fully documented. It is known that Japanese pearl divers, wearing goggles, practiced a form of skin diving in the 1920's. The techniques of the Japanese later became popular among sportsmen along the French Riviera. During World War II the Italian navy introduced the first frogmen, underwater demolition teams that made use of the type of equipment now popular with skin-diving enthusiasts.

More than 500 skin-diving clubs existed in the United States in the early 1960's. The International Underwater Spearfishing Association was formed in 1950. Many skin divers, individually and as club members, have turned their skills toward the preservation of marine life, assisting biologists in major research and conservation programs.

See also Swimming and Diving.

SLOAN, TOD, professional name of James Forman Sloan (1874–1933), American jockey, born near Kokomo, Ind. He rode both in the United States and England between 1889 and 1906. Sloan popularized the forward-seat, low-crouch position now used universally in thoroughbred flat racing. A heavy better, he made and spent a fortune in an era of comparatively small purses.

SNEAD [*snēd*], **SAMUEL JACKSON ("SLAMMIN' SAM")** (1912–), American professional golfer, born in Hot Springs, Va. He won fame for his flawless swing and for his earnings in tournament play, which totaled more than $300,000 and ranked among the greatest in golf history. Snead won the Professional Golfers' Association tournament in 1942, 1949, and 1951; Masters tournament in 1949, 1952, and 1954; British Open, 1946; Western Open, 1949 and 1950; and Canadian Open, 1938, 1940, and 1941.

SOAP BOX DERBY, annual contest for boys aged 11 to 15, who build and race gravity-propelled coasting cars of their own design. Its basic principle, as defined by the automobile manufacturer who has been the principal sponsor of the event for many years, is "to encourage a boy to build with his hands until the job is finished and then put his product to the test in fair competition with others."

The official title of the event is the All-American Soap

Opening ceremonies at the All-American Soap Box Derby, held at Akron, Ohio.

All-American Soap Box Derby, Inc.

Box Derby. The first national competition was held in Dayton, Ohio, in 1934. The location was changed in 1935 to Akron, Ohio, where the competition was held annually thereafter, except from 1942 to 1945, when it was suspended because of the war emergency. The site of the final races is a special coasting course in Akron, built in 1936 and known as Derby Downs. This three-lane racing strip is a paved track 975.4 ft. long. The incline is about 16% for a few feet near the starting line, drops to a 6% grade for most of the course, and then levels off at the finish line.

Prior to the finals at Derby Downs, officially sanctioned local elimination races are held in hundreds of U.S. and Canadian cities and towns and a lesser number of European ones. From about 50,000 original entrants, some 170 winners are selected to compete at Akron for the chance to win $15,000 in scholarships and other prizes. Additional trophies are awarded to the boy who records the best time in a single heat and to the boys whose cars are judged the best designed, best constructed, best upholstered, and best braked. A similar, affiliated competition was held annually in the 1960's in Duisburg, West Germany, to determine the German champion from about 10,000 entries.

Basic Rules. All rules are compiled and issued by the All-American Soap Box Derby, Inc., Derby Downs, Akron, Ohio. In the early 1960's the basic rules included the following: (1) All entrants race in one of two classes of competition, called class A (for boys aged 13 to 15) and class B (11 and 12). (2) Boys who have won an official Soap Box Derby are ineligible for further competition. The ban also applies to winning cars or parts thereof. (3) All work required in building the racing car must be performed by the entrant. (4) The entrant must drive his own car in an authorized race. A racing helmet must be worn, but goggles are optional. (5) The total cost of the car shall not exceed $20, exclusive of the wheels, axles, steering assembly, and paint. (6) The combined weight of the car and driver in both A and B classes must not be more than 250 lb. (7) Every car must pass official inspection before it may compete. (8) Cars must start by gravity from a standstill. Pushing is not allowed.

SOCCER [sŏk′ər], parent game of the football family. It is played by two teams, each of which attempts to score points by propelling a round ball into the other's goal. The ball is advanced principally by kicking. Unlike Rugby and American football, which derived from soccer, the latter prohibits use of the hands or arms in advancing the ball except by the goalkeeper when he is within a specific area. The ball is propelled by kicking it or by striking it with the head, shoulder, or other parts of the body excepting the hands and arms.

History. Although Great Britain may well lay claim to being the birthplace of the modern sport, historians have noted that games closely resembling it were played in many countries. One form was familiar in ancient Greece and Rome. Another was played at about the same time in China, where it was called *Tsu Ch'iu* (football). At the present time soccer is played in virtually every country in the world, and has the status of a national game in many of them. Everywhere but in North America, in fact, the word "football" signifies soccer. In England soccer is known as "association football," a name derived from the London Football Association, which in 1863 codified soccer rules and thus brought uniformity to a sport that had existed in diverse forms for many centuries. Until the origin of Rugby early in the 19th century and of American football some 30 years later, all football games were forms of soccer.

Modern soccer can easily claim to be the most popular sport in the world. In addition to being played widely, it attracts huge crowds to top games in Europe and South America. Europe has long been considered the stronghold of the game, with Great Britain as the principal bastion. English, Scottish, Irish, and Welsh emigrants helped introduce the game to North America in the late 19th century. Thereafter, emigrants from other European countries gave the game a vital lift both in the United States, where it made marked gains after World War II, and Canada. In the United States this surge of interest was reflected in the programs of colleges and secondary schools and in the spread of soccer on an amateur level outside schools.

Major Competitions. The top international competition, the World Cup tournament, represents a true world series

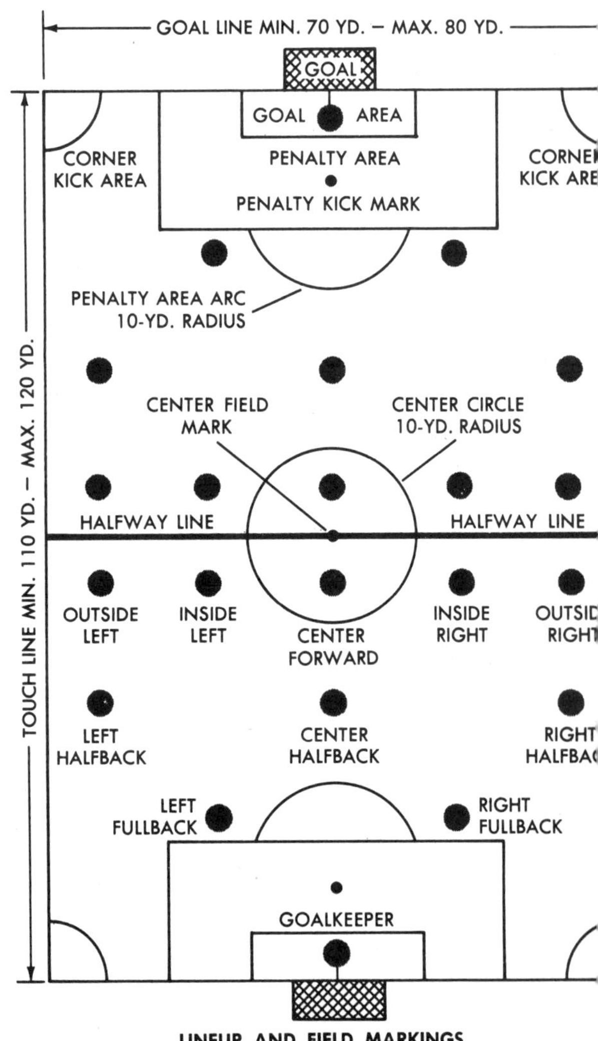

LINEUP AND FIELD MARKINGS

United Press International

A goalkeeper (*right*) blocks an attempt to score during a soccer match at Olympic Stadium, Berlin, Germany.

of the sport. This is conducted every four years in the even years when the Olympic Games are not held. A series of zone eliminations cuts the field to 16 teams, which then compete for the World Cup in soccer centers of Europe and the Americas. There are other international tournaments, including one in which national champions of European countries compete for the European Cup.

In the Olympic Games, where the game is listed officially as football, a series of eliminations on a zone basis is also employed to limit the field for final competition. As in all branches of Olympic competition, the teams are amateur. In other competition the major teams are professional.

Although there are many competitions in the United States, only two have national status. One, for the National Challenge Cup, is open to both amateur and professional teams. The other, for the National Amateur Cup, is restricted to amateurs. In 1959, series were initiated to determine the national collegiate champion and the champion among smaller colleges. Control of all forms of the game is exercised by the United States Soccer Football Association. The corresponding organization in Canada is the Dominion Football Association, which conducts annual national championship competition.

How the Game Is Played. The playing area is a rectangle of turf. For international matches, the field is 110 to 120 yd. long and 70 to 80 yd. wide. On each end line, midway between the side lines, is a goal consisting of uprights set 8 yd. apart and topped by a crossbar set 8 ft. above the ground. Surrounding each goal is a rectangular penalty area formed by a central segment of the end line; a line 44 yd. long and parallel to the end line; and two other parallel lines, 18 yd. long, that intersect the first pair. Within the penalty area the goalkeeper alone may use his hands and arms on the ball while in the act of defending his team's goal. A center line, parallel to the end lines, divides the field in half. The center of this line is the midpoint of a circle with a 10-yd. radius. Within this circle, play begins at the start of each period and immediately after a goal is scored.

Regulation soccer is played by 11-man teams. In addition to the goalkeeper, each team includes two fullbacks, who are stationed near their team's goal and have a basically defensive function; three halfbacks, whose positions at the start of play are between the fullbacks and the center line, and whose function is both offensive and defensive; and five forwards, stationed near the center line, who are the principal attacking players.

As in basketball and hockey, each team lines up in its own half of the playing area at the start of play, facing the opposing team's goal. Also as in those games, the object is to score points by putting the ball into the opposing team's goal while preventing the opposing team from scoring. When a member of a team succeeds in propelling the ball into the opposing team's goal, by kicking it or striking it with another legal part of the body, he scores a goal which counts one point. The game, consisting in international play of 45-minute halves with a 10-minute intermission, is won by the team that scores the greater number of points. Games involving school teams often are divided into 22-minute quarters or shorter periods.

The ball is round, inflated, and covered with leather or rubber. It weighs between 14 and 18 oz. and is between 27 and 28 in. in circumference. Players wear unpadded jerseys, shorts, shinguards beneath knee-length socks, and cleated shoes.

A single referee has complete charge of the game after play begins. (In high school and college games, two referees are employed.) Rules prohibit such illegal bodily contact as pushing, holding, striking, or kicking an opponent. Such offenses, and others of a technical nature, are punished by the award of penalty kicks to the wronged team. These permit a player of the offended team to kick the ball unmolested toward the opposing team's goal from a point 12 yd. directly in front of the goal. Again as in basketball or hockey, offensive play consists basically in advancing the ball into opposition territory through team play—principally by passing the ball from player to player in an effort to elude the defenders—and finally in kicking or heading the ball in the direction of the opponents' goal.

Andrew St. George—Magnum

International soccer match in Sausalito Stadium of Viña del Mar, one of South America's most popular resorts, on the Chilean coast.

Defensive players, meanwhile, seek to break up such invasion of their territory by intercepting the passes and by otherwise legally harrying the team trying to score.

SOFTBALL, game similar to baseball, first developed as an indoor recreation in the Midwest United States, in the late 19th century. There are two versions of softball's birth. One credits its invention to George W. Hancock of the Farragut Boat Club of Chicago in 1887. The other says Lewis Rober, a Minneapolis, Minn., fireman, invented it in 1895. It is certain that the first softball league was organized at Minneapolis in 1900 and its first rule book published there in 1906. Softball was known variously as kitten ball, diamond ball, and indoor-outdoor ball. The name softball was generally adopted in the 1930's.

Development. Softball began as an informal recreation, and the majority of games are still played that way. The Amateur Softball Association (ASA) had 500,000 players registered in 1965, but estimated the game was played by 25,000,000 people annually.

From its origins in Minneapolis, softball has experienced a gradual trend toward formal organization. The National Amateur Playground Association published a rule book at Chicago in 1908. The Playground Baseball Committee was formed at a meeting of the National Recreation Congress at Springfield, Ill., in 1923. Expanded in 1933 to become the Joint Rules Committee on Softball, it continues jurisdiction over how the game is played.

The National Diamond Ball Association, formed in 1923, sponsored the first national tournaments at Minneapolis in 1931 and at Milwaukee, Wis., in 1932, but only a few states sent representatives. A truly national organization awaited the birth of the Amateur Softball Association at Chicago in 1932. Leo Fischer, sports editor of *The Chicago American*, was the driving force behind the ASA, which sponsored its first world's championship tournaments for men and women at the World's Fair in 1933.

The ASA has become, for practical purposes, softball's sole governing body. It conducts six national tournaments each year, sponsors men's and women's all-star games,

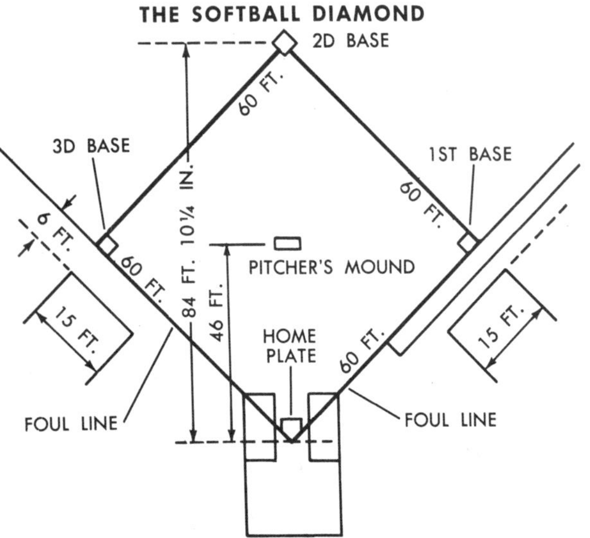

Delivering the pitch. Softball pitching differs from baseball pitching in that the ball must be thrown underhand. (CHARLES SUMNER)

and selects the U.S. representative for the annual international tournament, the first of which was held at Melbourne, Australia, in 1965.

The Game. For the most part, softball rules and techniques coincide with baseball. The principal differences are those of size. The softball field is smaller, with bases 60 ft. apart and pitching distances of 46 ft. for men and 38 ft. for women. The bat is smaller, with a maximum length of 34 in. and a maximum thickness of 2⅛ in. The game is only seven innings long. The ball is larger, 12 in. in circumference, whereas a baseball is 9 in.

The major difference in technique is that all pitching must be underhand, with the arm parallel to the body at time of delivery. Stealing bases is allowed, but the runner cannot leave his base until the pitcher releases the ball. Until 1946 softball had a tenth man on the field, but the position of shortfielder—a man who roamed just behind the infield to catch short fly balls—was abolished that year.

Despite the restrictions on delivery, pitchers dominate the game. The best of them can get the ball to home plate faster than the average baseball pitcher, owing to the shorter distance. This puts a great emphasis on bunting and place-hitting by the offense; a one-run lead is as valuable in top-grade softball as it once was in baseball. In tournament play, games with no score or even no hits are no rarity. Since pitchers do not twist their arms throwing curves and sliders, they can work longer (the record for one game is 42 innings) and oftener than in baseball.

This domination by pitchers led some leagues to institute a "slow pitch" rule, requiring the ball to be thrown with a visible arch to the plate. In this version of the game, bunting and base-stealing are prohibited and the shortfielder has been restored. The ASA ran a slow pitch tournament for men at Chicago in 1933 and has held one annually since 1953. An industrial division was added in 1956 and a women's division in 1961.

See also BASEBALL.

SPALDING, ALBERT GOODWILL (1850–1915), American baseball player and businessman, born in Byron, Ill. He was an outstanding pitcher for Boston of the National Association from 1871 to 1875. One of the organizers of the

National League in 1876, he pitched for its Chicago team and later served as manager and as an executive of the same team. In 1876 he and his brother founded A. G. Spalding and Brothers, a sporting-goods firm. He was elected to the National Baseball Hall of Fame in 1939.

SPEAKER [spē'kər], **TRISTRAM E. ("TRIS") (1888–1958),** American baseball player, born in Hubbard, Tex. Rated by many as the finest defensive outfielder of all time, Speaker, a left-handed batter, also had a lifetime batting average of .344. He played for Boston (1907–15), Cleveland (1916–26), Washington (1927), and Philadelphia (1928) of the American League. He also managed Cleveland (1919–26), and in 1920 his team won the World Series. Speaker won the AL batting championship in 1916 with an average of .386. His career total of 793 doubles stood as a major-league record in the early 1960's. Speaker, also called the "Gray Eagle," was elected to the National Baseball Hall of Fame in 1937.

SPEEDBALL, game that combines features of soccer and basketball with a few elements of American football, notably the punt and drop kick. It was invented in 1921 by Elmer D. Mitchell of the University of Michigan.

The game is usually played on a standard football field or one similar to it. Regulation teams are made up of 11 players: five forwards, three halfbacks, two fullbacks, and a goalkeeper. Speedball can be played with fewer men if the field is smaller than the standard football field. The ball may be either a regular soccer ball or a regulation speedball, which is slightly larger.

The object is to move the ball in the direction of the opponents' goal and score points. When the ball is in the air as a result of a kick or a pass (not having bounced from the ground), it may be caught and then thrown, punted, or drop-kicked. A single foot-dribbling step may be taken before executing any of those alternatives. When the ball is on the ground or has bounced from the ground, it must not be touched with the hands but must be dribbled with the feet or given impetus by the body, as in soccer. In general, the game is played as in basketball until the ball touches the ground. Then it is played like soccer until the ball is caught on the fly. At no time may any player run with the ball as in American football. Play begins with a kickoff, as in soccer. The regulation game comprises four 10-minute periods.

Scoring is accomplished by any one of five methods. A ball that is kicked, or propelled by another acceptable part of the body, between the goal posts under the crossbar is a field goal and scores three points. Catching a forward pass in the end zone is a touchdown and scores two points. Kicking the ball across the end line from within the end zone is known as an end kick and scores one point. A penalty kick (following a foul) that passes under the crossbar counts one point. One point is also scored if the ball is drop-kicked over the crossbar from a point outside the end zone.

See also BASKETBALL; FOOTBALL; SOCCER.

STAGG, AMOS ALONZO, SR., ("The Grand Old Man of Football") **(1862–1965),** American football coach, born in West Orange, N.J. He entered Yale University in 1884, where he pitched the baseball team to five successive championships and was named to the All-American football squad in 1889. In 1892 he became athletic director and coach of the newly organized University of Chicago, the first U.S. athletic coach with academic rank. His teams had a total won-lost-tied record of 229–108–27. They outscored their opponents 5,827 to 2,724, won a total of seven Western Conference (Big Ten) championships, and tied once for the national championship. Stagg also coached the Chicago baseball team to five championships.

Although the eastern teams dominated football, Stagg was noted for his strategy and generally became recognized as one of the country's leading originators of football. He developed the principle of the hidden ball, turtleback play, ends back play, end around play, man-in-motion play, fake place kick, "T" formation, and modifications of the forward pass. He also began player numbering, which was quickly adopted by all coaches across the nation. He invented the "tackling dummy" when he was a senior at Yale. After leaving Chicago in 1932, Stagg coached for 14 years at the College of the Pacific, Stockton, Calif. In 1943 he was voted "Coach of the Year" by the nation's coaches. Later he became advisory coach at Susquehanna University under his son, Amos Alonzo Stagg, Jr.

STENGEL [stĕng'gəl], **CHARLES DILLON ("CASEY") (1890–1975),** American baseball player and manager, born in Kansas City, Mo. After 14 years as an outfielder with five National League teams, Stengel began his managerial career in 1925 with Worcester, Mass., of the Eastern League. In nine years as a National League manager with the Brooklyn Dodgers (1934–36) and Boston Braves (1938–43), his teams finished no higher than fifth.

After winning a Pacific Coast League pennant with Oakland, Calif., in 1948, Stengel became manager of the New York Yankees. His first five teams (1949–53) set a record by winning both the American League pennant and World Series. Stengel's teams also won pennants in 1954–58 and 1960 and the World Series in 1956 and 1958.

Stengel was dropped as Yankee manager after the 1960 season, but returned to New York as first manager of the Mets in 1963. In two and a half seasons, Stengel could not get that club out of last place and he retired in Aug., 1965, after suffering a broken hip. Stengel was elected to baseball's Hall of Fame, Mar. 8, 1965, and installed on July 25 of that year.

SULLIVAN, JOHN LAWRENCE (1858–1918), American boxer, born in Boston and known as the "Boston Strong Boy." He won the heavyweight championship in 1882 by knocking out Paddy Ryan. This match and a notable one in 1889, in which he knocked out Jake Kilrain in 75 rounds, were fought without gloves under the London Prize Ring rules. In 1892 Sullivan was knocked out by James J. Corbett in 21 rounds in the first major bout under the Marquess of Queensberry code, which included use of gloves. Corbett thus became the recognized heavyweight champion under the new rules, though Sullivan was undefeated under the old code. A colorful, immensely popu-

Culver Pictures, Inc.

John L. Sullivan, heavyweight boxing champion (1882–92).

lar performer, Sullivan was largely responsible for the first surge of interest in the sport in the United States.
See also Boxing.

SURFBOARDING, also called surfing, the sport of riding a board on the fast-moving incline of a wave. It is one of the least complicated of water sports in that it requires no equipment other than the board. However, the sport demands an unusual sense of balance, timing, and co-ordination. Most surfboard riders are proficient swimmers who find the pastime an exciting test of aquatic skill.

Surfboarding originated in Hawaii, and is practiced by sportsmen primarily along the coasts of Australia, Brazil, and Peru. Within recent years it has become popular along portions of the California coast where long, rolling swells create an ideal "slide" toward shore.

Nature of the Board. A surfboard is generally between 9 and 10 ft. in length, rounded at both ends, giving it an elliptic shape. The center thickness of the board is usually 3 to 4 in. The nose and tail sections of a board are frequently tapered. Because of the taper, a board's extremities are not as thick as its center section, giving the board a slight arc, or "rocker." At its center point, the average board measures from 19 to 23 in. in width. Most surfboards are fitted at the tail with a small skeg, a miniature keel which helps stabilize the board.

Several types of board are presently in use. One is a surfboard of laminated redwood planks. Another is a lamination of redwood and balsa. The Malibu board, which finds favor among sportsmen on the West coast of the United States, is constructed of solid balsa planks. Lightweight plywood boards, forming a "hull," the inside

Grant—Globe

SURFBOARDING

This water sport requires a special board about 9 or 10 ft. long on which the surfer may lie, sit, kneel, or stand to ride a wave.

Above, contestants in the West Coast Surfboard Championships at Huntington Beach, Calif. The annual two-day event attracts surfers from California and Hawaii as well as many spectators.

Left, a surfer at the Huntington Beach competition rides a wave. Rules permit an entrant to ride three to six waves in a heat, and judges observe his form and skill.

of which is hollow, have become increasingly popular. Foam plastic boards are also popular because of their light weight.

Many boards, such as the Malibu, are covered with fiber glass cloth hardened with resin, which gives the surface a smooth, lustrous finish. The upper portions of a board are frequently coated with paraffin wax as a deterrent to slipping. The total weight of many boards is from 20 to 30 lb.

Technique of the Sport. A person who engages in the sport is a "surfer." He can ride his board by standing up, sitting down, kneeling, or lying, chest down, in the manner of a swimmer doing a breast stroke. In practice, a surfer swims with his board to a point offshore where one or more waves start their long, rolling sweep toward the beach. The surfer mounts his board by grasping its sides and sliding over the tail, in a prone position. A surfboard has a point of balance, generally a short distance behind its center, in relation to the size and weight of the swimmer.

If the surfer chooses to ride the board in a prone position, he lies, chest down, with chest and shoulders slightly raised. By doing a butterfly stroke, he can maneuver the board into a position where it will be headed toward shore at the precise moment when it is lifted by the impetus of the long, rolling wave. Before starting a ride, some surfers maneuver the board by sitting on it, slightly aft of center, with their legs dangling over the sides. By rotating their legs, they are able to jockey the board into a given position.

Surfboarding is dependent entirely upon one's ability to ride the momentum of a wave. Once under way, the surfer can make slight changes in the direction of the board by shifting his weight.

See also SWIMMING AND DIVING; WATER SKIING.

SWIMMING AND DIVING. Swimming as a competitive sport is the act of propelling the body through water with arm and leg motion and without artificial aid. It is also one of the world's most popular recreations. Diving is plunging into water in a prescribed manner involving three stages: the take-off, the maneuver in the air, and the entry into water.

History

Man probably learned to swim from observing animals. The Old Testament mentions swimming. Greek and Roman warriors were taught to swim as part of their training.

Origin of Competitive Swimming. Competitive swimming dates from 1862, when several clubs in England

FOUR BASIC SWIMMING STROKES

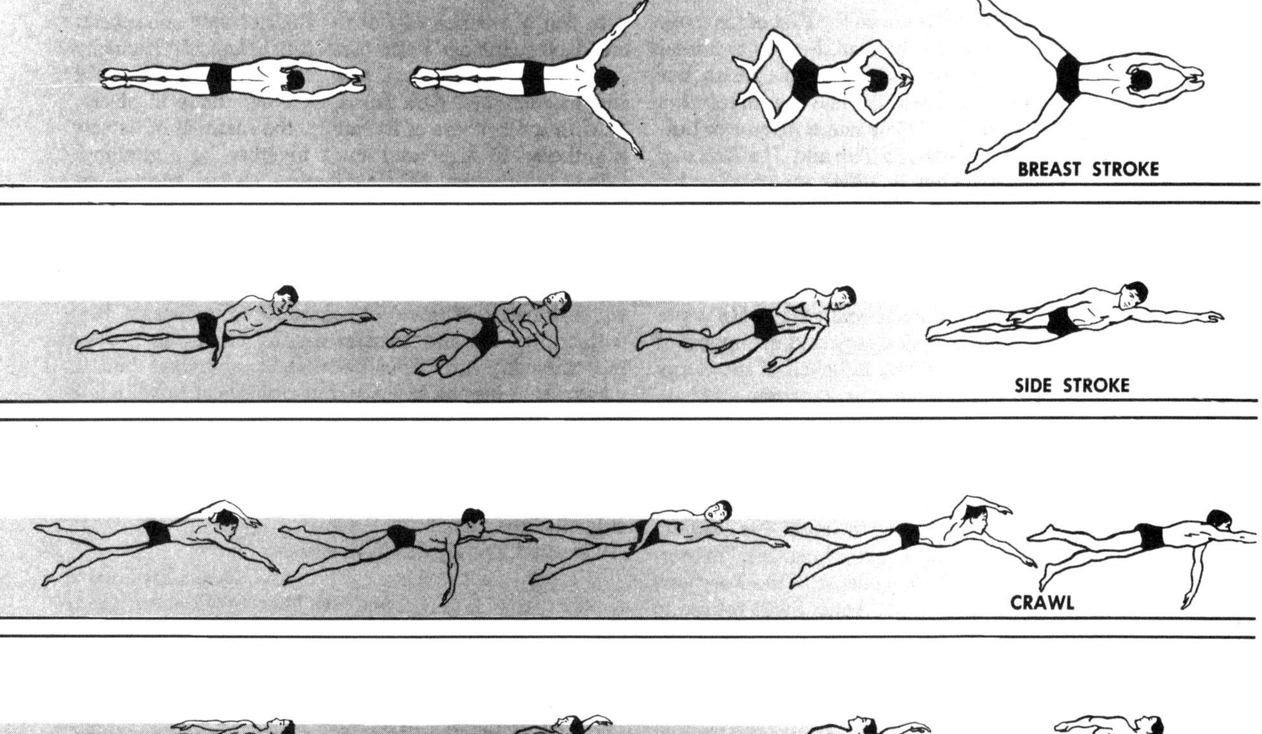

formed an association and conducted a meet. In 1875, Capt. Matthew Webb of England became the first person to swim across the English Channel. He used the breast stroke, the most popular stroke of that era. The first world record was established in 1878 by E. T. Jones of England, who swam 100 yd. in 68.5 seconds. American records date from 1883. Swimming received great impetus in the 1890's when the so-called Australian crawl was borrowed from South Seas natives. This stroke became universally used in free-style competition (in which any stroke is permissible) after its refinement by J. Arthur Trudgen of England, who introduced above-water arm action.

Types of Present-day Competitive Swimming. When the Olympic Games were revived in 1896, swimming became an Olympic sport for men. Women first swam in the Olympics in 1912.

In 1908 swimming was organized internationally under the Fédération Internationale de Natation Amateur (International Amateur Swimming Federation), or FINA. In the United States the sport came under the control of the Amateur Athletic Union and the National Collegiate Athletic Association. The AAU annually conducts separate outdoor and indoor championships for men and women, and the NCAA stages an annual indoor championship for men. The governing body in Canada is the Canadian Amateur Swimming Association, founded in 1909.

International competition is conducted (usually outdoors) in pools 50 meters (54.68 yd.) or 55 yd. in length. Most American pools are indoors and are 25 yd. long, and some are 20 yd. long. Since May 1, 1957, FINA has recognized world records for men and women only if made in pools 50 meters or 55 yd. long. The AAU recognizes records for men and women in three categories according to pool length: 20 yd., short course (25 yd.), and long course (50 meters or 55 yd.).

International records are recognized for the following types of competition: free style, breast stroke, butterfly stroke, backstroke, individual medley (which combines the four basic strokes), medley relay, and free-style relay.

Records seldom last more than a year or two because the sport is relatively young and techniques are constantly refined. New training methods, improvements in diet, and an extensive swimming program for children also have played a part in the continual assault on records. Many of America's outstanding male, and almost all female, swimmers are teen-agers. Few swimmers in America compete after their college years.

In the early years of the sport the dominant nations were Great Britain, Australia, and the United States. In the middle of the 20th century the leaders were Australia, the United States, and Japan. The outstanding American college teams included Yale, Ohio State, Michigan, Indiana, and Southern California.

Development of Diving. Competitive diving dates from the 17th century in Germany and Sweden, where gymnasts took their apparatus to beaches in the summer and practiced on land and over water. Most dives have counterparts in gymnasts' maneuvers, and many American gymnasts have also been divers of note. Diving was organized formally in Britain and the United States between 1895 and 1900 through the codification of rules and techniques.

Techniques

Free Style. A refined Australian crawl is universally used in free-style racing. It is the fastest stroke, providing a maximum of speed with a minimum of waste motion. With the body prone, face down (but turning regularly for breathing), the swimmer alternates arms in a pulling motion. An overarm motion is used, and the arms are returned over the surface of the water. The feet move in a flutter kick.

Backstroke. Lying on his back, the swimmer reaches back with his arms in a dorsal version of the crawl. Recovery is out of the water. He uses a flutter kick and generally a tumble turn.

Breast Stroke. The arms move simultaneously, forward and out, as the swimmer glides on the water, face down. The legs also move simultaneously in a froglike kick. All arm and leg action is underwater.

Butterfly Stroke. In this variant of the orthodox breast stroke, the arm action is underwater, the recovery over the water. The body lunges out of the water as the arms move forward quickly and together. A dolphin kick (synchronous action of the legs in up-and-down motion) is used. Racing exclusively with this stroke started in 1954.

Side Stroke. Lying on either side of his body, the swimmer alternately moves his arms forward and backward. At the same time he executes a scissors kick with his legs. The side stroke is not used in competition.

Diving. The diver leaps into the water, hands or feet first, in one of an almost limitless combination of somersaults and twists. There are six categories of dives: forward, backward, reverse (formerly known as gainer), inward (once called cutaway), twist, and handstand (performed from the platform only). Each contestant must perform a prescribed number of required dives and a prescribed number of optional dives.

Judges evaluate the excellence of each dive according to a point scale from 0 to 10. The score of each dive is multiplied by the degree of difficulty of the dive, as specified in the rule book. Dives are made in three positions: layout (in which the body is almost rigid), pike (in which the body is jackknifed) and tuck (in which the body is bunched, with knees and hips flexed). Competition is conducted from three height levels: 1-meter springboard, 3-meter springboard, and 10-meter platform. The heights represent the distances of the boards from the water.

Leading Figure

Swimmers (early years): J. Arth[illegible] Trudgen, J. H. Derbyshire, and Frederick Cavill, Great Britain; Richard Cavill, Australia; J. Scott Leary, Charles M. Daniels, and Duke Kahanamoku, United States.

Swimmers, free style: Johnny Weissmuller, Peter Fick, Clarence ("Buster") Crabbe, Jack Medica, Ralph Flanagan, Alan Ford, Dick Cleveland, Bill Smith, Wally Ris, Jimmy McLane, and Steve Clark, United States; George Young and Jim Thompson, Canada; John Marshall, Murray Rose, and John Konrads, Australia; Hironoshin Furuhashi, Japan.

Swimmers, breast stroke: Leonard Spence, John Higgins, Chet Jastremski, and Joe Verdeur, United States; Terry Gathercole, Australia.

FOUR DIVES

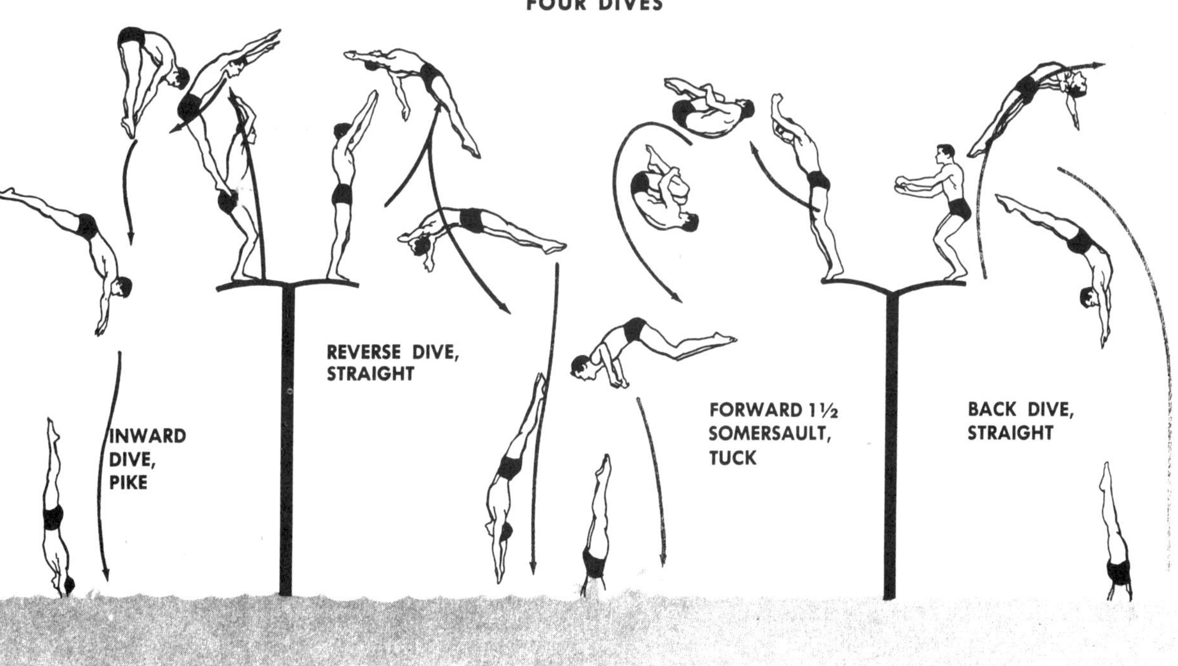

Swimmers, butterfly stroke: Bill Yorzyk and Mike Troy, United States.

Swimmers, backstroke: Adolph Kiefer, Allen Stack, Frank McKinney, and Charles Bittick, United States; John Monckton, Australia; Tommy Walker, Canada.

Swimmers (women), free style: Helene Madison, Gertrude Ederle, Florence Chadwick, Ann Curtis, and Chris von Saltza, United States; Dawn Fraser and Ilsa Konrads, Australia. Butterfly stroke: Nancy Ramey, United States. Backstroke: Eleanor Holm and Carin Cone, United States.

Divers: Dick Degener, Pete Desjardins, Al Patnik, Sammy Lee, Bruce Harlan, David ("Skippy") Browning, and Pat McCormick, United States.

Coaches: J. Arthur Trudgen and Sydney Cavill, Great Britain; Tommy Walker, Canada; Bob Kiphuth, Matt Mann, and Mike Peppe, United States.

See also Skin Diving; Surfboarding; Water Polo; Water Skiing.

T

TABLE TENNIS, often called "ping-pong," a game patterned after tennis, but played indoors on a table. The table measures 9 ft. long by 5 ft. wide. Its surface is 30 in. above the floor. A center line, ⅛ in. wide and parallel to the sides, divides the table for doubles play. A net, dividing the table into two equal areas, is strung across the table parallel to the ends. It is 6 in. high above all points of the playing surface. The ball is hollow celluloid and weighs approximately ⅒ oz. It is about 4½ in. in circumference. The wooden racket may be of any size, shape, or weight, but generally it has an oval blade whose diameters measure 6 and 6½ in. The average racket has a 4-in. handle and weighs about 5 oz. The striking surface is covered with pebbled rubber or with cork or sandpaper.

Rules. Table tennis may be played by two or four players. Play begins with the server tossing the ball into the air from the open palm of his free hand and hitting it with his racket so that it bounces on his side of the net, then over the net and into the receiver's court. The receiver must return the ball by hitting it over the net after it has bounced once. Volleying (striking the ball before it has bounced once on the table) in such an exchange is not permitted. Failure of a player to make a good service or return the ball properly counts one point for the opponent. Points are scored for both server and receiver. Service is alternated after five successive points are scored. The winner is the first to score 21 points, except when the score is tied at 20 all. Then play continues until one player wins two consecutive points. At such times service is alternated after every point.

The rules are similar for doubles except that service must be made to the proper half of the opponents' court. The server must hit the ball into the diagonally opposite area of the table. Service alternates between teams and between partners. Unlike play in other games employing rackets, partners must alternate in returning balls hit into their court during rallies.

History. A crude form of table tennis, using homemade

Brooks—Monkmeyer

TABLE TENNIS

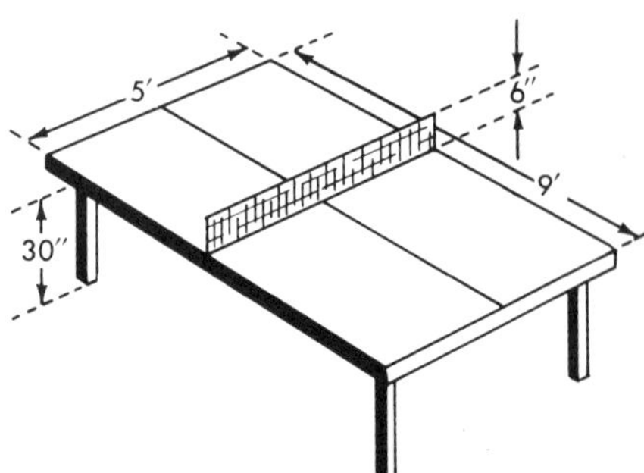

The table used in table tennis, or "ping-pong," measures 9 ft. by 5 ft. with a surface 30 in. from the floor. The top of the net is 6 in. above the surface. The center line divides the table for doubles play.

Left, a table tennis competitor in singles play. Using a wooden racket, he returns the celluloid ball to the opponent's court.

materials, was played in England about 1890. This game was only mildly popular until about 1899, when the celluloid ball replaced earlier ones made of cork or rubber. In the 20th century the game has enjoyed wide popularity throughout the world. It is often referred to as "ping-pong," after a proprietary version of table tennis. In 1926 the International Table Tennis Federation was organized as the world-wide governing body. In 1933 the U.S. Table Tennis Association was formed as one of its affiliates. Both Canada and the United States conduct national championship play. Winners of such national tournaments participate in international championship competition. Japan, Hungary, and Czechoslovakia have made especially strong showings in international play.

See also PADDLE TENNIS; RACKET GAMES; TENNIS.

TENNIS [tĕn'ĭs]. The word "tennis," in modern usage, signifies lawn tennis, which originated in 1873. A game that developed in the Middle Ages in Europe was "court tennis," or "royal" or "real" tennis. (For a description of that same, *see* RACKET GAMES.) Variants of lawn tennis, including paddle tennis and table tennis, are treated in separate articles under their own names.

Lawn tennis, the subject of this article, is a game played indoors or outdoors on a rectangular court by two persons (in singles) or by four of the same sex (women's and men's doubles) or by men and women partners (mixed doubles). The players use rackets to strike a ball back and forth across a net. The object is to score points by hitting the ball out of the opponent's reach, or in such a way that he cannot return it successfully.

How the Game is Played

Equipment. The modern racket is shaped like a frying pan and is usually about 27 in. long. Its oval head, used for striking the ball, is about 9 in. wide. Rackets are made of laminated wood, aluminum, steel, or alloys. The "head," or hitting area, is strung with a resilient fiber, usually gut or nylon, and the handle, or grip, is bound usually in leather. The ball is a hollow rubber sphere inflated under pressure and covered with fluffy felt. It measures about 2½ in. in diameter.

The Court. The court surface may be grass, clay, composition (frequently asphalt), cement, concrete, or wood. Major national championships, such as Forest Hills, Wimbledon, and Australia, are still played on grass, but the vast number of ordinary events are played on clay, cement, or wood, because grass is increasingly regarded as too unstable and too subject to changes in weather conditions. The court is 78 ft. long. In singles play the width is 27 ft. In doubles the width is increased to 36 ft. through the use of two parallel strips, or alleys, each 4½ ft. wide, on either side.

The net is strung across the midpoint of the court so that it parallels the base lines (end lines). The net is 3 ft. high in the center and 3½ ft. high at the net posts on either side of the court.

Each side of the court is divided into three areas. Two forecourt areas near the net are called the left and right service courts. These are equal in size, and their rear boundary is a line parallel to the net and 21 ft. from the net. In doubles these service courts are not widened to include the alleys. Behind these forecourts is a backcourt extending the width of the court.

Rules and Procedure of Play. In singles the players first toss a coin or a racket. The winner of the toss has his choice of naming the order of service or of selecting a given side of the court. The server takes his position just behind the base line, at a point between the center mark of the baseline and the right side line. He tosses the ball into the air and strikes it so that it goes over the net and into the service court diagonally opposite this position, while keeping his feet behind the baseline, and not jumping.

If the ball touches the net while going over, a "let" is called, and he must repeat the procedure. Otherwise, the server is given two chances to make a good serve (within the proper service court of his opponent). Failure to do so results in a "double fault" and a point being awarded to his opponent. The same player serves throughout an entire game, alternating positions on either side of the center mark as he serves. His service leading to the second point is made from the left side of the mark. After each game, service alternates between contestants. The players change sides (ends) of the court after odd-numbered games.

After a good serve has been delivered, the ball continues in play during an exchange (rally) that culminates in the scoring of a point, either by the server or the receiver. Except on a serve, the ball may be returned on the volley (before it has struck the court surface). In every case the ball must be returned before it has struck the surface twice. In rallies, net (or "let") balls (those tipping the net before landing on the other side of the court) are in play. Points are scored when a player is unable to return a ball in play before it has bounced twice, or when he commits an error. Errors include (1) returning the ball so that it strikes the net and fails to go over, and (2) hitting the ball outside the confines of the court (beyond the opponent's baseline or the side lines).

Dimensions of a regulation-size tennis court.

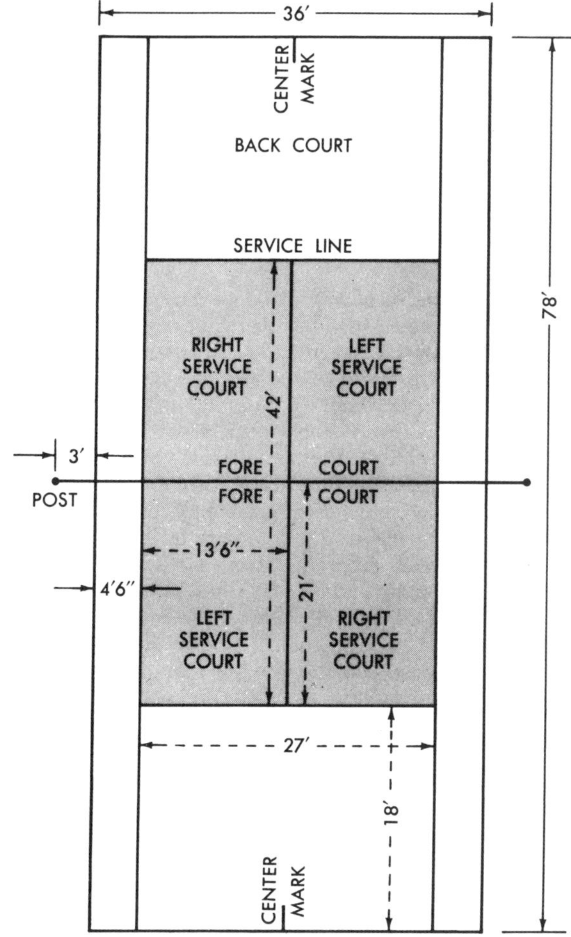

Scoring is a little anachronistic, hailing back to the origins of the game. The first point is called 15, the second 30, the third 40, and the fourth "game." The word "love" signifies no points. A game is won by the first player to score four points except in the following situation. A score of 40 all is called "deuce," and in such a situation one player must win two points more than his opponent to win the game. The player who first wins six games wins a "set." An exception to this rule occurs when each player has won five games. Then the winner of the set is the first player to win two games more than his opponent.

A match consists of a specified number of sets, usually the best of three or, in major championships, of five sets. In most countries a rest period of 10 minutes is allowed between the third and fourth sets of a best-of-five sets match, but this does not apply at Wimbledon.

Doubles play involves no special rules except that the court surface is larger. Partners alternate in serving complete games when it is their team's turn to serve. During rallies either member of a team may make a return. Players are not required to alternate in that respect.

In recent years different scoring methods have been used to bring to an end ("sudden death") championship matches. At 6-all, or 8-all, in a set the contestants play either the best of seven points or else the player who first reaches seven points, providing there is a two-point margin, wins.

History of the Game

Lawn tennis is only indirectly descended from court tennis, which is played indoors in a walled court. However, court tennis at one time must often have been played outdoors, and in 1873 an English army officer, Maj. Walter Clopton Wingfield, took this variation to its logical conclusion by introducing, in Wales, his version of an outdoor game, which he patented as "Sphairistike." Items covered by his patent rights included nets, posts, rackets, balls, and a set of rules. His court was shaped like an hourglass, narrower at the net than in the backcourt area. The net was hung high, as in badminton, a game Wingfield had learned in India, and additional nets, called "side curtains," were employed.

The game, which was more vigorous than croquet and capable of being enjoyed by persons of either sex, soon found a popular following in Europe. Each locality employed its own variations of Wingfield's rules, but gradually the net was lowered, the side-nets removed, and the rules formalized. The Marylebone Cricket Club, the international governing authority of cricket, undertook to

Bill Tilden during the finals of the U.S. men's singles in 1925. Tilden was probably the outstanding tennis player of the first half of the 20th century. (UPI)

Frank Sedgman of Australia at Wimbledon in 1949. He won the Australian men's singles championship in 1949 and 1950. (UPI)

Helen Hull Jacobs, U.S. women's singles champion from 1932 to 1935, also won fame in international play. (WIDE WORLD)

Australian world champion Rod Laver won the U.S. Open, Australian Open, French Open, and Wimbledon in 1969. (UPI)

Jean Borotra, tennis champion from France, hits an overhand smash during a championship game at Wimbledon, England. (WIDE WORLD)

Althea Gibson at Wimbledon in 1958. In 1957 and 1958 she won the U.S. and the Wimbledon women's singles. (UPI)

codify the rules of lawn tennis (as Sphairistike came to be called) against Wingfield's opposition.

Finally, in 1877, the game became truly standardized. The All England Croquet Club in Wimbledon, whose revenues were declining as tennis became more popular than croquet, set aside part of its lawns for a tennis court. By then virtually all that remained of Wingfield's game was the net and alternate name. The modern court was devised along with the rules of play and scoring.

Spread of the Game. Even before the first All-England championships at Wimbledon—still the major annual event—in 1877, the game had found its way abroad. In 1874 Mary Outerbridge saw it played in Bermuda and introduced it to the United States. The first U.S. court was set up on the grounds of the Staten Island (N.Y.) Cricket and Baseball Club. About the same time, William Appleton of Boston obtained a set of Wingfield's "Sphairistike" and took it to his summer home in Nahant, Mass. The game grew as popular in the United States as in England, and with the same resultant confusion.

In 1880 a championship competition was held on Staten Island, but players from Boston refused to enter. All-

SOME BASIC TENNIS GRIPS

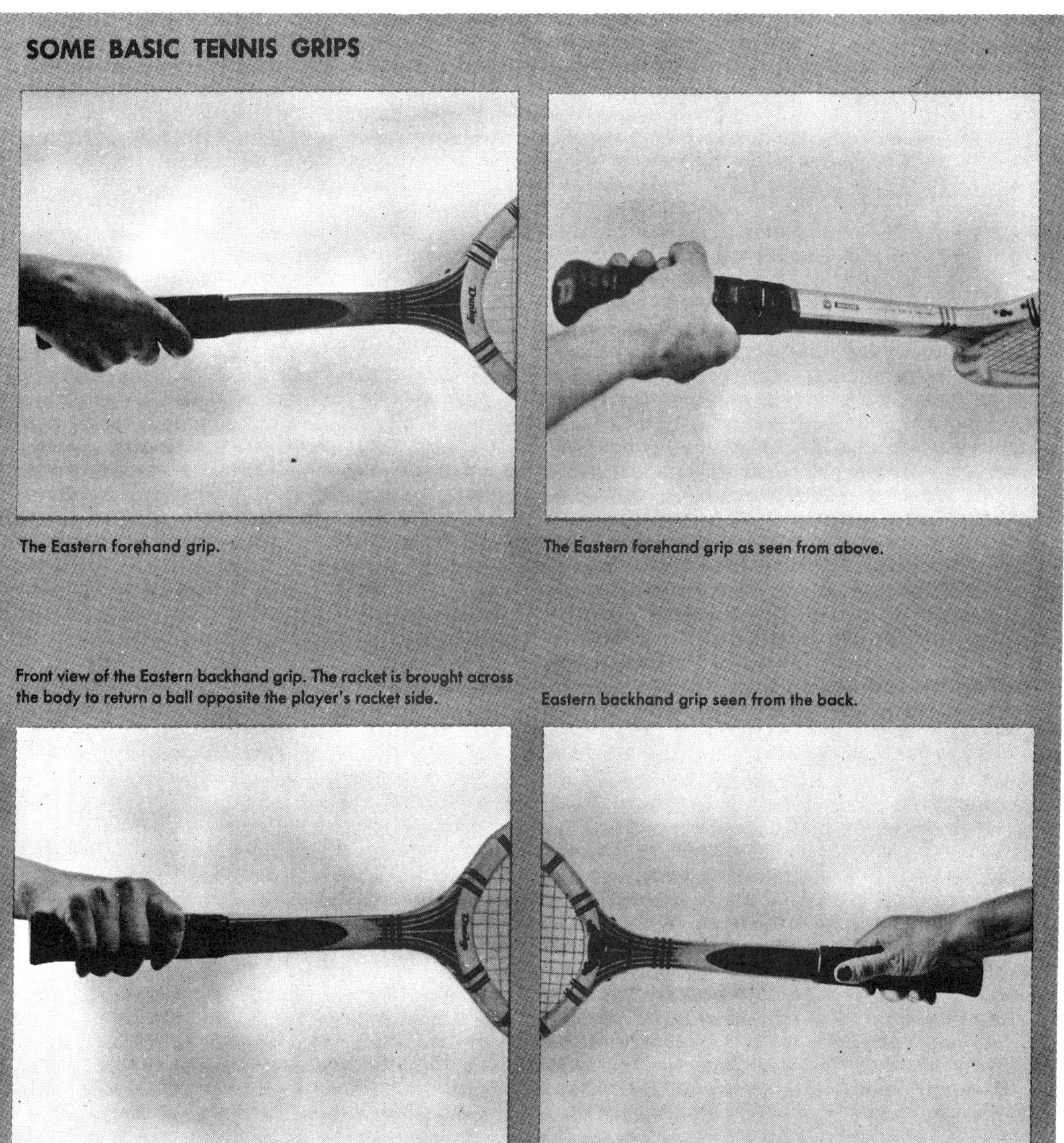

The Eastern forehand grip.

The Eastern forehand grip as seen from above.

Front view of the Eastern backhand grip. The racket is brought across the body to return a ball opposite the player's racket side.

Eastern backhand grip seen from the back.

England rules were employed, and the winner was an Englishman, O. E. Woodhouse. Shortly thereafter, James Dwight, who had played on Appleton's court, persuaded a number of U.S. clubs to join in organizing a governing body. In 1881 the United States National Lawn Tennis Association (now the United States Lawn Tennis Association) was formed. The first U.S. championship was conducted in the same year in Newport, R.I. The winner was Richard D. Sears, a protégé of Dwight.

Lawn tennis came to Canada about the time it was introduced to the United States. Beginning in 1885 annual competitions for a challenge cup were held. In 1890 the Canadian Lawn Tennis Association was founded, and in that year it began holding tournaments.

Beginning of International Competition. Like the United States, England had a seven-time national champion, William Renshaw. With his twin brother, Ernest, his partner in doubles, William Renshaw added both new strokes and strategy to both the singles and doubles form of lawn tennis in the 1880's. Before long outstanding American players, including Dwight and Sears, were journeying to Wimbledon to test their skill against their British contemporaries. The International Lawn Tennis Federation was formed in 1913.

Other countries also took up the game. Lawn tennis was first played in Australia in 1879, and today it is perhaps the most widely played game in the world.

Davis Cup. The spark was provided by a young American, Dwight Filley Davis, who conceived the idea of offering a cup as a prize to amateur competitors in international play. The Davis Cup was first competed for at Longwood, Mass., in 1900, when the U.S. team defeated Britain's. The competition, which is now open to men's teams throughout the world, has been an annual event since that time with the exception of 1901 and 1910 and the periods of World Wars I and II. Under past rules, the country holding the cup met the winner of competition among all of the challenging countries. But in 1971 it was decided that the holder, the United States, should play right through, and that this new rule should stand. In all rounds, four singles matches and one doubles match are played. Entrants from each competing country include two singles players and a doubles team, which may include the singles players.

In the early 1960's Australian and U.S. teams had compiled the most successful records in Davis Cup play since its inception and had dominated it since the 1930's. Britain and France also had had spells of success. In the late 1960's and 1970's, because of loss of players to the ranks of professionals (who are ineligible to play), the English-speaking countries began to yield to others.

Wightman Cup and Other Major Amateur Competitions. The Wightman Cup was donated in 1923 by Hazel Hotchkiss Wightman, an outstanding American player of that period. It is competed for annually by U.S. and British women's teams. By the 1970's, U.S. representatives had established a wide margin of superiority in the series. In 1963 the Federation Cup, a women's competition embracing all nations and competed for by teams of three players, who contest two singles and one doubles, was inaugurated. America and Australia have also dominated this event.

The All-England championships at Wimbledon attract world-wide attention annually in five divisions of major competition—men's singles, men's doubles, women's singles, women's doubles, and mixed doubles. The U.S. national championships at Forest Hills, N.Y., are conducted similarly, and at each competition senior and junior events also are held. In these and most other countries a variety of national championships are also played on red clay or cement and indoors on wood.

Play in these tournaments is not limited to players of the countries that conduct them. The international nature of such competition was emphasized in 1938 when Don Budge, of the United States, became the first player to score a "grand slam" of titles in one year, by winning at Wimbledon and Forest Hills as well as in France and

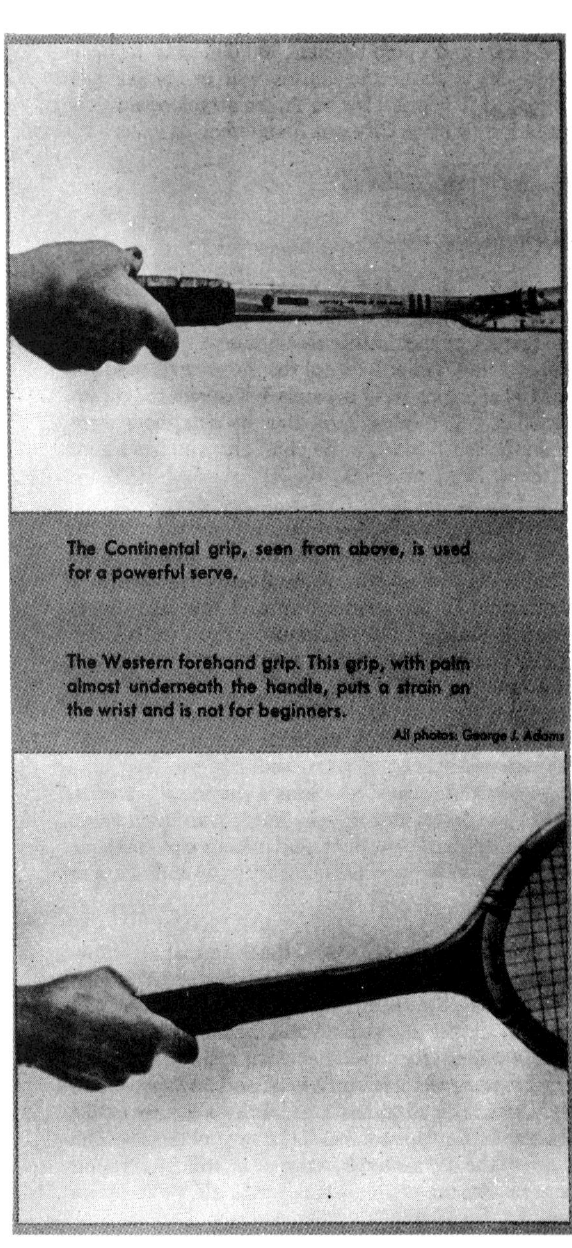

The Continental grip, seen from above, is used for a powerful serve.

The Western forehand grip. This grip, with palm almost underneath the handle, puts a strain on the wrist and is not for beginners.

All photos: George J. Adams

Australia. In 1962 and 1969, Rod Laver, of Australia, became the first player to do it twice.

"Open" Competition. Tennis, being a game that attracts many spectators, always was open to commercial exploitation. From the 1920's leading players received large sums of "expenses" under the table, although this was against the rules of the International Federation. The blatant hypocrisy of the practice offended many people. Accordingly, in 1967 the British Lawn Tennis Association, at the risk of expulsion from the International Federation, declared the game "open" to amateurs and professionals alike, thereby bringing the money above the table. The rest of the world followed suit in 1968, and thereafter most major championships were open to all to win substantial sums in prize money.

In the meantime a profound change had overtaken professional tennis following the formation of a Dallas-based group called World Championship Tennis. By the early 1970's the Texas group had 32 leading players under contract. The group's interests clashed with the amateur bodies' views on how the game should be conducted, and there were threats and counter-threats until an uneasy compromise was reached whereby the professionals, as well as competing in their own world championship, also were allowed to play in Federation-backed events.

TENNIS ELBOW, painful condition of the outer aspect of the elbow, possibly involving inflammation of a bursa (one of the fluid-filled sacs which are located at points of friction in the body). The condition is seen not only in tennis players, but also in fencers, golfers, butchers, and carpenters. The grip is weak, and the patient experiences pain upon attempting to pick up or turn objects. Treatment consists of rest and injections of cortisone and related drugs.

THORPE, JAMES FRANCIS ("JIM") (1888–1953), American athlete, born in a one-room cabin near Shawnee, Okla., of an Indian mother and a father who was part Irish. He was given the tribal name of Wa-Tho-Huck, or Bright Path. Twenty-four years later, at the closing ceremonies of the 1912 Olympics, the King of Sweden addressed him as "Sir," adding "you are the greatest athlete in the world." By that time the lithe, great-grandson of the Sac and Fox warrior Chief Black Hawk had been named to the All-American football team and had won both the pentathlon and decathlon at the 1912 Olympics. Subsequent disclosure of a brief, summer fling at professional baseball, while still in college, cost him all his Olympic medals and honors. After his amateur days Thorpe played in the major leagues as an outfielder. In 1950, in a national poll conducted by the Associated Press, he was named the outstanding athlete of the first half of the 20th century.

Most football followers think Thorpe's greatest day came in 1911 in a game against Harvard when the brilliant halfback for Carlisle, a high school for Indian boys, kicked four field goals to beat the Ivy Leaguers, 18–15. Thorpe's personal choice was the 1912 game against Army, when he caught a kick on his own 5-yd. line and raced 95 yds. for a touchdown that was nullified by a penalty. Army kicked again. This time Thorpe caught the ball on the goal line and threaded his way for 100 yds. and a touchdown that counted. Carlisle won, 27–6.

TILDEN, WILLIAM TATEM, JR. ("BIG BILL") (1893–1953), American tennis player, born in Germantown, Pa. He became interested in tennis in his early boyhood when he played on his family's private court. When he was seven years old he won his first tournament. He entered the nationals when he was 18 and won the mixed doubles title at 20, with Mary K. Browne as his partner. In 1918, with Vincent Richards, Tilden took the national men's doubles title and the following year was runner-up for the national singles championship. After winning the singles in 1920 for the first time, he then dominated the amateur tennis scene for the next decade. A member of the Davis Cup team that won the world championship from Australia that year, Tilden was the foremost figure in successively defending the Cup until 1927. In all, Tilden won the national men's doubles title five times (1918, 1921, 1922, 1923, 1927) and the singles seven times (1920–25, 1929). At Wimbledon he won the singles title three times (1920, 1921, 1930).

After Tilden was banned from amateur tennis in 1928 for writing articles about the Wimbledon tournaments, the French insisted that he be reinstated in order to play against René Lacoste in the Davis Cup matches. Lacoste won the singles title in 1926 and defeated Tilden in the Davis Cup in 1927. Tilden was reassigned his amateur status. He turned to professional tennis in 1931, and went on to win a host of championships for two decades.

TITTLE, Y(ELBERTON) A(BRAHAM), (1926–), American professional football quarterback, born in Marshall, Tex. He first attracted national attention while at Louisiana State University. Professionally he played for the Baltimore Colts (1948–50), San Francisco Forty-niners (1951–60), and New York Giants (1961–65). He led the Giants to three straight National Football League Eastern Division championships in 1961, 1962, and 1963. When he retired he held a number of NFL records, including most touchdown passes in one season (36) and most touchdown passes (212).

TRACK AND FIELD, a series of competitive events that comprise one of the oldest of all sports. They comprise running for speed, jumping for height or distance, and throwing for distance—activities vital to ancient man for survival. These events make up the most universal and most important sport internationally. It is conducted almost exclusively on an amateur basis. Since the revival of the Olympic Games in 1896, track and field has been the major sport in this worldwide athletic program. No official world-championship competition is conducted in track and field, but Olympic winners are regarded as unofficial world champions.

The European, British Commonwealth, and Pan-American champions are determined in other major competitions. Like the Olympics, they are held every four years. Almost every nation in the world has provided outstanding track and field athletes. The United States has been a world leader for a century. The Soviet Union instituted a crash program in the 1950's to develop talent and quickly became a world leader.

United Press International

Above, Henry Carr, Arizona State University, in the 200-yd. sprint.

United Press International

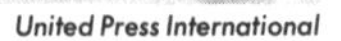

United Press International New York Daily News

Above, U.S. athletes Rafer Johnson (*left*) putting the shot in the Olympic Games and Ralph Boston (*right*) making a broad jump.

Left, Donald Meyers, University of Colorado, making a 16-ft.-1½-in. pole vault.

History

Track and field was a major sport in ancient Greece, where the Olympic Games originated, and champions were national heroes. When the Romans conquered Greece, they, too, took up the sport. Track and field was introduced to England (where it became known as "athletics") in the 12th century. It gained momentum in the 19th century.

In 1834 the English set up standards of minimum performance for qualification for major competition. In 1864 Oxford met Cambridge in the first intercollegiate meet. In 1866 the first English championships were held.

In 1868 the New York Athletic Club staged the first meet in the United States. It was held indoors and also marked the first use of spiked shoes in track and field events. In 1875 a group of American colleges, mostly from the Northeast, formed the Intercollegiate Association of Amateur Athletes of America (better known as the IC4-A). In 1876 the first IC4-A championship meet was held, along with the first competition to determine U.S. champions. The latter was open to collegians and all other amateur athletes. IC4-A meets were held annually thereafter. In 1888 the Amateur Athletic Union of the United States (AAU) was formed. It subsequently codified rules for amateur sports. The AAU immediately became the ruling body for track and field in the United States and staged national championship meets outdoors and indoors. The Amateur Athletic Union of Canada, governing body of the sport in that country, dates from the same period.

In 1896, in the first modern Olympic Games, the United States won 9 of the 12 track and field events. In 1913 came another impetus to the sport—the founding in Berlin of the International Amateur Athletic Federation. This organization governs the sport internationally and passes on all world records.

In 1920 the National Federation of State High School Athletic Associations was formed in Chicago. This federation exercises administrative control over track and field, among other sports, but does not conduct national championship competition. In 1921 the National Collegiate Athletic Association held its first national championship meet, which became an annual event. The NCAA membership now includes almost all major colleges and many small ones.

On May 6, 1954, Roger Bannister, an English medical student, achieved one of the great feats in sports history. He won a 1-mi. race at Oxford, England, in 3 minutes 59.4 seconds, the first time a mile had been run in less than 4 minutes. During the next eight years the 4-minute mile was bettered more than 90 times by more than 30 runners, but Bannister will always be honored as the pioneer.

In 1961 a revolution was fomented by the NCAA in an effort to wrest control of American amateur sports from the Amateur Athletic Union. The NCAA contended that it did not have equitable representation in AAU policy making. The AAU denied it. With the support of the group governing high school sports, the NCAA established the United States Track and Field Federation and the frame-

EVOLUTION OF WORLD RECORDS

RUNNING EVENTS	1900	1910	1920	1930	1940	1950	1960	1970
100 yd.	0:09.8	0:09.6	0:09.6	0:09.4	0:09.4	0:09.3	0:09.3	0:09.1
100 meters	0:10.8	0:10.8	0:10.6	0:10.4	0:10.2	0:10.2	0:10.0	0:09.9
200 meters	0:22.2	0:21.6	0:21.6	0:20.6	0:20.3	0:20.2	0:20.0	0:19.5
220 yd.	0:21.2	0:21.2	0:21.2	0:20.6	0:20.3	0:20.2	0:20.0	0:19.5
400 meters	0:49.4	0:49.2	0:48.2	0:47.0	0:46.0	0:45.9	0:44.9	0:43.8
440 yd.	0:47.8	0:47.8	0:47.4	0:47.4	0:46.4	0:46.0	0:45.7	0:44.7
800 meters	2:01.4	1:52.8	1:51.9	1:50.6	1:46.6	1:46.6	1:45.7	1:44.3
880 yd.	1:53.4	1:52.8	1:52.2	1:51.6	1:49.2	1:49.2	1:46.8	1:44.9
1,500 meters	4:06.0	4:03.4	3:54.7	3:49.2	3:47.8	3:43.0	3:35.6	3:33.1
1 mi.	4:15.6	4:15.6	4:12.6	4:10.4	4:06.4	4:01.4	3:54.5	3:51.1
2 mi.	9:17.4	9:09.6	9:09.6	9:01.4	8:53.2	8:42.8	8:32.0	8:19.6
3 mi.	....	14:17.6	14:17.6	14:11.2	13:42.4	13:32.4	13:10.8	12:50.4
5,000 meters	....	....	14:36.6	14:28.2	14:08.8	13:58.2	13:35.0	13:16.6
10,000 meters	....	....	30:58.8	30:06.6	29:52.6	29:21.2	28:18.8	27:39.4

HURDLES	1900	1910	1920	1930	1940	1950	1960	1970
120-yd. high	0:15.2	0:15.0	0:14.4	0:14.4	0:13.7	0:13.5	0:13.2	0:13.2
110-meter high	0:15.4	0:15.0	0:14.8	0:14.4	0:13.7	0:13.5	0:13.2	0:13.2
200-meter low	....	0:24.6	0:24.6	0:23.0	0:22.3	0:22.3	0:21.9	0:21.9
220-yd. low	0:23.6	0:23.6	0:23.6	0:23.0	0:22.5	0:22.3	0:21.9	0:21.9
400-meter	0:57.6	0:55.0	0:54.0	0:52.0	0:50.6	0:50.6	0:49.2	0:48.1
440-yd.	0:57.2	0:56.8	0:54.2	0:52.6	0:52.6	0:51.9	0:49.7	0:49.3

RELAYS	1900	1910	1920	1930	1940	1950	1960	1970
400-meter	....	....	0:42.2	0:40.8	0:39.8	0:39.8	0:39.5	0:38.2
440-yd.	....	....	0:42.8	0:41.0	0:40.5	0:40.5	0:39.6	0:38.6
800-meter	....	1:36.0	1:27.8	1:25.8	1:25.0	1:24.0	1:22.6	1:21.7
880-yd.	....	....	1:27.8	1:25.8	1:25.0	1:24.0	1:22.6	1:21.7
1,600-meter	....	....	3:16.6	3:13.4	3:08.2	3:08.2	3:02.2	2:56.1
1-mi.	....	....	3:18.0	3:13.4	3:10.5	3:09.4	3:05.6	3:02.8
2-mi.	....	7:53.0	7:50.4	7:41.9	7:35.8	7:34.5	7:19.4	7:14.6
4-mi.	....	....	17:51.2	17:21.4	17:16.2	16:42.8	16:25.2	16:09.0

FIELD EVENTS	1900	1910	1920	1930	1940	1950	1960	1970
High Jump	6-5⅝	6-5⅝	6-7 5/16	6-8¼	6-10⅜	6-11	7-3¾	7-5¾
Pole Vault	11-10½	12-10⅞	13-5	14-1½	15-1⅛	15-7¾	15-9¼	17-10¼
Broad Jump	24-7½	24-11¾	24-11¾	26-0⅛	26-8¼	26-8¼	26-11¼	29-2½
Triple Jump	48-6	50-11	50-11	50-11¼	52-5⅞	52-5⅞	55-10¼	57-¾
Shot-put	48-2	51-0	51-0	52-7½	57-1	58-10½	65-10	71-5½
Discus Throw	118-9	139-10½	156-1⅜	169-8⅞	174-2½	186-11	196-6½	224-5
Hammer Throw	167-4½	184-8	189-6½	189-6½	192-6⅞	196-5½	230-9	245
Javelin Throw	....	188-0	216-10⅜	239-3¼	258-2⅜	258-2⅜	282-3½	304-1

work for federations in basketball and gymnastics. Federations also were planned in other sports.

How Events Are Contested

The track events in track and field consist of running contests, mainly without obstacles. They also include obstacle (hurdle and steeplechase) and walking races. The field events consist of jumping (high jump, pole vault, broad jump, and triple jump, formerly known as the hop, step, and jump) and throwing (shot-put, discus throw, javelin throw, hammer throw, and weight throw).

Races are usually run over an oval track measuring 440 yd. or 400 meters in circumference. Races up to 440 yd. often start from a straightaway leading into a long side of the track. These races may end on the main track or on another straightaway. The track surface is hard and usually composed of cinders or a composition. Some tracks outside North America have running surfaces of grass. Races start with the firing of a gun and end when the first finisher snaps a thin tape, stretched across the finish line, with his chest. In handicap races the "scratch" man (the one rated the best) starts at the normal starting line and the others start from predetermined handicap positions in front of him.

Most field events usually are held in the track infield, with the other events in a nearby area. Jumpers, on completing their jumps, drop into pits of sawdust or other soft material. Race distances and jumping performances are measured in feet and yards in the United States, Canada, Great Britain, and Commonwealth nations. Most other countries use the metric system. Separate world records are listed for races conducted at distances measured in yards and in meters.

Uniforms. Shorts and sleeveless shirts are worn. Some athletes prefer to compete without socks. Shoes usually carry special track spikes. Some distance runners race in bare feet, and some high jumpers wear only one shoe.

Track Events

These vary greatly both in length of course and conditions of competition.

Sprints. These are races up to and including 220 yd. The runner starts from a crouch, usually with his feet braced against starting blocks.

Longer Races. The start is from a crouch or standing position. A gun is fired or a bell sounded when the leader begins the last lap.

Hurdle Races. These are events up to 440 yd. over vertical barriers 30 to 42 in. high. The height depends on the distance of the course and the age and sex of hurdlers.

Steeplechases. These races, usually 3,000 meters, involve at least 28 hurdle and 7 water jumps.

Relays. Teams of four (sometimes more) runners each compete against each other. Except in medley relays, each runner runs the same distance. Each runner passes on to the next man on his team a baton almost 12 in. long and weighing 2 oz. or less.

Cross-country. This is distance running on an undulating course—dirt, grass, or both—with natural obstacles. It was introduced in England in the 19th century. It is a popular college sport in the United States, where many runners use it in the autumn to remain in condition for winter and summer track competition. Technically it is not a part of track and field, but only related.

Otis Davis wins for the U.S. team as he crosses the finish line in the 400-meter relay race of the Olympic Games.

Annan Photo Features

Marathon. This is a road race of 26 mi. 385 yd. There is no recognized world record because courses vary. The best runners usually complete a race in 2 hours 20 minutes or faster. The best-known marathon in the United States is the Boston Athletic Association event each April. The event commemorates the legendary feat of Pheidippides, who reputedly traveled from Marathon to Athens in 490 B.C. to announce the Greek victory over the Persians.

Walking. Competitive walking, known in England for centuries, was introduced to the United States in the 19th century. This sport enjoys greater popularity in Europe than in North America. Road races are common. World records are recognized for competition over standard running tracks at distances from 2 mi. to 50,000 meters (about 31 mi.). The walker uses a long stride and swings his hips in an exaggerated motion. He must keep a toe of one foot on the ground until the heel of the other foot touches the ground, thus the term "heel-and-toe" walking. A fast walker can cover a mile in well under 7 minutes.

Field Events

Within this category are events in which the contestant jumps for distance (measured either vertically or horizontally) or throws various objects for distance (measured horizontally).

Broad Jump. This is a horizontal jump for distance, preceded by a long run-up. The successful competitor must have the speed of a sprinter.

WORLD RECORDS

(Recognized by the International Amateur Athletic Association)

FLAT RACING

Event	Time	Name	Nation	Date
100 yd.	0:09.1	Bob Hayes	U.S.	6-21-63
	0:09.1	Harry Jerome	Canada	7-15-66
	0:09.1	Jim Hines	U.S.	5-13-67
	0:09.1	Charlie Greene	U.S.	6-15-67
	0:09.1	John Carlos	U.S.	5-10-69
220 yd.	0:19.5	Tommie Smith	U.S.	5-7-66
220 yd. (turn)	0:20.0	Tommie Smith	U.S.	6-11-66
440 yd.	0:44.7	Curtis Mills	U.S.	6-22-69
880 yd.	1:44.9	Jim Ryun	U.S.	6-10-66
1 mi.	3:51.1	Jim Ryun	U.S.	6-23-67
2 mi.	8:19.6	Ron Clarke	Australia	8-24-68
3 mi.	12:54.4	Ron Clarke	Australia	7-5-66
6 mi.	26:47.0	Ron Clarke	Australia	7-14-65
10 mi.	46:44.0	Ron Hill	Britain	11-9-68
15 mi.	1:12:48.2	Ron Hill	Britain	7-21-65
1 hr.	12 mi. 1478 yd.	Gaston Roelants	Belgium	10-28-66
100 meters	0:09.9	Jim Hines	U.S.	6-20-68
	0:09.9	Charlie Greene	U.S.	6-20-68
	0:09.9	Ronnie Ray Smith	U.S.	6-20-68
	0:09.9	Jim Hines	U.S.	10-14-68
200 meters	0:19.5	Tommie Smith	U.S.	5-7-66
200 meters (turn)	0:19.8	Tommie Smith	U.S.	10-16-68
400 meters	0:43.8	Lee Evans	U.S.	10-18-68
800 meters	1:44.3	Peter Snell	New Zealand	2-3-62
	1:44.3	Ralph Doubell	Australia	10-15-68
1,000 meters	2:16.2	Jurgen May	E. Germany	7-20-65
	2:16.2	Franz-Josef Kemper	W. Germany	9-21-66
1,500 meters	3:33.1	Jim Ryun	U.S.	7-8-67
2,000 meters	4:56.2	Michel Jazy	France	10-12-66
3,000 meters	7:39.6	Kipchoge Keino	Kenya	8-27-65
3,000 meter steeplechase	8:24.2	Jouko Kuha	Finland	7-17-68
5,000 meters	13:16.6	Ron Clarke	Australia	7-5-66
10,000 meters	27:39.14	Ron Clarke	Australia	7-14-65
20,000 meters	58:06.2	Gaston Roelants	Belgium	10-28-66
25,000 meters	1:15:22.6	Ron Hill	Britain	7-21-65
30,000 meters	1:32:25.4	Jim Hogan	Britain	11-12-66

RELAYS

Event	Time	Name	Nation	Date
400 meters	0:38.2	National Team	U.S.	10-20-68
440 yd.	0:38.6	U. of Southern California	U.S.	6-17-67
800 meters	1:22.1	San Jose State College	U.S.	5-13-67
880 yd.	1:22.1	San Jose State College	U.S.	5-13-67
1,600 meters	2:56.1	National Team	U.S.	10-20-68
1 mi.	3:02.8	National Team	Trinidad	8-13-66
3,200 meters	7:08.6	National Team	W. Germany	8-13-66
2 mi.	7:14.6	National Team	W. Germany	6-13-68
6,000 meters	14:49.0	National Team	France	6-25-65
4 mi.	16:09.0	U. of Oregon	U.S.	5-12-62

HURDLES

Event	Time	Name	Nation	Date
120 yd.	0:13.2	Martin Lauer	W. Germany	7-7-59
	0:13.2	Lee Calhoun	U.S.	8-21-60
	0:13.2	Earl McCullouch	U.S.	7-16-67
	0:13.2	Erv Hall	U.S.	6-19-69
110 meter	0:13.2	Martin Lauer	W. Germany	7-7-59
	0:13.2	Lee Calhoun	U.S.	8-21-60
	0:13.2	Earl McCullouch	U.S.	7-16-67
200 meters	0:21.9	Don Styron	U.S.	4-2-60
200 meters (turn)	0:22.5	Martin Lauer	W. Germany	7-7-59
	0:22.5	Glenn Davis	U.S.	8-20-60
220 yd.	0:21.9	Don Styron	U.S.	4-2-60
400 meters	0:48.1	Dave Hemery	Britain	10-15-68
440 yd.	0:49.3	Gerhardus Potgeiter	S. Africa	4-16-60

FIELD EVENTS

Event	Distance (feet, inches)	Name	Nation	Date
High Jump	7-5¾	Valeri Brumel	U.S.S.R.	7-21-63
Pole Vault	17-10¼	John Pennel	U.S.	6-21-69
Broad Jump	29-2½	Bob Beamon	U.S.	10-18-68
Triple Jump	57-0¾	Viktor Saneyev	U.S.S.R.	10-17-68
Shot-Put	71-5½	Randy Matson	U.S.	4-22-67
Discus Throw	224-5	Jay Silvester	U.S.	9-18-68
Hammer Throw	245-0	Anatoli Bondarchuk	U.S.S.R.	9-20-69
Javelin Throw	304-1	Jorma Kinnunen	Finland	6-18-69
Decathlon	8,319 points	Kurt Bendlin	W. Germany	5-13 & 14-67

Annan Photo Features

John Thomas, U.S. high jumper in the Olympic Games, clears the bar at 2-meter height in the qualification jumps.

Triple Jump (formerly Hop, Step, and Jump). From a running start, the competitor takes a hop, stride, and jump in succession. This is actually a combination of three leaps, and the object is to cover the greatest possible distance horizontally.

High Jump. This is a vertical jump for height over a crossbar set on upright standards. A short run-up precedes the jump.

Pole Vault. The procedure in this event is similar to that in the high jump except that a pole is used for elevating the body, and a longer and faster run-up is necessary. Poles are made of fiberglass, aluminum, steel, or bamboo.

Shot-put. With a thrusting motion, during which the wrist is held rigid, the contestant hurls a 16-lb. iron or brass ball. High school athletes use a 12-lb. shot, women an 8.8-lb. one.

Discus Throw. In this event the contestant, after spinning his body to gain leverage, throws a wooden platter having a smooth metal rim. The discus measures 8½ to 9 in. in diameter and weighs 4 lb. 6½ oz. (3 lb. 9 oz. for high school competition).

Javelin Throw. This involves throwing a pointed spear (javelin) after a long run-up. The javelin is made of metal or solid wood with a metal point. Its total length is 8½ to 9 ft., and its weight at least 1¾ lb.

Hammer Throw. After spinning the body to gain leverage, the contestant hurls an iron or brass ball attached to a handle by a chain. The ball weighs 14.992 lb. The total weight of the ball, handle, and chain is 16 lb. and their maximum length is 48 in.

Weight Throw. Following a series of body spins, the contestant hurls an iron or brass ball attached to a grip. The total weight is 35 lb. in outdoor competition and 56 lb. in indoor.

Decathlon

Competition in 10 events in 2 days makes up the decathlon. Events of the first day are the 100-meter dash, broad jump, shot-put, high jump, and 400-meter run. Those of the second day are the 110-meter high hurdles, discus throw, pole vault, javelin throw, and 1,500-meter run. This grueling event is considered a true test of the all-round athlete.

Pentathlon. This event, now discontinued in the Olympic Games but included in some North American and European competitions, comprises the broad jump, javelin throw, 200-meter dash, discus throw, and 1,500-meter run. The modern pentathlon includes cross-country running together with four events not in track and field: horseback riding, fencing, pistol shooting, and swimming.

Other Competition

Indoor Meets. Indoor track meets have become a winter fixture in the United States and are increasing in Canada, Britain, Germany, Japan, and the Soviet Union. The tracks are made of banked boards (usually measuring 11 laps to a mile), flat boards (usually 8 laps to a mile), or a mixture of dirt and cinders (usually 8 laps to a mile). Five annual indoor meets attract capacity or near-capacity crowds to Madison Square Garden in New York City. Relay races are a popular feature. The International Amateur Athletic Federation does not recognize world indoor records. The Amateur Athletic Union recognizes American indoor records. Track experts maintain a list of unofficial world indoor records for competition on board tracks or from board take-offs.

Professional. There has been little professional track. Sprinters, especially in Australia, have competed professionally, and so have walkers in the United States. But attempts to stage professional meets or series of meets have failed.

Women's. Women's track and field has been an Olympic sport since 1928. It enjoys far more popularity in Europe than in the United States. The Soviet Union has produced many fine women athletes, and Australia is noted for its sprinters. Leading athletes from the United

States have included Wilma Rudolph Ward, Mildred ("Babe") Didrikson, Stella Walsh, Dorothy Dodson, Alice Coachman, Earlene Brown, and Frances Kaszubski.

Outstanding Athletes

(Americans unless otherwise noted)

Sprints: Bernard ("Barney") Wefers, Charles Paddock, Ralph Metcalfe, Jesse Owens, Norwood ("Barney") Ewell, Dave Sime, Bobby Morrow, Frank Budd.

440-Yd. Run: Lawrence Myers, James ("Ted") Meredith, Ben Eastman, Bill Carr, Herb McKenley (British West Indies), George Rhoden (British West Indies), Otis Davis, Curtis Mills.

880-Yd. Run: Mel Sheppard, James ("Ted") Meredith, Johnny Woodruff, John Borican, Mal Whitfield, Tom Courtney, Peter Snell (New Zealand), Jim Ryun.

1-Mi. Run: Walter George (Great Britain), G. W. Orton, Joie Ray, Glenn Cunningham, Gil Dodds, Gunder Haegg (Sweden), Wes Santee, Roger Bannister (Great Britain), John Landy (Australia), Ron Delany (Ireland), Herb Elliott (Australia), Peter Snell (New Zealand), Jim Beatty, Dyrol Burleson, Jim Ryun.

Distance Races: Don Lash, Greg Rice, Horace Ashenfelter, Paavo Nurmi (Finland), Sandor Iharos (Hungary), Vladimir Kuts (Soviet Union), Emil Zatopek (Czechoslovakia), Murray Halberg (New Zealand), Ron Clarke (Australia), Ron Hill (United Kingdom).

Marathon: Clarence DeMar, John J. Kelley.

Hurdles: Percy Beard, Arky Erwin, Fred Wolcott, Harrison Dillard, Jack Davis, Hayes Jones, Glenn Davis,

Soviet javelin thrower Yanis Lusis set an Olympic javelin record of 90.10 meters at the 1968 Olympic Games in Mexico. (SOVFOTO)

Soviet female long jumper N. Kroyter jumps 6 meters 38 cm. to victory in international track and field competition. (SOVFOTO)

Gert Potgieter (South Africa), Dave Hemery (United Kingdom).

Steeplechase: Joe McCluskey, Zdzislaw Krzyszkowiak (Poland), Jouko Kuha (Finland).

Walking: Henry Laskau, Christoph Hohne (East Germany).

High Jump: I. K. Baxter, Harold Osborn, Cornelius Johnson, Dave Albritton, Les Steers, John Thomas, Charlie Dumas, Valeri Brumel (Soviet Union).

Pole Vault: Charles Hoff (Norway), Cornelius Warmerdam, Bob Richards, Don Bragg, John Uelses, John Pennel.

Broad Jump: M. W. Ford, DeHart Hubbard, Jesse Owens, Ralph Boston, Igor Ter-Ovanesyan (Soviet Union), Bob Beamon.

Triple Jump: D. F. Ahearn, Bill Brown, Adhemar da Silva (Brazil), Ira Davis, Viktor Saneyev (Soviet Union).

Shot-put: F. L. Lambrecht, G. R. Gray, Parry O'Brien, Bill Nieder, Dallas Long, Randy Matson.

Discus Throw: Martin Sheldon, A. W. Mucks, Fortune Gordien, Al Oerter, Jay Silvester.

Javelin Throw: G. A. Bronder Jr., Matti Jarvinen (Finland), Franklin ("Bud") Held, Jorma Kinnonen (Finland).

Hammer Throw: J. S. Mitchel, John Flanagan, Pat Ryan, Imre Nemeth (Hungary), Hal Connolly, Vasili Rudenkov (Soviet Union), Anatoli Bondarchuk (Soviet Union).

Weight Throw: C. A. J. Queckberner, J. S. Mitchel, Pat McDonald, Frank Berst, Henry Dreyer, Bob Backus.

Decathlon: Jim Thorpe, Bob Mathias, Rafer Johnson, Vasili Kuznetsov (Soviet Union), William A. Toomey.

See also OLYMPIC GAMES; PAN AMERICAN GAMES.

TRAMPOLINE, an elevated, resilient bed or net employed by tumblers as a springboard. Rebound tumbling is one of the several activities that make up the sport of gymnastics. The rebound tumbler performs acrobatic stunts of his choosing on this web-constructed canvas bed, which enables him to spring as high as 20 ft.

The origin of rebound tumbling is somewhat obscure. It was devised in France in the 18th or 19th century by professional acrobats and became popular in circuses. It gained a wide American following in the 1930's and 1940's. In 1954 competitive rebound tumbling in the United States came under the control of the Amateur Athletic Union. The National Collegiate Athletic Association administers the sport on a college level. In Canada the governing body is the Canadian AAU. There is no Olympic or other international competition, however, because the International Federation of Gymnastics does not sanction the sport.

The trampoline is a rectangular sheet of canvas with minimum measurements of 12 by 5½ ft. This is mounted on a metal frame. Frame pads on all sides protect the athlete from injury. Male rebound tumblers wear tights and women wear leotards. Men and women compete separately. The AAU rules, revised in 1962, call for one series of stunts, limited to 12 bounces (contacts with the bed), for each athlete. The series is preceded by a "reasonable number" of preparatory bounces, with the counting of bounces toward the maximum of 12 starting with the first stunt.

The stunts are formed from almost limitless combinations of somersaults and twists. Outstanding rebound tumblers have performed triple somersaults (without twists) and three and one-half twists with one somersault. Their stunts are highly similar to those of divers, and numerous athletes have excelled in both sports. Rebound tumbling is scored by four judges. Each athlete starts with a maximum score of 10 points from each judge. The judges then deduct points for lack of difficulty in stunts and deficiencies in form or smoothness.

TRAPSHOOTING. *See* SKEET AND TRAPSHOOTING.

TRAYNOR [*trā'nər*], **HAROLD JOSEPH ("PIE")** (1899–1972), American baseball player, born in Framingham, Mass. He is generally regarded as the outstanding third baseman in the history of the sport. He played for Pittsburgh of the National League throughout his entire major-league career (1920–37). He also managed this team from 1934 through 1939. Traynor had a NL career batting average of .320. In 1948 he was elected to the National Baseball Hall of Fame.

TROTTING. *See Horse Racing.*

TUNNEY [*tŭn'ē*], **JAMES JOSEPH ("GENE")** (1897–), American boxer, born in New York City. He left school at 15 to become a boxer and retired at 30 as the undefeated world heavyweight champion. He won the world heavyweight title from Jack Dempsey in Philadelphia on Sept. 23, 1926, through a 10-round decision, and retained it in the famed long-count fight in Chicago on Sept. 22, 1927. Fighting desperately in the latter bout to regain the title, Dempsey cornered Tunney in the seventh round and smashed him to the floor with a series of rights. Dempsey virtually stood over his prostrate foe, in violation of the rules, and it was an estimated 5 seconds before the referee could convince Dempsey to move to a neutral corner. Tunney had about 14 seconds, in contrast to the legal 10, to recover his senses. In the eighth round Tunney floored Dempsey, and went on to win, again by decision.

Tunney knocked out Tom Heeney of New Zealand in 11 rounds on July 26, 1928, and retired from professional boxing the next day. He served with the Marines in World War I and with the naval forces in World War II. After his retirement from the ring, Tunney achieved further success as a corporation executive.

TURNVEREIN [*to͝orn'fĕ-rīn*], German gymnastic club. Founded in Berlin by Friedrich Ludwig "Father" Jahn in 1811, the organization was designed to strengthen, through gymnastic exercises, the physical force and moral will of the German people in the period of Napoleonic domination. Under Jahn's tutelage the Turnverein remained a patriotic organization not only during the war of liberation against the French (1813–15) but also in the postwar period. In this period it became a center of nationalist agitation against the localism of the German rulers. Transplanted to the United States by German immigrants during the 19th century, it still flourishes as a social club.

U

UNITED STATES OLYMPIC COMMITTEE. *See* OLYMPIC GAMES.

VARDON, HARRY (1870–1937), English golfer. He won 62 major tournaments, including the British Open in 1896, 1898, 1899, 1903, 1911, and 1914. He also won the U.S. Open in 1900. A graceful player and a master of iron shots, Vardon is credited with popularizing the overlapping grip. The trophy awarded annually to the member of the Professional Golfers' Association of America with the lowest average score in PGA-approved events is named after Vardon.

VOLLEYBALL, game played indoors or outdoors by teams whose members seek to score points in the course of hitting a ball back and forth across a net. The playing area is a rectangular court measuring 60 by 30 ft., which is divided into halves by a center line. The net extending across the center line is 3 ft. in width. Its top edge is 8 ft. from the court surface. For women's play the net is lowered 6 in., and for children's play, 1 ft. On each side of the court is a restraining line 7½ ft. from, and parallel to, the center line. The ball is a leather-covered rubber sphere inflated to a circumference of between 26 and 27 in. It weighs between 9 and 10 oz.

Each team has six players. Three, stationed in the area near the net, are designated "right forward," "center forward," and "left forward." Stationed behind in a corresponding arrangement are three players known as "backs." At every change of service the players rotate clockwise so that each has an opportunity to serve.

Rules and Procedures. Play begins with service by the right back. He throws the ball into the air and hits it with his hand, fist, or arm so that the ball travels over the net into the opponents' court. The serve is made from the zone immediately behind the end line. Once the ball has been struck by the server, he may step into the court. At any time in the game, if a serve goes out of bounds, fails to clear the net without striking the net, goes into the net, or hits any obstruction before clearing the net, it is void. Then the opposing team gains the right to serve, but no points are scored, since points are scored only by the serving team. A ball that has been legally served must be returned by the opposing team before it strikes the court. If it is not, or if the ball is hit into the net or out of bounds, the serving team scores a point and retains the service. When the serving team fails to return the ball under such conditions, it loses the service.

In making a return, a team member may not catch the ball. Using one or two hands, he must hit it over the net or to a teammate. The ball may be struck three times before it is returned over the net by a given team, except that no player may strike it twice in succession. Generally team members avail themselves of the three opportunities for contact with the ball before the return. Frequently a back taps the ball to a teammate who then "sets up" the ball for another teammate near the net. The third player strikes it forcefully into the opponents' court. This procedure (spiking) by the third player makes return of the ball difficult. After a serve has been made, players may move to any section of the court and are eligible for all play with one exception. A back may not spike the ball in front of the restraining line. No player may touch the net or cross the center line.

The winner is decided on the basis of a specified point total (usually 15) or a time limit (8 minutes, calculated solely as time during which the ball is actually in play). In the first case, if the score is 14 all, one team must gain a 2-point advantage in order to win. When a time limit is observed, the winner is the side that is ahead by two or more points the first time the ball becomes dead (when a new serve is called for) after the expiration of 8 minutes. If one team has less than a 2-point lead, unlimited overtime is played until such a margin is achieved.

History. Volleyball was invented by William G. Morgan

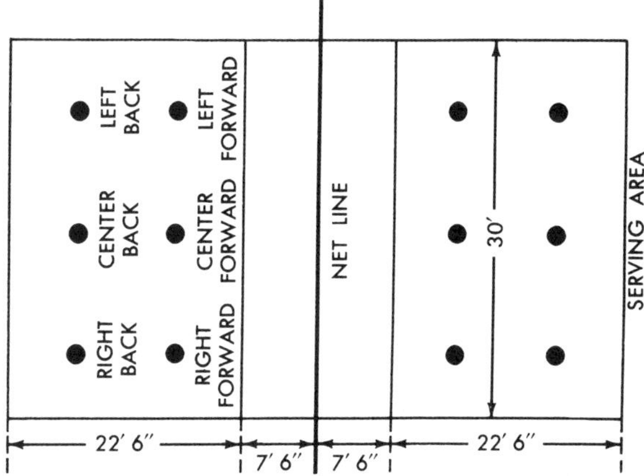

French forwards (right of net) spike the ball to the Japanese side during an international volleyball match held in Paris, France. (PICTORIAL PARADE)

in 1895, when he was a physical director for the YMCA in Holyoke, Mass. His object was a game, not too strenuous in nature, that would be suitable for older men. During World War I and II it was popular among U.S. service personnel, who helped to make it an international sport. The United States Volleyball Association, with headquarters in New York, is the governing body of the sport in U.S. competition. In the 1960's men's volleyball was part of the Olympic Games, and men's and women's competition was included in the Pan American Games.

WAGNER [wăg'nər], **JOHN PETER ("HONUS") (1874–1955),** American baseball player, born in Carnegie, Pa. In the opinion of most qualified observers he was the foremost shortstop in the history of the game. In 21 National League seasons with Louisville (1897–99) and Pittsburgh (1900–17) he compiled a career batting average of .329. A right-handed batter, he won eight NL batting championships between 1900 and 1911 and hit over .300 in 17 consecutive seasons. Both feats stood as league records in the early 1960's. Despite his heavy-set, ungainly frame, he was an outstanding defensive player, and his speed won for him the nickname "Flying Dutchman." He was elected to the National Baseball Hall of Fame in 1936.

WALCOTT, JERSEY JOE, professional name of Arnold Raymond Cream, Jr. (1914–), American boxer, born in Camden, N.J. He began his career about 1930, twice unsuccessfully challenged Joe Louis for the heavyweight championship, and in 1951 won the title from Ezzard Charles. He lost it to Rocky Marciano the next year.

WARNER, GLENN SCOBEY ("POP") (1871–1954), American football coach, born in Springville, N.Y. He served as a head coach for 44 years and was one of the sport's great innovators. As an undergraduate he was an all-round athlete at Cornell University. Warner served as head football coach at the University of Georgia (1895–96), Cornell (1897–98 and 1904–6), Carlisle Indian School (1899–1903 and 1907–14), University of Pittsburgh (1915–23), Stanford University (1924–32), and Temple University (1933–38). At Carlisle he produced 13 All-American players, including the renowned Jim Thorpe. Among Warner's many great teams were Stanford's Rose Bowl elevens of 1925, 1927, and 1928. His most notable inventions were the single wing back and double wing back formations. *See also* FOOTBALL.

WATER POLO, a typical goal-type game with one notable difference: it is played in water. It combines many of the characteristics of hockey, soccer, basketball, and polo, but is rougher than any of them. The object of water polo, as in other games in this broad family, is to score points (goals) by putting the ball into the opponent's goal. The ball, inflated and covered by leather, is the size of a soccer ball (between 27 and 28 in. in circumference). Water polo usually is played in a pool, but also can be played in a roped-off area of open water.

The game started in England in the 1870's and was introduced in the United States in the 1880's. In 1897 the rules were codified in the United States. In 1900 water polo was first played in the Olympic Games. In 1906 the sport in the United States came under the control of the Amateur Athletic Union.

In water polo's early years two types evolved—"softball" and "hardball." The softball version, in which the ball was not fully inflated, was perhaps the roughest of all sports. It lost favor internationally but had a small but dedicated following in the United States until the 1940's. Hardball water polo, the type preferred in Europe, was adopted eventually throughout the world.

Basic Rules and Procedure. The game is played in a rectangular area 19 to 30 yd. long and no more than 20 yd. wide. The water must be at least 3 ft. deep and usually is deeper in most or all of the playing area. At each end of this area, at least 1 ft. from the boundary, is a 10-ft.-wide netted goal. The goal rises at least 3 ft. out of the water. An attacking player scores by putting the ball into the goal with hand, foot, or head.

Each team uses seven players—a goalkeeper, three forwards (mainly for offense), and three backs (mainly for defense). Substitution is limited. The game is played in 10-minute halves.

The ball is moved by being balanced on one hand, passed, or dribbled (kept in front of the body). Only the goalkeeper may use two hands on the ball. The defense may tackle only the player with the ball.

Hungary, through the years, has been a leader in the sport. The Illinois Athletic Club and the New York Athletic Club have been traditional leaders in the United States. Water polo is governed internationally by the Fédération Internationale de Natation Amateur.

WATER SKIING, an international sport whose growth has paralleled the growth and popularity of motorboating in North America and Europe. Unlike the snow skier, whose weight and momentum carry him down a slope, the water skier is dependent upon a boat to tow him. The widespread use of fast, maneuverable small craft has led to the present-day status of water skiing as a participant and spectator sport.

Water skiing traces its origin to Fred Waller, an inventor from Huntington, N.Y., who was granted the first patent for water skis in 1924. Until his introduction of skis, many water-sport enthusiasts were towed behing motorboats on a single flat board, or aquaplane. Waller applied the concept of two narrow boards, attached by a bridle, which became the forerunner of modern water skis.

A few wealthy Europeans, vacationing along the French and Italian coasts of the Mediterranean, engaged in water skiing in the late 1920's. The sport was introduced at Juanles-Pins, a French resort, in the summer of 1930, according to Leo Roman, director of the École de Ski Nautique, one of the Continent's first water-ski schools. The advent of fast, relatively inexpensive outboard boats gave impetus to the sport in the late 1940's. Although no official tally is available, it is estimated that more than 1,000,000 North Americans are water skiers.

Equipment. The equipment used by a water skier includes the boat used to tow him, a towline, a buoyant jacket or vest (worn as a safety measure), and his skis. Present-day skis include a conventional type ranging from 5 ft. to 5 ft. 9 in. in length; elliptical "banana" skis, used for tricks; jumping skis, with reinforced tips; a single slalom ski; and shoe skis, which usually measure no more than 15 in. in length and are used primarily in exhibition skiing. Resilience and durability are the characteristics of a water ski. The most popular skis are made of ash or hickory or of plywood combining ash, hickory, and mahogany.

Virtually any motorboat capable of a speed of more than 20 mph can be used to tow a water skier. At slower speeds the skier has a tendency to "plow," or settle into the water. Speeds of at least 35 mph are necessary for a skier to show good form in jumping or in the slalom.

Small craft designed specifically as ski boats are usually fast "planing" hulls that ride on the surface of the water and have a high degree of maneuverability. The crew of a boat used in towing includes the driver and a lookout, who keeps the skier and traffic under observation.

Hundreds of water-ski clubs exist throughout North America, and numerous high schools and colleges have courses in the sport as a form of extracurricular activity or as an integral part of their programs in physical education. *See also* SURFBOARDING.

WEIGHT LIFTING. The early history of this sport is not well documented, but weight lifting is known to be of ancient origin. According to legend, Egyptian and Chinese athletes demonstrated their strength by lifting heavy objects nearly 5,000 years ago. During the era of the ancient Olympic Games a Greek athlete of the 6th century B.C., Milo of Croton, gained fame for feats of strength, including the act of lifting an ox onto his shoulders and carrying it the full length of the stadium at Olympia, a distance of more than 200 yd.

During the following centuries the sport continued to be practiced in many parts of the world. When the Olympics were revived in 1896 weight lifting was included in the program of the modern games. Until 1948 the sport was closely contested in these competitions by German, Austrian, Italian, French, and Egyptian athletes. In that year U.S. weight lifters began to assert leadership. In the decade that followed they won 12 Olympic gold medals and established more than 50 world records in other international weight-lifting competition. Beginning in the 1950's the Soviet Union's weight lifters made great strides forward, notably in the Olympic Games of 1956 and 1960. In large measure this was due to the Soviet Union's overall excellence in organizing sports and to its subsidization of athletic programs. In the early 1960's more than 200,000 competitive weight lifters were registered in the Soviet Union, compared with approximately 5,000 in the United States. Other Communist-dominated countries, especially Poland and Hungary, followed the Soviet program during the same period and began to offer serious challenges in international weight lifting.

Basic Lifts. Beginning with the 1936 Olympic Games, three two-hand lifts were established as the basis of official competition throughout the world. (In some other competition one-hand lifts are also practiced.) The three are known as the (1) clean and press, (2) snatch, and (3) clean and jerk. In each case the only equipment required is a bar bell, the bar of which is made of high-grade spring steel not exceeding 7 ft. 2½ in. in length. To each end of the bar are added cast-iron disks varying in weight from 2½ to 45 lb. Through such additions weights of any desired poundage are possible. At the conclusion of all three lifts, the contestant is standing erect with the bar bell at full arms' length overhead.

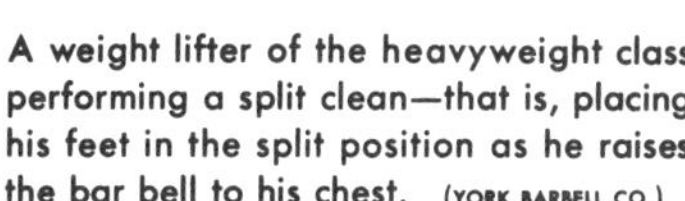

A weight lifter of the heavyweight class performing a split clean—that is, placing his feet in the split position as he raises the bar bell to his chest. (YORK BARBELL CO.)

The clean and press is performed in two movements. The first, in which the bar bell is raised from the platform to the chest, is the part of the lift known as the clean. In the second stage the contestant stands erect and, after a momentary pause following the clean, lifts the bar bell vertically to full arms' length overhead. This must be accomplished without excessive back bending and without any bending at the knees. Also forbidden are heel and toe raising, obvious jerking of the body, and pausing in bringing the bar bell to its final position.

The snatch is executed by lifting the bar bell from the platform to full arms' length overhead in one rapid, continuous movement. Either the "split" or "squat" styles may be employed. The split, in which one foot is placed forward and the other to the rear, is the more reliable. The squat, in which the body is lowered under the bar bell by bending at the knees prior to the lift, is perhaps more efficient but also more precarious. Causes for disqualification during the execution of this lift are touching the platform with the knee or knees and causing the bar bell to pause in its ascent.

The clean and jerk is a two-movement lift. Unlike the clean and press, it does not restrict leg action. In the first phase the bar bell is lifted from the platform to the chest in a single movement performed by either the split or squat styles. At the conclusion of this first movement the contestant is standing erect. In the second phase he employs alternate bending and straightening of the legs, in short, rapid movements, and a rapid push upward with the arms to raise the bar bell overhead. At the conclusion he balances the weight at full arms' length with his legs spread apart in a split position, and then stands erect. The main causes for disqualification are touching the platform with the knees and permitting the elbows to touch the legs.

Conduct of Competition. Contestants usually participate on a square platform, each side of which is 4 meters (13.12 ft.). This is constructed of heavy lumber and laid flat on a stage or on the floor of a gymnasium or ring. Stepping off the platform during the execution of a lift is cause for disqualification.

The weight of the bar bell is progressively increased by the addition of multiples of 5 lb. Contestants are permitted three attempts in each of the three basic lifts. The final score of a contestant is the sum of his best efforts in each, each effort being the equivalent of the poundage lifted. In the 1960 Olympic Games, for example, the Russian heavyweight Yuri Vlasov achieved a record aggregate score of 1,184¼ lb. His best individual efforts were: clean and press, 396¾ lb.; snatch, 341½ lb.; and clean and jerk, 446 lb.

Three officials judge the competition. A referee, seated facing the contestant, and two judges seated on either side of the referee signify approval or disapproval (satisfactory or unsatisfactory execution of a lift) by means of white and red lights, respectively. All lights flash simultaneously, and a majority decision prevails in the event of lack of unanimity. The referee signals a lifter to begin the press by clapping his hands. The same signal is used to instruct him to lower the bar bell to the platform upon satisfactory completion of a lift.

U.S. competitions are conducted in accordance with rules set down by the Amateur Athletic Union. The AAU is a member of Fédération Internationale Halterophile et Culturiste (International Federation for Weight Lifting and Physical Culture), the governing body of international competition.

Classes of Competition. Contestants compete in seven classes according to their body weight. The classes and maximum weight for each are as follows: bantamweight (123½ lb.), featherweight (132¼ lb.), lightweight (148¾ lb.), middleweight (165¼ lb.), light heavyweight (181¾ lb.), middle heavyweight (198¼ lb), heavyweight (any weight over 198¼ lb.).

WEISSMULLER [*wīs'mŭl-ər*], **JOHN ("JOHNNY")** (1904–), American swimmer and actor, born in Windber, Pa. He was voted the outstanding swimmer of the first half of the 20th century in a poll of U.S. sports writers. In the 1920's he held every world free-style record from 100 yd. to a half mile. He won two events in the 1924 Olympic Games and another in the 1928 Olympics. Through a motion-picture career beginning in 1932, Weissmuller became equally famous as Tarzan in numerous films based on the Edgar Rice Burroughs adventure series.

WENE, SYLVIA (1930–), American bowler, born in Philadelphia. She was the first woman to roll three perfect (300) games in major competition and was the foremost challenger to Marion Ladewig's supremacy in women's bowling in the 1950's and 1960's. In 1955 she won the women's championship in the annual all-star tournament of the Bowling Proprietors' Association of America. In 1960 she again won that title during competition in which she bowled the third perfect game of her career. Only 4 ft. 11 in. tall, she was one of the smallest bowlers to attain national recognition.

WILLARD, JESS (1883–1968), American boxer, born in Pottawatomie County, Kans. Known as "the great white hope," he won the heavyweight championship in 1915 by knocking out Jack Johnson, the first Negro heavyweight champion, in the 26th round. Willard, who was 6 ft. 6½ in. tall and weighed 250 lb., was in turn dethroned by Jack Dempsey in 1919. At the conclusion of three rounds of that bout, his seconds threw a towel into the ring to signify his surrender.

WILLIAMS, THEODORE SAMUEL ("TED") (1918–), American baseball player, born in San Diego, Calif. A left-handed-hitting outfielder, he played for Boston of the American League throughout his major-league career (1939–60), which was interrupted by service as a Marine Corps flyer in World War II and the Korean War. His feats as a batter included compiling a career major-league average of .344 and hitting 521 home runs. Between 1941, when Williams hit .406, and 1958, he won six American League batting championships. He was voted the league's most valuable player in 1946 and 1949. Lanky and high-strung, Williams was one of the most colorful players in modern baseball, and his feuds with Boston sports writers and fans made him one of the most controversial. In 1966 he was elected to the Baseball Hall of Fame.

WILMAN, JOSEPH ("JOE") (1905–), American bowler, born in Fontanet, Ind. He won the all-events championships of the American Bowling Congress tournaments in 1939 and 1946. He also was a member of teams that won ABC five-man titles in the tourneys of 1942 and 1954. In annual all-star tournaments conducted by the Bowling Proprietors' Association of America, Wilman won the men's title in 1945, and teamed with Johnny Small to win the doubles title in 1946. In 1946 he was named "bowler of the year" by the Bowling Writers' Association of America.

WIMBLEDON [*wĭm'bəl-dən*], residential area and shopping center in the London borough of Merton. A former borough of Surrey county, it was incorporated into London and merged with two other boroughs as a result of the London Government Act of 1963. Wimbledon is most famous for the All-England Lawn Tennis Championships, which have been held here annually since 1877. In Wimbledon Common, one of the many open spaces and sports grounds in the area, are remains of ancient fortifications.

WINTER SPORTS. The activities covered in this article are practiced principally in the colder regions of North America and Europe. Separate articles are devoted to the more widespread winter sports—skating, skiing, and ice hockey—and to bobsledding and curling.

Dog-sled Racing. For many years sleds pulled by dogs have provided a vital form of transportation in Canada and northern United States, notably Alaska. The owners' pride in their dogs led to racing, usually for wagers. Another outgrowth of this pride was the dog-sled derby, which is often over a course of 100 mi. or more. In most races a sled is pulled by five dogs, although three to seven sometimes are used. A good team can attain a speed of about 10 mph in a relatively short race. One crack team covered 100 mi. in 18 hours nonstop. In sprints, dog sleds have traveled as fast as 25 mph.

Monkmeyer Press Photo Service

A winter hike in New Hampshire. The broad wood and leather snowshoes support the men on the surface of the snow.

Morris—Black Star

Skate sailing on Lake Hopatcong, New Jersey. The kite-shaped sail has a hole for the skater to see through.

The dogs employed are Siberian Huskies (which normally weigh between 35 and 60 lb. each), Alaskan Malamutes (50–85 lb.), Eskimos (50–85 lb.), and Chinooks (90–120 lb.). They usually are willing workers, but it is important that they be not struck with a whip. They are inclined to sulk and buck when whipped. Among the famous drivers of racing dog sleds were Leonhard Sepalla of Alaska and Emilie St. Goddard of Canada.

Iceboating or Ice Yachting. This spectacular and dangerous sport has an exceptionally dedicated following in northern North America and northern Europe. Specially built craft, mounted on steel runners and equipped with sails, travel over ice. They have attained speeds of 143 mph officially and 160 mph unofficially. A jet-propelled ice yacht was said to be capable of going 250 mph. In its traditionally popular form the sport employs boats powered by sails, however.

Iceboating originated in northern Europe and is prob-

Annan Photo Features

An entrant in a Canadian dog-sled race crosses a ditch at the 12-mi. point. The driver is using a six-dog team and lightweight sled.

Philip Gendreau

An iceboat of the Skeeter type speeds into a turn.

Contestants leap forward with their iceboats from the lineup for a race on Lake St. Clair, Mich., as the official on the right gives the starting signal by firing a small cannon.

Pix, Inc.

ably of ancient origin, though the first record dates from the 18th century. A book published in 1768, Fredrik Hendrik Chapman's *Architectura navalis mercatoria*, contained an illustration of a Dutch sloop, mounted on a wooden plank with runners at each end, for traveling on ice. These boats also were known in the 18th century in the areas comprising modern Finland and Latvia.

The first ice yachts in the United States were built in

the latter part of the same century. By 1870 the sport was well established on the Hudson River and nearby rivers in New Jersey. The early racers were large, heavy, and cumbersome. Their many wooden parts led to inefficiency in operation. In 1879 the *Robert Scott* was built, and it became the prototype for the so-called Hudson River class, which comprises the sport's larger craft. It was sleek and designed in general to be lighter, faster, and more maneuverable than earlier iceboats.

The Wisconsin-type boat, employing an almost triangular mainsail, was developed early in the 20th century. In 1931 Starke Meyer of Milwaukee, Wis., made a significant contribution to iceboating design by moving the rudder to the front of the craft, thus eliminating spin. This gradually led to the development of a smaller class of iceboat, the Skeeter, which became by far the most popular. Employing only 75 sq. ft. of sail, boats in this category are fast, inexpensive, and easy to transport. It was largely through this class that the sport had a great increase in popularity. The North Atlantic coastal area and the region of the Great Lakes basin are the major North American locales for participation in the sport.

In 1912 the Northwestern Ice Yachting Association was founded at Oshkosh, Wis. It standardized rules and established classes of racing according to sail area. In 1937 the Eastern Ice Yachting Association was formed and adopted almost identical classes. In 1940 the International Skeeter Association was organized to control competition in that category. The sport is governed in Europe by the European Ice Yachting Union, founded in 1928.

Skate Sailing. This is the sport of sailing on ice skates. Although the skater never goes directly with the wind to his back because of the difficulty in maintaining control that such a procedure would present, he has attained speeds up to 60 mph. The sail is held by the skater in such a way that the wind strikes it at an angle. The sail is never held flat, in back of him, so that the wind hits it directly.

A form of skate sailing can be traced back to the Middle Ages. The sport had its real start in Scandinavia, where ski sailing became a popular variation. Skate sailing was introduced to the United States in the 1890's and found avid support in the areas around New York City and the Great Lakes.

The skater wears long racing skates. The sails are made of cloth (nylon or some variation) and are triangular, rectangular, or kite shaped. The sail area generally is 50 to 70 sq. ft. The sail is stretched on a cross frame of light spars. This frame rests on the skater's shoulder, with its angle controlled by hand.

The Skate-Sailing Association of America was founded in 1922 to set standards for competition. It permits use of skates up to 18 in. in length. It limits the sail area to 1 sq. ft. for each 2½ lb. of the skater's weight. Races are conducted over triangular courses. The outstanding American skate sailor was Clarence W. Capes, who held the national title throughout most of the period from 1928 until 1942, when he retired.

Snowshoeing. Snowshoeing is a method of walking or running on deep snow by wearing on each foot a light wooden frame with strips of leather stretched across it. The frames sometimes are as long as 5 ft. The weight is distributed over a wide area, allowing the wearer to stay atop the snow. A typical snowshoe somewhat resembles a tennis racket with a disproportionately short handle.

Snowshoeing is centuries old in Europe. Canadian Indians independently invented snowshoes hundreds of years ago. Racing in snowshoes is common in Canada and the northern United States, and it is a traditional feature at winter carnivals. The sport is especially popular in Lewiston, Maine, and in Quebec City, Montreal, and St. Hyacinthe in the Province of Quebec. Competition in the United States and Canada is governed by the International Snow-Shoe Congress. Speed records include 13.2 seconds for 100 yd. and 5 minutes 18.6 seconds for 1 mi.

Tobogganing. A toboggan is a flat-bottomed, sledlike vehicle without runners. It is made of strips of wood fitted together, with the front pieces curved up and back. It generally is 3 to 8 ft. long and 15 to 36 in. wide. The North American Indians originated the toboggan, using it to haul packs over snow. In its sports use the toboggan coasts down slides or hills covered with natural or artificial snow or ice. It has been timed in races at more than 61 mph. A team usually consists of four riders, with the one in the back steering with ropes. Tobogganing is popular, especially as a recreation sport, in northern United States, Canada, and Switzerland. Tobogganing is the father of the more glamorous and dangerous sport of bobsledding.

See also BOBSLEDDING; CURLING; ICE HOCKEY; OLYMPIC GAMES; SKATING; SKIING.

Philip Gendreau

Children tobogganing down a snow-covered slide in Massachusetts.

WRESTLING, a body-contact sport in which two contestants grapple on a mat, each attempting to pin the other. It is at least 5,000 years old. It was an honored sport in ancient Greece and Rome, and a form of wrestling was incorporated into the Olympic Games about 708 B.C. International competition was known in the Middle Ages. In a celebrated match in 1520, King Francis I of France ac-

Columbia University

The top man has a body press on his opponent in an intercollegiate match.

Top man is blocking the opponent's single leg hold.

Top man uses front-body scissors on his opponent.

Top man has a quarter-nelson hold on his opponent.

cepted the challenge of King Henry VIII of England and pinned him.

Basic Types. Two basic types of wrestling have survived —free style (also known as catch-as-catch-can) and Greco-Roman. (*Sumo*, the national sport of Japan, is a major variation, but relatively unknown in the Western world.) Free-style wrestling is the type employed by professionals the world over and by amateurs, including collegians, in the United States and Canada. Greco-Roman, unlike free style, permits no holds below the waist and no leg holds. It has become rare in North America but enjoys popularity in Europe.

Evolution of Professional Wrestling. Professional wrestling had its major development in North America. The sport was known among the American Indians before the white man set foot on the continent. The Greco-Roman style was the more common North American form until the 19th century.

Tom Jenkins, a Cleveland rolling-mill worker, was the first noted American professional free-style champion. However, the foremost figure in the rise of professional wrestling was Frank Gotch, who dethroned Jenkins in 1905 and dominated the sport until he retired in 1913. Gotch was comparatively small and light, but his scientific methods more than overcame those handicaps. He won 154 of his 160 matches.

After Gotch retired, American professional wrestling underwent a great change. By the 1930's it had become more theater than a highly skilled and scientific sport. Except for rare interludes, the outcome of at least 99% of all matches was predetermined. The purpose was to entertain. A wrestler's success depended much less on his wrestling ability than on his acting ability. Like actors, wrestlers became typed as heroes or villains. There were wrestlers with bleached blond hair, masks, beards, and ballet slippers (and some were unshod). There were midget and women wrestlers. There were tag-team matches (two or more men to a side) and free-for-alls. There were wrestling rules, but the villains violated them freely by kicking, gouging, biting, and hair pulling. It was all an act. Seldom did a wrestler intentionally injure or even hurt an opponent.

A large audience was developed for these spectacles. Interest in them reached its zenith immediately after World War II, when matches saturated the new medium of television. Attendance at U.S. matches exceeded 20,000,000 in 1948 alone. Wrestling had its ups and downs after that but never completely lost its hold on the public. Antonino Rocca, an Italian-born Argentine who became a U.S. citizen, was the most popular and prosperous wrestler in this boom era. He earned upward of $150,000 a year.

Amateur Wrestling. During this metamorphosis amateur wrestling remained a pure sport. In 1903 the Intercollegiate Wrestling Association was formed in the United States. In 1904 wrestling became a full-scale Olympic sport. In 1919 U.S. interscholastic competition began in Oklahoma.

The International Amateur Wrestling Federation was founded by 65 nations in 1920 and became the world ruling body. The best amateur wrestlers have come from the Soviet Union, Turkey, and Iran.

Amateur wrestling in the United States is controlled by the National Collegiate Athletic Association (for collegians) and the Amateur Athletic Union (for noncollegiate competition). The strongholds of college wrestling include Oklahoma State University (formerly Oklahoma A. and M. College), the University of Oklahoma, Lehigh University, Cornell College (Mount Vernon, Iowa), and Iowa State Teachers College.

College and AAU competition is governed by approximately similar rules. The colleges conduct bouts in 10 classes with the following weight limits: 115 lb., 123, 130, 137, 147, 157, 167, 177, 191, and unlimited. The AAU weight classes usually vary from the foregoing by a few pounds. The colleges conduct only free-style competition. Each bout is scheduled for three rounds of three minutes each. Tournament finals may last longer.

The bout is contested on a mat at least 24 ft. square. (The professionals use boxing rings.) The wrestler wears full-length tights with outside trunks, a sleeveless shirt, and sneakers.

A college bout is ended by a fall—when one man's shoulders are pinned to the mat for two seconds. If neither man is pinned, the bout is decided by a system involving point scoring. These points are awarded by the referee during competition for such accomplishments as gaining advantages of position, takedowns, near falls, and escapes. Only in a dual meet can a bout end in a draw. In tournaments, if the wrestlers are tied in points after two extra two-minute rounds, the referee and two judges select a winner on the basis of wrestling ability in the overtime rounds.

The amateur wrestler has many holds at his disposal. Some, notably those in the scissors family, involve primarily the use of legs. Most, including the arm lock, leg lock, chin lock, and those in the nelson family, involve the use of arms.

Punishing and dangerous holds are barred under college rules. These include the front headlock, straight head scissors, over-scissors, strangle hold, body slam, toe hold, full nelson, and some hammer locks.

See also JUJITSU.

Sumo wrestling. The first man to be thrown from the ring or touch the ground with any part of his body but his feet loses the match. (BURT GLINN—MAGNUM)

YOUNG, DENTON TRUE ("CY") (1867–1955), American baseball player, born in Gilmore, Ohio. A right-handed pitcher, he compiled a record total of 511 victories during his major-league career. His other feats that still remain records include winning 20 or more games in a single season 16 times and 30 or more games 5 times. During Young's 22 years in the major leagues he played for Cleveland of the National League (1890–98), St. Louis of the National (1899–1900), Boston of the American (1901–8), Cleveland of the American (1909–11), and Boston of the National (1911). His victories included three no-hit games. In 1937 he was elected to the Baseball Hall of Fame.

Z

ZAHARIAS [zə-hĕ′rē-əs], **MILDRED DIDRIKSON ("BABE")** (1914–56), American athlete, born in Port Arthur, Tex.

She was voted the outstanding woman athlete of the first half of the 20th century in an Associated Press poll. As "Babe" Didrikson she distinguished herself in track and field by setting world records in the javelin throw and 80-meter hurdles in the 1932 Olympic Games. In 1938 she married the noted wrestler George Zaharias. An outstanding performer in basketball, baseball, and billiards, she later concentrated on golf, where she won 17 consecutive tournament victories, including the U.S. women's National Amateur in 1946. A year later, she became the first American to win the British Women's Amateur tournament. She also won the U.S. Women's Open tourneys in 1948, 1950, and 1954.

Index

INDEX

INDEX